MICROCOMPUTER
GRAPHICS

Art, Design and
Creative Modelling

A picture is worth a thousand words
A picture is worth 1024 words

Ancient and modern renditions
of a famous Chinese proverb

MICROCOMPUTER GRAPHICS

Art, Design and Creative Modelling

Michael Batty

LONDON
Chapman and Hall

First published in 1987 by
Chapman and Hall Ltd
11 New Fetter Lane, London EC4P 4EE

© 1987 M. Batty

Printed in Great Britain at the University Press, Cambridge

ISBN 0 412 28530 4 (Hardback)
0 412 28540 1 (Paperback)

British Library Cataloguing in Publication Data

Batty, Michael
  Microcomputer graphics: art, design and
  creative modelling. – (Chapman & Hall
  computing)
  1. Computer graphics.   2. Microcomputers
  – Programming
  I. Title
  006.6'86   T385
  ISBN 0–412–28530–4
  ISBN 0–412–28540–1 Pbk

Contents

Preface

The two most important technologies developed during the last 50 years have been the television and the computer. Individually, they have already realized enormous potential but their increasing interdependence is enabling a whole range of unanticipated applications in which access to computers is through the medium of television and vice versa. Computer graphics represents the cutting edge of these developments. A decade ago, the use of computers to produce graphical imagery was still the domain of specialist computer scientists, but with dramatically falling costs of computer memory, graphical applications are fast becoming the dominant mode of computation. Indeed, one of the ironies of the microrevolution has been that the best general purpose graphics applications are those which are possible using low cost microcomputers, usually available on a personal basis in the home or in the workplace.

In a field in which the hardware is changing so rapidly, it might seem a little hazardous to attempt to write a book on microcomputer graphics. Yet despite the proliferation of texts in this field, the ideas underlying computer graphics are evolving much more slowly. In fact, the current spate of books on computer graphics mirrors the earliest texts written in the late 1960s. The emphasis is still on geometry with the high point of computer graphics being three-dimensional representation in a two-dimensional medium, thus reflecting the origins of the subject area in engineering rather than in the arts. In the intervening years, only the hardware has changed.

I intend taking a different tack in this book by emphasizing some of the less conventional concepts and theories behind computer graphics, yet ideas which I hope will last a good deal longer than the microcomputer hardware on which I have chosen to implement these various techniques. There are two main principles which I have adopted in this exposition. First, in educating myself in computer graphics, I have always been amazed by how dry and non-visual many of the textbooks appear; this has always struck me as puzzling in a field so dedicated to articulating visual imagery. My second point is complementary and revolves around the relatively standard set of ideas which dominate computer graphics.

I am a firm believer that if the field is explored in more visual terms, conventional ideas involving geometry will be complemented by a whole range of design principles, equally important to computer graphics. Thus I have set out here to provide a gentler introduction and extension to the usual ideas found in computer graphics books. Geometry is still central but to this, I have attempted to embrace a variety of ideas involving pattern, structure, composition, symmetry and suchlike which are more in the domain of art than in engineering. Hence the subtitle of this book in which art, design and creativity represent the way in which microcomputer graphics is to be treated.

I will spend some time in the first chapter describing the various ways in which computers can be used in art, but to anticipate a strong theme which runs throughout this book, computer art is developed here as creative modelling where pictures and design are intricately woven within the programs and algorithms which produce them. Indeed, the correspondence between picture structure and program structure is an all-important characteristic of every application presented here, and it enables each idea to be represented in three ways: as a formal structure, as a computer program, and as a computer graphic.

Notwithstanding my emphasis on ideas and my exposition of computer graphics through design principles, hardware can never be forgotten, for graphics always depends upon the constraints imposed by the available hardware. All artists and designers know what they are able to achieve in various contexts with particular materials, and this is just as true of computer art and graphics as other design situations. Picture detail, colour, resolution, and other aspects of representation all depend on the hardware, and thus computer art will depend on the ingenuity of the artist-programmer in enabling certain sorts of pictures to be produced on certain sorts of machines. Indeed the emphasis here on two-dimensional flat landscapes rather than three-dimensional representations is particularly well-suited to a hardware which is heavy on screen memory but light on memory for graphics programming.

This book has primarily been written for students who wish to explore computer graphics at a comparatively elementary level, and who require fairly immediate applications which emphasize pictorial designs. Computer scientists may be interested in the emphasis on design principles and picture composition but there is little emphasis here on graphical algorithms *per se*. This book is largely tailored to artists and designers who require a gentle but firm introduction to the potential of microcomputing in art, to those studying computer programming who require graphics applications at a relatively elementary but intelligible level, and to those who wish to begin exploring how formal design principles can be articulated through computer programming.

A prerequisite to using this book is familiarity with the Basic computer programming language. As the programs reproduced here are in BBC Basic, familiarity with a structured Basic would be more useful. For students who have access to a BBC microcomputer, the applications and programs included here are immediate, but those unfamiliar with BBC Basic, can still use the book to explore design principles. Indeed, it is a straightforward matter to translate the programs here which are never longer than 165 lines to other versions of Basic which run on other machines. Essentially the book can be used as a text for any course in computer graphics where the emphasis is on using microcomputers, and where the bias is towards design rather than computation *per se*. The book is structured from simple to complex, from introductory ideas and techniques which act as the parts of some greater whole to pictures which are produced by replicating and combining techniques as soon as they are introduced. Many different groups might use this book. For example, it can be used as a graphics text for final-year high school students studying computing, and first-year university students of computer science who require an easy introduction to graphics applications, or for artists and designers wanting the same but at a later stage in their college education. I have used sections of the book in my courses to final-year students of architecture and town planning, and this suggests other groups.

Although the book covers all aspects of a computer graphics course which typically deals with two- and three-dimensional geometry, as well as animation, readers may wish to select certain sections for study. The first four chapters of the book could be used as an elementary exposition of computer graphics without embarking on the mathematically more involved area of three-dimensional representation. The book could be used for more specialist introductions to fractal geometry and graphics (Chapter 5) or to animation (Chapter 7). At a more detailed level, readers interested in computer landscapes would find the book useful, particularly Chapters 4 and 5, while there are applications in architecture, planning and geography which are useful if used selectively. However, I believe the treatment is elementary enough to be of interest to many groups from a variety of backgrounds but at the same time, advanced enough to point the way to thoroughly professional applications.

Computer graphics is one of those areas which sits astride the sciences and the arts and necessarily involves a synthesis of analytic and creative thinking. I am a firm believer that there are disciplines and subject areas not primarily involved in computer graphics which are able to make a contribution to it, such as my own area of town planning. This is an eclectic area drawing on many disciplines but the synthesis it provides its students is well-suited to the ideology of computer graphics. I hope some of this comes across in the book. On a more personal level, many people have helped me during the last ten years by focusing my interest on computer graphics, but in a sense, seeds were sown through my undergraduate education in design in the Department of Town and Country Planning in the University of Manchester in the early 1960s.

My present abode in the University of Wales Institute of Science and Technology has provided a very congenial environment in which to develop these ideas, particularly because of its emphasis on decentralized but large-scale computing. My departmental colleagues have provided a constant source of inspiration through their criticism and dialogue. The Department of Town Planning's technical staff, Tracy Dinnick, Andrew Edwards, Martin Morris and Nathan Webster helped produce the artwork and photographs, while my secretary, Beryl Collins, typed the manuscript. My wife Sue, and son Daniel have been especially tolerant of my hectic lifestyle which embodies a curious mix of travel and professional research with running a university department. Only they know how this book was written by being squeezed into a multitude of spare moments. To them, I have a special debt.

Finally, I have been much influenced by the place where I live. South Wales in the mid-1980s has all the paradoxes of late 20th century Britain but, culturally, it is undeniably different from all the other places I have lived. The Vale of Glamorgan across which I drive to work each day as well as the mining valleys to the north have their own strange beauty which I hope is reflected in some of the pictures produced here. This more than anything else reflects my thesis that the computer is a unique medium which enables us to enrich ourselves in a variety of novel and surprising ways.

Welsh Saint Donats
Cowbridge, South Glamorgan   *April 1986*

1

Introduction: the evolution of computer art and graphics

Computer art challenges our traditional beliefs about art:
how art is made, who makes it, and what is the role of
the artist in society.

(Ruth Leavitt, *Artist and Computer*, 1976)

One of the first public demonstrations of the use of computers involved the arts. In December 1951, Jay Forrester, the Director of the Whirlwind computer project at the Massachusetts Institute of Technology, was interviewed by Ed Murrow on his popular TV show *See It Now*. Forrester demonstrated how the Whirlwind computer could simulate a bouncing ball and display its path on an oscilloscope attached to the machine. In the same show, Whirlwind was used to simulate the trajectory of a rocket and the demonstration was concluded with the computer playing its own version of *Jingle Bells* (Peterson, 1983). Such applications however were by no means unique even in 1950. Several of the two dozen or so machines then available had oscilloscopes attached for purposes of monitoring their internal functioning and the realization that computers could be used for graphics was thus immediate. Scientists in the University of Cambridge recall a program which animated a highland dance routine running on the EDSAC computer in 1950 (Jankel and Morton, 1984). And the earliest known exhibits of computer art involved developments of this type of oscillography by Ben Laposky who began demonstrating his designs based on 'electronic light' in the early 1950s (Laposky, 1976).

   Yet despite such promising beginnings, the use of computers in graphics and art progressed rather slowly. Early applications to art and design were pioneered largely by computer scientists as an adjunct to more mainstream scientific activities, although there were developments in line-drawing graphics for engineering purposes by companies such as Boeing. It was not really until the development of minicomputers in the early 1960s that computer graphics became a serious pursuit. The development of *Sketchpad*, essentially the first interactive drawing package, by Ivan Sutherland (1963) represented a landmark, and in the 1960s a small community of artists and scientists dedicated to exploring the potential of computers in the arts began to flourish. Most of the graphic art which emerged was based on line drawing using pen plotters, and its predominant characteristic was the emphasis on geometrical abstraction. Indeed, Negroponte (1979) in commenting on this generation of computer art likened it to a 'Calcomp contest' after the company which produced most of the then available plotters and which also sponsored an annual competition among graphics users. In 1968, when the London Institute of Contemporary Arts staged its exhibition *Cybernetic Serendipity*, most of the works shown reflected a constructivist emphasis, with most of the exhibitors being computer scientists and programmers first, artists second (Reichardt, 1968). At this time, computers had made little impact on the visual arts, and their potential for influencing traditional art still lay largely unrealized.

In the last decade, the scene has changed dramatically, largely due to the development of the microprocessor, and the continually falling cost (and increasing size) of computer memory. In the 1960s, ways of displaying computer graphics were mainly restricted to paper or to developments of the cathode ray tube (CRT) to display line drawings. These display devices were and continue to be known as vector graphics devices after the method of displaying lines as vectors which are directly traced out on the phosphor of the display screen. However, the development of cheap memory in the 1970s made possible the widespread application of the raster scan technology used in television. Instead of tracing out each line individually on the screen, the raster scan system prints the picture line by line from the top to the bottom of the screen, refreshing the image by continually scanning the area of computer memory which contains the picture. In this system, the picture itself is stored in an area of the computer's memory known as the screen memory or frame buffer. A close correspondence between the picture on the screen and this memory area of the computer is thus implied, and this has led to major developments in colour rendering and animation.

Computer art has changed accordingly. It is no longer dominated by line drawings and much of the heavy formal emphasis has disappeared. A new generation of art has emerged in which greater realism is possible. In fact, what has happened is that the most advanced computer art has taken on a surrealist quality. Colour is sharp, perhaps too sharp for many tastes, and there is much complexity in picture composition. Colour photographs from VDUs (Visual Display Units) have replaced the Calcomp style plots of the 1960s. Moreover, the widespread diffusion of microcomputers has blurred the community of artists, making computer art accessible to everyone. For the first time, there is the sudden possibility of major advances in computer art in many diverse contexts. But with this proliferation of computers, and the development of computer memories reserved for pictures, has come the need for much clearer perspectives on the meaning and scope of computer art. Before we proceed to outline such principles, it is thus worth defining the varieties of computer art which have already evolved.

1.1 VARIETIES OF COMPUTER ART: PROGRAMMING AND PAINTING

In one sense, the debate over computer art is part of the wider debate about 'what is art?'. This debate focuses on the issues raised by Ruth Leavitt (1976) in the quotation which opens this chapter, and it involves not only what is art but who it is for. In particular, views differ as to whether art is primarily for the individual, the artist, the patron, the connoisseur or for society at large, whether art is a public or private domain, whether art should be judged in terms of the process of its making or its end product, or some combination of both. What is obviously clear is that computer art is very different from conventional art on all these points. Both the process of producing computer art, and its product whether on paper or on the display screen, differ fundamentally from the conventions of traditional art, not only in terms of the medium and the technology, but also in the ways experience and intuition in art are enabled through the medium of the computer. Indeed it is the *sine qua non* of this book that computer art is different from conventional art and must thus be judged in a different way.

Varieties of computer art can be classified into many different types. In terms of its *product*, the distinction between *computer graphics* and *computer art* is an obvious one with graphics implying a more definite scientific purpose in contrast to art which is more personal, expressive and recreationally inspired. But the boundary is blurred, graphics merges into art in the computer world and vice versa. In terms of *processes*, there is a major distinction between *passive* and *interactive* (active) computer art. The crudest categorization of this distinction is to consider passive computer art as art in which the artist embodies all his or her intuition in the computer program that produces art, in contrast to interactive art in which the artist continually modifies the program and the resulting picture, embodying intuition into the product through learning about how picture and program structure interact. A twist in this distinction between passive and interactive art involves viewing computer art as primarily *painting* or as primarily *programming*. In its extreme, art as programming involves designing procedures and algorithms which simulate and model picture structure while art as painting involves replacing the canvas with the computer screen and using a predetermined drawing system within which to generate the image. Of course, combinations of programming and painting do exist, particularly in some computer-aided design, but the distinction is useful in serving to focus the subject matter of this book and the type of art and graphics to be explored.

Some computer artists consider that traditional artists are best served by the computer and by computer scientists through the development of painting systems. David Em is one such artist who uses James Blinn's drawing system at the Jet Propulsion Laboratory in Pasadena, to great effect (Deken, 1983; Michie and Johnston, 1984). In contrast, computer art based on the mathematical modelling of picture structure can best be seen in the works of Alan Norton and Richard Voss of IBM in their simulations of both abstract and real landscapes using fractals (Mandelbrot, 1982). In fact, both these positions are extremes for even in the development of passive computer art, simulations of picture structure are made over and over again until the artist/programmer is satisfied that the best product has emerged. There is a third category of computer art which involves both programming and painting, and this involves using computers to construct drawings, usually on paper, which are subsequently coloured or painted in the traditional way. The production of such drawings may be either passive or interactive and in a way, computers are used to construct the skeleton or framework of a drawing before it is rendered. The most well-known exponent of such art is Harold Cohen whose programming ideas embody the rudimentary ideas of an artificial intelligence embodying creativity (Reffin–Smith, 1984).

This latter category is more a type of computer-assisted art in that the resulting art represents a mixture of new and traditional products and processes. In fact, artists have long been concerned with using computers in diverse ways in the production of art objects. Edward Ihnatowicz's (1976) *Senster* is an example of a computer-controlled kinetic sculpture exhibiting 'intelligence' in its motion. Computers have been used to enable designs for a variety of objects which are then manufactured in conventional fashion. Ness's work with sculptures based on random computer designs is an example (Franke, 1971). In this domain, computers are clearly being used in an experimental fashion, as a way of exploring design possibilities as well as new art forms; yet this emphasis on experimentation runs deep throughout computer art; it may even be due to the comparatively primitive state in which computer art presently exists, for one's ability to produce art clearly depends on the extent to which the medium is known. Computers are still unknown mediums in comparison with traditional ways of producing art. Throughout this book the art produced has been the subject of extensive experimentation in matching picture to program structure, and vice versa.

The dependence of computer art on its technology is thus central to the type of art produced. We have already indicated that until the age of cheap computer memory (that is, before the mid-1970s), computer art was dominated by line drawings whose form showed the underlying clever mathematics more than any wider considerations of picture structure. In fact, the most primitive of such art involved output devices other than plotters and oscilloscopes. Plotters and oscilloscopes were never widely available then but line printers were and were thus extensively exploited as a medium for crude computer art. I first saw computer art of this kind in the late 1960s in the

University of Cambridge School of Architecture where line-printer plots of the Mona Lisa, and Marilyn Monroe adorned the walls. This type of art is of the most literal kind – the computer program is the picture and vice versa. To illustrate what is involved, Program 1.1 presents a listing which draws the cartoon character 'Mickey Mouse'. This program could have been printed

Program 1.1   'Mickey Mouse' line printer program-plot
© 1987 The Walt Disney Company

```
 10 MODE3
 20 PRINT
 30 PRINT
 40 PRINT
 50 PRINT"              XXXXXXXXX"
 60 PRINT"             XXXXXXXXXXXXXX"
 70 PRINT"            XXXXXXXXXXXXXXXX"
 80 PRINT"            XXXXXXXXXXXXXXXX"
 90 PRINT"            XXXXXXXXXXXXXXXX"
100 PRINT"            XXXXXXXXXXXXXX"
110 PRINT"             XXXXXXXXXXXXXXXXXXXXX"
120 PRINT"                XXXXX        X    XX"
130 PRINT"      XXXXXXXXX    XXXXXX     XX     XXX X"
140 PRINT"      XXXXXXXXXXX XXXXXXX    X        *   X"
150 PRINT"      XXXXXXXXXXXX XXXXXXX         *** *** X  XX"
160 PRINT"      XXXXXXXXXXXXXXXXXXXXXX      **** **** X XXXX"
170 PRINT"      XXXXXXXXXXXXXXXXXXXXXX      ***** *** XXXXXX"
180 PRINT"      XXXXXXXXXXXXXXXXXX    XX     ****      XX X"
190 PRINT"      XXXXXXXXXXXX X                        X"
200 PRINT"      XXXXXXXXXXX  X    XX                  X"
210 PRINT"      XXXXXXXX    X      XX              XX"
220 PRINT"              XXX      XXX            XX          ==="
230 PRINT"             XXXXX  XXXXXXXXXXXXX                 ====="
240 PRINT"                 XXXXXXXXXXXXXX                   ====="
250 PRINT"                 XXXXXXXXXXXXXXXXXXXXXXXX   XXXX========="
260 PRINT"                 XXXXXXXXXXXXXXXXXXXXXXXX    ========="
270 PRINT"                 XXXXXXXXXXXXXXXX      XXXX  ========="
280 PRINT"                 XXXXXXXXX      ааа аа X XX========="
290 PRINT"                   XXXXX        аааа ааа X  ========="
300 PRINT"                   XXXXX        ааа  аа X   ========="
310 PRINT"                   XXXX          а      X   ========="
320 PRINT"                   XX                   X   ========="
330 PRINT"                   X                    X    ======="
340 PRINT"                   X                   XX    ====="
350 PRINT"                 X                 X   X"
360 PRINT"                XXX               XX XXXX"
370 PRINT"              XX  XXXXX         XXXX"
380 PRINT"            XXXX  XXXXXXXXXX"
390 PRINT"          XXXX      XXXXX XXXX"
400 PRINT"      XXXXXXXXX        XXXXX XXXX"
410 PRINT"   XXXXXXXXX          ===XXXXX XXXX"
420 PRINT"   XX          X       =     X    =    ==аааааааааа"
430 PRINT"   XXXXXXXXXX         аааааааааааа=ааааааааааааааааааа"
440 PRINT"             ааааааааааааааа   ааааааааааааааааа"
450 PRINT"            ааааааааааааааааааа ааааааааааааааа"
460 PRINT"            ааааааааааааааааааа  аааааааааааа"
470 PRINT"             ааааааааааааааааааааааааааааа"
480 PRINT"               ааааааааааааа"
490 PRINT
500 PRINT
```

through the computer as a figure and it is easy to see that as the listing is processed by the computer, the design is then plotted (or rather printed) on paper. Running the program and displaying it on a VDU does not provide a useful picture, for this sort of art is prior to the medium of the display screen. We need not dwell on this for very long but it is important to note that this program has no structure. The computer simply acts as a medium for displaying a picture whose structure is directly translated from the artist's imagination to the output of the program. In a sense, this is the essence of computer painting systems but it is not the kind of art we will be presenting here.

The art in this book is essentially passive art in terms of our previous characterization. It is art based on matching picture structure to program structure and vice versa, it is art as computer programming, it is art in which mathematical modelling and simulation is central and essential. Furthermore, it is art which has only been possible since the development of cheap computer memory but it is also the art which is the most exciting and dramatic in terms of its future, largely unknown possibilities. This is an art form with a liberating effect in that conventional forms of drawing skill are not a prerequisite to the production of form. Some will object that this is not art, that art would be best left to those working traditionally but through new mediums. But this gets back to the debate over 'what is art?', and in any case I subscribe to Marshall McLuhan's definition of art as ". . . anything you can get away with" (McLuhan and Fiore, 1967). Replacing the canvas with the computer screen is not the type of art developed here. Computer art in this context focuses on the processes of creating pictures from program to output, and this requires a thorough knowledge of the elementary principles of picture structure and program structure which will be developed in this book.

1.2   THE CONTROVERSY OVER COMPUTER ART AND GRAPHICS

Throughout history, artists have always exploited the latest technology and thus it is somewhat surprising that there has been so little interaction between the art and computer communities. This is perhaps due to the longstanding myth, which continues to perpetuate in our society, that the computer will eventually 'usurp' most traditional human activities. The spectre of the computer itself creating art, art which is 'non-human', is a myth which is hard to dispel, notwithstanding the fundamentally flawed nature of this kind of argument. Yet what has been produced so far has clearly not lived up to its original promise, and it has almost appeared to those with little knowledge of the limitations of computer systems, that such art is already non-human. Reffin–Smith (1984) confirms the usual response when he says ". . . computer-art is and has been, by and large, boring nonsense". Negroponte (1979) is equally critical but more pointed in his response: he says:

Rarely have two disciplines joined forces seemingly to bring out the worst in each other as have computers and art . . . . While the intentions may be good, the results are predominantly bad art and petty programming. In almost all cases the signature of the machine is far more apparent than the artist's.

There is no single issue in the development of computer art which can account for such harsh criticism. The first important point however relates to the fact that for the most part, computer art has been produced by computer scientists, only occasionally artists, but invariably it has been criticized by traditional artists. Secondly, criticisms have rarely been directed at the overall process but at its product. There has been little artistic appreciation of the qualities of linking program to picture structure, and thus the criticism so far has been partial and incomplete. Thirdly, it is very early days in this field as yet. The dramatic change from the first-generation Calcomp-style line-drawing art to the raster graphics art of the 1980s, is almost too much to absorb. The new generation of art pioneered by artists like David Em and physicists like Mel Prueitt has an entirely different style and feel from that produced a generation earlier. And finally there has not been much computer art so far. As Carl Sagan (1984) has so cogently pointed out ". . . try imagining where computer art will be, not 10000 years from now, but in a mere 20 or 30".

These however are pragmatic considerations. There are deep differences between computer and traditional art which will become clearer only as we engage in more and more computer art. The medium is obviously different, as is the environment in which the artist makes use of materials. The temporal quality of such art is different. Computer art is repeatable, reproducible for ever through its digital imagery and thus the question of what is the *original* is problematic. Indeed computer art is more like music in that the program represents the score and the computer the instrument on which it is played. It has the same everlasting quality in that it can be played over and over again and there is even the possibility that it can be played 'differently' on different types of computer. But the correspondence with music is imperfect. For painting systems, the programmer might be likened to the composer and the artist to the musician but this is clearly not the case for passive computer art where programmer and artist are the same.

Nevertheless music is perhaps the closest of the arts to computer art and this also extends to the possession of such art. Jankel and Morton (1984) say: "The clearest way computer art can be possessed is in the way that music can be possessed – through the means of playing it." But performance and possession are again superficial qualities. There is a sense in which the structures which run through music are beginning to find themselves in the principles of computer art as well as in the principles of computer programming (Hofstadter, 1979) and these will become clearer as the argument progresses.

Some argue that computer art demystifies; for by concentrating on the process – by laying bare the skeleton on which visual imagination is developed through computer programming – the way the product emerges can be clearly traced. But the intuitions which pave the way from process to product still remain inaccessible inside the heads of computer artists. More likely, computer art liberates rather than demystifies. It enables those with little or no manual dexterity to express their visual imaginings through explicit thinking and logical problem-solving. Prueitt (1984), a physicist by training but with latent and unrealized artistic talent, argues this point when he says: ". . . computer art may be closer to the human mind and heart than other forms of art. That is, it is art created by the mind rather than the body". And in this lies the way forward, for the development of elementary principles for and of computer art will enable such expression to begin.

1.3   ELEMENTARY PRINCIPLES OF COMPUTER ART AND GRAPHICS

The key organizing concept in this book is that picture structure and program structure are in various ways complementary as has already been implied; but this correspondence is always more than it seems. In this type of computer art, it is not possible to define whether the artist thinks first in terms of pictures or in programs. One is not necessarily logically prior to the other. In art, the tendency is to think of the picture influencing the method of its construction – the program, but who can say whether the artist thinks in terms of the picture in the first instance. This is a strange looping which has long gone unremarked in computer art but it is essential to expose it early for it influences much of what follows. Essentially it means that those who wish to judge the art in this book by looking at the pictures will only see and hear half the story. The other half is in the programs, but, to appreciate the whole, both must be considered: programs run and pictures generated.

In emphasizing structure defined here as order-in-representation, the idea of system is all important. Pictures and programs viewed as systems are composed of parts or elements whose arrangement and interaction form the system of interest. Pictures and programs can be decomposed or disaggregated into their constituent parts which act as the building blocks in composing or aggregating the overall structure. The building blocks are often referred to as primitives in contrast to whole pictures or programs which are called universals. Subsystems of building blocks are sometimes referred to as segments which emerge from decomposition or composition of the system through its structural hierarchy. This discussion might imply that treating pictures and programs as systems leads to a full understanding of structure but this can never be the case. It is axiomatic in systems theory that 'the whole is greater than the sum of the parts', that there are always additional synthesizing elements in any system which remain elusive to mechanical procedures for decomposition and composition.

What we are really saying here is that despite the emphasis in this kind of computer art on structure and the way in which visual imagination can be encoded through algorithms, the deeper intuitions and experiences which characterize traditional art, also characterize computer art. It is important at the outset for readers to be convinced that this book will never provide recipes for the production of good art, although it will tell you how to proceed in producing well-structured art. The best art, like the best of any kind of design, remains the prerogative of the gifted designer. There is nothing here that will tell you how to create the masterpiece, for that depends on inspiration for which there is no formal recipe. Nevertheless, the elementary principles to be enunciated here will at least enable you to get started.

There is more to computer art than just pictures and programs. How the picture unfolds and evolves once the program has been started up provides another dimension for appreciation. As you will see if you run any of the programs in this book, this style of computer art is kinetic, and thus there is structure in the way the picture is composed in real time on the display device. Picture structure and program structure cannot be fully experienced simply by understanding the program and linking this to the picture. It is necessary to actually experience the program working to gain a fuller understanding. The constraints of the technology are also central to this appreciation, for many things the artist/programmer might wish to do are limited by the hardware available. Colour and spatial (screen) resolution are obvious limits but the real point is that certain types of art are appropriate to certain types of machine. Realizing the potential of the art depends upon knowing the technology. In a rapidly changing context, this can often be forgotten.

Structure itself can be introduced in many ways but in computer graphics and art it is usually through the computer language used. Different languages represent different degrees of structure but for the type of art presented here, deeper structures are introduced through the way structure in the language is exploited, and this in itself is a design problem. The building blocks of computer language are often incorporated into procedures or (sub) routines, and their assemblage in an hierarchical system usually reflects some decomposition of the visual elements comprising the picture. The early chapters of this book emphasize these building blocks or primitives, and how they might be put together to form subsystems or segments of simple pictures. Simple hierarchies also characterize these designs.

A related principle which is central to computer art involves replication, or iteration as it is usually called. The great strength of computer art is the ability to replicate detail in great abundance and to achieve representations which are quantitatively much richer and more precise than other forms of artistic expression. Whether such expressions are qualitatively richer takes us back to the controversy but it is important to grasp the point that iteration is central to the way building blocks and primitives are used in programming. Other principles which involve manipulating the primitives such as the generation of regular and broken symmetries, and the transformation of forms also embody important ideas reflecting the potential of computer art. Many of these involve making life easier for the artist, for example by generating one side of a design and transposing it by reflection to produce the whole design or by generating many similar designs using the same graphical building block. But such techniques also enable new designs to be innovated. In particular, the ability to transform in countless ways enables new insights to be achieved which would not otherwise have emerged without the power of the computer. These principles are central to what follows but readers can gain a cursory impression of these ideas by looking at the collections of early computer art in the books by Reichardt (1968), Franke (1971), Leavitt (1976) and Malina (1979) and at the later art in the more recent books by Deken (1983), Prueitt (1984) and Jankel and Morton (1984).

Another feature of computer art involves the question of randomness. Nothing is truly random in the sense of chaotic for this would be meaningless in this context. Randomness is usually invoked within some predetermined structure to enable differences in form and perhaps style to emerge when the same computer program is run over and over again. In fact in this book we will use a constrained form of randomness many times. For example the picture on the cover of this book contains a multitude of random choices but these do not affect its overall form or its style, only its local detail. There are however other reasons why computer artists invoke the concept of randomness. First, there are situations where it is simply impossible to decide on the best or correct form for an object and thus a random choice is made. Secondly, randomness tempers repeatability and sameness, and this makes the running of a computer program a little more unpredictable and hence interesting (Mezei, 1976; Nees, 1968). And thirdly, randomness gives the possibility of better art. In some of the pictures that follow, some of the compositions are better balanced than others produced by running the same program. Excellent examples of such random effects exist in the work of many computer artists such as Harold Cohen, Leslie Mezei, George Ness and Michael Noll, and a study of these works serves to underscore the importance of randomness in computer art (Reichardt, 1968; Malina, 1979).

The art produced here is clearly more accessible than that produced by conventional means, at least in terms of its making, if not its understanding; for the correspondence of picture and program structure enables the relationship between them to be better understood. Jankel and Morton (1984) emphasize this when they say:

> Skilful use of a well-chosen procedure as a building block in the construction of a program is the very essence of good computer programming. Similarly the careful design and repeated use in various ways of one geometrical figure is a way to produce a visually pleasing pattern.

In talking about computer languages which enable this approach to be developed, they continue by pointing to the highly-structured language Logo:

> Logo allows the one activity to depend on the other and rewards the author of a well-structured program with a beautiful picture, and, conversely, requires that those who wish to produce beautiful pictures should write beautiful programs.

But we must be careful not to overplay this point for the process of producing good computer art requires thousands of decisions about style and form which like any design activity go unrecorded and will never be accessible to mechanistic routine.

To conclude this section, it is worth presenting an example of another principle of computer art involving experimentation and the necessity of improving the quality of program and picture structure through interactive use. The design we have chosen is a famous one from the late constructivist period of modern art by Josef Albers. It consists of an Escher-like construction resembling the wire frame of two interlocking rectangular blocks which are joined together and presented in a perspective which is suggestive of an impossible structure. The impossibility of the object is heightened by the fact that its central horizontal panel linking the two blocks is solid, thus hiding the frame lines. Entitled 'Structural Constellation' and first exhibited in 1957, the design represents a classic visual illusion. We have designed a program which produces Albers' original design and then enables the user to examine the effects of different illusions due to filling other panels of the blocks. The program which is listed as Program 1.2, is composed of two main parts: it first constructs the original design in steps, and then lets the user explore the various illusions in repeated random fashion.

The program consists of a main program in lines 10 to 220 which controls these operations, a procedure in lines 240 to 280 which draws the outline (wire frame) of any one of the structure's panels, and set of data (lines 300 to 350) which give the coordinates of the points defining the panels which constitute the wire frame. After initializations up to line 40, these coordinates are read in in nested FOR–NEXT loops between lines 50 and 80, and then plotted as six panels in the loop in lines 90 to 100. Each of the panels is actually plotted in a call to PROCDRAW (lines 240 to 280) which in turn is based on the standard sequence of commands to draw a four-sided object: an initial MOVE command followed by four DRAW commands. The original frame of the object is then completed with additional lines being drawn in lines 110 and 120. Each stage in the construction is held until the user presses any key to continue, thus illustrating the build up of the form.

The heart of the experimentation resides in a REPEAT–UNTIL loop in lines 140 to 210. The first time through, this loop hides the lines behind the panel in Albers' original design; in lines 150 to 160 this panel is blanked out and then edged in line 170. At this point, Albers' original design is on the screen.

Program 1.2   An 'abstract' line drawing program

```
10 REM Josef Albers' Structural Constellation
20 MODE1
30 DIM X%(4,6),Y%(4,6)
40 VDU23,1,0;0;0;0;29,175;40;
50 FOR K%=1 TO 6
60    FOR I%=1 TO 4
70       READ X%(I%,K%),Y%(I%,K%)
80       NEXT I%:NEXT K%
90 FOR K%=1 TO 6
100   PROCDRAW(K%):AA=GET:NEXT K%
110 MOVE X%(1,1),Y%(1,1):DRAW X%(1,4),Y%(1,4)
120 MOVE X%(3,2),Y%(3,2):DRAW X%(3,3),Y%(3,3)
130 AA=GET:L%=6:GCOLO,0
140 REPEAT
150    MOVE X%(1,L%),Y%(1,L%):MOVE X%(2,L%),Y%(2,L%)
160    PLOT85,X%(4,L%),Y%(4,L%):PLOT85,X%(3,L%),Y%(3,L%)
170    GCOLO,3:PROCDRAW(L%):AA=GET
180    FOR K%=1 TO 6
190       PROCDRAW(K%):NEXT K%
200    L%=RND(6):GCOLO,0
210    UNTIL FALSE
220 END
230 :
240 DEFPROCDRAW(K%)
250 MOVE X%(1,K%),Y%(1,K%)
260 DRAW X%(2,K%),Y%(2,K%):DRAW X%(3,K%),Y%(3,K%)
270 DRAW X%(4,K%),Y%(4,K%):DRAW X%(1,K%),Y%(1,K%)
280 ENDPROC
290 :
300 DATA 400,100,460,410,210,530,150,220
310 DATA 340,290,400,600,150,720,90,410
320 DATA 710,410,770,720,520,840,460,530
330 DATA 780,220,840,530,590,660,530,350
340 DATA 340,290,530,350,590,660,400,600
350 DATA 460,410,710,410,460,530,210,530
```

Pressing any key leads to restoration of the original frame (lines 180 to 190) and random determination of the next (of six) panels to blank out (line 200). In line 210, this sequence repeats itself indefinitely. There are several issues to explore here. The question must be asked 'Why did Albers choose this particular construction rather than any of the others which can be explored in this program?' Did Albers see the design as a wire frame from a particular position and did he realize that the illusion could be heightened by choosing this position carefully? These are the sorts of issue which can be explored in this program, and Fig. 1.1 shows the sorts of design including the original, which are produced.

The program itself represents the picture structure only in the crudest of ways in this case, for the picture is largely encoded in the data and the essence of the program is the REPEAT–UNTIL loop which aids experimentation. Nevertheless many extensions of this kind of experimental art are possible

Fig. 1.1 Structural constellations, after Josef Albers

1.5   OUTLINE OF THE BOOK

In the next chapter, we introduce these building blocks of computer art in the form of the graphics primitives of BBC Basic as well as the kinds of geometrical prerequisites which utilize the primitives. The prerequisites involve basic methods for drawing circles and related shapes, and elementary trigonometry is thus central to their treatment. Immediately we introduce ways in which the building blocks can be assembled to create natural patterns, and thus readers can indulge in quite respectable design almost straightaway. In Chapter 3, however, we take these ideas much further by introducing techniques for repeating as well as transforming simple shapes into more complicated designs. Our mathematics becomes a little more complex but the level achieved enables us to produce simple landscapes and natural forms such as butterfly designs, as well as mixes of colours and shades to produce heightened effects.

Complete but elementary picture structures are first dealt with in Chapter 4 where a variety of depth-cue techniques approximating perspective are introduced. Picture structure is built up through program structure by organizing programs to reflect the way painters paint from background to foreground, and this enables a variety of natural landscapes to be generated. Here for the first time, we introduce the formal idea of recursion – that is, successive repetition and transformation of simple features which in combination produce more complex forms. These are illustrated by various tree designs. Recursion and randomness are continued in Chapter 5 where more formal picture structures simulating abstract forms such as river systems to more realistic scenes such as mountain ranges, are illustrated. This chapter enables us to explore the way irregularity can be simulated through programs which use randomness and recursion in their formal expression. It is here that we provide a major contrast between the simpler and more conventional geometry and trigonometry of regular forms and the emerging geometry of the irregular as expressed in that new branch of mathematics called fractal geometry.

Complex picture structures form the subject matter of Chapter 6 and this takes us closest to the realm of computer graphics. Here we deal with three-dimensional representations of objects stored in the computer, and their transformation and projection onto the two-dimensional screen. There is little we can approximate here and thus the mathematics of the process are elaborated and algorithms for securing true perspective and hidden line elimination are explored. Less natural forms are pictured through programs which show how artificial objects can be viewed from any position. At this point, we have also reached the limit of what we can achieve in complete programs and thus we continue to elaborate more complex picture structures by stringing separate picture and program segments, thus building up more complex designs. This in fact is the way of professional computer graphics.

The last substantive chapter represents a change in direction – from art and graphics where space is of the essence to art and graphics which unfold in real time. We deal with computer movie-making in the form of simple cartooning and animation. A variety of animation techniques are introduced with an emphasis on defining the most appropriate contexts in which these methods can be used to effect slow and fast animation; and, as in the previous chapter, several animation techniques are combined to produce more complex computer movies. By the end of this book, all the ideas of contemporary computer graphics and art will have been sketched as informally as possible, and the stage has been set for readers to produce their own. Where the subject is likely to go from here and where readers themselves should go are issues which are raised in a short conclusion. But by this time, if the messages and challenges of this book have been taken up, readers should be far away producing art which is many times better than the rudimentary pictures and programs illustrated here.

2

Graphics primitives and geometrical prerequisites

> By a *hierarchic system*, or hierarchy, I mean a system that
> is composed of interrelated subsystems . . . it is somewhat
> arbitrary as to where we leave off the partitioning and
> what subsystems we take as elementary.
>
> (Herbert A. Simon, *The Sciences of the Artificial*, 1969)

We have already discussed the importance of computer language for computer art and graphics, and an obvious beginning involves exploring how the computer language we are going to adopt deals with graphics operations. We are assuming that readers have a sufficient knowledge of the language Basic to be at ease with its extension to graphics use, and we have already noted that the variant of Basic we are using – BBC Basic – is a highly-structured, graphics orientated version of this language. In this chapter, we will show how this language can be extended to deal with graphics operations, but for readers who are unfamiliar with this variant of Basic it may be necessary to consult an introductory programming text such as McGregor and Watt (1983) or more likely, the User Guide for the BBC Microcomputer (Coll, 1982).

In fact, we will have recourse to mention the User Guide on several occasions as our concern here is not with languages *per se* but with applications, and thus there will be many graphical operations available in BBC Basic which we will not deal with comprehensively. Nevertheless, in this chapter we will begin by exploring the most elementary aspects of such operations and to this end we will concern ourselves with *graphics primitives* – basic operations such as DRAW, PLOT and MOVE which are embodied in the machine's hardware, and *geometrical prerequisites* – simple mathematical techniques essential to designing creative software which utilizes these primitives. These prerequisites will involve us in describing shapes and designs using elementary trigonometry and coordinate geometry.

We will begin with a brief description of the way graphics can be displayed on the screen and how the screen's resolution, colour and memory requirements can be adjusted. Graphics primitives commands in BBC Basic will be introduced, and then the mathematics of using these commands to plot points and to draw and fill shapes such as circles and ellipses will be developed. Throughout this book, the emphasis will be upon using techniques to produce designs almost as soon as we introduce them, and thus towards the end of this chapter we will be in a position to use these methods to construct simple pictures. In fact, the earliest computer art was of a very abstract kind, based on manipulating objects which could be described using the kinds of regular shapes presented in this chapter. We will thus conclude the chapter with some examples of this kind of art on the BBC Micro.

2.1   THE GRAPHICS SCREEN: MODE, COLOUR AND RESOLUTION

The area of RAM (Random Access Memory) in the BBC computer which is concerned with graphics is known as the frame buffer. This memory stores a frame which is almost literally a screenfull of graphics data. A portion of the two-dimensional graphics screen thus occupies a portion of the graphics memory, the screen being said to be memory-mapped or bit-mapped. This kind of machine architecture is usually associated with a technique of graphics display called *raster scan* which takes the graphics memory and displays it a line at a time on the screen. Further details of the way the graphics memory is organized will not concern us here but the important point to note is that on this computer, the size of the memory given over to graphics can be adjusted. The Basic command MODE which is followed by a specific number enables this adjustment to take place, and we thus refer to the machine as being in different modes which in turn enable different types of graphics to be developed.

The most basic unit of screen memory which the user can manipulate is called a picture element or *pixel* for short. The more pixels on the screen, the finer the resolution or detail which can be displayed and thus the key function of MODE is to change the number of pixels. In general more pixels will involve more memory but life is never as simple as this because the pixels can be coloured differently. It is easiest to think of a pixel as a kind of switch which can be 'on' or 'off', 'on' being associated with one colour, 'off' with another. Thus the most basic mode of screen memory would consist of a set of pixels with two colours usually black and white. More colours involve more memory, and different modes on the BBC computer will therefore reflect a particular combination of numbers of pixels, and colours, thus implying a certain memory size or memory requirement.

There are eight modes on the BBC computer, numbered 0 to 7 of which five (MODES 0, 1, 2, 4 and 5) are reserved for graphics. The other three modes are text modes in which high resolution graphics is not possible although in MODE 7, the so-called teletext mode which is the default mode on power-up (when the computer is switched on), it is possible to develop 'chunky' or block graphics. In fact, many computer games are developed in this mode but for the kind of design envisaged here this mode is not suitable and will not be discussed further.

The best way to illustrate the characteristics of each mode is to list their properties as in Table 2.1. The first column shows the mode number: MODE 0, MODE 1, etc. thus represent the Basic commands which set the mode. The pixel resolution given in the second column represents the measure of resolution in the X, then Y direction. Throughout this book points on the graphics screen will be referred to as x, y coordinates, the x index being in the horizontal direction, the y in the vertical direction. A screen mode of 640×256 pixels therefore means that the screen has 640 pixels in the X direction, 256 in the Y direction, giving $640 \times 256 = 163\,840$ pixels in all. The number of colours available in each mode is given in the third column. Working out the memory requirements of each graphics mode is straightforward. One pixel which can exist in two states or two colours requires 1 bit. The BBC computer is an 8-bit micro, 8 bits constituting 1 byte. The number of memory locations is measured in bytes, thus to convert the pixel resolution level to memory required, we divide the second column by 8. To work out the memory required by colour, we divide the third column by 2 and we then multiply the two results together. For example, for MODE 1, we get $[(320 \times 256)/8] \times [4/2] = 20\,480$ memory locations. We refer to 1024 memory locations as 1K, hence the memory required for MODE 1 is $20480/1024 = 20$K. Similar calculations for each mode give the memory requirements in the fourth column of Table 2.1.

The teletext mode, MODE 7, is also listed as having a 'graphics' capability in Table 2.1, but as already mentioned, this involves a rather special and restrictive form of graphics and will not be referred to further. Finally, the classic trade-off between level of resolution (pixel size) and colour is illustrated in the table, showing that as the number of colours increases, the resolution

Table 2.1   Characteristics of the machine's modes.

Mode	Number of pixels	Number of colours	Memory requirements	Screen resolution
0(g)	640×256	2	20K	2×4
1(g)	320×256	4	20K	4×4
2(g)	160×256	16	20K	8×4
3(t)	—	2	16K	—
4(g)	320×256	2	10K	2×4
5(g)	160×256	4	10K	8×4
6(t)	—	2	8K	—
7(T)	80×75	16	1K	—

g: graphics mode; t: text mode; T: teletext mode.

must drop to retain the same memory requirements (see for example, the transition from MODE 0 to MODE 1 to MODE 2). Note also that as the basic BBC computer has only 32K RAM of which some 28K is available if a disc-filing system is installed, graphics use eats up memory. Thus the computer programs required to develop graphics must be efficiently organized to fit in the remaining area of RAM, once the screen memory has been fixed by the MODE command.

The screen, although measured in pixels, is not in fact addressed in this way from Basic. There is a standard screen coordinate system which is independent of mode and this enables graphics programs to be run in any of the available modes. The default coordinates are measured from the origin 0, 0 which is located in the bottom left-hand corner, and range to 1279 in the X (horizontal) direction and to 1023 in the Y (vertical) direction. Thus a point on the screen in any graphics mode is given by x,y where $0 \leqslant x \leqslant 1279$ and $0 \leqslant y \leqslant 1023$. Figure 2.1 illustrates this range. Thus the screen coordinates must fall into these ranges for visible lines, points etc. to be plotted on the screen. Usually, objects to be drawn are measured in a different set of coordinates often relevant to the object itself, rather than the screen, and thus these *object*, or *world* coordinates as they are sometimes referred to, must be transformed to the *screen* coordinate system before plotting. We will see an example of this in Program 2.2 reproduced a little later in this chapter. In the next chapter, and in Chapter 6 where three-dimensional pictures are treated, we will explore such transformations in depth but meanwhile it is important to note that such transformations are often necessary for the most basic of designs.

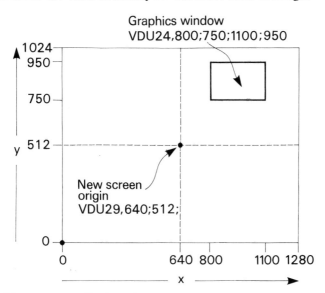

Fig. 2.1   The screen coordinate system

World coordinates are transformed to screen coordinates by software but it is the hardware which transforms the screen to pixel coordinates. For example in MODE 0, we have a resolution of 640 pixels in the X direction, 256 in the Y. With the screen coordinates measured over a range of 1280 units in the X and 1024 in the Y direction, clearly two units in the X direction correspond to a single pixel, while four in the Y direction correspond to a pixel. In other words, any values of x and y in the range $0 \leqslant x < 2$ and $0 \leqslant y < 4$ are associated with the pixel in the bottom left-hand corner of the screen. To find out the level of screen resolution associated with any pixel, we divide 1280 by the number of pixels in the X direction associated with an appropriate mode, and 1024 by the number of pixels in the Y direction. This gives screen resolution which is the number of screen coordinate units covered by a single pixel in a given mode. We have listed this as the fifth column in Table 2.1.

Finally in this section, we must briefly mention how text is reproduced in the various modes. In each of the graphics modes 0, 1, 2, 4 and 5, there are 32 lines (rows) of text which fill a screen, while in the text modes 3, 6 and 7 there are 25 lines. In MODE 0, there are 80 characters per line, in MODE 1 and MODE 4, 40 characters per line and in MODE 2 and MODE 5, 20 per line. In MODE 3, there are 80 and in MODE 6 and MODE 7, 40 characters per line. Text is located by row and column numbers measured from the top left-hand position of the screen, not the bottom left. In general, we will not be programming much text in this book but occasionally it will be necessary to define an area of the screen for text – a text window – and then we will need to refer to the text size in terms of row and column position.

2.2   MANIPULATING AND COLOURING THE GRAPHICS SCREEN

There are a whole series of commands in BBC Basic which enable the default settings of the machine to be changed. For graphics, these commands are called VDU commands and in this section, we will be using them to show how the screen coordinate system can be shifted, how windows (rectangular areas smaller than the screen) can be defined, and how colours can be switched. To shift the origin of the screen to a new position within the original set of screen coordinates, we use the command

    VDU29,X;Y;

where X and Y are the screen coordinates of the original system which position the new origin. For example, VDU29,640;512; changes the origin point 0,0 to the point 640,512 which is the centre point of the screen. Once this command is executed, the new origin becomes the point 0,0 and all screen coordinates are now defined relative to this. In this example which is shown on Figure 2.1, the screen is divided into the four quadrants with the following range: $-640 \leqslant x \leqslant 640$ and $-512 \leqslant y \leqslant 512$. Judicious use of VDU29 thus enables objects to be shifted around the screen without any actual transformation of their coordinates.

The default graphics screen is the whole screen but sometimes it is necessary to define an area smaller than this in which a picture or some text is to be displayed. In fact, such windows, as they are called, can be used to break down a complex picture into segments and can thus be used to build up graphical structure. Graphics windows are defined using the VDU24 command which is given as

VDU24, leftX; bottomY; rightX; topY;

where the window is $(rightX - leftX) \times (topY - bottomY)$ in size. Clearly $rightX \geqslant leftX$ and $topY \geqslant bottomY$ for the window to be defined. The window in Fig. 2.1 is given by VDU24,800;750;1100;950; which is in terms of the original screen coordinates. Note that if the screen coordinate system is changed using VDU29 first, then VDU24 will operate on the new system.

As soon as the graphics window is set up, whatever is drawn on the screen will only appear in the window. Anything drawn outside the window will be invisible and what is more, no error will be reported. Thus there is no need to 'clip' lines so that only those in the window area are plotted. Clipping can be a tedious and sometimes complicated process and on many display devices such as direct view storage tubes, and even some micros such as the Apple II, clipping is essential if errors are to be avoided. The BBC machine avoids all this. A text window is defined using the VDU28 command but X and Y are now measured in text coordinates, from the top left position which is 0,0 and in the character coordinates referred to earlier. This command is

VDU28, leftX, bottomY, rightX, topY

and it will be used occasionally in later chapters where text is required to control the graphics.

The most complicated feature of the graphics screen undoubtedly concerns colour which as we have already seen involves a tradeoff between level of resolution and the screen memory required. Each graphics mode supports a given number of colours which have default hues. These values in turn can be altered by switching them to those in a standard palette of 16 colours. The VDU19 command is required to effect this switching. The default colours are referred to as *logical* colours while the standard palette contains *actual* colours. There is also a distinction between foreground and background colours in each mode. Foreground colours are indexed in the range 0, 1, . . . while background colours begin in the range 128, 129, . . . The greatest range of colours can range from 0 to 15, the background from 128 to 143. The best way of showing the colour organization in each mode is through Table 2.2 which shows the logical colour numbers and hues for the five graphics modes.

Table 2.2 Logical colour numbers and colour hues in the graphics modes.

Modes		Foreground numbers	Background numbers		Colour hues
0 and 4		0	128		Black
(2 colours)		1	129		White
1 and 5		0	128		Black
(4 colours)		1	129		Red
		2	130		Yellow
		3	131		White
2	S	0	128		Black
(16 colours)	T	1	129		Red
	A	2	130		Green
	N	3	131		Yellow
	D	4	132		Blue
	A	5	133		Magenta
	R	6	134		Cyan
	D	7	135		White
		8	136	F	Black/White
	P	9	137	L	Red/Cyan
	A	10	138	A	Green/Magenta
	L	11	139	S	Yellow/Blue
	E	12	140	H	Blue/Yellow
	T	13	141	I	Magenta/Green
	T	14	142	N	Cyan/Red
	E	15	143	G	White/Black

In a suitable mode, selecting a foreground or background colour involves executing the command

    GCOL0, logical-colour-number

and then every graphics operation following this command will use this colour where appropriate. If the colour is a foreground colour, commands such as DRAW will plot lines in this colour, while, if the colour is a background colour, this can be set by the command CLG (which clears the graphics screen). Note that the first number following GCOL which is 0 enables absolute colour to be plotted. Other values will be introduced in later chapters, particularly in Chapter 7 when animation through colour switching is presented. In the case of text, the command

    COLOUR logical-colour-number

accomplishes the same type of setting. Text which is in the foreground will be displayed in the given colour while the text background can be set by following the COLOUR command with the command CLS (clear the screen). Further details and a more extensive treatment are given in the User Guide.

Table 2.2 also indicates that for MODE 2, the logical palette of colours is identical to the actual palette. Thus in this mode, no switching of colours is necessary. However in the two and four colour modes, any of these 16 actual colours can be assigned to a logical colour using the command

   VDU19,log,act;0;

where the logical colour number (log) is switched to an actual colour number (act). For example, in MODE 1, the logical foreground colour 2 is yellow. If it is desired to assign this colour number to blue which is actual colour number 4, then VDU19,2,4;0; will ensure this. We would then have a colour assignment in this mode consisting of a black background (log = 0; default colour), red (log = 1; default colour), blue (log = 2; act = 4) and white (log = 3; default colour). To change more than one colour we can string the VDU19 commands together as

   VDU19,log,act;0;19,log,act;0; . . . .

Much more can be said about colour. The User Guide provides a comprehensive summary but we will postpone more detailed presentations until we require them in later chapters.

We are now in a position to develop our first program. This program requests the user to input a number of rectangles whose size is computed randomly which are then plotted on the screen as graphics windows. This illustrates how blocks of colour on the screen can be defined quickly and built up to generate more complex patterns. The listing is given in Program 2.1. In these early programs, we will discuss the structure in detail but as ideas are developed throughout the book and as the programs become longer, we will leave it to the reader to work through the programs as 'exercises'.

Program 2.1   Graphics windows

```
10 REM Graphics Windows
20 INPUT "NO.OF WINDOWS = ",N%
30 MODE1
40 VDU23,1,0;0;0;0;
50 VDU19,1,4;0;19,2,5;0;19,3,6;0;
60 FOR I%=1 TO N%
70   REPEAT
80     XL%=RND(1280):XR%=RND(1280)
90     YB%=RND(1024):YT%=RND(1024)
100    UNTIL XL%<XR% AND YB%<YT%
110   VDU24,XL%;YB%;XR%;YT%;
120   GCOL0,128+RND(3):CLG
160   AA=GET:NEXT I%
170 END
```

Line 20 requests the user to input N% rectangles, MODE 1 is selected in line 30, while the cursor is switched off using VDU23,1,0;0;0;0; in line 40. Colour assignments to blue, magenta and cyan are made in line 50. A FOR–NEXT loop between lines 60 and 160 ensures N% windows are defined. Their dimensions are fixed randomly in a REPEAT–UNTIL loop in lines 70 to 100 which guarantees consistent dimensions. The window is defined in line 110 and its colour is fixed randomly and established as a background colour in line 120. Line 160 requires the user to press any key before the next window is defined and plotted. Typical output from the program is presented in Fig. 2.2. The kind of design generated is reminiscent of early 20th century abstract painting such as that produced by Mondrian. Experiment with the program by changing its colours in line 50. A slightly more complex task might be to use the structure of the program to define similar designs using text windows.

2.3 BASIC GRAPHICS COMMANDS

The most basic commands involve moving to a position on the graphics screen

Fig. 2.2 Graphics windows

and drawing a line from this position to another. The positions are described using screen coordinates *x,y*. For example

    MOVE X1,Y1 : DRAW X2,Y2

positions an invisible cursor at point *X1,Y1* and then draws a line in the current foreground colour to point *X2,Y2*. Points *X1,Y1* and *X2,Y2* must lie on the graphics screen for the whole length of the line to be visible. To illustrate this, consider again the program in Program 2.1 which defines graphics windows. Replace line 120 with the following lines 120 to 150

    120 GCOL0,RND(3)
    130 FOR J%=1 TO 300
    140   DRAW RND(1280),RND(1024)
    150   NEXT J%

In each graphics window, the program now draws 300 randomly positioned lines across the default screen, many of which will cut the graphics window thus illustrating how the window clips lines, as well as demonstrating the speed of the DRAW command.

Although MOVE and DRAW will be widely used in this book, a more versatile set of commands are the PLOT commands which include line, point and fill operations. These commands have the following form

    PLOTnumber,X,Y

which operate a particular PLOT function (given by the number) at coordinate *X,Y*. There are many different PLOT commands: PLOT5,X,Y for example is equivalent to DRAW X,Y. However, as we use only a few of the possible commands in this book, we will not list the whole set here but simply refer the reader to pages 319–321 of the User Guide where a complete description is provided. In the sequel, we will need to plot a dot or point at *X,Y* and this is given by PLOT69,X,Y. Random points many of which occur in our graphics window are given by replacing line 120 in Program 2.1 with

    120 GCOL0,RND(3)
    130 FOR J%=1 TO 1000
    140   PLOT69,RND(1280),RND(1024)
    150   NEXT J%

and running the new program. Plotting a dotted (broken) line from the previous coordinates to *X,Y* involves using PLOT21,X,Y. Random dotted lines in the graphics window are plotted if line 120 of Program 2.1 is now replaced with

    120 GCOL0,RND(3)
    130 FOR J%=1 TO 1000
    140   PLOT21,RND(1280),RND(1024)
    150   NEXT J%

In fact, these three modifications to Program 2.1 begin to hint how shading techniques might be developed and the results of running these programs produce interesting designs in their own right.

The most useful PLOT command in this book in fact involves filling shapes with colour rather than drawing to or at a single set of coordinates. The most elemental closed shape (polygon) is the triangle and this is the shape used in BBC Basic for colour fill. The appropriate command is PLOT85,X,Y which works by filling in the triangle given by point X, Y and the *two previous* points defined in the computer program. As an example, type into your computer

MODE 1 : MOVE 100,400 : MOVE 900,200 : PLOT85,200,800

and note how the triangle with vertices (100,400), (900,200) and (200,800) is filled with the current foreground colour, in this case white. The essence of using this command to fill complex polygons is therefore to break up the shape into triangles and to use PLOT85. It is not just a matter of defining complex shapes by triangles, however, for the way in which the points defining these triangles are coded is of critical importance. Points can often be coded in a sequence which enables strings of PLOT85 commands to be used without the need for MOVE or other graphics operations. Whether this is possible, depends upon the complexity of the shape and the ingenuity of the designer. We will see many examples of various types of coding in this book but first let us demonstrate how several of these basic commands can be embodied in a simple program.

We have written a program, shown in Program 2.2 which draws one of the heads sketched by the famous German artist Albrecht Durer in the late 15th century (Strauss, 1972). The program uses two colours in the higher resolution MODE 0, of which the foreground colour is assigned red in line 40. The main characteristic of the program is the way the head, shown in Fig. 2.3(a) is coded, and then drawn. The head is divided into four segments, each segment being a natural subdivision of the shape which can be plotted as a continuous line described by a string of coordinates *x,y*. The need for such segmentation relates to the fact that there is no way the complete head can be drawn as a continuous line. The first segment involves the face which is stored as 31 pairs of coordinates, the second the eye area – eight pairs of coordinates, the third the front of the neck – two pairs of coordinates, and last the back of the head – fifteen pairs of coordinates. These are stored in the program as DATA statements in lines 190 to 370.

The coordinates of the four segments are read in and drawn in the FOR–NEXT loop between lines 70 and 160. In line 80, the number of coordinates associated with the segment is read in; then the first pair of coordinates is read in and the cursor moved to this point in line 90. The rest of the coordinates are read in in line 110 and drawn to in line 120, within the FOR–NEXT loop beginning at line 100. There are two important features to

Program 2.2   The Durer head

```
 10 REM Head by Albrecht Durer
 20 MODE0
 30 VDU23,1,0;0;0;0;
 40 VDU19,1,1;0;
 50 T=4:XX%=90:YY%=50
 60 A%=T*(100+XX%):B%=T*(60+YY%)
 70 FOR I%=1 TO 4
 80    READ N%:READ X%,Y%
 90    MOVE T*(X%+XX%),T*(Y%+YY%)
100    FOR J%=2 TO N%
110       READ X%,Y%
120       DRAW T*(X%+XX%),T*(Y%+YY%)
150       AA=GET
160       NEXT J%:NEXT I%
170 END
180 :
190 DATA 31
200 DATA 138,61,140,53,146,55,156,54
210 DATA 147,120,144,131,130,140,110,143
220 DATA 90,142,80,140,75,130,73,105
230 DATA 70,90,60,95,50,90,48,80
240 DATA 51,70,60,68,58,60,60,50
250 DATA 70,34,90,19,110,10,120,12
260 DATA 140,13,142,30,139,33,142,44
270 DATA 135,44,148,44,146,55
280 DATA 8
290 DATA 120,96,130,99,142,98,138,90
300 DATA 128,89,136,85,138,90,136,77
310 DATA 2
320 DATA 100,14,96,0
330 DATA 15
340 DATA 144,131,140,140,130,150,110,166
350 DATA 80,173,60,173,30,164,10,148
360 DATA 1,130,1,110,9,80,20,56
370 DATA 20,44,15,30,11,10
```

note. First, the coordinates of the head in the DATA statements are different
from the screen coordinates ultimately used. Thus these 'world' coordinates
must be transformed to screen coordinates to centre the head on the screen
and scale it to reasonable size. The scaling parameter is set as *T* in line 50 and
the centring (displacement) parameters as *XX%* and *YY%* in the same line.
Thus whenever the world coordinates *x* and *y* are used, they are displaced by
XX% and *YY%*, and scaled by *T*. Try changing these values to assess their
effect. Set *T* = *1* and *XX%* and *YY%* as 0 and watch the head appear in the
bottom left-hand corner of the screen. Secondly we do not store the
coordinates, for as soon as they are read in, the program uses them. In later
programs, we will see the need to store these as arrays as we do with the Welsh
dragon in the next chapter.

The other reason why the head has been coded in four segments relates to
the need to demonstrate the fill command PLOT85. The first segment of 31

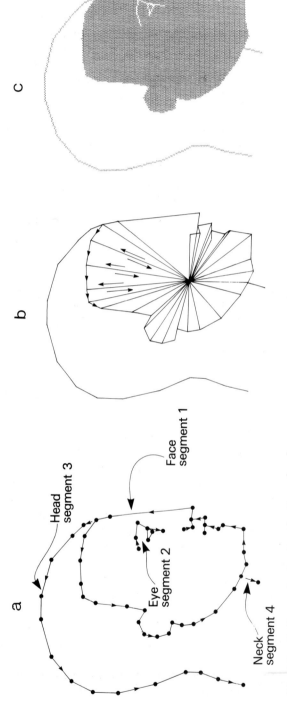

a

Head
segment 3

Face
segment 1

Eye
segment 2

Neck
segment 4

b

c

Fig. 2.3 Coding and colouring the Durer head

pairs of coordinates defining the face is a closed polygon. We can thus divide the polygon up into triangles and fill it by filling each triangle. As the face is roughly a convex polygon, one way of filling it is to define an interior point and splay the triangles around this point as shown in Fig. 2.3(b). By moving in sequence to an edge point, then to the interior, then to the next edge point, back to the interior point and so on, a sequence of MOVE, then PLOT85 commands will fill the shape. The order is shown by the arrows in Fig. 2.3(b) which illustrates the counter-clockwise direction of fill. To achieve this, Program 2.2 can be altered by replacing line 120 with the following lines

```
120 X%=T*(X%+XX%):Y%=T*(Y%+YY%)
130 IF I%=2 THEN GCOL0,0 ELSE GCOL0,1
140 IF I%=1 THEN MOVE A%,B%:PLOT85,X%,Y% ELSE DRAW X%,Y%
```

As the face will be the only segment of the head filled, line 140 checks to see whether the segment requires the DRAW or PLOT85 command. As the fill is in red, the eye must now be in black and line 130 ensures this. Note that the interior point is already set in the original program as line 60. This method of coding and filling is not necessarily the fastest but it is generally the easiest to construct and we will see it used several times in this book. Indeed, in the sections that follow where regular shapes such as circles and ellipses are developed, this interior-exterior fill procedure will be illustrated again. The filled head is shown in Fig. 2.3(c).

2.4   THE ELEMENTARY MATHEMATICS OF POINTS, CIRCLES AND ELLIPSES

The position of a point, given in two-dimensional space by the coordinates x,y is always measured relative to some other point, usually a fixed point such as the origin 0,0. In the subsequent treatment, we will assume that all the points given by x,y are in relation to the origin, and simply note that if any displacement from the origin is required, all we need to do is to add this displacement to the points. A typical point x,y is illustrated in Fig. 2.4 where it is clear that there are several ways in which the point can be located. Using the conventional right-angle triangle description, we refer to the vertical distance y as the perpendicular, the horizontal distance x as the base, and the distance from 0,0 to x,y as the hypotenuse R. These distances are related by Pythagoras's Theorem which states mathematically that

$$R^2 = x^2 + y^2. \tag{2.1}$$

If any two distances in equation (2.1) are known, this functional relationship can be manipulated to find the third unknown distance.

The second type of relationship in Fig. 2.4 involves defining the relationship between any two of these distances in terms of a parameter. The most well-

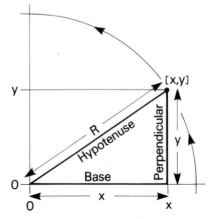

Fig. 2.4   Description of a point in the *x–y* coordinate system

known way is to calculate the ratios of these distances which give rise to standard trigonometric functions. First the ratio of the base to the hypotenuse, $x:R$, gives the cosine defined as

$$\cos(\theta) = \frac{\text{base}}{\text{hypotenuse}} = \frac{x}{R} \qquad (2.2)$$

where θ is the angle between the base and hypotenuse which clearly varies with the ratio x/R. In similar fashion, the ratio of perpendicular to hypotenuse gives the sine function

$$\sin(\theta) = \frac{\text{perpendicular}}{\text{hypotenuse}} = \frac{y}{R} \qquad (2.3)$$

and the ratio of perpendicular to base which is also the ratio of the sine to cosine is given by the tangent

$$\tan(\theta) = \frac{\text{perpendicular}}{\text{base}} = \frac{y}{x} = \frac{\sin(\theta)}{\cos(\theta)}.$$

These functions, particularly the cosine and sine, embody key relationships in computer graphics and will be employed extensively throughout this book.

The first basic shape we will explore is the circle, which as Fig. 2.4 illustrates can be described by tracing out the path of the point *x,y* keeping *R* fixed and making one complete revolution of the angle θ. One revolution is measured from 0 to 360 degrees or in radians (which is the measure usually employed by computers) from 0 to 2π radians. The points on the circumference of the circle always satisfy equation (2.1) which can be rearranged using equations (2.2) and (2.3) to give

$$\frac{x^2+y^2}{R^2}=\frac{x^2}{R^2}+\frac{y^2}{R^2}=\cos^2(\theta)+\sin^2(\theta)=1. \qquad (2.4)$$

$\cos^2(\theta)$ and $\sin^2(\theta)$ are the squares of the cosine and sine functions in equations (2.2) and (2.3). R is now the fixed radius of the circle. It is more usual however to compute the coordinates x and y using the parametric forms in equations (2.2) and (2.3) directly. Then

$$x = R\, \cos(\theta) \qquad (2.5)$$

and

$$y = R\, \sin(\theta) \qquad (2.6)$$

and these are the equations used most frequently in this book to trace out points defining the circumference of a circle.

Equations (2.1) to (2.6) enable us to specify a slightly more general shape called the ellipse in which the ratios in equations (2.2) and (2.3) are given in terms of R_x and R_y specific to the x and y coordinate directions. Defining these ratios as

$$\cos(\theta) = \frac{x}{R_x} \qquad (2.7)$$

and

$$\sin(\theta) = \frac{y}{R_y}, \qquad (2.8)$$

the functional form for the ellipse following equation (2.4) is

$$\frac{x^2}{R_x^2}+\frac{y^2}{R_y^2}=1 \qquad (2.9)$$

and the parametric form

$$x = R_x\, \cos(\theta) \qquad (2.10)$$

and

$$y = R_y\, \sin(\theta). \qquad (2.11)$$

Note that when $R_x = R_y = R$, equations (2.7) to (2.11) collapse to (2.2) to (2.6) respectively and thus any program to draw an ellipse can be used to draw a circle when $R_x = R_y$.

A program to draw an ellipse where the user can input the lengths R_x and R_y which we refer to as radii, is shown in Program 2.3. This program draws the circumference of the ellipse using equations (2.10) and (2.11) to compute points x and y for given increments to the angle θ which varies from 0 to 2π (one revolution). The origin is first fixed at the centre of the screen in line 40 and text and foreground colours set as red in line 50. A REPEAT–UNTIL loop from lines 60 to 200 enables the user to run the program indefinitely inputting different shapes and sizes of ellipse in lines 70 and 80. The increment in the

Program 2.3   Slow ellipse drawing

```
 10 REM Slow Ellipse Drawing
 20 MODE1
 30 VDU23,1,0;0;0;0;
 40 VDU29,640;512;
 50 COLOUR1:GCOL0,1
 60 REPEAT
 70    INPUT"RADIUS OF X AXIS = ",RX
 80    INPUT"RADIUS OF Y AXIS = ",RY
 90    TIME=0
100    N%=60:DT=2*PI/N%
110    MOVE RX,0:TH=0
120    FOR I%=1 TO N%
130       TH=TH+DT
140       X%=RX*COS(TH)
150       Y%=RY*SIN(TH)
160       DRAW X%,Y%
170       NEXT I%
180    PRINT"TIME TAKEN = ";TIME
190    A=GET:CLS
200    UNTIL FALSE
210 END
```

angle θ is set in line 100 as $2\pi/60$ and the points computed using equations (2.10) and (2.11) in the FOR–NEXT loop from lines 120 to 170. This program also computes the time taken to draw the ellipse using the BBC computer's clock which measures time in hundredths of a second and which is set to 0 in line 90 and printed in line 180. Three features are worthy of note. In line 110, the first graphics command moves the cursor to the right-hand edge of the ellipse before drawing commences in sequence in line 160. Secondly, the computations are in real numbers but the coordinates $X\%$ and $Y\%$ are set as integers because the screen resolution is finite. This mixing of integer and real numbers will be a feature of many of the programs developed here and it reflects decisions concerning the nature of the computations involved and the effects of rounding errors. Finally, this program is independent of the mode in that the increments to the angle θ are not computed with the screen resolution in mind. The increments are small enough in fact to approximate the curve of the ellipse by straight lines but they have not been fixed in terms of the pixel resolution. In Section 2.6 we will see how questions of resolution can become important in determining the visual acceptability of a drawing.

2.5   FAST GENERATION OF CIRCLES AND ELLIPSES

Using equations (2.10) and (2.11) to compute x and y represents an extremely slow way of generating an ellipse because the computation of $\cos(\theta)$ and $\sin(\theta)$ for every value of θ is expensive in terms of computer time. A much faster method is available using elementary results from trigonometry and this enables the calculations to be speeded up considerably. Consider then the sequence of computations of points x_n, y_n and x_{n+1}, y_{n+1} in Program 2.3 where the first pair of coordinates is associated with the angle θ and the second pair with $\theta + \Delta\theta$, the angle plus its increment $\Delta\theta$. These coordinates are computed as

$$x_n = R_x \cos(\theta) \qquad \text{and} \qquad y_n = R_y \sin(\theta), \qquad (2.12)$$

$$x_{n+1} = R_x \cos(\theta + \Delta\theta) \quad \text{and} \quad y_{n+1} = R_y \sin(\theta + \Delta\theta). \qquad (2.13)$$

The cosine and sine functions in equations (2.13) can be expanded using the following standard trigonometric results

$$\left.\begin{array}{l} \cos(\theta + \Delta\theta) = \cos(\theta)\cos(\Delta\theta) - \sin(\theta)\sin(\Delta\theta), \\[2mm] \sin(\theta + \Delta\theta) = \sin(\theta)\cos(\Delta\theta) + \cos(\theta)\sin(\Delta\theta). \end{array}\right\} \qquad (2.14)$$

Substituting equations (2.14) into equations (2.13) and simplifying using equations (2.12) gives formulae for the recursive generation of the coordinate points. Then

$$\begin{aligned} x_{n+1} &= R_x \cos(\theta)\cos(\Delta\theta) - R_x \sin(\theta)\sin(\Delta\theta), \\[2mm] &= x_n \cos(\Delta\theta) - y_n \frac{R_x}{R_y} \sin(\Delta\theta), \end{aligned} \qquad (2.15)$$

$$\begin{aligned} y_{n+1} &= R_y \sin(\theta)\cos(\Delta\theta) + R_y \cos(\theta)\sin(\Delta\theta), \\[2mm] &= y_n \cos(\Delta\theta) + x_n \frac{R_y}{R_x} \sin(\Delta\theta). \end{aligned} \qquad (2.16)$$

Equations (2.15) and (2.16) show that if we know the values of $\cos(\Delta\theta)$ and $\sin(\Delta\theta)$, we can compute the whole sequence of points x_n $(n=2,3,\ldots)$, y_n $(n=2,3,\ldots)$ from the starting point x_1, y_1.

Equations (2.15) and (2.16) can be succinctly summarized in matrix form as

$$[x_{n+1} y_{n+1}] = [x_n y_n] \begin{bmatrix} \cos(\Delta\theta) & \dfrac{R_y}{R_x}\sin(\Delta\theta) \\[4mm] -\dfrac{R_x}{R_y}\sin(\Delta\theta) & \cos(\Delta\theta) \end{bmatrix}.$$

We have written equations (2.15) and (2.16) in this form to show that the recursive calculation of the point x_{n+1}, y_{n+1} is essentially based on a transformation of the point x_n, y_n, where the 2×2 matrix in large square brackets above acts as the transformation operator. Those unfamiliar with matrix operations can ignore this for the time being but it will be reintroduced in the next chapter and again in Chapter 6 where brief digressions on matrix operations are included. If $R_x = R_y$, then the above transformation collapses to the standard transformation of any point into another. In this case, it is sufficient to note that the ratios R_y/R_x and R_x/R_y stretch the points away from the pure circle form to an ellipse.

We have adapted Program 2.3 to that listed in Program 2.4 where equations (2.15) and (2.16) are now used instead of equations (2.10) and (2.11). The first nine lines of the program are the same as the previous one. Line 100 is the same except the ratio R_x/R_y has been computed. In line 110, the starting points for x and y are fixed and in 120, the increment $\Delta\theta$ is used to compute the functions $\cos(\Delta\ell)$ and $\sin(\Delta\theta)$, these then being modified by the appropriate radii ratios. Lines 130 to 170 involve the recursive transformation of points and the drawing operation. Note that the values of x and y are now real values X and Y, not integer as in Program 2.3 due to the need to compute the transformations of these points in real terms.

Program 2.4 is over three times as fast as Program 2.3. If you run both programs, the slower one draws an ellipse in about 3.2 seconds, the faster one in just under 1 second, this difference being accounted for mainly through the number of computations of the sine and cosine functions. In the sequel, we will use both methods in fact, but sometimes speed is important in developing a picture. If the development of the picture is unimportant or boring, then speed in constructing the picture is of the essence. Often we will find that the development of the picture is an art form in its own right – kinetic art – but for circles or ellipses, this is not usually the case.

Before we move on to techniques for filling these regular shapes, it is worth noting one other method for generating ellipses. First, let us find the change in

Program 2.4   Fast ellipse drawing

```
 10 REM Fast Ellipse Drawing
 20 MODE1
 30 VDU23,1,0;0;0;0;
 40 VDU29,640;512;
 50 COLOUR1:GCOLO,1
 60 REPEAT
 70    INPUT"RADIUS OF X AXIS = ",RX
 80    INPUT"RADIUS OF Y AXIS = ",RY
 90    TIME=0
100    N%=60:DT=2*PI/N%:A=RX/RY
110    X=RX:Y=0:MOVE X,Y
120    C=COS(DT):S=SIN(DT):SS=S/A:S=S*A
130    FOR I%=1 TO N%
140       T=X*C-Y*S
150       Y=Y*C+X*SS:X=T
160       DRAW X,Y
170       NEXT I%
180    PRINT"TIME TAKEN = ";TIME
190    A=GET:CLS
200    UNTIL FALSE
210 END
```

x and y, called dx and dy, with respect to the change in the angle θ, called dθ. Differentiating equations (2.10) and (2.11) with respect to θ gives the following standard results:

$$\frac{dx}{d\theta} = -R_x \sin(\theta) = -y \frac{R_x}{R_y} \tag{2.17}$$

and

$$\frac{dy}{d\theta} = R_y \cos(\theta) = x \frac{R_y}{R_x}. \tag{2.18}$$

If we approximate dx, dy and dθ as Δx, Δy and $\Delta\theta$, then an algorithm for updating given values of x_n and y_n which uses discrete approximation to equations (2.17) and (2.18) can be based on the following equations

$$x_{n+1} = x_n + \Delta x = x_n - y_n \frac{R_x}{R_y} \Delta\theta \tag{2.19}$$

and

$$y_{n+1} = y_n + \Delta y = y_n + x_n \frac{R_y}{R_x} \Delta\theta. \tag{2.20}$$

It is clear that as $\Delta\theta \to d\theta$, equations (2.19) and (2.20) converge to (2.15) and (2.16). In fact, equations (2.19) and (2.20) have often been used as the basis of a circle generator which is embodied in hardware (Newman and Sproull, 1979), but as a circle/ellipse generator in high level language, $\Delta\theta$ has to be very small before a satisfactory approximation to the shape is generated. Tests of this procedure on the BBC computer in BBC Basic suggest that the previous method based on equations (2.15) and (2.16) is superior in all cases.

2.6   TECHNIQUES FOR FILLING CIRCLES AND ELLIPSES

So far we have introduced techniques for drawing circles and ellipses which do not depend on the mode, that is upon the level of resolution of the screen and our approach has exclusively emphasized the efficiency of mathematical technique. We will continue this approach here, but at the end of this section we will introduce a technique for filling an ellipse which depends on adapting the technique to the hardware of the display device. The first method of filling an ellipse has already been introduced when we filled the Durer head. This method is based on finding an interior point and revolving around this using a succession of MOVE followed by PLOT85 commands. In the case of a circle or an ellipse, the obvious interior point is the centre, in this case the origin 0,0. To accomplish the fill, all we need do is to replace the draw command in either Program 2.3 or 2.4 with the fill sequence. Then for Program 2.3, replacing line 160 with

160 MOVE0,0:PLOT85,X%,Y%

and for Program 2.4, line 160 with the same

>160 MOVE0,0:PLOT85,X,Y

generates the fill. The sequence of coordinates accessed in these operations is illustrated in Fig. 2.5(a).

Although this is the traditional method, there is a method which is closer to the way shapes are shaded by hand and which involves only half the number of coordinate point computations as those contained in Programs 2.3 and 2.4. Imagine you are shading an ellipse by hand. If you are right-handed, you would probably fill in the shape from left to right using continuous upright strokes. This method works the other way, assuming you are left-handed because the angle of revolution increases in a counter-clockwise direction. The essence of the idea which is illustrated in Fig. 2.5(b) involves computing a point x,y, then filling the triangle formed by that point, the previous point and the symmetric reflection of the computed point, that is $x, -y$. This involves the same number of plot commands as in the first method but only half the number of coordinate calculations for now the revolution of θ is only from 0 to π. The method is technically more efficient than the previous one.

The program for this cross fill method is listed in Program 2.5. This program is based on the calculation of the coordinates using equations (2.15) and (2.16) and is thus similar to Program 2.4. Line 100 indicates that only half the number of angular increments need be computed and this is accomplished by the FOR–NEXT loop in lines 140 to 180. To start the procedure, a separate fill

Program 2.5   Cross fill method

```
10 REM Fast Draw,Cross Fill
20 MODE1
30 VDU23,1,0;0;0;0;
40 VDU29,640;512;
50 COLOUR1:GCOLO,1
60 REPEAT
70    INPUT"RADIUS OF X AXIS = ",RX
80    INPUT"RADIUS OF Y AXIS = ",RY
90    TIME=0
100   N%=30:DT=PI/N%:A=RX/RY
110   C=COS(DT):S=SIN(DT):SS=S/A:S=S*A
120   X=RX*C:Y=RY*S
130   MOVE RX,0:MOVE X,Y:PLOT85,X,-Y
140   FOR I%=2 TO N%-1
150     T=X*C-Y*S
160     Y=Y*C+X*SS:X=T
170     PLOT85,X,Y:PLOT85,X,-Y
180     NEXT I%
190   PLOT85,-RX,0
200   PRINT"TIME TAKEN = ";TIME
210   AA=GET:CLS
220   UNTIL FALSE
230 END
```

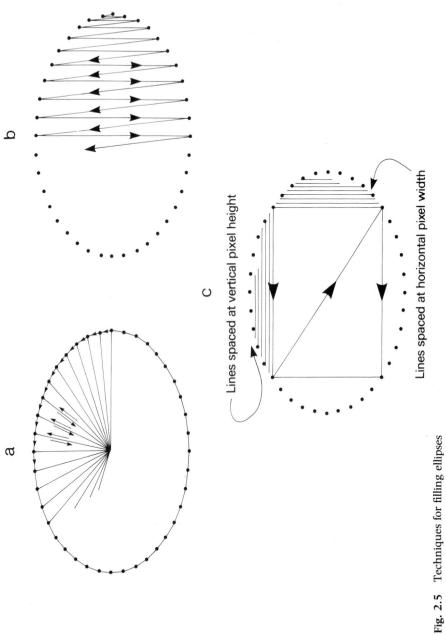

Lines spaced at vertical pixel height

Lines spaced at horizontal pixel width

Fig. 2.5 Techniques for filling ellipses

sequence is required in line 130 and one is required to finish this in line 190. Thus the FOR–NEXT loop involves two less plot sequences then the number of angular increments. In line 170, two PLOT85 commands indicate the reflective symmetry of the method. There is no dramatic difference in the speed of the two fill methods based on Program 2.4. The second cross fill method is up to 30% faster for ellipses with the major axis up to 100 screen units in size but above this, the centre fill method is faster. This is due to the fact that the speed of the PLOT85 command depends on the shape of the triangle. For long thin triangles which occur in the cross fill method as the ellipses increase in size, the PLOT85 commands become much slower. This indicates that shape, as well as technique can be important in computer graphics. The decision to use one or other of these fill procedures will thus in the last analysis be based on the ease of coding and/or ease of drawing the shape.

We have seen that the PLOT85 command can be quite a slow way of filling a shape and in comparison, other operations such as MOVE and DRAW are extremely fast. One strategy to fill a shape would thus be to minimize use of the fill commands and use the DRAW commands as much as possible to fill in the remaining areas. As the DRAW command operates at the pixel level, that is it switches on a line of pixels, the level of screen resolution will clearly affect the technique. The essence of the technique to be suggested is to fill in a rectangle within the ellipse using two PLOT85 commands and then to colour the remaining unfilled areas using DRAW commands. An illustration of the method is given in Fig. 2.5(c).

The coordinates of a rectangle which fits the ellipse most efficiently are given by

$$x = R_x \cos(45°) = R_x/\sqrt{2}$$

and

$$y = R_y \sin(45°) = R_y/\sqrt{2} .$$

The corner points of the rectangle are given by (x,y), $(-x,y)$, $(-x,-y)$ and $(x,-y)$. The remaining areas at the top and bottom, and left and right of the rectangle are filled using DRAW commands. First, the x coordinate is incremented at the pixel resolution level which in MODE 1 is four screen units, from x to R_x and y is computed as follows: from equation (2.4), if x is known, then

$$\sin^2(\theta) + \frac{x^2}{R_x^2} = 1$$

and thus

$$\sin(\theta) = \sqrt{\left[1 - \left(\frac{x}{R_x}\right)^2\right]}.$$ (2.21)

From equation (2.11) and using (2.21), y is thus computed as

$$y = R_y \sqrt{\left[1 - \left(\frac{x}{R_x}\right)^2\right]} \qquad (2.22)$$

and lines are then drawn from x,y to $x,-y$ on the right of the rectangle, and from $-x,y$ to $-x,-y$ on the left. This is continued until R_x and $-R_x$ are reached.

The same procedure is then operated for units of y from y to R_y which involve computing x from the analogous equation to (2.22)

$$x = R_x \sqrt{\left[1 - \left(\frac{y}{R_y}\right)^2\right]} \qquad (2.23)$$

and drawing lines from x,y to $-x,y$ and $x,-y$ to $-x,-y$ until R_y and $-R_y$ are reached. These ideas are encoded in the listing presented as Program 2.6. The first nine lines are the same as in earlier programs. Lines 100 to 120 involve the computation of the corner points of the rectangle and its filling using two PLOT85 commands. The FOR–NEXT loop between 130 and 170 involves incrementing x to R_x, calculating y using equation (2.22) (in line 140) and drawing lines on the right and left of the rectangle. The FOR–NEXT loop in

Program 2.6   Fast fill method

```
10 REM Fast Ellipse Fill
20 MODE1
30 VDU23,1,0;0;0;0;
40 VDU29,640;512;
50 COLOUR1:GCOL0,1
60 REPEAT
70    INPUT "RADIUS OF X AXIS = ",RX
80    INPUT "RADIUS OF Y AXIS = ",RY
90    TIME=0
100   XY%=RX/SQR(2):YX%=RY/SQR(2)
110   MOVE XY%,YX%:MOVE XY%,-YX%
120   PLOT85,-XY%,YX%:PLOT85,-XY%,-YX%
130   FOR X%=XY%+4 TO RX STEP 4
140     Y%=RY*SQR(1-(X%/RX)^2)
150     MOVE X%,Y%:DRAW X%,-Y%
160     MOVE -X%,Y%:DRAW -X%,-Y%
170   NEXT X%
180   FOR Y%=YX%+4 TO RY STEP 4
190     X%=RX*SQR(1-(Y%/RY)^2)
200     MOVE X%,Y%:DRAW -X%,Y%
210     MOVE X%,-Y%:DRAW -X%,-Y%
220   NEXT Y%
230   PRINT"TIME TAKEN = ";TIME
240   AA=GET:CLS
250 UNTIL FALSE
260 END
```

lines 180 to 220 does the same for the top and bottom of the rectangle using x computed from equation (2.23).

This program is much faster than the previous two. For shapes up to $R_x, R_y = 100$, it is at least three times as fast while for radii up to 300, it is over 1.5 times as fast. For really large shapes with R_x and $R_y > 700$ screen units, then the traditional centre fill based on Program 2.4 is faster while the cross fill in Program 2.5 is rather inefficient due to large narrow areas to be filled. What this section has shown is that graphics programming depends on the efficiency of mathematical technique *and* the limitations of the hardware. Efficient coding and sequencing of the graphics operations is also important and although there are broad principles to be followed, every design will have unique features which can be exploited in its programming.

2.7   CREATING NATURAL PATTERNS FROM SIMPLE SHAPES

At this point, we have introduced enough technique to begin to construct some colourful and interesting designs which illustrate elementary principles of picture structure. First we will introduce a program to plot randomly positioned ellipses of variable size and different colour on the screen. The essence of this program involves replicating the fast ellipse drawing algorithm based on the cross fill technique in Program 2.5 an indefinite number of times by defining it as a procedure and providing it with randomly chosen parameters. In this way, the picture can be regarded as being composed of segments, each segment being an ellipse called from a given position in the main program.

The listing for the random ellipses program is given in Program 2.7. The procedure to draw and fill the ellipse is defined in lines 150 to 250. This is similar to lines 110 to 190 in Program 2.5 but note that as the cosine and sine functions are the same for each ellipse, they are defined only once in the main program at line 60. In the main program, colour assignments are made in lines 40 and 50 while the randomly configured ellipse is set up and plotted in a REPEAT–UNTIL loop between lines 70 and 120. Line 80 centres the ellipse in a random position on the screen, line 90 chooses a random colour, and line 100 chooses random axes lengths R_x and R_y between certain limits. A typical design is shown in Fig. 2.6. Although ellipses individually have little form, together they are sometimes suggestive of abstract landscapes and the chosen colours in Program 2.7 – blue background with ellipses coloured in magenta, cyan and white occasionally produce wistful looking scenes.

To generate more realistic natural shapes, we can extend our ellipse program to produce a spiral which is one of the basic models for the growth of biological forms (Thompson, 1961). Essentially, a spiral is a circular or elliptical plot which does not close upon itself but increases or decreases without bound. There are two basic types. First a spiral whose radius increases

Program 2.7 Random ellipses

```
10 REM Random Ellipses
20 MODE1
30 VDU23,1,0;0;0;0;
40 VDU19,0,4;0;19,1,5;0;
50 VDU19,2,6;0;19,3,7;0;
60 DT=PI/30:C=COS(DT):S=SIN(DT)
70 REPEAT
80    VDU29,RND(1280);RND(1024);
90    GCOLO,RND(3)
100   RX=20+RND(150):RY=20+RND(150)
110   PROCSHAPE
120   UNTIL FALSE
130 END
140 :
150 DEFPROCSHAPE
160 A=RX/RY:SX=S/A:SY=S*A
170 X=RX*C:Y=RY*S
180 MOVE RX,O:MOVE X,Y:PLOT85,X,-Y
190 FOR I%=2 TO 29
200    T=X*C-Y*SY
210    Y=Y*C+X*SX:X=T
220    PLOT85,X,Y:PLOT85,X,-Y
230    NEXT I%
240 PLOT85,-RX,O
250 ENDPROC
```

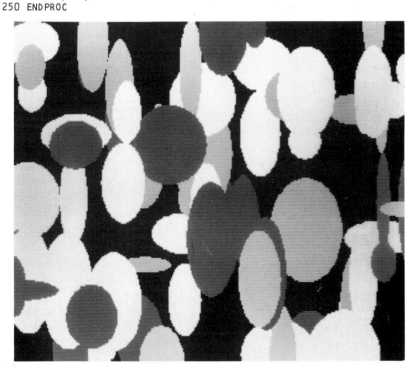

Fig. 2.6 Random ellipses

or decreases linearly or arithmetically – the equable or Archimedean spiral which coils like a rope; and secondly, the equiangular spiral whose radius changes geometrically. Here we will concern ourselves only with the Archimedean spiral which represents the trace of x,y coordinates defined by

$$x = R_x \theta \cos(\theta), \text{ and } y = R_y \theta \sin(\theta). \tag{2.24}$$

Program 2.8 which is modelled on the earlier ellipse programs enables the user to plot an increasing elliptical (or circular where $R_x = R_y$) spiral. The spiral is drawn out from the origin 0,0 and lines 110 and 120 show that the radii of the X and Y axes increase linearly as the product of the angle and the start radii R_x and R_y. The spiral is plotted for ten revolutions, that is from θ starting at 0 to 20π. We have only shown the traditional and slowest method for computing the x,y coordinates in equation (2.24) but it is possible to derive a recursive form for x,y analogous to the derivation which led to equations (2.15) and (2.16) earlier. This is left as an exercise for the reader. To understand the spiral, experiment with Program 2.8 by changing the way the parameter θ affects the radii in equation (2.24).

We are now going to make what might seem like a massive leap in using our spiral program to create certainly more realistic and possibly 'beautiful' designs. If you look at the petals forming a flower, you will see that they are arranged in a spiral-like fashion around the centre, reflecting the growth of the plant. What we are going to do is create the illusion of petals forming a rose by using our spiral program. There are three main issues to resolve. First, we do not want the spiral to be completely regular so if we perturb each coordinate x,y slightly from its pure value (computed from equations (2.24)), this will add to its realism. The form will be random in detail but regular overall. Secondly, we want to colour in the spiral using the centre fill technique but changing the colours periodically to reflect shades of petals. If we plot an increasing spiral,

Program 2.8   The Archimedean spiral

```
10 REM Archimedean Spiral
20 MODE1
30 VDU23,1,0;0;0;0;
40 VDU29,640;512;
50 COLOUR1:GCOL0,1
60 REPEAT
70    MOVE0,0
80    INPUT "START X RADIUS = ",RX
90    INPUT "START Y RADIUS = ",RY
100   FOR I=0 TO 20*PI STEP 0.1
110      X%=RX*I*COS(I)
120      Y%=RY*I*SIN(I)
130      DRAW X%,Y%
140   NEXT I
150   AA=GET:CLS
160   UNTIL FALSE
170 END
```

the inner trace will be obliterated by the PLOT85 command as the form spirals outward. Therefore if we plot a decreasing spiral the inner spirals will overplot the outer but preserving the spiral form. Finally, we will edge the spiral in black thus ensuring that its form is clear.

The program is listed as Program 2.9. It plots randomly positioned, randomly sized, filled spirals in red, white and blue which resemble rosettes rather than roses. It has the same general structure as Program 2.7 except that the spiral is not contained in a separate procedure but is in the main body of the program. The decreasing spirals are in fact circular, not elliptical. The user inputs the number of rosettes required in line 20 and colour assignments are made in line 50. The rosettes are set up and plotted in the FOR–NEXT loop which is between lines 60 and 200. Line 70 fixes the radius and two colours for each rosette randomly while line 80 determines its position on the screen. Lines 90 and 100 set up parameters which determine the number of revolutions of the spiral, the start colour and contain a move command to the centre. The FOR–NEXT loop between 110 and 200 controls nine colour changes for the spiral (made in line 120) while the FOR–NEXT loop between 130 and 200 randomly fixes the length of the spiral over which a particular colour operates. The decreasing radius R is randomly calculated and perturbed in line 150, x,y coordinates computed in 160 and a portion of the spiral filled in 170. In line 180, that portion of the spiral is edged in black, and the colour shifted back in line 190. If you need to see how the procedure works more slowly insert the new line 185 AA = GET, which will enable you to control the speed of the plot. A typical picture generated by this short program is illustrated in Fig. 2.7.

Program 2.9   Random rosettes

```
 10 REM Random Rosettes
 20 INPUT "NO.OF ROSETTES = ",NUM%
 30 MODE1
 40 VDU23,1,0;0;0;0;
 50 VDU19,1,1;0;19,2,4;0;19,3,7;0;
 60 FOR J%=1 TO NUM%
 70   Z=RND(2)+RND(1)+1.5:C1%=RND(3):C2%=RND(3)
 80   VDU29,RND(1280);RND(1024);
 90   N=2*PI:M=10*N:MOVE0,0
100   IK=0:L%=C2%:GCOLO,L%:XX%=0:YY%=0
110   FOR K%=1 TO 9
120     IF L%=C1% THEN L%=C2% ELSE L%=C1%
130     FOR I=0 TO 1.7*PI+RND(1.2*PI) STEP 0.2
140       IK=IK+0.2
150       R=(Z/(1+RND(1)/4.5))*(M-IK)
160       X%=R*COS(IK):Y%=R*SIN(IK)
170       MOVE 0,0:PLOT85,X%,Y%
180       GCOLO,0:MOVE XX%,YY%:DRAW X%,Y%
190       GCOLO,L%:XX%=X%:YY%=Y%
200       NEXT I:NEXT K%:NEXT J%
210 END
```

Fig. 2.7   Random rosettes

2.8   EARLY COMPUTER ART

There are no exercises in a book such as this one but readers are encouraged to explore these ideas further by modifying the programs and extending them. All the programs are short enough to be typed into the machine with only a little effort, and the only way to learn about computer art and graphics is through trial and error. For example, there are decisions in the rosettes program concerning the shapes generated which could only have been made by sitting at the terminal and exploring appropriate parameter values. Trial and error leads to insights which in turn enable visual anticipation of what computers might produce. This is the real excitement of computer graphics and art which combines fanciful imaginings with stolid technique.

We will conclude this chapter with a couple of examples of early computer art which build on the techniques developed so far. Twenty years ago, most computer art was based on line drawings which could be displayed on direct view storage tubes or reproduced on plotters. Designs based on trigonometric manipulations were the order of the day and only when raster graphics terminals became widely available in the late 1970s did a new realism enter the field. Nevertheless, the early art was often ingenious and produced fascinating abstract designs. In 1967, the astrophysicist, Fred Whipple (1968) published some of his own art which was based on randomly constructed, and randomly coloured polygons. Although his art was not produced by computer, he outlined a simple algorithm for constructing a random polygon which we have programmed here. He called his technique 'stochastic painting'.

Whipple constructed his polygons by ensuring that each internal angle of the polygon was less than π radians, and closing the polygon once the computed side was pointing in the direction of the original side. The length of each side was also chosen randomly within given limits. The kind of convex polygon produced is illustrated in Fig. 2.8. After the second side has been calculated, it is necessary to test whether or not the third or subsequent sides point towards the original side in the polygon. We thus need to calculate whether or not this side intersects the first side, and to do this we need a little more coordinate geometry.

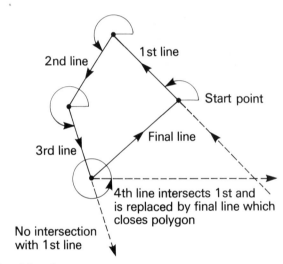

Fig. 2.8 Whipple's polygon construction

Using the equation for a straight line, any point x_a, y_a on the line or its projection can be computed from

$$\left.\begin{array}{l} x_a = x_1 + F_a(x_2 - x_1) \quad \text{and} \\ \\ y_a = y_1 + F_a(y_2 - y_1) \end{array}\right\} \tag{2.25}$$

where (x_1, y_1) and (x_2, y_2) represent the first and last points on the given line. If $0 \leqslant F_a \leqslant 1$, the point (x_a, y_a) lies on the line. If $F_a > 1$, the point lies forward of the line, beyond (x_2,y_2) and if $F_a<0$, the point lies backward of the line. Consider a second line defined by (x_3,y_3), (x_4,y_4) and F_b. If these two lines or their projections intersect, then

$$\left.\begin{array}{l} x_1 + F_a(x_2 - x_1) = x_3 + F_b(x_4 - x_3) \quad \text{and} \\[6pt] y_1 + F_a(y_2 - y_1) = y_3 + F_b(y_4 - y_3). \end{array}\right\} \tag{2.26}$$

F_a and F_b can be found by solving equations (2.26) as

$$F_a = \{(y_3 - y_1)(x_4 - x_3) - (x_3 - x_1)(y_4 - y_3)\}/G \tag{2.27}$$

$$F_b = \{(x_2 - x_1)(y_3 - y_1) - (y_2 - y_1)(x_3 - x_1)\}/G \tag{2.28}$$

where G is defined as

$$G = (y_2 - y_1)(x_4 - x_3) - (x_2 - x_1)(y_4 - y_3).$$

If $G=0$, the two lines are parallel. Further details of these derivations are provided by Mufti (1982).

All we need note is that if the second line points towards or intersects the first, then F_b in equation (2.28) will be greater than zero. Equation (2.27) will

Program 2.10   Stochastic painting

```
10 REM Stochastic Painting
20 MODE1
30 VDU23,1,0;0;0;0;
40 VDU19,1,4;0;19,2,6;0;19,3,1;0;
50 Z%=60:D1%=100:D2%=100
60 REPEAT
70    GCOLO,RND(3):A=RND(360)
80    X1%=RND(1279):Y1%=RND(1023):MOVE X1%,Y1%
90    PROCLINE
100   X2%=X1%+DX%:Y2%=Y1%+DY%:X%=X2%:Y%=Y2%
110   MOVE X1%,Y1%:PLOT85,X%,Y%:XB%=X%:YB%=Y%
120   PROCLINE
130   X%=XB%+DX%:Y%=YB%+DY%
140   PROCINTER(X2%,Y2%,X1%,Y1%,XB%,YB%,X%,Y%)
150   IF Q>0 THEN PLOT85,X1%,Y1% ELSE GOTO 110
160   UNTIL FALSE
170 END
180 :
190 DEFPROCLINE
200 AI=RAD(Z%+RND(Z%)):D%=D1%+RND(D2%):A=A+AI
210 DX%=D%*COS(A):DY%=D%*SIN(A)
220 ENDPROC
230 :
240 DEFPROCINTER(X1%,Y1%,X2%,Y2%,X3%,Y3%,X4%,Y4%)
250 XA%=X3%-X1%:XB%=X2%-X1%:XC%=X4%-X3%
260 YA%=Y3%-Y1%:YB%=Y2%-Y1%:YC%=Y4%-Y3%
270 DEN%=(-XB%*YC%+YB%*XC%)
280 Q=(XB%*YA%-YB%*XA%)/DEN%
290 ENDPROC
```

not be required as it is of no consequence whether the intersection is forward or backward of the first side of the polygon. The program we have written is based on Whipple's algorithm with closure of the convex polygon as soon as a computed side yields a value of F_b which is positive. The structure of the program is based on choosing a random position on the screen for each polygon, determining the orientation and length of the first and subsequent sides randomly, and testing, using equation (2.28), as to whether or not the third or a later side intersects the first. As soon as $F_b > 0$, the computed side is abandoned and the polygon is closed. The polygon is coloured by filling triangles centred on the original vertex position. These triangles (and polygon sides) are constructed in a counter-clockwise direction.

The listing is given as Program 2.10. The orientation, length and end coordinates of each polygon side are fixed in the procedure PROCLINE in lines 190 to 220, while the intersection of any two lines is determined using computations in the procedure PROCINTER in lines 240 to 290. Colour assignments and limits on the interior polygon angles and side lengths are first fixed in lines 40 to 50. A REPEAT–UNTIL loop between lines 60 and 160 constitutes the main body of the program in which the polygon is constructed

Fig. 2.9 Stochastic painting

and coloured. Line 70 determines polygon colour and its initial orientation while line 80 positions the initial vertex on the screen. The first side is calculated and drawn in lines 90 to 110, the second in line 120. The intersection test is computed and checked in lines 140 and 150. If the line is pointing towards the first side, the polygon is closed in line 150 and a new polygon started. If however the line is not in the direction of the first, the program returns to line 110, plots the side, computes another and continues with the test. Note that between lines 100 and 130, start and end coordinates of the current line are updated. Running the program produces pictures such as that in Fig. 2.9. You can change the shape of the polygons by altering the parameters in line 50.

Our last example is an illustration of a computer program written by Kolomyjec (1976) which produces a simple but effective line drawing. This program subdivides a square on the screen into smaller squares, positions a circle randomly within each smaller square and draws lines at regular intervals around the circumference of the circle to regular intervals around the edges of the square in which the circle is located. The program is listed in Program 2.11. In lines 20 to 50, the user is asked to input the number of

Program 2.11   Kolomyjec's organic illusion

```
10 REM Kolomyjec's Organic Illusion
20 INPUT "NO.OF SUBDIVISIONS = ",N%
30 MODE0:L%=900:M%=10
40 VDU23,1,0;0;0;0;
50 INC=L%/N%:XB%=(1280-L%)/2:YB%=(1024-L%)/2
60 Y%=YB%
70 FOR I%=1 TO N%
80    X%=XB%
90    FOR J%=1 TO N%
100      RZ%=0.33*INC:R=(RZ%+RND(RZ%))/2
110      XO%=X%+RZ%+RND(RZ%):YO%=Y%+RZ%+RND(RZ%)
120      Z%=INC/M%:SI=90/M%
130      ANG=180:KJ%=1:JK%=1
140      PROCSHAPE(X%,Y%,Z%,0,ANG,JK%*SI)
150      PROCSHAPE(X%+INC,Y%,0,Z%,ANG+KJ%*90,JK%*SI)
160      PROCSHAPE(X%+INC,Y%+INC,-Z%,0,ANG+KJ%*180,JK%*SI)
170      PROCSHAPE(X%,Y%+INC,0,-Z%,ANG+KJ%*270,JK%*SI)
180      X%=X%+INC:NEXT J%
190    Y%=Y%+INC:NEXT I%
200 AA=GET:MODE7:GOTO 20
210 END
220 :
230 DEFPROCSHAPE(XA%,YA%,XI%,YI%,SA,SI)
240 FOR K%=1 TO M%
250    MOVE XO%+R*COS(RAD(SA)),YO%+R*SIN(RAD(SA))
260    DRAW XA%,YA%
270    XA%=XA%+XI%:YA%=YA%+YI%:SA=SA+SI
280    NEXT K%
290 ENDPROC
```

subdivisions of the large square which apply to both the X and Y axes, and the various subdivision lengths are computed. FOR–NEXT loops between lines 70 and 190, and 90 and 180 determine the calculations and drawing operations for each smaller square starting at the bottom left-hand corner and progressing horizontally, then vertically up the screen.

The parameters of each circle – its radius, its position in each square, and the increments of the circle's angle, and the square's subdivided side are computed in lines 100 to 120. In line 130, the starting orientation of the line drawing is fixed and the parameters *KJ*% and *JK*% determine the direction in which the line drawing proceeds around the circle. In lines 140 to 170, a procedure PROCSHAPE is called four times, each of which draws *M*% (= 10) lines from regular positions on the circumference of the circle to regular positions on the relevant side of the square. The computation of these positions and the drawing operation are given in PROCSHAPE which is defined in lines 230 to 290. The program as set up draws lines in a counter-clockwise direction around both the circle and the square, producing the regular 'moonscape' shown in Fig. 2.10.

To produce what Kolomyjec called his 'Organic Illusion' all that is required is

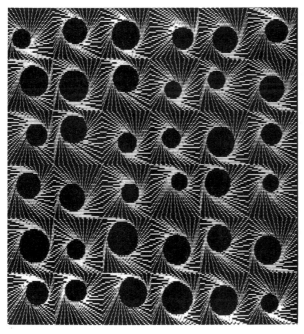

Fig. 2.10   Illusion of Moonscape

to alter the program to draw the lines around the circle in a clockwise direction, keeping the counter-clockwise direction around each small square the same. This can be done by changing line 130 in Program 2.11 to

130 ANG=RND(360):KJ%= −1:JK%= −1

and noting that the picture produced is similar to that shown on page 48 of Kolomyjec's chapter in Leavitt's (1976) book. All sorts of other designs can be produced with this program if the directions of plotting around the square and circle are changed and this provides an amazing illustration of the power and simplicity with which single parameters can control the visual form of an object. Finally, it is worth emphasizing that these last programs have introduced procedures which are used to replicate shapes in building up more complex patterns. In one sense, these procedures act as segment generators of the picture structure. In the next chapter, we will take these ideas further and explore them in more depth.

3

Combining and transforming regular shapes into simple designs

> We shall strictly limit ourselves to cases where the
> transformation necessary to effect a comparison shall be
> of a simple kind . . .
>
> (D'Arcy Thompson, *On Growth and Form*, 1961)

Although we mainly dealt with the geometry and programming of basic shapes such as circles and ellipses in the last chapter, we did touch upon, albeit briefly, the rudiments of picture structure. For example, we replicated simple shapes many times at random positions on the screen using different colours and sizes, thus building up composite designs, and we also introduced irregularities into our regular geometry producing natural forms such as rosettes. What we did not attempt to do was combine several basic shapes into more complex designs. It is the purpose of this chapter to extend our comprehension of picture structure in this way and to introduce principles of graphic design which involve generating complexity from combinations of simple objects.

The other purpose of this chapter is to present the formal ideas involved in transforming basic shapes. This will involve us in moving shapes to any position on the two-dimensional screen and we will present the classic operations of scaling, translation and rotation. We will illustrate these ideas by combining circles and ellipses through their transformation into flower-like designs, and this will provide us with the necessary preliminaries for dealing with three-dimensional design in Chapter 6. In this chapter, we will first explore ways of combining shapes based on rectangular and circular forms and we will show how these elements can be put together to create designs for flags. Flags provide excellent illustrations for simple graphic design and we will present a variety of flag programs incorporating rectangles, circles, stars and stripes which yield familiar forms. We will introduce transformations informally, first in the context of flag designs but then we will present the formal mathematics of transformations which involve matrices. The flower pictures which follow will involve demonstrations of these various transformation techniques.

Transformations and combinations of shapes are by no means the only ways of generating more complex forms, and thus we will present extensions of standard trigonometric functions which enable more convoluted shapes to be generated. These polar plots, as they will be referred to, are still regular but mathematically more complex. Their introduction will show how regular forms can generate irregularities such as discontinuities in shape, and we will illustrate these by plotting butterfly designs and forming cloud sculptures. Finally, in our quest to enhance the realism of our pictures, we will show how new colours can be mixed from the standard palette, and how colours can be combined to enable shading.

In this chapter, our programs will be a little longer and more involved than those previously so we will comment on them less, leaving readers to work through them, and to use the principles involved to generate their own personal computer art. We will still however describe the key techniques and illustrate their operation using diagrams, screen shots and printer plots.

3.1   CIRCULAR DESIGNS: RAYS AND STARS

The simplest possible combination of two elementary shapes involves the circle and the rectangle, and an obvious combination – the circle in the centre of a larger rectangle – yields the Japanese flag, one of the simplest and perhaps most memorable of all national flags. To draw the flag, we will require routines for both the circle and the rectangle and although we will introduce a special routine for drawing a rectangle a little later, in this instance we will define the rectangle using a graphics window.

Although the national flag is quite simple, the other Japanese flag which is memorable is the ensign, which incorporates the sun of the national flag with rays radiating over the length and breadth of the flag. This design in fact is quite tricky because although the rays are spaced at regular angular increments around the sun, the sun is off-centre and thus the rays are thicker on the right-hand side of the flag. Rather than code the position of the rays round the rectangle of the flag, what we can do is plot the rays to a distance much greater than the length of the flag, all around the sun, and then 'clip' the rays to fit in the rectangle of the main flag. Using a graphics window for the rectangle means that rays outside the window will not show up. The idea of plotting the ensign in this way and clipping it to fall in the window is illustrated in Fig. 3.1.

This rather neat idea of combining two shapes illustrates a general principle of design; that is, the procedure used to design a shape does not only depend on the intrinsic properties of that shape but on how the shape relates to the whole.

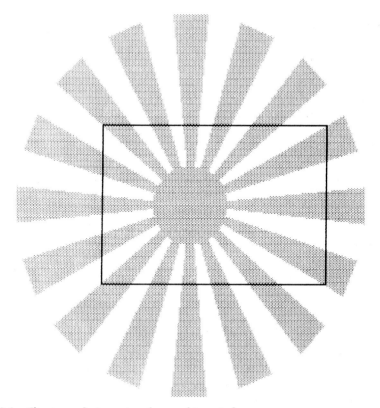

Fig. 3.1   Clipping a design using the graphics window

How one finds such procedures depends on intuition and on experience rather than on any standard rules. We have written a program which plots both the Japanese national flag and the ensign, and this is listed as Program 3.1. The program assigns mode, colour, origin and size in lines 20 to 60, and then sets up a graphics window in line 70 which it clears to white in line 80. A circle is then plotted in red in the centre of the window using PROCCIRCLE which is called in line 90. This procedure, defined in lines 200 to 260 is based on the slow draw, centre fill method which is quite acceptable for this type of pedagogic illustration.

   The graphics window is then cleared in line 100, and the red circle, now smaller in radius and displaced to the left a little is plotted from line 110. The FOR–NEXT loop in lines 130 to 160 computes the position of each ray from the centre of the sun and plots the ray using a PLOT85 command in line 150. The radius of these rays is much larger than the window which effectively clips the rays to their correct size. Note that this program plots the circle by converting degrees to radians, and plots the rays using radians directly. You can watch

Program 3.1   The Japanese flag and ensign

```
 10 REM Japanese Flag and Ensign
 20 MODE1
 30 VDU23,1,0;0;0;0;
 40 VDU19,2,7;0;
 50 VDU29,640;512;
 60 XS%=600:YS%=(2/3)*XS%
 70 VDU24,-XS%/2;-YS%/2;XS%/2;YS%/2;
 80 GCOL0,130:CLG:GCOL0,1
 90 PROCCIRCLE(0.3*YS%,0,0)
100 AA=GET:CLG:Z=0.12
110 PROCCIRCLE(0.25*YS%,-Z*XS%,0)
120 AI=RAD(5.6):A=RAD(90)/4:R=0.8*XS%
130 FOR I=0 TO 2*PI STEP A
140    MOVE -Z*XS%,0:MOVE -Z*XS%+R*COS(I-AI),R*SIN(I-AI)
150    PLOT85,-Z*XS%+R*COS(I+AI),R*SIN(I+AI)
160    NEXT I
170 AA=GET:MODE7
180 END
190 :
200 DEFPROCCIRCLE(R%,XA%,YA%)
210 MOVE XA%+R%,YA%
220 FOR I=0 TO 360 STEP 12
230    XX=R%*COS(RAD(I)):YY=R%*SIN(RAD(I))
240    MOVE XA%,YA%:PLOT85,XA%+XX,YA%+YY
250    NEXT I
260 ENDPROC
```

the program at work without the effect of clipping by leaving out line 70. The two flags produced are illustrated in Fig. 3.2.

   Another basic design element in a flag is the star which once again uses circular rotation as its organizing concept. Here we will plot a five point star but it is a simple matter to extend these ideas to stars with different numbers of points. In fact the five point star is one of the more complex to fill as we will see. The five points are fixed at regular increments in a circle of given radius which means the angle θ between each point at the centre of the star is $\theta = 2\pi/5 = 72°$. We will write a general procedure for plotting such a star which will enable a star of any radius and orientation to be constructed. We will also fix the five sets of x,y coordinates defining the points in two five element arrays whose coordinates will be calculated using the recursive circle generator method based on equations (2.15) and (2.16) given in the last chapter. These coordinates need to be stored in this fashion because of the manner in which the star is filled. The coordinate points are stored in a counter-clockwise direction and the sequence of accessing them and filling the star using MOVE and PLOT85 commands is as follows: *M1, M0, P3, P5, M0, P2, P4, M0, P1* where the numbers refer to the order of points, *0* refers to the centre of the star, *M* refers to a move command, and *P* to a PLOT85 command. The triangles filled in this way appear to constitute the most efficient filling

Fig. 3.2   The Japanese flag and ensign

sequence; it is left as an exercise for the reader to determine if the star can be constructed using a lesser number of graphics commands.

These ideas are embodied in the program which is listed as Program 3.2. First note that the coordinates of the five points are defined counter-clockwise in $X\%(5)$ and $Y\%(5)$ which are in turn defined in line 30. In fact, arrays defined in this way contain six elements which are accessed 0, 1, . . . , 5, but as in this case, it is sometimes easier for illustrative purposes to simply refer to the nonzero accessed elements 1, . . . , 5. Program 3.2 is rather simple in

Program 3.2   A five point star

```
10 REM Five Point Star
20 MODE1
30 DIM X%(5),Y%(5)
40 VDU23,1,0;0;0;0;
50 VDU19,0,6;0;19,1,4;0;
60 GCOLO,1:VDU29,640;512;
90 PROCSTAR(300,RAD(90))
100 GCOLO,0
110 FOR I%=1 TO 5
120    MOVE 0,0:DRAW X%(I%),Y%(I%)
130    NEXT I%
140 AA=GET:MODE7
150 END
160 :
170 DEFPROCSTAR(R%,A)
180 AI=RAD(72):C=COS(AI):S=SIN(AI)
190 X%(1)=R%*COS(A):Y%(1)=R%*SIN(A)
200 FOR I%=2 TO 5
210    X%(I%)=X%(I%-1)*C-Y%(I%-1)*S
220    Y%(I%)=X%(I%-1)*S+Y%(I%-1)*C
230    NEXT I%
240 MOVE X%(1),Y%(1):MOVE 0,0
250 PLOT85,X%(3),Y%(3):PLOT85,X%(5),Y%(5)
260 MOVE 0,0:PLOT85,X%(2),Y%(2)
270 PLOT85,X%(4),Y%(4)
280 MOVE 0,0:PLOT85,X%(1),Y%(1)
290 ENDPROC
```

structure. After assignments up to line 60, the procedure PROCSTAR whose arguments are the circle radius, and the orientation of the first point of the star, is called. In lines 100 to 130, the spokes of the star are drawn in the background colour to give it a little relief. The procedure itself is defined in lines 170 to 290. In lines 180 and 190, the first point of the star and the angular increment are determined, while lines 200 to 230 define the other four points recursively. Lines 240 to 280 give the plotting sequence using these coordinates which was outlined above. The output of this program is given in Fig. 3.3.

As in the case of our random ellipses and random rosettes programs in Chapter 2, we can easily construct a random stars program. If we replace lines 60 to 140 with the following program lines

```
 60 VDU19,2,0;0;19,3,1;0;
 70 REPEAT
 80    GCOLO,RND(3):VDU29,RND(1279);RND(1023);
 90    PROCSTAR(50+RND(200),RAD(RND(360)))
100    GCOLO,0
110    FOR I%=1 TO 5
120       MOVE 0,0:DRAW X%(I%),Y%(I%)
130       NEXT I%
140    UNTIL FALSE
```

Fig. 3.3   A five point star

random stars are plotted, at different sizes in different colours on the screen. At first, these stars produce a rather pleasant form, which is well-defined but as more and more stars are plotted, the picture becomes formless and somewhat confused. This illustrates another important principle of picture structure: that is, picture quality depends on simplicity of form, which in turn often depends upon how well articulated the various segments or shapes are in relation to one another.

3.2   FLAGS AS ELEMENTARY PICTURE STRUCTURES

In this section, we will continue the idea of composing pictures from simple shapes but we will emphasize two related features which dominate all the art produced in this book. The first feature relates essentially to the hardware we are working with and in particular to the way the graphics memory is organized and displayed. The frame buffer is displayed continually at a rate of 30 times per second and as this memory is updated, the display changes to reflect this. In essence, this means that the previous memory does not have to be deleted but that new graphics instructions simply write out the previous ones. Now pictures are often produced using the same idea: the artist paints the background first, progressively moving to the foreground, increasing the level of detail, and simply painting over what has been painted already. If the picture can thus be organized into a clear sequence of background to foreground graphics commands, the computer program, and thus memory display can thus be organized to reflect this order. We have already seen simple examples of this in the various designs produced in the last chapter, and particularly in our program plotting the Japanese flag where the rectangular background is produced first with the sun (and its rays) overplotted as the foreground.

The second feature involves the related idea of successively approximating a complex shape by overplotting a sequence of simple shapes. This idea can even be seen as one in which one shape can be used to 'rub out' unwanted detail from another. We can illustrate this and the previous idea using the example of the Turkish flag which is composed of a white crescent and star set on a red background. The crescent can be constructed by plotting a white circle and then plotting a smaller circle in the background colour whose left-most edge touches the edge of the larger circle. The smaller circle effectively removes an inner portion of the circle thus forming the crescent. The order for plotting the Turkish flag is as follows. The flag itself is plotted first as a red rectangle, then a large white circle is plotted, followed by an overplot of a smaller red circle which forms the crescent, and finally the star is plotted. The sequence is straightforward and each shape can be drawn using appropriate procedures which determine the segments of the final picture.

The flag is computed and plotted in the program listed as Program 3.3. The circle and star procedures, PROCCIRCLE and PROCSTAR are defined in lines 280 to 480 and are as described previously. A procedure PROCSQUARE is given in lines 230 to 260 which plots a rectangle using two MOVE commands, followed by two PLOT85 commands: this is the most efficient sequence to fill a rectangle as two triangles. The main program is obvious in that after assignments are made up to line 80, the rectangle, the crescent formed from two circles and the star are plotted by calling the appropriate procedures in lines 100, 130, 160 and 190. The only point to note is that the five point star is orientated with its first point set at RAD (110), thus it is not quite upright. The graphics output is illustrated in Fig. 3.4. If you need to illustrate the way the crescent is formed, change GCOL0,1 in line 150 to CGOL0,0.

We are now going to present two flag designs which are considerably more complicated in that they demand much trickier combinations of basic shapes. The first is the 'Stars and Stripes', the national flag of the United States of America. This flag is composed of 13 alternating red and white stripes with a blue canton – the rectangular panel set in the top left-hand corner of the main flag – on which 50 white stars are arranged in regular grid form. We can use the rectangle procedure PROCSQUARE introduced in the Turkish flag program

Program 3.3   The Turkish flag

```
 10 REM Turkish Flag
 20 MODE1
 30 DIM X%(5),Y%(5)
 40 VDU23,1,0;0;0;0;
 50 VDU19,2,7;0;
 60 VDU29,640;512;
 70 XS%=600:YS%=400
 80 XX%=XS%/2:YY%=YS%/2
 90 GCOL0,1
100 PROCSQUARE(-XX%,-YY%,XS%,YS%)
110 XX%=-XX%/2:YY%=0:MOVE XX%,YY%
120 R%=XS%/6:GCOL0,2
130 PROCCIRCLE(R%,XX%,YY%)
140 XX%=XX%+(R%/4):R%=3*R%/4
150 MOVE XX%,YY%:GCOL0,1
160 PROCCIRCLE(R%,XX%,YY%)
170 MOVE 0,0:R%=XS%/15
180 A=RAD(110):GCOL0,2
190 PROCSTAR(R%,A)
200 AA=GET:MODE7
210 END
220 :
230 DEFPROCSQUARE(X%,Y%,N%,M%)
240 MOVE X%,Y%+M%:MOVE X%+N%,Y%+M%
250 PLOT85,X%,Y%:PLOT85,X%+N%,Y%
260 ENDPROC
270 :
280 DEFPROCCIRCLE(R%,XA%,YA%)
290 MOVE XA%+R%,YA%
300 FOR I=0 TO 360 STEP 24
310   XX=R%*COS(RAD(I)):YY=R%*SIN(RAD(I))
320   MOVE XA%,YA%:PLOT85,XA%+XX,YA%+YY
330   NEXT I
340 ENDPROC
350 :
360 DEFPROCSTAR(R%,A)
370 AI=RAD(72):C=COS(AI):S=SIN(AI)
380 X%(1)=R%*COS(A):Y%(1)=R%*SIN(A)
390 FOR I%=2 TO 5
400   X%(I%)=X%(I%-1)*C-Y%(I%-1)*S
410   Y%(I%)=X%(I%-1)*S+Y%(I%-1)*C
420   NEXT I%
430 MOVE X%(1),Y%(1):MOVE 0,0
440 PLOT85,X%(3),Y%(3):PLOT85,X%(5),Y%(5)
450 MOVE 0,0:PLOT85,X%(2),Y%(2)
460 PLOT85,X%(4),Y%(4)
470 MOVE 0,0:PLOT85,X%(1),Y%(1)
480 ENDPROC
```

Fig. 3.4   The Turkish flag

to plot both the stripes and the canton, and the star procedure PROCSTAR to set up the pattern of stars. Thus the structure of the flag program is fairly simple although the pattern of stars is rather complex. In the program, rather than plotting the stripes individually, we plot the whole flag first in the first stripe colour, reduce the size of the flag from the top by one stripe in depth and plot the flag in the other stripe colour, and continue this progressive reduction in flag size and colour switch until the last stripe is plotted. This provides a pleasing kinetic effect. The canton is then plotted using PROCSQUARE, and two overlapping grids are set up to control the positioning of each star plot. The first grid consists of a net of 5 lines with 6 star positions generating 30 stars, the second a net of 4 lines with 5 positions generating 20 stars, this latter grid being symmetrically offset within the former grid.

The program is listed as Program 3.4. The previous procedures generating rectangles and stars are listed as PROCSQUARE and PROCSTAR in lines 390 to 560. The main program involves the usual types of assignment up to line 90 and then in the FOR–NEXT loop between lines 120 to 160, PROCSQUARE is used to generate the 13 stripes in alternating red and white. The canton is plotted through lines 170 to 200, and then the two intersecting grids of stars are set up in the FOR–NEXT loop bounded by lines 230 and 350. The vertical direction of the grid and star plot is controlled by another FOR–NEXT loop (lines 270 to 350) while an inner FOR–NEXT loop in lines 290 to 330 controls the horizontal plot direction. Within these loops, PROCSTAR is called at the appropriate positions. The flag which results is shown in Plate 1.

These programs are longer than those in Chapter 2 but their structure is

Program 3.4   The US national flag

```
 10 REM The US National Flag
 20 MODE1
 30 DIM X%(5),Y%(5)
 40 VDU23,1,0;0;0;0;
 50 VDU19,2,7;0;19,3,4;0;
 60 VDU29,640;512;
 70 YS%=650:XS%=1.9*YS%
 80 YI%=YS%/13:YB%=YS%
 90 XX%=XS%/2:YY%=YS%/2
100 REM Stripes Plotted as Rectangles
110 KK%=1:GCOLO,KK%
120 FOR K%=1 TO 13
130   PROCSQUARE(-XX%,-YY%,XS%,YB%)
140   IF KK%=1 THEN KK%=2 ELSE KK%=1
150   YB%=YB%-YI%:GCOLO,KK%
160   NEXT K%
170 REM Plots the Canton
180 YB%=7*YI%:YY%=YY%-YB%
190 XS%=(38/95)*XS%:GCOLO,3
200 PROCSQUARE(-XX%,YY%,XS%,YB%)
210 REM Plots Two Grids of Stars
220 GCOLO,2:XI%=XS%/6:YI%=YB%/5
230 FOR J%=1 TO 2
240   IF J%=1 THEN XZ%=7:YZ%=6 ELSE XZ%=6:YZ%=5
250   IF J%=1 THEN XW%=0:YW%=0 ELSE XW%=XI%/2:YW%=YI%/2
260   Y1%=YS%/2+512-YW%-YI%/2
270   FOR K%=1 TO YZ%-1
280     X1%=-XX%+640+XW%+XI%/2
290     FOR KK%=1 TO XZ%-1
300       VDU29,X1%;Y1%;
310       PROCSTAR(YS%/50,RAD(90))
320       X1%=X1%+XI%
330     NEXT KK%
340     Y1%=Y1%-YI%
350   NEXT K%:NEXT J%
360 AA=GET:MODE7
370 END
380 :
390 DEFPROCSQUARE(X%,Y%,N%,M%)
400 MOVE X%,Y%+M%:MOVE X%+N%,Y%+M%
410 PLOT85,X%,Y%:PLOT85,X%+N%,Y%
420 ENDPROC
430 :
440 DEFPROCSTAR(R%,A)
450 AI=RAD(72):C=COS(AI):S=SIN(AI)
460 X%(1)=R%*COS(A):Y%(1)=R%*SIN(A)
470 FOR I%=2 TO 5
480   X%(I%)=X%(I%-1)*C-Y%(I%-1)*S
490   Y%(I%)=X%(I%-1)*S+Y%(I%-1)*C
500   NEXT I%
510 MOVE X%(1),Y%(1):MOVE 0,0
520 PLOT85,X%(3),Y%(3):PLOT85,X%(5),Y%(5)
530 MOVE 0,0:PLOT85,X%(2),Y%(2)
540 PLOT85,X%(4),Y%(4)
550 MOVE 0,0:PLOT85,X%(1),Y%(1)
560 ENDPROC
```

quite clear, and the use of procedures enables the reader to trace their operation easily. We have also repeated the procedures we have used in earlier programs to avoid the necessity of turning back to previous programs when keying them into the computer. Nothing is more infuriating than having to construct a program from several sources, and thus in the spirit of this book that any reader can key in any of the programs produced in less than 60 minutes, we will continue to list the complete program regardless of whether or not we have already listed some of its procedures. All our flag designs so far are regular and consist of combining basic procedures. We have taken the designs from Pedersen's (1971) *International Flag Book* but we would encourage the reader to use these procedures to construct more regular flag designs involving interesting patterns of crescents, stars, circles, stripes and such like which are listed in Pedersen's book. The national flags of Burma, China, Pakistan and Tunisia would be worth constructing, while flags such as the Swiss, Finnish and French flags are simpler involving just PROCSQUARE. The Union Jack could also be constructed (a program is available in Cownie, 1982) while more ambitious readers might attempt to construct flags using, say the six point Star of David which is part of the Israeli flag.

To conclude this section, we will examine a program for the Welsh flag which illustrates flags with irregular designs, although this will be the first of several programs in this book which are influenced by my living in Wales in the mid-1980s. In the time-honoured way, most artists, even – perhaps especially – computer artists, are influenced by the surroundings! The essence of the Welsh flag is two rectangles adjoining each other along the horizontal, the upper rectangle being white, the lower one green. Astride the join lies the red Welsh dragon which like the Durer head in Chapter 2, is an irregular shape requiring data and a special coding.

The dragon itself takes up most of the data and graphics commands in the program. It has been divided into 25 distinct segments which in total involve 226 pairs of x-y coordinates. The 25 segments have been defined as natural partitions of the dragon which enable the cross fill method to be used for filling. The 226 coordinate pairs are stored in arrays $X\%(225)$ and $Y\%(225)$ while the number of pairs in each segment are given in the array $N\%(24)$. The pairs are run-coded, that is the $N\%(0)$ coordinates in the first segment occupy $X\%(0)$ to $X\%(N\%(0)-1)$ and $Y\%(0)$ to $Y\%(N\%(0)-1)$, the second $N\%(1)$ coordinates in the second segment occupy space $X\%(N\%(0))$ to $X\%(N\%(0)+N\%(1)-1)$ and $Y\%(N\%(0))$ to $Y\%(N\%(0)+N\%(1)-1)$, and so on. From this, it is clear that

$$\sum_{I=0}^{24} N\%(I) = 226$$

and that whenever a segment I is plotted, it needs to be accessed by examining the range of coordinates between locations $N\%(I-1)$ and $N\%(I)$ in the $X\%$ and $Y\%$ arrays.

Unlike the Durer head, it is not possible to find suitable interior points in the segments of the dragon, thus the centre fill method has not been used. Cross fill is used instead, just as if you were shading the dragon by hand, and the way this is achieved is illustrated for the segmented dragon in Fig. 3.5. For each segment, two MOVE commands are made to the first two pairs of coordinates and the fill then proceeds sequentially using PLOT85 commands. A second feature of the program involves the need to transform the original coordinate coding into coordinates consistent with the screen system, and this involves both translation and scaling of the object coordinates. The original frame within which the dragon was symmetrically placed measured 1400×900 units, and the first task is to translate this frame and the dragon into one centred about the coordinates 700×450, the new origin of the system. To scale the frame to screen units, the x direction can arbitrarily take precedence, the maximum unit length here being 1280. Thus after translation, the x,y coordinates are scaled by $1280/1400$. The combined translation-scaling operations for object coordinates x,y into screen coordinates x',y' are thus given as

$$x' = \frac{1280}{1400}(x - 700), \quad \text{and } y' = \frac{1280}{1400}(y - 450).$$

Finally, in the program we will scale and translate these screen coordinates x' and y' further to show how different sized flags can be plotted.

The program is listed in Program 3.5. The main program between lines 10 and 270 is structured into procedures which in sequence read in, transform,

Fig. 3.5   Coding the Welsh dragon

Program 3.5   The Welsh flag

```
 10 REM Transformations of the Welsh Flag
 20 DIM X%(225),Y%(225),N%(24)
 30 MODE5
 40 VDU23,1,0;0;0;0;
 50 VDU19,2,2;0;
 60 M%=24:MN%=225
 70 REM Reads in Data
 80 PROCINDATA
 90 REM Plots Welsh Flag with Captions
100 PROCTEXT1
110 VDU29,X0%;Y0%;:XJ=1:YJ=1
120 PROCFLAG(XJ,YJ)
130 PROCTEXT:G=INKEY(200):CLG
140 REM Plots Flags of Different Sizes
150 FOR XJ=0.4 TO 1 STEP 0.2
160   FOR YJ=0.4 TO 1 STEP 0.2
170     PROCFLAG(XJ,YJ):G=INKEY(100)
180     CLG:NEXT YJ:NEXT XJ
190 REM Plots 9 Flags on the Screen
200 XJ=0.3:YJ=0.3
210 FOR IX%=213 TO 1279 STEP 426
220   FOR IY%=171 TO 1023 STEP 341
230     VDU29,IX%;IY%;
240     PROCFLAG(XJ,YJ)
250     NEXT IY%:NEXT IX%
260 AA=GET:MODE7
270 END
280 :
290 REM Reads Coordinates of the Dragon
300 DEFPROCINDATA
310 FOR I%=0 TO M%
320   READ N%(I%)
330   NEXT I%
340 ZX%=1279:ZY%=1023:XD%=1400
350 YD%=900:X0%=ZX%/2:Y0%=ZY%/2
360 TRANS=ZX%/XD%:YADJ%=YD%*TRANS/2
370 FOR I%=0 TO MN%
380   READ X%(I%),Y%(I%)
390   X%(I%)=X%(I%)*TRANS-X0%
400   Y%(I%)=Y%(I%)*TRANS-YADJ%
410   NEXT I%
420 ENDPROC
430 :
440 REM Plots a Flag of Size XJ_YJ
450 DEFPROCFLAG(XJ,YJ)
460 GCOL0,3:REM Plots Flag Top in White
470 XC%=X0%*XJ:YC%=YADJ%*YJ
480 PROCSQUARE(-XC%,0,2*XC%,YC%)
490 GCOL0,2:REM Plots Flag Bottom in Green
500 PROCSQUARE(-XC%,-YC%,2*XC%,YC%)
510 GCOL0,1:REM Plots Dragon in Red
520 Q%=0
530 FOR I%=0 TO M%
540   IF I%=M% THEN GCOL0,3
550   FOR K%=0 TO N%(I%)-1
```

Program 3.5   continued

```
560      X=X%(Q%)*XJ:Y=Y%(Q%)*YJ
570      IF K%=0 OR K%=1 THEN MOVE X,Y ELSE PLOT85,X,Y
580      Q%=Q%+1
590      NEXT K%:NEXT I%
600 ENDPROC
610 :
620 REM Plots a Rectangle
630 DEFPROCSQUARE(X%,Y%,N%,M%)
640 MOVE X%,Y%+M%:MOVE X%+N%,Y%+M%
650 PLOT85,X%,Y%:PLOT85,X%+N%,Y%
660 ENDPROC
670 :
680 REM Plots Welsh Caption
690 DEFPROCTEXT1
700 VDU5:MOVE 200,48
710 PRINT"COFION O GYMRU":GCOL1,1
720 MOVE 192,40:PRINT"COFION O GYMRU"
730 ENDPROC
740 :
750 REM Plots English Caption
760 DEFPROCTEXT
770 MOVE -632,512
780 PRINT"GREETINGS FROM WALES"
790 GCOL1,2:MOVE -640,504
800 PRINT"GREETINGS FROM WALES"
810 ENDPROC
820 :
830 REM Segment Coordinate Data
840 DATA 15,14,12,14,6,4,5,3,3,3,13,25
850 DATA 5,5,3,15,4,15,9,15,5,7,9,14,3
860 DATA 670,440,587,651,682,470,693,685
870 DATA 730,478,731,692,762,505,765,708
880 DATA 807,510,803,718,835,535,840,728
890 DATA 861,545,860,730,905,549
900 DATA 1030,785,860,730,965,741,868,700
910 DATA 961,710,868,675,1009,708,875,651
920 DATA 943,663,881,625,938,638,889,610
930 DATA 970,618,890,590
940 DATA 587,651,670,440,599,492,685,320
950 DATA 547,461,566,294,515,448,498,296
960 DATA 496,452,460,300,480,464,410,324
970 DATA 410,324,480,464,368,427,482,502
980 DATA 383,498,492,530,419,562,518,570
990 DATA 400,623,534,602,401,660,539,632
1000 DATA 411,679,560,651
1010 DATA 475,662,555,687,521,652,558,673
1020 DATA 560,651,580,685
1030 DATA 401,660,318,668,400,623,320,630
1040 DATA 318,550,320,595,347,568,410,602
1050 DATA 419,562
1060 DATA 410,602,400,623,320,613
1070 DATA 320,613,270,622,280,630
1080 DATA 253,668,265,615,296,638
1090 DATA 685,320,670,440,760,345,750,469
```

Program 3.5 continued

```
1100 DATA 828,365,794,485,858,354,861,500
1110 DATA 945,332,920,485,970,382,970,450
1120 DATA 990,425
1130 DATA 920,485,970,450,975,500,1000,462
1140 DATA 1020,510,1040,470,1068,500,1070
1150 DATA 468,1095,493,1085,460,1115,472
1160 DATA 1095,445,1128,440,1098,430,1115
1170 DATA 400,1090,418,1082,380,1075,415
1180 DATA 1050,385,1060,423,1032,405,1060
1190 DATA 449,1028,435,1070,468,1040,470
1200 DATA 1068,500,1095,493,1100,524,1130
1210 DATA 518,1118,540
1220 DATA 1085,570,1118,540,1145,565,1172
1230 DATA 540,1205,590
1240 DATA 1118,540,1172,540,1145,475
1250 DATA 300,549,252,540,318,520,275,518
1260 DATA 310,495,254,482,308,465,250,450
1270 DATA 368,427,252,421,310,408,280,390
1280 DATA 312,380,251,380,295,360
1290 DATA 368,427,310,408,410,324,390,310
1300 DATA 370,208,372,241,395,188,396,255
1310 DATA 410,212,425,240,434,201,445,240
1320 DATA 460,192,465,238,495,200,480,250
1330 DATA 515,232,498,296,566,294
1340 DATA 515,232,495,200,532,228,540,198
1350 DATA 560,240,558,185,580,260,594,210
1360 DATA 605,235
1370 DATA 634,239,650,200,682,245,690,210
1380 DATA 718,243,728,205,740,249,750,201
1390 DATA 756,260,765,200,780,241,790,210
1400 DATA 800,238,810,200,820,228
1410 DATA 828,365,761,280,760,345,694,290
1420 DATA 685,320
1430 DATA 792,322,761,280,800,302,756,260
1440 DATA 825,295,780,241,815,265
1450 DATA 858,354,945,332,852,295,990,318
1460 DATA 875,280,990,285,935,265,965,230
1470 DATA 923,232
1480 DATA 831,232,843,200,860,248,870,210
1490 DATA 898,235,902,200,923,232,940,205
1500 DATA 965,230,979,201,1000,240,1000
1510 DATA 188,1020,242,1030,215
1520 DATA 421,652,449,643,435,629
```

and store the object coordinates (PROCINDATA), set up text (PROCTEXT1 and PROCTEXT), plot a full screen flag (PROCFLAG), and then plot a variety of flag sizes with shrunk and stretched x,y directions finishing with a full screen design involving nine identical flags, arranged in a 3×3 grid. Assignments are first made in the main program up to line 60 and then PROCINDATA is called (line 80). This procedure listed in lines 290 to 420 first reads in the number of coordinates associated with the 25 segments (lines 310 to 330), then reads in the 226 pairs of coordinates and effects the above transformations (lines 370 to 410). All the data are read from DATA statements which comprise nearly half the program in lines 830 to 1520.

The full screen flag is first plotted in PROCFLAG (line 120) above and below which are set the text captions in Welsh (PROCTEXT1 called in line 100) and English (PROCTEXT called in line 130). These procedures listed respectively in lines 680 to 730 and 750 to 810, write text at the graphics cursor using VDU5 in line 700, and achieve a three-dimensional effect by displacing and writing the same captions again using the GCOL1 command. We have only used GCOL0 type statements so far but for the moment, simply accept that this command with logical operator 1 achieves the desired effect. More of this later especially in Chapter 7 on animation.

PROCFLAG itself is listed in lines 440 to 600. This procedure first calls PROCSQUARE (the usual listing given in lines 620 to 660) twice, first in white, then in green thus forming the main body of the flag. The dragon is plotted in lines 520 to 590 which involves accessing the coordinates in each of the 25 segments in the given order using two nested FOR–NEXT loops. The usual move-plot sequence associated with cross fill is given in line 570. If you have understood our remarks on coding the dragon given earlier, you will have no difficulty in understanding lines 520 to 590. Note how the counter $Q\%$ in this routine enables the appropriate coordinates to be accessed. Finally PROCFLAG is provided with two arguments XJ and YJ which represent the scaling values to be applied to the screen coordinates $X\%$ and $Y\%$: these are determined in the main program.

Back in the main program, these XJ and YJ values are determined directly in two nested FOR–NEXT loops in lines 150 to 180 and this enables a variety of scaled flags (some 16 in all) to be displayed. Finally, nine small Welsh flags are displayed simultaneously in regular positions on the screen using two nested FOR–NEXT loops in lines 210 to 250. The flag is shown in Plate 2. This program illustrates a number of key points. The limits on resolution are clearly displayed in that in the last nine small flags, the dragons are blurred: they are still distinct but only just and it is an open question as to whether or not your prior experience of the flag in this program increases their recognition. The other important illustrative point involves the need to structure the program to achieve ease of transformation. In a sense, the flag itself is relegated to procedures while the main program controls size, position, transformation and general input/output. This kind of structure becomes essential as the graphics becomes more complicated. There is however a limit to what we can achieve in building structure this way. We require more technique and thus we will now turn formally to a study of transformation.

3.3   THE MATHEMATICS OF TWO-DIMENSIONAL TRANSFORMATIONS

There are three elementary transformations which together are both necessary and sufficient to transform any point in any position in two-dimensional space to any other position. These transformations are referred to as *translation, scaling* and *rotation*. We have already encountered translation and scaling in an informal context in Program 2.1 which drew the Durer head, and in the previous section in Program 3.5 which drew the Welsh flag. And as we shall see in a moment, our concern for rotating points to trace out circles, ellipses and spirals in this and the last chapter has indirectly introduced us to ideas about rotation, particularly in Program 2.4 which dealt with the recursive generation of points describing the circumference of an ellipse. In this section and the next, we will tie these ideas together more systematically in a formal treatment of transformations.

A point given by coordinates x,y will be called x_n,y_n before its transformation and x_{n+1},y_{n+1} after transformation. The operation of translation is straightforward in that it involves a movement in the horizontal or x coordinate direction and one in the vertical or y coordinate direction. Then

$$x_{n+1} = x_n + T_1 \quad \text{and} \quad y_{n+1} = y_n + T_2, \tag{3.1}$$

where T_1 and T_2 are positive or negative displacements in the x and y directions respectively. Scaling involves a multiplicative rather than additive operation which is given as

$$x_{n+1} = S_1 x_n, \quad \text{and} \quad y_{n+1} = S_2 y_n, \tag{3.2}$$

where S_1 and S_2 are the appropriate x and y coordinate scalars which can take on any real values. Both these transformations in equations (3.1) and (3.2) were illustrated in the Durer head and Welsh dragon programs but what is less obvious there and clearer now, is that the order of these operations is critical. Applying equation (3.1) first and equation (3.2) second will generally result in different coordinates from the reverse operation, and thus it is necessary to be clear about the correct order for any given problem.

By far the trickiest transformation is the third operation – *rotation*. We measure the rotation of a point using the conventional counter-clockwise angular variation over the range $0 \leqslant \theta \leqslant 2\pi$ where θ is measured in radians or $0 \leqslant \theta \leqslant 360$ where θ is now measured in degrees. The complete rotation of a point is through 2π radians or 360 degrees and this brings the point back to its original position. The best way to visualize the meaning of rotation is through the diagram in Fig. 3.6. We will first make some elementary points about the representation of coordinates and angular variation. If we have a point given by (x_n,y_n), we can conceive of this point as being the amalgam of two points $(x_n,0)$ and $(0,y_n)$: these two points are identified in Fig. 3.6. We will now rotate these three points through θ degrees in counter-clockwise fashion. The circles in Fig. 3.6 indicate the trace of rotation for each point. It is clear that for point $(x_n,0)$ the angle of rotation is measured from the horizontal while for $(0,y_n)$ it is measured from the vertical. These angles are obviously equal. It can be

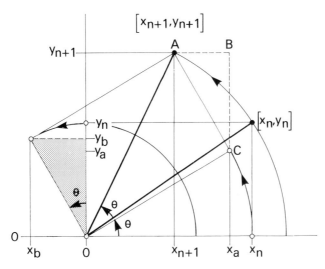

Fig. 3.6   Rotating a point through θ degrees

formally shown that the rotation angle from (x_n,y_n) to (x_{n+1},y_{n+1}) is the same as these angles because these points are all perpendicular to one another. An investigation of how (x_n,y_n) transforms to (x_{n+1},y_{n+1}) can thus begin by showing how $(x_n,0)$ and $(y_n,0)$ transform under the same rotation.

The point $(x_n,0)$ transforms to (x_a,y_a) in Fig. 3.6 and this new point is given using standard circular rotation from equations (2.5) and (2.6) as

$$x_a = x_n \cos(\theta). \quad \text{and} \quad y_a = x_n \sin(\theta). \tag{3.3}$$

Points $(0,y_n)$ transform to (x_b,y_b) in similar fashion as

$$x_b = y_n \sin(\theta), \quad \text{and} \quad y_b = y_n \cos(\theta). \tag{3.4}$$

Let us now construct the triangle ABC which relates point (x_a,y_a) to point (x_{n+1},y_{n+1}). A casual inspection of this triangle in Fig. 3.6 shows that x_{n+1} can be derived by subtracting the distance AB from x_a and y_{n+1} can be obtained by adding BC to y_a. Now it is clear that ABC is congruent with the triangle formed by the rotation of the point $(0,y_n)$ which is stippled in Fig. 3.6. From these comparisons, it is clear that $AB=x_b$ and $BC=y_b$. Thus the point x_{n+1},y_{n+1} is given as

$$x_{n+1} = x_a - x_b, \quad \text{and} \quad y_{n+1} = y_a + y_b. \tag{3.5}$$

Using equations (3.3) and (3.4) in equation (3.5) leads to the computable forms

$$x_{n+1} = x_n \cos(\theta) - y_n \sin(\theta), \tag{3.6}$$

$$y_{n+1} = x_n \sin(\theta) + y_n \cos(\theta). \tag{3.7}$$

Equations (3.6) and (3.7) have the same structure as equations (2.15) and (2.16) which were derived using standard trigonometric results. In fact, when $\Delta\theta = \theta$ and $R_x = R_y$ in equations (2.15) and (2.16), equations (3.6) and (3.7) result. In many books on computer graphics (see for example Harrington, 1983), rotation is defined using the logic behind equations (2.15) and (2.16) rather than the more long-winded method developed here.

It is very important to acquire some feel for rotation and thus we have written a simple program which enables the user to rotate a square box through any angle. The program is listed in Program 3.6. The box coordinates are given in the program in lines 60 and 70 and stored in $X\%$ and $Y\%$ arrays. In line 80, a procedure PROCDRAW is called from lines 210 to 260, which moves to the top left corner of the box (point 4) and draws to points 1,2,3 and back to 4 in that order. Dotted axes are set up defining the four quadrants in lines 90 and 100 (the origin 0,0 is at the centre of the screen) and the user is requested to input the angular rotation in line 110. The coordinates are transformed using equations (3.6) and (3.7) in lines 130 to 160 and the rotated box is then redrawn in line 170. The program is looped so the user can repeat the whole process again using another angle of rotation, and so on. The program could easily be adapted to draw a more complex shape and rotate it, and the other operations – translation and scaling could be added. More exercises for the reader.

Program 3.6   Rotating a square box

```
 10 REM Rotating a Square Box
 20 MODE1
 30 VDU23,1,0;0;0;0;
 40 VDU29,640;512;
 50 DIM X%(3),Y%(3)
 60 X%(0)=100:X%(1)=300:X%(2)=300:X%(3)=100
 70 Y%(0)=100:Y%(1)=100:Y%(2)=300:Y%(3)=300
 80 GCOLO,1:PROCDRAW
 90 MOVE 0,400:PLOT21,0,-400
100 MOVE 500,0:PLOT21,-500,0
110 INPUT TAB(8,0)"ANGLE OF ROTATION = ",TH
120 TH=RAD(TH):C=COS(TH):S=SIN(TH)
130 FOR I%=0 TO 3
140    X=X%(I%)*C-Y%(I%)*S
150    Y%(I%)=X%(I%)*S+Y%(I%)*C:X%(I%)=X
160    NEXT I%
170 GCOLO,3:PROCDRAW
180 AA=GET:CLG:GOTO 60
190 END
200 :
210 DEFPROCDRAW
220 MOVE X%(3),Y%(3)
230 FOR I%=0 TO 3
240    DRAW X%(I%),Y%(I%)
250    NEXT I%
260 ENDPROC
```

3.4 THE MATRIX REPRESENTATION OF TRANSFORMATIONS

The various transformations introduced here in equations (3.1) to (3.7) are essentially *linear* transformations involving no more than simple additive and multiplicative operations. In fact, more complex nonlinear transformations such as those used to transform biological forms under various conditions of growth and evolution, will not be examined in this book (Thompson, 1961) although such transformations are clearly important in advanced treatments of computer graphics. The linear nature of our transformations means that they can be represented using a more parsimonious and efficient notation system which is based on linear or matrix algebra. At this point, we must digress a little and briefly introduce the ideas behind matrices and vectors. Readers are warned that the treatment here is cursory and therefore you are recommended to look at fuller treatments in books such as Myers (1982; Chapter 5) and Harrington (1983; Chapter 4).

Consider two variables x and y which are both linear functions of two other variables a and b. We can write these functions as

$$\left.\begin{array}{l} x = aA + bB \\ y = aC + bD \end{array}\right\} \tag{3.8}$$

The parameters A, B, C and D are the appropriate linear scalars in equations (3.8). Now we can represent these sets of variables and parameters in the following form

$$\boldsymbol{g} = [x \quad y], \quad \boldsymbol{h} = [a \quad b] \quad \text{and} \quad \boldsymbol{Q} = \begin{bmatrix} A & C \\ B & D \end{bmatrix}$$

where $\boldsymbol{g}$ and $\boldsymbol{h}$ are called 1 (row) × 2 (column) *row vectors* and $\boldsymbol{Q}$ is a 2 (row) × 2 (column) matrix. We can represent equations (3.8) in vector–matrix form using the above definitions as

$$[x \quad y] = [a \quad b] \begin{bmatrix} A & C \\ B & D \end{bmatrix} \tag{3.9}$$

which has the general structure of $\boldsymbol{g} = \boldsymbol{hQ}$.

Relating equations (3.9) to (3.8) is fairly straightforward. When two matrices or a vector and a matrix as in equation (3.9) are multiplied together, an element in a given row and column of the resultant vector or matrix, in this case $\boldsymbol{g}$, is formed by taking each element in the same row of the first matrix or vector, multiplying it by each element in the column of the second matrix or vector, and adding the results. For example the first element in $\boldsymbol{g}$, that is the first row-column element x, is formed by multiplying each element of the first and only row of $\boldsymbol{h}$ by each element in the first column of $\boldsymbol{Q}$: then $x = aA + bB$

which is the first line of equations (3.8). In fact, performing the same operations on the second column of Q leads to the second line of (3.8). What these operations imply is that the dimensions of our matrix multiplications must be consistent. Then an $n \times m$ matrix can only be postmultiplied by an $m \times n$ matrix so that the size of the rows and size of the columns of the first and second matrices respectively match. In our case, we will only ever be dealing with square matrices so this issue will not arise explicitly. Finally, it is worth noting that we can extend the logic of equation (3.9) to a general multiplication involving more than two row or column elements. Then

$$[g_1 \quad g_2 \quad \cdots \quad g_n] = [h_1 \quad h_2 \quad \cdots \quad h_m] \begin{bmatrix} q_{11} & q_{12} & \cdots & q_{1n} \\ q_{21} & q_{22} & \cdots & q_{2n} \\ \cdot & \cdot & & \cdot \\ \cdot & \cdot & & \cdot \\ \cdot & \cdot & & \cdot \\ q_{m1} & q_{m2} & \cdots & q_{mn} \end{bmatrix}$$

which has the structure $g = hQ$ and can be summarized as

$$g_j = \sum_{i=1}^{m} h_i q_{ij}, \quad j = 1, 2, \ldots, n.$$

We will need this generalization in a moment but first let us put our three transform operations into matrix form.

Translation in equations (3.1) can now be written as

$$[x_{n+1} \quad y_{n+1}] = [x_n \quad y_n] + [T_1 \quad T_2], \tag{3.10}$$

while the scaling transformation in equations (3.2) can be formed from

$$[x_{n+1} \quad y_{n+1}] = [x_n \quad y_n] \begin{bmatrix} S_1 & 0 \\ 0 & S_2 \end{bmatrix}, \tag{3.11}$$

where the 2×2 matrix is called a scalar diagonal matrix. Rotation in equations (3.6) and (3.7) has the same form as equation (3.9), that is

$$[x_{n+1} \quad y_{n+1}] = [x_n \quad y_n] \begin{bmatrix} \cos(\theta) & \sin(\theta) \\ -\sin(\theta) & \cos(\theta) \end{bmatrix}, \tag{3.12}$$

where equation (3.12) has the same structure as the matrix equation summarizing equations (2.15) and (2.16) in Chapter 2.

Equations (3.10) to (3.12) are consistent with one another but the real purpose of matrix representation is to examine the broader structure at the vector–matrix level, to explore issues involving the order of transformations, and to provide composite equations. To synthesize all three operations in general form we need to expand these matrix operations to what is known as *homogeneous form*. Essentially representing coordinates in this form involves adding a third variable which acts as an overall scaling/translating device. This third variable is usually set as having no overall effect but it can be used to adjust the overall scale. We thus need to represent our vectors with 1×3 dimension and matrices as 3×3, the first two rows and columns representing the individual rotation and scaling effects as in equations (3.11) and (3.12) above, and the third row-column as the overall scaling and individual translation effects.

We will now write our generalized transformation in this form as

$$[x_{n+1} \quad y_{n+1} \quad 1] = [x_n \quad y_n \quad 1] \begin{bmatrix} a_{11} & a_{12} & 0 \\ a_{21} & a_{22} & 0 \\ a_{31} & a_{32} & 1 \end{bmatrix} \qquad (3.13)$$

where the 1×3 vector on the left-hand side of equation (3.13) is referred to as p_{n+1}, the right-hand vector as p_n, and the 3×3 transformation matrix as A. The general structure of this homogeneous transformation is thus $p_{n+1} = p_n A$; a_{11}, a_{12}, a_{21} and a_{22} can reflect the scaling and rotation effects in equations (3.11) and (3.12), a_{31} and a_{32} the translation effects in equations (3.10), and the variable $(a_{33} =)$ 1 the overall scaling effect which could be set at a value different from unity. We can represent the three elementary transformations – translation, scaling and rotation – by the 3×3 matrices called T, S and R respectively. Then

$$T = \begin{bmatrix} 1 & 0 & 0 \\ 0 & 1 & 0 \\ T_1 & T_2 & 1 \end{bmatrix}, \quad S = \begin{bmatrix} S_1 & 0 & 0 \\ 0 & S_2 & 0 \\ 0 & 0 & 1 \end{bmatrix}, \quad \text{and } R = \begin{bmatrix} \cos(\theta) & \sin(\theta) & 0 \\ -\sin(\theta) & \cos(\theta) & 0 \\ 0 & 0 & 1 \end{bmatrix}$$

Use of these matrices in the general matrix equation in (3.13) will give the operations in equations (3.10) to (3.12) with the third dummy variable as 1. Readers are advised to work out $p_{n+1} = p_n T$, $p_{n+1} = p_n S$ and $p_{n+1} = p_n R$ if they are unfamiliar with this kind of algebra, and check these results against equations (3.1), (3.2), (3.6) and (3.7).

Matrix operations only show their true worth when they are used to explore the structure of a sequence of transformations. We have already noted that the order of such a sequence is of importance and we will conclude this section with an example related to transforming the box which is presented in Program 3.6. In that program, the box is not located at the origin of the system. If we want to rotate the box itself about one of its points we must in fact make that point the origin before we effect the rotation. In short, we must translate all points to a new origin based on the point in question, rotate the object, and then translate back to the original coordinate system. In terms of the above matrix operations, our sequence would be

$$p_{n+1} = p_n TRT^{-1}, \tag{3.14}$$

where T^{-1} is the inverse of the original translation matrix T. This inverse simply moves each point back into the same system from which it was originally moved.

In the case of rotating our box, let us assume that the point about which we are rotating is T_1 units along the x axis and T_2 along the y. Then our sequence of operations following equation (3.14) is as follows:

$$[x_{n+1} \quad y_{n+1} \quad 1] = [x_n \quad y_n \quad 1]$$

$$\begin{bmatrix} 1 & 0 & 0 \\ 0 & 1 & 0 \\ -T_1 & -T_2 & 1 \end{bmatrix} \begin{bmatrix} \cos(\theta) & \sin(\theta) & 0 \\ -\sin(\theta) & \cos(\theta) & 0 \\ 0 & 0 & 1 \end{bmatrix} \begin{bmatrix} 1 & 0 & 0 \\ 0 & 1 & 0 \\ T_1 & T_2 & 1 \end{bmatrix}$$

$$= [x_n \quad y_n \quad 1] \begin{bmatrix} \cos(\theta) & \sin(\theta) & 0 \\ -\sin(\theta) & \cos(\theta) & 0 \\ T_1 - T_1 \cos(\theta) & T_2 + T_2 \cos(\theta) & 1 \\ + T_2 \sin(\theta) & -T_1 \sin(\theta) & \end{bmatrix}$$

We can further simplify these matrix equations by multiplying out the vector-matrix operation explicitly. This leads to

$$[x_{n+1} \quad y_{n+1} \quad 1] = [(x_n - T_1)\cos(\theta) - (y_n - T_2)\sin(\theta) + T_1,$$
$$(x_n - T_1)\sin(\theta) + (y_n - T_2)\cos(\theta) + T_2, \ 1]$$

where the order of the transformations is clear from the resulting equations. In fact, it is unlikely that programs would be written for microcomputers which make explicit use of matrix operations unless the sequences of transformation involved many (more than five) operations. However for more general graphics packages such as those based on the GKS (Graphical Kernel System) or CORE systems, explicit use of matrices enables their application to diverse operating environments (Harris, 1984; Harrington, 1983). In this book, we will only use matrices to demonstrate ideas, not in programming graphical operations.

3.5   DESIGNS BASED ON TRANSFORMATIONS

A useful way to begin to illustrate transformations is to take a simple but memorable object, stretch it, shrink it and rotate it about its centre. The Durer head introduced in Program 2.2 in the last chapter is an ideal example, and we will use this in showing how an object can be transformed. In fact, this head is of special importance in this context because Albrecht Durer himself was an early exponent of the art of transforming objects to enable their properties to be discovered (Thompson, 1961; Tobler, 1983). What we have done here is to enhance Program 2.2 into a simple transformation program in which the transformation is controlled by the user. The transformation is based on two of the elementary operations – scaling and rotation – and the formulae to produce these transforms are based on the matrix equation $p_{n+1} = p_n SR$.

Our program is listed as Program 3.7 which defines a text window at the bottom of the screen through which the user enters scale and rotation parameters. The program plots a grid of 4×3 heads, all with possibly different transformations specified by the user, so that comparisons of different rotations and scales can be made. The Durer head itself is also scaled and translated from its object to screen coordinates in Program 2.2 and this is also required here, although the origin of the head's coordinates relative to the screen is now located at the centre of the head. This enables rotation around the head's centre and saves space on the screen. The grid of locations of each head is controlled by the FOR–NEXT loops in lines 70 and 80, and in lines 90 and100 the scaling and rotation angle are input. The points defining the head are specified in DATA statements as previously and are read in afresh each time a new head is to be plotted.

The coordinates are transformed twice: first from object to screen coordinates and then from original screen to transformed screen coordinates. The way the object to screen transformations occur is the same as in Program 2.2 but the screen transformations themselves are accomplished through function statements defined in lines 250 and 260. These various transformations are accomplished in lines 150 and 190 for the object to screen and lines 160 and 200 for the screen to screen transformations. A typical picture from the program is presented in Fig. 3.7 for a variety of rotations and scaling. The program enables you to specify your own transformations, but to see more detail it would be necessary to draw a larger head. Taking out the FOR–NEXT loops beginning in lines 70 and 80 and ending at line 220, changing the scalar T and translators $XX\%$ and $YY\%$ in line 50, and setting a new origin for the screen coordinates in line 20 would accomplish this.

So far we have not shown how transforming a shape can result in a more complex design but it is fairly obvious that if the transformation is accomplished regularly or systematically in spatial terms, the original shape can be moved in a variety of ways and used as a module in more complex constructions. We will first illustrate this idea by extending our program to draw the ellipse in Chapter 2 (Program 2.4) to one which both draws and transforms the ellipse. This program, like the previous one transforming the Durer head, is under user control; that is the user can specify the original axes

Program 3.7   Transforming the Durer head

```
10 REM Transforming the Durer Head
20 MODE0
30 VDU23,1,0;0;0;0;
40 VDU19,1,1;0;
50 T=1.4:XX%=77:YY%=88
60 VDU28,0,31,79,29
70 FOR Y0%=870 TO 0 STEP -309
80   FOR X0%=160 TO 1280 STEP 320
90     INPUT "X SCALAR = ",SX,"Y SCALAR = ",SY
100    INPUT "ANGLE OF ROTATION = ",TH
110    TH=RAD(TH):C=COS(TH):S=SIN(TH)
120    RESTORE:VDU29,X0%;Y0%;
130    FOR I%=1 TO 4
140      READ N%:READ X%,Y%
150      XC%=T*(X%-XX%):YC%=T*(Y%-YY%)
160      X%=FNTRX:Y%=FNTRY:MOVE X%,Y%
170      FOR J%=2 TO N%
180        READ X%,Y%
190        XC%=T*(X%-XX%):YC%=T*(Y%-YY%)
200        X%=FNTRX:Y%=FNTRY:DRAW X%,Y%
210      NEXT J%:NEXT I%:CLS
220    NEXT X0%:NEXT Y0%
230 END
240 :
250 DEFFNTRX=XC%*SX*C-YC%*SY*S
260 DEFFNTRY=XC%*SX*S+YC%*SY*C
270 :
280 DATA 31
290 DATA 138,61,140,53,146,55,156,54
300 DATA 147,120,144,131,130,140,110,143
310 DATA 90,142,80,140,75,130,73,105
320 DATA 70,90,60,95,50,90,48,80
330 DATA 51,70,60,68,58,60,60,50
340 DATA 70,34,90,19,110,10,120,12
350 DATA 140,13,142,30,139,33,142,44
360 DATA 135,44,148,44,146,55
370 DATA 8
380 DATA 120,96,130,99,142,98,138,90
390 DATA 128,89,136,85,138,90,136,77
400 DATA 2
410 DATA 100,14,96,0
420 DATA 15
430 DATA 144,131,140,140,130,150,110,166
440 DATA 80,173,60,173,30,164,10,148
450 DATA 1,130,1,110,9,80,20,56
460 DATA 20,44,15,30,11,10
```

of the ellipse and rotate and draw it in any number of positions. The listing in Program 3.8 shows that 60 points on the circumference of the ellipse are first generated using the recursive transformation given in equations (2.15) and (2.16), the radii of which are input by the user in lines 70 and 80. As soon as the points are generated they are stored in arrays $X(60)$ and $Y(60)$. The transformation of these points is achieved in the REPEAT–UNTIL loop bounded

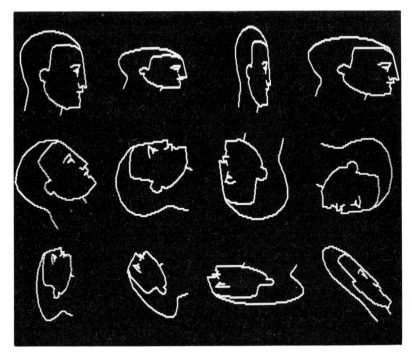

Fig. 3.7   Transformations of the Durer head

by lines 170 and 280. The user inputs the angle of rotation in line 180 and the rotation is accomplished, and the ellipse plotted using equations (3.6) and (3.7) in the FOR–NEXT loop between lines 230 and 270.

The rotated and original ellipses stay on the screen, showing the user the effect of various angles of rotation. The loop is ended when the input angle is set as 0, and then the program returns to demand parameters for a new start ellipse. It is important to note that the ellipse is rotated, not about its centre but about its smallest x coordinate: this is where the horizontal axis cuts the left edge of the ellipse. If the horizontal axis is larger than the vertical axis, rotation is reminiscent of the petals of a flower whereas if the vertical axis is larger than the horizontal, the rotation will produce shapes more reminiscent of cog wheel like designs. This program enables designs to be developed interactively: readers are advised to rotate ellipses for situations where $R_x \gg R_y$ and $R_y \ll R_x$ in equal angular increments, that is for say $\theta = 30$, 60, 90, . . . degrees.

The kind of experimentation suggested with Program 3.8 has been formalized into the design program listed as Program 3.9. We have clarified Program 3.8 by organizing the ellipse generation, and transformation (rotation) as procedures (PROCSETUP and PROCTRANSF respectively). We

Program 3.8 Rotating ellipses

```
10 REM Rotating Ellipses
20 MODE1:VDU28,0,1,39,0
30 DIM X(60),Y(60)
40 VDU23,1,0;0;0;0;
50 VDU29,640;512;
60 REPEAT
70   INPUT TAB(8)"RADIUS OF X AXIS = ",RX
80   INPUT TAB(8)"RADIUS OF Y AXIS = ",RY
90   DT=2*PI/60:A=RX/RY
100  C=COS(DT):S=SIN(DT):SX=S/A:SY=S*A
110  XA=RX:YA=0:MOVE XA+RX,YA
120  FOR I%=1 TO 60
130    T=XA*C-YA*SY
140    YA=YA*C+XA*SX:XA=T
150    X(I%)=XA+RX:Y(I%)=YA:DRAW XA+RX,YA
160  NEXT I%
170  REPEAT
180    CLS:INPUT TAB(9)"ANGLE OF PIVOT = ",TH
190    TH=RAD(TH):CC=COS(TH):SS=SIN(TH)
200    XA=X(60)*CC-Y(60)*SS
210    YA=X(60)*SS+Y(60)*CC
220    MOVE XA,YA
230    FOR I%=1 TO 60
240      XA=X(I%)*CC-Y(I%)*SS
250      YA=X(I%)*SS+Y(I%)*CC
260      DRAW XA,YA
270    NEXT I%
280  UNTIL TH=0
290  AA=GET:CLG
300  UNTIL FALSE
310 END
```

also require a routine to fill an ellipse and we have specified this as a procedure (PROCFILL) which uses the cross fill method. What Program 3.9 does is to set up an ellipse with major and minor axes whose size is specified by the user, and then rotates this ellipse over one revolution (360 degrees) at $N\%-1$ equal angular increments where the user inputs $N\%$. In fact, because the design is flower-like, $N\%$ is considered to be the number of petals of the flower. Finally, the centre of the flower is filled out using the ellipse generating routine to produce a circle.

As in the US, Turkish and Welsh flag programs earlier in this chapter, the generating, drawing, filling and transforming operations are contained in procedures. PROCSETUP in lines 230 to 310 recursively generates the 60 pairs of ellipse coordinates, PROCTRANSF (lines 330 to 390) rotates the ellipse coordinates by the given angular increment, and PROCFILL (lines 410 to 490) plots the ellipse using the cross fill method. The main program essentially consists of a REPEAT–UNTIL loop (lines 50 to 200) which generates the flower designs. The input parameters are requested in lines 60 to 80, and the original

Program 3.9   Exploring patterns of ellipses

```
10 REM Exploring Patterns of Ellipses
20 MODE1
30 DIM X(60),Y(60)
40 VDU23,1,0;0;0;0;
50 REPEAT
60    INPUT TAB(10),"RAD OF X AXIS = ",RX
70    INPUT TAB(10),"RAD OF Y AXIS = ",RY
80    INPUT TAB(10),"NO. OF PETALS = ",N%
90    VDU29,640;512;:GCOLO,1
100   PROCSETUP(RX,RY):PROCFILL
110   TH=2*PI/N%
120   FOR K%=1 TO N%-1
130      PROCTRANSF(TH):PROCFILL
140      NEXT K%
150   IF RX>=RY THEN Z=RY ELSE Z=RX
160   Z=Z*1.25:RX=Z:RY=Z
170   VDU29,640-RX;512;:GCOLO,2
180   PROCSETUP(RX,RY):PROCFILL
190   AA=GET:CLS
200   UNTIL FALSE
210 END
220 :
230 DEFPROCSETUP(XX,YY)
240 DT=2*PI/60:A=XX/YY:XA=XX:YA=0
250 C=COS(DT):S=SIN(DT):SX=S/A:SY=S*A
260 FOR I%=1 TO 60
270   T=XA*C-YA*SY
280   YA=YA*C+XA*SX:XA=T
290   X(I%)=XA+XX:Y(I%)=YA
300   NEXT I%
310 ENDPROC
320 :
330 DEFPROCTRANSF(TH)
340 C=COS(TH):S=SIN(TH)
350 FOR I%=1 TO 60
360   T=X(I%)*C-Y(I%)*S
370   Y(I%)=X(I%)*S+Y(I%)*C:X(I%)=T
380   NEXT I%
390 ENDPROC
400 :
410 DEFPROCFILL
420 MOVE X(60),Y(60):MOVE X(1),Y(1)
430 PLOT85,X(59),Y(59)
440 FOR I%=2 TO 29
450   PLOT85,X(I%),Y(I%):J%=60-I%
460   PLOT85,X(J%),Y(J%)
470   NEXT I%
480 PLOT85,X(30),Y(30)
490 ENDPROC
```

ellipse set up and filled in red by procedure calls in line 100. The FOR–NEXT loop in lines 120 to 140 transforms and fills the ellipse N% − 1 times, and in lines 150 to 180, a circular centre is fixed, set up and filled in yellow. Some typical designs are illustrated in Fig. 3.8 where the effects of different sized major and minor ellipse axes on their rotation are clearly visible.

We are at last in a position to generate some rather pleasing designs using the ellipse transformation program. As in the case of our random ellipses, rosettes and stars programs, we can use the basis of Program 3.9 to generate different sized, positioned and coloured flower-like forms on the screen. What we have done is to relegate the whole ellipse transformation algorithm of Program 3.9 to a set of nested procedures. PROCELLIPSE calls PROCSETUP, PROCFILL and PROCTRANSF in the order required to generate and plot a flower. The main program is thus concerned with determining the parameters of the ellipse – flower designs – essentially the radii of the axes and the number of petals – and randomly locating the centre of each flower on the screen.

The program which is listed as Program 3.10, contains a very elaborate sequence for determining the parameters of each flower. As the setting up and plotting of the flower in lines 160 to 550 is almost identical to the listing in Program 3.9, we will only concentrate on the additional procedures required to determine the type of flower plotted. Two broad types of flower are possible – one with a few, thick petals and one with many thin petals. These are determined randomly in PROCORD and PROCUNU listed in lines 570 to 600, and 620 to 650 respectively. In both these procedures, a random choice is made to determine whether $R_x > R_y$ or vice versa. These are fixed in PROCFOR and PROCBAK respectively (listed in line 670 to 710, and 730 to 770) which determine the ultimate shape of the flower. Finally, the actual size of each flower is determined from functions listed in lines 790 to 820 which are called from PROCFOR and PROCBAK.

This program is one of the most highly structured in this book and to understand its structure further, the flow chart presented in Fig. 3.9 provides a chronology of its logic. This illustrates the need for structure even in relatively simple programs, and as a general rule, this logical structure will reflect the graphical structure of the resulting picture. A typical picture resulting from the program is shown in Fig. 3.10. The pastel shades give the picture a quiet soft feel and it is interesting that the original definiteness of the flower forms does not give way to chaos as more and more flower forms are constructed. The art becomes more diffuse certainly but the image changes, becomes more abstract and this is the sort of kinetic art which would probably be acceptable for however long the program had been running. The longest we have run this program is 12 hours and the only constraint on this kind of display we have encountered involves possible overheating of the machine. Visually, this is the first true kinetic art in this book for it always produces an acceptable design.

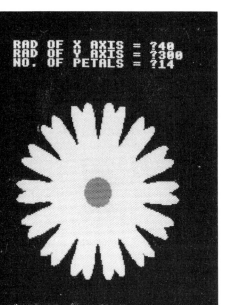

RAD OF X AXIS = ?40
RAD OF Y AXIS = ?300
NO. OF PETALS = ?14

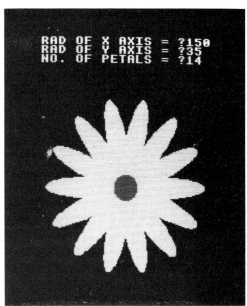

RAD OF X AXIS = ?150
RAD OF Y AXIS = ?35
NO. OF PETALS = ?14

RAD OF X AXIS = ?80
RAD OF Y AXIS = ?300
NO. OF PETALS = ?12

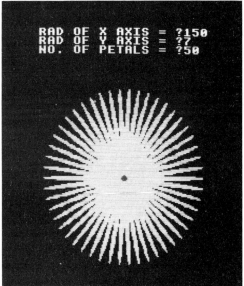

RAD OF X AXIS = ?150
RAD OF Y AXIS = ?7
NO. OF PETALS = ?50

g. 3.8   Flower-like designs based on ellipse rotations

Program 3.10   Let a thousand flowers bloom

```
 10 REM Let A Thousand Flowers Bloom
 20 MODE1
 30 VDU23,1,0;0;0;0;
 40 DIM X(30),Y(30)
 50 VDU19,0,5;0;19,1,6;0;
 60 VDU19,2,4;0;19,3,2;0;
 70 REPEAT
 80    M%=RND(2)
 90    IF M%=1 THEN PROCORD ELSE PROCUNU
100    X0=RND(1279):Y0=RND(1023)
110    VDU29,X0;Y0;
120    PROCELLIPSE(X0,Y0,RX,RY,N%)
130    UNTIL FALSE
140 END
150 :
160 DEFPROCELLIPSE(X0,Y0,XX,YY,N%)
170 GCOL0,RND(3):PROCSETUP(XX,YY)
180 PROCFILL:TH=2*PI/N%
190 FOR K%=1 TO N%-1
200    PROCTRANSF(TH):PROCFILL
210    NEXT K%
220 IF XX>=YY THEN Z=YY ELSE Z=XX
230 Z=Z*1.25:XX=Z:YY=Z
240 VDU29,X0-XX;Y0;:GCOL0,0
250 GCOL0,0
260 PROCSETUP(XX,YY):PROCFILL
270 ENDPROC
280 :
290 DEFPROCSETUP(XX,YY)
300 DT=2*PI/30:A=XX/YY:XA=XX:YA=0
310 C=COS(DT):S=SIN(DT):SX=S/A:SY=S*A
320 FOR I%=1 TO 30
330    T=XA*C-YA*SY
340    YA=YA*C+XA*SX:XA=T
350    X(I%)=XA+XX:Y(I%)=YA
360    NEXT I%
370 ENDPROC
380 :
390 DEFPROCTRANSF(TH)
400 C=COS(TH):S=SIN(TH)
410 FOR I%=1 TO 30
420    T=X(I%)*C-Y(I%)*S
430    Y(I%)=X(I%)*S+Y(I%)*C:X(I%)=T
440    NEXT I%
450 ENDPROC
460 :
470 DEFPROCFILL
480 MOVE X(30),Y(30):MOVE X(1),Y(1)
490 PLOT85,X(29),Y(29)
500 FOR I%=2 TO 14
510    PLOT85,X(I%),Y(I%):J%=30-I%
520    PLOT85,X(J%),Y(J%)
530    NEXT I%
540 PLOT85,X(15),Y(15)
550 ENDPROC
```

Program 3.10 continued

```
560 :
570 DEFPROCORD
580 R%=4+RND(4):N%=7+RND(7):M%=RND(2)
590 IF M%=1 THEN PROCFOR ELSE PROCBAK
600 ENDPROC
610 :
620 DEFPROCUNU
630 R%=15+RND(10):N%=30+RND(30):M%=RND(2)
640 IF M%=1 THEN PROCFOR ELSE PROCBAK
650 ENDPROC
660 :
670 DEFPROCFOR
680 M%=RND(2)
690 IF M%=1 THEN RX=FNSF ELSE RX=FNBF
700 RY=RX/R%
710 ENDPROC
720 :
730 DEFPROCBAK
740 M%=RND(2)
750 IF M%=1 THEN RY=FNSB ELSE RY=FNBB
760 RX=RY/R%
770 ENDPROC
780 :
790 DEFFNSF=50+RND(30)
800 DEFFNBF=120+RND(40)
810 DEFFNSB=80+RND(40)
820 DEFFNBB=200+RND(50)
```

3.6 POLAR GEOMETRY AND COMPUTER SCULPTURE

We have generated complexity through building more intricate designs out of simpler modules, such as in the case of our flowers program, but we have not yet shown how we can develop intricate shapes through the use of more elaborate mathematical functions. We will do this here. Instead of putting simple functions together in terms of their graphical form on the screen, we will put functions together at the algebraic level whose form is a direct consequence of the mathematics. We have already seen elementary examples of this in modification of our circle generators to embrace ellipses, and our further elaboration of these to form spirals. A similar kind of development will be presented here.

Let us write the equations which generate coordinates x and y using more general forms of the standard trigonometric functions. Then

$$x = f(R_x, \theta)\cos(\theta), \text{ and } y = g(R_y, \theta)\sin(\theta), \tag{3.15}$$

where the functions $f(R_x, \theta)$ and $g(R_y, \theta)$ suggest that the 'radii' associated with each coordinate are unspecified functions of the fixed or constant radii R_x and R_y, and the angle of rotation θ around the origin or pole. In this form, these types of relations are referred to as polar functions although strictly speaking,

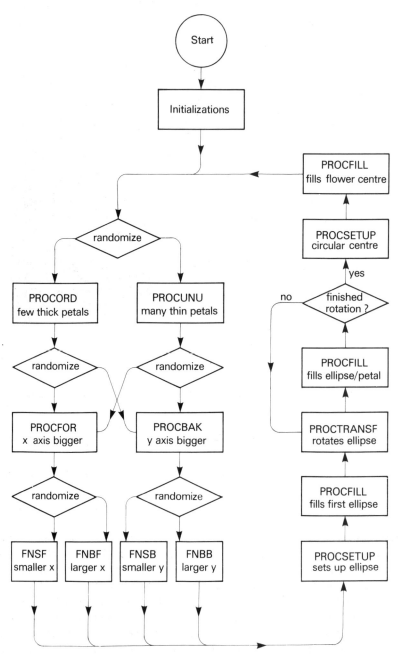

Fig. 3.9 Logical flow of control in randomly generated flower-like designs

Fig. 3.10 Let a thousand flowers bloom

all the rotational functions we have dealt with so far are part of this class. We can easily generate our standard forms from the general equations in (3.15). For example, a circle results when $R = f(R_x, \theta) = g(R_y, \theta)$, an ellipse when $R_x = f(R_x, \theta)$, $R_y = g(R_y, \theta)$, an Archimedean circular spiral when $R\theta = f(R_x, \theta) = g(R_y, \theta)$, and so on.

The function which we will work with which can generate extraordinarily elaborate designs is given by

$$x = R \sin(\alpha\theta)\cos(A\theta), \text{ and } y = R \sin(\alpha\theta)\sin(B\theta), \qquad (3.16)$$

where α, A and B are parameters taking on any positive value. Many other similar functions are possible and some are explored by Kosniowski (1983) to whose book readers are referred. Here however let us first note that if A and B are set equal to unity and θ is varied over one revolution $0 \leqslant \theta \leqslant 2\pi$, we generate designs which are reminiscent of our flower-like forms in the previous section. For $\alpha = 1$, we generate flower-like designs whose number of petals is 2α, while for $\alpha = 3, 5, 7, \ldots$ (odd values), we get flowers with α petals. As α gets larger, the petals become increasingly spikey. For α set as an integer value, we get closed shapes which normally will be complete for θ varying over one revolution. For real values of α, symmetric polar plots also result but the range over which θ must vary in order to converge on a closed shape is usually unknown in advance.

A simple program to explore plots of equations (3.16) is listed in Program 3.11. The program is straightforward based on slow computation of the coordinates and requiring the user to input parameter values α, A and B. Note that the functions $f(R_x,\theta) = g(R_y,\theta)$ are defined in lines 180 to 190 and thus the reader can easily modify this program to explore other functions such as those listed in Kosniowski (1983). If the parameter values A and B depart very much from unity, we begin to get plots with pronounced turning points, and in many cases, the turning point is so extreme, that the plots appear to contain major discontinuities. To explore the mathematics of such functions, we would need to use catastrophe and bifurcation theory but it is sufficient to note here, that such functions can be used to generate what 'appears' irregular and discontinuous despite its regular generation. If you set $5 \leqslant \alpha \leqslant 7, 1 \leqslant A \leqslant 5$, and $2 \leqslant B \leqslant 6$, the plots produced look like butterflies; they have all the features of winged insects and this suggests that we can use such functions to generate quite elaborate designs.

For this range of α, A and B, we have written a program listed in Program 3.12 which plots 12 'butterflies' arranged in a 4 × 3 grid on the screen. The 12 sets of parameters are read from DATA statements at the end of the program in lines 310 to 330. If you have explored Program 3.11, the shapes produced may well resemble all kinds of natural features but a way of filling them in, colouring them, is not obvious. There are clearly unseen advantages in building up complexity more simply than this, as we did in the previous section. But all is not lost because one possible method of filling is to

Program 3.11   Polar plots

```
 10 REM Polar Plots
 20 MODE1
 30 VDU23,1,0;0;0;0;
 40 VDU29,640;512;
 50 INPUT TAB(10)"RADIUS PARAMETER = ",ALPHA
 60 INPUT TAB(10)"X-AXIS PARAMETER = ",A
 70 INPUT TAB(10)"Y-AXIS PARAMETER = ",B
 80 GCOLO,1:S=300:MOVE0,0
 90 FOR I=0 TO 2*PI STEP 0.05
100   R=FNSIN(ALPHA,I)
110   X%=S*R*COS(A*I)
120   Y%=S*R*SIN(B*I)
130   DRAW X%,Y%
140   NEXT I
150 AA=GET:CLS:GOTO 50
160 END
170 :
180 DEF FNSIN(ALPHA,Z)
190 =SIN(ALPHA*Z)
```

Program 3.12 Butterflies

```
 10 REM Butterflies
 20 MODE1
 30 VDU23,1,0;0;0;0;
 40 FOR L%=1 TO 2
 50   CLS:RESTORE
 60   IF L%=1 THEN GCOLO,1:T=120 ELSE T=12
 70   IF L%=2 THEN MODE2:VDU23,1,0;0;0;0;
 80   YO%=854:YI%=341:XI%=320
 90   FOR N%=1 TO 3
100     XO%=160
110     FOR M%=1 TO 4
120       VDU29,XO%;YO%;
130       READ A,B,ALPHA
140       FOR S=T TO 120 STEP 12
150         IF L%=2 THEN GCOLO,RND(7)
160         SS=360/S:MOVEO,0
170         FOR I=0 TO 360 STEP SS
180           Z=RAD(I):R=FNSIN(ALPHA,Z)
190           X%=S*R*COS(A*Z)
200           Y%=S*R*SIN(B*Z)
210           DRAW X%,Y%
220         NEXT I:NEXT S
230       XO%=XO%+XI%:NEXT M%
240     YO%=YO%-YI%:NEXT N%
250   AA=GET:NEXT L%
260 END
270 :
280 DEFFNSIN(ALPHA,Z)
290 =SIN(ALPHA*Z)
300 :
310 DATA 1,3,5,2,3,5,4,3,5,1,2,6
320 DATA 3,2,6,1,4,6,3,4,6,5,4,6
330 DATA 1,2,7,1,4,7,2,4,7,1,6,7
```

plot the function by gradually increasing its fixed radius R in such a way that the figure is filled. For the fill to be complete, the change in R should be about the same as the pixel resolution in the smaller of the two directions.

This method of filling implies a long, laborious procedure but it can be turned to advantage. What Program 3.12 does is to plot the outline of the butterflies first in MODE1 and then replot them at a lower level of resolution in MODE2, gradually increasing the radius R until it reaches that of the outline plots in MODE1. As it changes the radius, the program also selects one of seven colours at random and what results are amazingly colourful butterfly designs. In the program, the FOR–NEXT loop from lines 40 to 250 controls the MODE of plotting, while the loops bounded by lines 90 to 240, and 110 and 230 control the position of each butterfly on the screen. For MODE1, the FOR–NEXT loop between lines 140 and 220 which gradually increases the radius, only operates for the maximum radius. The loop between lines 170 and 220 controls the angular revolution and the plotting within which is embedded the polar function which in turn is set in lines 280 and 290. The outlines of the butterflies are shown in Fig. 3.11, while the coloured designs which, some might say, are quite beautiful, are illustrated in Plate 3. Note that the colour filling procedure takes about 12 minutes in contrast to plotting their outline which takes only 2 minutes.

We can now augment our polar functions so that we can plot smaller circles or ellipses within the outline or envelope of larger circular forms. The coordinate functions are given as

$$x = (R_1 + R_2)\cos(\theta) - R_2 \cos\left(\frac{R_1 + R_2}{R_2}\theta\right), \qquad (3.17)$$

$$y = (R_1 + R_2)\sin(\theta) - R_2 \sin\left(\frac{R_1 + R_2}{R_2}\theta\right). \qquad (3.18)$$

Equations (3.17) and (3.18) essentially boil down to the plotting of smaller circles with radius R_2 within the envelope of a larger circle with radius $(R_1 + R_2)$. The speed of variation of the smaller circle plot is $(R_1 + R_2)/R_2$ times faster than that of the larger circle plot, and this leads to cusp-like plots within the larger circle.

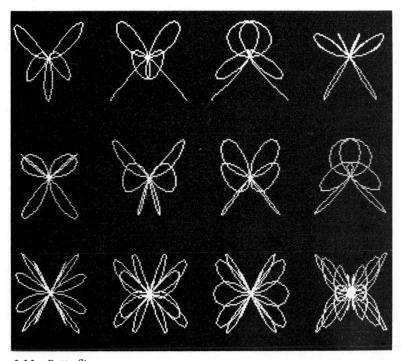

Fig. 3.11   Butterflies

To generate cusps which connect over one angular revolution, it is necessary that $(R_1 + R_2)/R_1$ be an integer; thus in the program we will introduce, the user is requested to input the number of cusps n from which R_2 is determined as

$$R_2 = R_1/n. \tag{3.19}$$

The cusps look like clouds but are a little too regular. If the large radius associated with the y axis is set as $(R_1 - R_2)$, that is equation (3.18) becomes

$$y = (R_1 - R_2)\sin(\theta) - R_2 \, \sin\left(\frac{R_1 + R_2}{R_2} \, \theta\right), \tag{3.20}$$

then an ellipse-shaped cloud will result.

A program to plot these forms is listed as Program 3.13. In line 50, the user is requested to input the radius R_1, and then in line 60, requested to specify a regular (circular) or irregular (ellipsoid) shape. In short, an affirmative answer to this question selects equation (3.18), a negative answer (3.20). The number of cusps is input in line 80, and the various parameters as well as R_2 from equation (3.19), calculated in line 90. The FOR–NEXT loop between lines 110 and 150 computes the polar functions and plots the shape. As usual the program can be used to generate a variety of designs. You can generate shamrocks, and other flower-like designs as well as cloud forms. Try generating an irregular shape with one cusp ($N\% = 1$) and see what you get. The best cloud-like forms are generated with five, six or seven cusps within the irregular (ellipsoid) envelope.

We will now plot some cloud formations which have a 'cumulus-like' structure. The idea for these cloud pictures has been taken quite unashamedly from Cownie's (1982) brilliant Windy Fields program but we have

Program 3.13   Cusp catastrophes

```
10 REM Cusp Catastrophes
20 MODE1
30 VDU23,1,0;0;0;0;
40 VDU29,640;512;
50 INPUT TAB(10)"RADIUS PARAMETER = ",A
60 INPUT TAB(4)"REGULAR SHAPE ? TYPE YES OR NO ",Q$
70 IF LEFT$(Q$,1)="Y" THEN K=1 ELSE K=-1
80 INPUT TAB(11)"NUMBER OF CUSPS = ",N%
90 B=A/N%:H=A+B:F=A+K*B:G=H/B
100 GCOLO,1:MOVE A,0
110 FOR I=0 TO 2*PI STEP 0.1
120    X%=H*COS(I)-B*COS(G*I)
130    Y%=F*SIN(I)-B*SIN(G*I)
140    DRAW X%,Y%
150    NEXT I
160 AA=GET:CLS:GOTO 50
170 END
```

incorporated a simple three-dimensional effect which gives a 'sculptured' look to the picture. We plot randomly positioned white clouds on a light blue background towards the top of the screen, and achieve the three-dimensional effect by edging the left side and base of the cloud in black. This is done by first plotting the cloud in black and then plotting the same cloud in white but this time displaced slightly towards the 'north-east' of the screen. The cloud formation emerges spontaneously as clouds are overplotted. Once this has been built up, a dark blue sea is put across the bottom half of the screen, and the clouds are gradually scrolled down to the sea, the sky ending up all white. Here is the simplest of animation, involving a clouding-over of the sky. The way the clouds are sculpted and the sky scrolled down provides yet another nice example of kinetic art.

The program is listed in Program 3.14. It incorporates the key elements of Program 3.13, and achieves the displacement effect by changing the origin of each cloud by the given distance. The plotting is accomplished using the centre fill technique: the cloud is sufficiently convex in shape to avoid any overplotting of the edges. Between 13 and 24 clouds are plotted to build up the formation in the FOR–NEXT loop between lines 60 and 180. Most of the top of the screen is thus white cloud and this enables the scrolling down to all white

Program 3.14   Cloud sculptures

```
 10 REM Cloud Sculptures
 20 MODE1
 30 VDU23,1,0;0;0;0;
 40 VDU19,0,6;0;19,1,0;0;
 50 VDU19,2,7;0;19,3,4;0;
 60 FOR K%=1 TO 12+RND(12)
 70   X0%=RND(1279):Y0%=700+RND(400)
 80   A=60+RND(75):B=A/(3+RND(4))
 90   H=A+B:G=H/B:F=A-B
100   FOR L%=1 TO 2
110     GCOL0,L%:VDU29,X0%;Y0%;:MOVE A,0
120     FOR I=0 TO 2*PI STEP 0.1
130       X%=H*COS(I)-B*COS(G*I)
140       Y%=F*SIN(I)-B*SIN(G*I)
150       MOVE0,0:PLOT85,X%,Y%
160     NEXT I
170     X0%=X0%+4+RND(4):Y0%=Y0%+4+RND(4)
180   NEXT L%:NEXT K%
190 REM Clouding Over
200 VDU28,0,31,39,13
210 COLOUR131:CLS
220 AA=GET:VDU26
230 VDU28,0,12,39,0:COLOUR130
240 FOR J%=1 TO 50
250   VDU11:AZ=INKEY(50)
260   NEXT J%
270 AA=GET:GOTO 20
280 END
```

to be achieved consistently colourwise. The blue sea is defined by a text window in line 200, and the sky is then defined by a text window in line 230 and scrolled down to its white background using the VDU11 command which is set in the FOR–NEXT loop between lines 240 and 260. A typical picture before the scrolling down or clouding over occurs is illustrated in Plate 4. Note the use of the text windows to define colour and to encase areas built up by graphics commands but then manipulated using text commands. Plate 4 is our first landscape and some of the techniques used will be further developed in the next chapter.

3.7 SIMPLE COLOUR MIXING AND SHADING

In this chapter, extending the realism and complexity of our pictures has been mainly accomplished by manipulating shapes. Indeed much of this and the last chapter has been concerned with geometry. But there is a limit to how far we can go with techniques without compensating with ideas about enhancing the realism of our pictures in terms of colour, texture, light and shade. Here we will examine simple colour mixing and shading which will also involve questions of texture and lighting, somewhat unwittingly perhaps.

The trade-off between number of colours available and level of resolution was examined in Chapter 2, and although MODE2 offered us a palette of 16 colours, eight of these involved alternating absolute colours by flashing; thus strictly the BBC computer can offer only eight absolute colours. Three primary colours – red (R), green (G) and blue (B) are available through the hardware and these are mixed in pairs to form complementaries – cyan ($=G+B$), magenta ($=R+B$) and yellow ($=R+G$). All the colours are combined to produce white ($=R+G+B$) and none of the colours produce black. There are of course techniques available to control the way the colour guns operate on the machine but these are beyond the scope of this book and in any case, would involve machine code and assembler. Thus to mix any of these eight default colours here, we will have to achieve this through high level software – Basic – and this will involve generating patterns of pixels in various colour mixes.

The colour mixing we will present will be based on switching on adjacent pixels in different colours, thus achieving over a much larger area than a single pixel, an *impression* of a different colour. For example with eight colours, we can mix each of the eight colours with the other seven, thus producing $(8 \times 7)/2 = 28$ distinct shades, with the original eight making 36 colours in all. In MODE1, there are six shades plus four original colours making ten in all; in MODE0 there is only one shade plus two colours making three in all. There are a few well-defined colour models which should tell us what colour results when one mixes colours in this fashion. However, these are beyond the scope of this book and in any case, the rather rudimentary way of mixing at the pixel level would be sufficient to invalidate many of these. Thus our foray into colour mixing will be entirely *ad hoc.* Lastly, we have found that mixing more than two colours in any mode is problematic and it is difficult to derive general rules. Therefore we will confine ourselves to mixes composed of only two colours.

The key to our colour mix lies in the PLOT21 command which switches on every alternate pixel in the given foreground colour. If we plot such a line either horizontally or vertically in one colour and then displace the plot line one pixel in the direction of the line and plot in a second colour, we will achieve the mix on a single line. By moving to the next line (up or down, right or left), and repeating this operation but switching the colours around enables a pixel to have different coloured pixels horizontally and vertically adjacent to it. By 'weaving' our colours in this way, we can build up shades which are fairly evenly patterned. We are however restricted to the horizontal and vertical directions in which the pixels are laid out with the most tractable accessibility, and thus the patterning will be affected by curvature of the screen etc.

We have written a program to plot three horizontally adjacent rectangles of colour which form the design for the familiar Tricolour flags. In the program listed in Program 3.15, we have coded the Irish flag – green, white and orange. The orange colour in the third panel of the flag is produced by mixing red and yellow using the above 'weaving' technique. The flag is set on a black

Program 3.15 The tricolour

```
 10 REM The Tricolour
 20 DIM COL%(3)
 30 READ M%,S1%,S2%
 40 READ COL%(0),COL%(1),COL%(2),COL%(3)
 50 MODE M%:VDU29,640;512;
 60 VDU23,1,0;0;0;0;
 70 X%=-300:Y%=-150:XA%=200:YA%=300
 80 GCOLO,COL%(0)
 90 PROCSQUARE(X%,Y%,XA%,YA%)
100 GCOLO,COL%(1)
110 PROCSQUARE(X%+XA%,Y%,XA%,YA%)
120 DRAW -X%,Y%:DRAW -X%,-Y%:DRAW -X%-XA%,-Y%
130 FOR I%=-X%-XA% TO -X% STEP S1%
140    GCOLO,COL%(2):PLOT21,I%,Y%
150    GCOLO,COL%(3):MOVE I%,Y%+S2%
160    PLOT21,I%,-Y%:MOVE I%+S1%,-Y%
170    C%=COL%(2):COL%(2)=COL%(3):COL%(3)=C%
180    NEXT I%
190 AA=GET:MODE7
200 END
210 :
220 DEFPROCSQUARE(X%,Y%,N%,M%)
230 MOVE X%,Y%+M%:MOVE X%+N%,Y%+M%
240 PLOT85,X%,Y%:PLOT85,X%+N%,Y%
250 ENDPROC
260 :
270 DATA 2,8,4,2,7,1,3
```

background, thus there are five colours in total and this means MODE2 must be used. In Program 3.15, mode and pixel resolution in the x and y directions are read in from a DATA statement on line 30, and in line 40, the colours of the first panel, of the second and the two required to mix the third panel are also read in and stored in an array. The familiar PROCSQUARE listed in lines 220 to 250 is called to plot the first and second panels in lines 90 and 110, and in line 120, the third panel is edged in the second panel colour. The FOR–NEXT loop from lines 130 to 180 controls the alternative pixel colour mixing which involves moving successively to adjacent pixels to start the PLOT21 commands in alternate colours.

We can obviously use Program 3.15 to plot other tricolours in different modes but most tricolours do not involve any colour mixing (Pedersen, 1971). The most appropriate use of the program therefore is to use it to explore various palette mixes in MODE2. If we set the first panel one colour, the second another, and set the two mixture colours the same as these first two, we will see the effect of mixing the two colours of the first two panels in the third. Replacing line 40 by

40 INPUT COL%(0),COL%(1):COL%(2)=COL%(0):COL%(3)=COL%(1)

we can use the program in MODE2 to read in the two colours to be mixed. If we also inserted the program in an appropriate loop, the user could then explore all combinations (shades) of colour in MODE2. To do the same for the other modes, would require assignment of actual to logical colours but this is also straightforward.

To show how effective colour mixing can be, we will return to our Cloud Sculpture program (Program 3.14) and replace the clouding over sequence (lines 190 to 260) with

```
190  REM Mixing a New Sea Colour
200  Y%=300:C1%=2:C2%=3:N%=4:M%=4
210  VDU29,640;Y%;:MOVE −640,Y%
220  FOR J%=−640 TO 640 STEP N%
230    GCOL0,C1%:PLOT21,J%,−Y%:MOVE J%,−Y%+M%
240    GCOL0,C2%:PLOT21,J%,Y%:MOVE J%+N%,Y%
250    C%=C1%:C1%=C2%:C2%=C%
260  NEXT J%
```

This uses the technique of Program 3.15 to colour the sea a mixture of dark blue and white which emerges in MODE1 as a kind of purple. In fact, this does not really resemble the sea because of the peculiar herringbone pattern that results due to the machine's hardware. Nevertheless, experimentation with different mixes in MODE1 does show that many more than four colours can be used and sometimes to great effect.

We will conclude this chapter with another technique of combining colour which emphasizes shading. Choosing two colours which might represent the extreme ends of some colour continuum, we can combine these in such a way that one colour dominates in one direction, the other in the other direction with the continuum between both being modelled with an appropriate mix. In our clouds program (Program 3.14), we could colour the sea so that it was blacker towards the bottom left-hand corner, bluer towards the top right. To do this we can first determine a point in the sea randomly; if another position in the possible range of points within the sea were chosen, and if the sum of the two coordinates defining this point were less than the sum of the coordinates defining the first point, one colour could be used; if not, the other. The first point could then be plotted in the assigned colour. If a very large number of points were plotted in this way, the sea would change from one colour near the minimum sum of coordinates to the other near the maximum. If we replace lines 190 to 260 in Program 3.14 with

```
190 REM Shading the Sea
200 VDU29,0;0;:X%=1279:Y%=600
210 VDU24,0;0;X%;Y%;:GCOL0,129;CLG
220 REPEAT
230     X0%=RND(X%):Y0%=RND(Y%):Z0%=RND(X%)+RND(Y%)
240     IF Z0%>X0%+Y0% THEN GCOL0,1 ELSE GCOL0,3
250     PLOT69,X0%,Y0%
260 UNTIL FALSE
```

this will achieve such a shading. Note that a graphics window is defined in one of the colours (black in this instance) for the sea, and then points are plotted either in black or blue dependent upon the test condition in line 240 using the PLOT69 command in line 250. After about 1 hour, the shading is near complete although we have not determined a test for its completion.

This has been a long chapter but we now have sufficient technique and insight into rudimentary computer art and graphics, to begin to construct some dramatic scenes. Landscapes offer great potential at this stage and therefore in the next chapter, we will explore how we can model trees, hills, lakes and other material features pertaining to distant, almost flat landscapes which contain little enough perspective to make their construction elementary.

4

Elementary picture structures: two-dimensional 'flat' landscapes

> Suppose I want to understand the 'structure' of
> something. Just what exactly does this mean? It means,
> of course, that I want to make a simple picture of it,
> which lets me grasp it as a whole. And it means, too,
> that as far as possible, I want to paint this picture out of
> as few elements as possible. The fewer elements there
> are, the richer the relationships between them, and the
> more of the picture lies in the 'structure' of these
> relationships.
>
> (Christopher Alexander, *The Timeless Way of Building,* 1979)

As soon as we talk of pictures, we talk of perspective, of regular geometrical distortion which enables us to reproduce three-dimensional reality on a two-dimensional surface. In this chapter, we will begin to tackle such reproductions although our concern will be to simulate the most simple of pictures, introducing a variety of 'tricks' to give our pictures perspective. In the previous chapter, the designs we developed were truly flat and contained no sense of perspective; here we will continue to work with 'flat' pictures although we will 'cue in' depth or perspective, generating what some refer to as '$2\frac{1}{2}$-dimensional' images. Fully-fledged perspective modelling requires considerably more mathematics than we have introduced so far and thus we will postpone such discussion until Chapter 6.

Several new themes will emerge in this chapter. We will show how pictures can be constructed from program modules or segments, complexity being built up through combining different techniques and/or replicating the same technique many times. Many of our pictures will have structures which closely correspond to the structures of the computer programs used in their generation. Landscapes are ideally suited to demonstrate this point in that their visual structure is usually straightforward, and rather good impressionistic and abstract art can be generated quickly and simply. We will also be concerned with the techniques used to generate different types of landscape: not only soft 'rural' landscapes but also harder 'urban' landscapes. To achieve this, we will use *colour* and *geometry* judiciously to give both soft and hard impressions, and to emphasize specific qualities of the picture.

Three other considerations must be stressed at this stage. In computer art, so many intuitive decisions are made when building up a picture that it is impossible to specify all but the most critical. The computer artist David Em in an interview with Peter Sorensen (1984a) bears this out when he says: "When you make a picture . . . you make millions of little decisions that you don't think about until you have to start specifying them". Throughout this book and particularly in this and later chapters, there is no way all the necessary decisions in producing good or bad computer art can be recorded, and it is important to recognize this. The second point relates to the power of mathematics in generating pictures. As implied in Chapter 1, 'true' computer art is not drawing using the medium of the computer but mathematical modelling of picture structure. This controversial thesis begins to be illustrated in this chapter where the power of the machine to generate designs recursively, and the need to understand the mechanisms of both nature and society are essential to the simulation of satisfying pictures. This is particularly clear when the 'parameters' of the models governing picture structure are manipulated, as they can be in the case of the tree structures shown here. Finally, the process of constructing pictures is, as is clear from earlier chapters, an art form in itself, and this implies that the way the picture is computed must be subject to aesthetic principles.

Landscapes dominate this chapter and we begin with programs to construct soft landscapes composed of gently rolling hills, lakes, roads and trees based on techniques involving sine waves and ellipses. We will also introduce a crude animation here involving switching the colours of our landscapes to give the impression of seasonal change. Hard landscapes follow involving city building using the graphics window technique. Trees will also recur throughout this chapter, and soft, elliptical trees will be contrasted with those based on more natural processes, on branching which in turn introduces the basic computer programming idea of recursion. Programs for designing branching structures, and using these designs to simulate savannah-like landscapes, and rolling 'English' countryside will be presented. Finally non-recursive tree designs – palms – will be introduced and used to simulate subtropical scenes.

Although a sense of realism flows throughout the programs developed here it is only a sense, for the pictures produced are impressionistic and abstract. As all artists and philosophers know, the quest for realism is inevitably an elusive one, and art is thus a combination of what the artist sees, his or her skill at reproducing it and the constraints which the medium imposes. This is as true of computer art as any other art and in this chapter, we will begin to see how the computer imposes its own qualities on the pictures produced. One final point before we launch into our landscape modelling and this involves the programs themselves. These are clearly longer than in previous chapters, sometimes taking up two or three pages of the book. Nevertheless, in the spirit of this book that everything you see is created from the programs given, and that it rarely takes more than an hour or so to key in and debug even the longest program, we urge readers to bear with the longish listings and to continually reflect on the detail generated in comparison to program length.

4.1   TEMPORAL PRIORITY AND THE PAINTER'S ALGORITHM

In Chapter 3, we showed that as a consequence of the way the frame buffer is organized, as soon as a segment or element of a design is generated in the program, it replaces any element which already resides in the same place within the buffer. In short, new pictorial detail overplots the detail already present. In developing an algorithm from this notion, we can do no better than quote Harrington (1983, p. 294):

> The algorithm gets its name from the manner in which an oil painting is created. The artist begins with the background. He can, if he wishes, fill the entire canvas with the background scene. The artist then paints the foreground objects. There is no need to erase portions of the background, the artist simply paints on top of them. The new paint covers the old so that only the newest layer of paint is visible. A frame buffer has this same property.

Making a virtue out of a necessity is a time-honoured technique of computer graphics, and the painter's algorithm orders the elements of the picture in the sequence in which they are to be plotted over one another. For example, in hiding lines in constructing three-dimensional objects, the lines are ordered not according to the order in which they are generated but in the sequence in which they need to be plotted. We will discuss such ordering in Chapter 6 but here the simplest possible ordering is used by the algorithm – ordering according to the position in the computer program and the time when the element is generated on the screen. The priority is therefore *temporal* (Foley and Van Dam, 1982); picture elements are ordered according to the order in which the commands in the computer program are executed. Pictorial detail is quite literally 'pasted on top' of previous detail (Cownie, 1982). The burden of temporal priority is of course the fact that previously generated detail is lost and the picture cannot usually be manipulated. The algorithm is more suitable for art than graphics, and it also enables a 'kinetic' sense to be imparted to the creation of any picture.

A typical landscape can be constructed according to this process. The background is first fixed and then the horizon, middle and foregrounds created in that order. Hills might form the horizon leading down to grassy fields in the foreground, colours changing from darker to lighter. Finally, the picture can be edged or framed, usually by darker forms. We will use this sequence extensively here. We will construct a program in MODE1 using four colours – cyan or light blue for the background sky, white and dark blue for the distant hills and green for the foreground. To give more excitement to structure, we could shade the various 'grounds' in the picture using different mixes of these colours in the manner also illustrated by Cooper (1984), stressing the vertical dimension to give an impression of scale. Rather than developing such detail through software, it is possible to exploit the machine's hardware in a non-standard way which involves the colour operation commands. But first we will digress slightly to present this technique as it is important to the programs we will be outlining.

The command – GCOL n,col – enables a colour switching operation n based on an absolute colour col, to be performed on the graphics screen. So far the operation number n has been that involving no logical colour switching ($n = 0$) and we have already said that we will not discuss the other standard operations ($n = 1, 2, 3$ or 4) until Chapter 7 where these ideas will be illustrated in relation to animation. However, experiment shows that for values of $n \geqslant 11$, interesting and unusual vertical hatches of colour, from those defined for that MODE, can result, and even more intriguing patterns are formed when these are plotted over one another. We have written a program, listed as Program 4.1 which enables the user to consider the effects of various GCOL operations from $n = 0$ to $n = 255$. What we are interested in here is finding high-order GCOL operation numbers which give vertical patterns and colour mixes which might be characteristic of different landscape effects such as lines of trees, field patterns and so on.

Program 4.1 plots four vertical rectangles of colour – dark blue, cyan, green and white which are the colours to be used in our soft landscapes, using GCOL 0,col and then overplots the same four coloured rectangles in the horizontal direction using GCOL n,col where $n = 0$ to 255. The plotting is accomplished left to right, and then bottom to top of the screen. The program moves from n to $n + 1$ upon pressing any key, and it can be used to explore operation numbers which give the required effects. What the program does not show, however is the effect of one high order GCOL plot over another, that is the effect of GCOL m, col-one on GCOL, n, col-two where $m, n \neq 0$. It is also clear from the program that some high order GCOL operations lead to unpredictable fill sequences, and the program does not show all the effects on the frame buffer such as some of the strange layering effects seen in subsequent programs. There is little need to comment on Program 4.1 except to note that a block of colour is plotted using the standard process of filling a rectangle with two MOVE and two PLOT85 commands given in PROCBLOCK in lines 210 to 250.

We can use higher order GCOL operations to plot blocks of vertical hatch

Program 4.1   Exploring GCOL numbers

```
 10 REM Exploring GCOL Numbers
 20 MODE1:VDU5
 30 VDU19,0,4;0;19,1,6;0;
 40 VDU19,2,2;0;19,3,7;0;
 50 FOR L%=0 TO 255
 60    X%=100:Y%=900:MOVE X%,Y%
 70    FOR C%=0 TO 3
 80       GCOLO,C%
 90       PROCBLOCK(0,-800,100,0,100,-800,200,0)
100    NEXT C%
110    X%=50:Y%=850:MOVE X%,Y%
120    FOR C%=3 TO 0 STEP-1
130       GCOL L%,C%
140       PROCBLOCK(800,0,0,-100,800,-100,0,-200)
150    NEXT C%
160    MOVE 850,1000:GCOLO,3:PRINT L%
170    AA=GET:CLS:CLG
180    NEXT L%
190 END
200 :
210 DEFPROCBLOCK(X1%,Y1%,X2%,Y2%,X3%,Y3%,X4%,Y4%)
220 MOVE X%+X1%,Y%+Y1%
230 PLOT85,X%+X2%,Y%+Y2%:PLOT85,X%+X3%,Y%+Y3%
240 X%=X%+X4%:Y%=Y%+Y4%:MOVE X%,Y%
250 ENDPROC
```

across the screen, and to overplot giving the impression of lines of trees and distant forests in the middle ground. The shape of these various blocks of colour can be computed from the following general function

$$y_{n+1} = \alpha[y_n - kr(5)] + (1-\alpha)[y_s + Y\sin(\theta_n)] \qquad (4.1)$$

where y_{n+1} and y_n are the vertical screen coordinates associated with horizontal coordinates x_{n+1} and x_n respectively, y_s is a basic screen coordinate of constant level for any x_n, and θ_n is the angular variation associated with x_n. Equation (4.1) enables a variety of bounding lines to be computed with coordinates x_n, y_n where x_n varies across the horizontal spread of the screen. If the parameter $\alpha = 1$, the first term in square brackets on the RHS of equation (4.1) only applies and this generates an upward or downward slope, or horizontal line depending on the value of k. If $\alpha = 0$, then the second square bracketed term applies and this can simulate a sinewave around the base value of y_s ($\theta = 0$) whose period is controlled by the angular variation θ_n and whose amplitude is fixed by Y.

When $\alpha = 1$, k can be positive, negative or zero, leading respectively to a downward, horizontal or upward sloping line, left to right across the screen. The term $r(5)$ indicates that for any x_n, a random number is chosen between 1 and 5 (in BBC Basic this is the function RND(5)), and thus the line if sloping is unlikely to be straight. Note that we could simulate a mix of lines and sinewaves if $\alpha \neq 0$, 1, although in the programs here $\alpha = 0$, 1, and $k = 0$, 1, -1. Finally x_n is varied regularly in steps of 20 screen units, that is $x_n =$ [0, 20, 40, . . .] and a block of colour is plotted across the screen using a sequence of x,y coordinates in PLOT85 commands, a typical example of which would be PLOT85, x_n,y_n: PLOT85, x_{n+1}, 0: PLOT85, x_{n+1},y_{n+1}, and so on. The angular variation of θ_n can itself be varied but in the programs here it is based on increments of 10 degrees for each increment of 20 horizontal (x) screen units.

A program based on plotting blocks of colour in this fashion, making use of some high order GCOL operations, and using temporal priority is presented in the listing in Program 4.2. Thirteen lines of 'hills' are plotted from background to foreground with different values of α, k, and y_s, as well as different GCOL operations and colours. Various initializations are first made in program lines 10 to 80. Then the essence of the main program is given by the FOR–NEXT loop in lines 90 to 140 in which k and α are randomly chosen, the GCOL

Program 4.2   Temporal priority: back-to-front landscapes

```
 10 REM Temporal Priority
 20 REM Back-to-Front Landscapes
 30 MODE1
 40 VDU19,0,6;0;19,1,4;0;
 50 VDU19,2,2;0;19,3,7;0;
 60 VDU23,1,0;0;0;0;
 70 K%=0:CK%=0:N%=30:G%=0
 80 YS%=685+K%*RND(N%)
 90 FOR H%=0 TO 12
100    READ COL%,G%
110    PROCHILLS(YS%,COL%,G%,K%,CK%)
120    YS%=YS%-(10+RND(N%))
130    K%=2-RND(3):CK%=2-RND(2)
140    NEXT H%
150 AA=INKEY(600):RUN
160 END
170 :
180 REM Plots a Wave or Line of Colour
190 DEFPROCHILLS(YS%,COL%,J%,K%,CK%)
200 GCOL J%,COL%
210 DT=RAD(10):TH=RAD(RND(360))
220 S=SIN(DT):C=COS(DT):SS=SIN(TH):CC=COS(TH)
230 SI%=RND(100):YN%=CK%*YS%+(1-CK%)*(YS%+SI%*SS)
240 MOVE 0,0:MOVE 0,YN%
250 FOR I%=20 TO 1280 STEP 20
260    SN=SS*C+CC*S:CC=CC*C-SS*S:SS=SN
270    YN%=CK%*(YN%-K%*RND(5))+(1-CK%)*(YS%+SI%*SS)
280    PLOT85,I%,0:PLOT85,I%,YN%
290    NEXT I%
300 ENDPROC
310 :
320 DATA 3,0,1,0,3,0,1,0,1,70,0,143,1,70
330 DATA 1,143,2,0,2,179,2,143,2,70,2,0
```

operation and colour numbers read from DATA statements (line 100) and the plotting and calculation of the colour block done in PROCHILLS which is called in line 110. y_s is successively lowered in line 120 reflecting the progression from background to foreground. PROCHILLS itself is given in lines 190 to 300. In lines 210 to 230, the amplitude and various angular trigonometric values are fixed while the FOR–NEXT loop in lines 250 to 290 controls the values of x_n, from 20 to 1280 in steps of 20. The recursive procedure given in Chapter 2 for updating the sine function is used in line 260, the function computed in line 270, and the appropriate strip from the colour block plotted in line 280.

Quite dramatic landscapes can result from running this program. The broad sequence of colours is white, dark blue and green on the light blue background, white representing the snow line, dark blue distant hills, occasionally distant lakes and green the grassy foreground. The mixture of high order GCOL operations with the zero GCOL operation yields impressions of distant hills, mixed with forests, woods and grasslands. From a cold start (switching on the machine), rather nice landscapes result on the 3rd and 6th run of the program. A typical output is illustrated in Fig. 4.1. Similar landscapes generated using sinewaves have been used by Cooper (1984) as the basis for silk-screen prints. There is clearly plenty of scope for experiment here and readers are urged to alter the DATA statements in lines 320 and 330 to explore how different colours and GCOL operations can lead to different pictures.

4.2   SOFT LANDSCAPES

It is already clear that temporal priority represents an obvious way to structure our computer landscape painting and now we can be concerned with extending the realism of the kind of scenes produced in Fig. 4.1. Random combinations of the composite function given in equation (4.1) lead to soft countryside, rolling hills and gently sloping grasslands. There is nothing harsh about the kinds of pictures generated for the colours chosen are also soft. In short, it is the combination of sinewave geometry and colours which gives the landscape its flavour. What we will do here is to augment the picture by giving it real depth – by adding a road which disappears into the distance, and by plotting trees which increase in size as the foreground is approached. As yet in our landscapes there is little depth for the 'hills' are too far away, and insofar as there is any sense of scale, it is colour, not geometry which imparts this. We will cue in depth by controlling the vertical dimension more strongly than the horizontal, and we will add to the realism of the picture by shading some trees with a mixture of two colours, affecting texture rather than colour *per se.*

We will extend the temporal priority of our soft landscapes of the previous section by structuring the program according to the following sequence: sky→hills→lake→treeline→grasslands→road→trees.   The   sky   will   be determined by the background colour while the hills, lake, treeline and

Fig. 4.1   Hillscape

grasslands are fixed using calls to PROCHILLS. The road will be computed and plotted in the procedure PROCROAD and the trees will be plotted using calls to PROCTREE, and shaded if necessary with PROCTSHADE and PROCLINE. We will now present the way in which these procedures operate before the full listing is examined.

PROCHILLS is essentially the same as that in Program 4.2 with the same arguments but it is only called four times by the main program; first with a high order GCOL operator, dark blue colour and sinewave form to generate the wooded distant hills, second to generate a horizontal dark blue lake, third with a high order GCOL operator and green colour to produce the nearer woodland and finally to produce a green grassland as the foreground. Whereas the first two calls are controlled in terms of the form generated, the last two are not, but are randomly formed thus allowing slopes, flatlands or rolling hills to be simulated. There is only one change from Program 4.2 and that is that the upper y_n coordinates of each colour block are stored in a 65 element array $YH\%$ ($N\%$) associated with x coordinates at 20 screen units apart so that the extent of the last 'ground' plotted – the foreground – is available to control the subsequent road and tree plotting.

PROCROAD has a similar structure to PROCHILLS in that a sinewave is used to compute the coordinates of the twisting road, the difference being that the amplitude of the wave is fixed horizontally not vertically. In fact, two sinewaves are computed, one displaced horizontally from the other, the displacement increasing as the foreground is approached, thus simulating perspective. The area between the waves is filled in solid white completing the depth cue. The tree plotting is in fact more complicated for many trees are plotted and shading can be involved. In essence, each tree is modelled as an ellipse and computed using the fast draw, centre fill technique of Chapter 2. The procedure PROCTREE plots and fills an ellipse and puts a stem on it. This occurs only in the green foreground and as the bottom of the screen is approached, the trees get larger. The trees are also positioned to avoid the road.

A white tree is first plotted and then the tree is displaced slightly, always to the right, and a coloured or shaded tree of the same size is then plotted, the white edging giving another cue to depth. If the tree is shaded, this is accomplished in PROCTSHADE and PROCLINE which uses the 'weaving' technique of Program 3.15 to mix the two blue colours. The trees are only plotted from the upper edge of the foreground given in the $YH\%$ array and they are placed randomly in the horizontal direction. In the vertical sequence they are plotted from the top to the bottom of the screen reflecting the temporal priority. A check is made to see if the tree overplots the white road, and the nature of the check also enables trees to avoid the white edge of other trees, thus orientating the whole landscape towards the bottom right of the screen. The temporal priority contained in the program is graphically illustrated in the picture flow chart in Fig. 4.2 which presents the typical sequence of procedure calls for a landscape based on unshaded trees.

The complete program is listed in Program 4.3, and although this is one of the longest programs in this book with 133 lines, it has a clear structure which we will comment on briefly, leaving readers to explore its finer points. After initializations up to line 80, lines 90 to 200 are straightforward. PROCHILLS is called four times with random parameters and with the base level y_s successively reduced and PROCROAD is then called in line 200. PROCHILLS listed in lines 550 to 680 is the same as the procedure in Program 4.2 except for the addition of line 650 in which $YH\%$ is set. PROCROAD in lines 700 to 840 involves the computation of a vertically varying sinewave in lines 780 to 830 which is displaced by an increasing amount as it approaches the bottom of the screen (line 790) and filled in using PLOT85 commands in lines 810 and 820. Note that the road 'disappears' at the upper edge of the green foreground, the position of which is chosen randomly within the middle area of the screen (line 730).

Much of the remaining program – lines 210 to 430 in the main program and the procedures from line 860 to the end – deal with tree plotting. We will deal with the main program first. In line 230, the number of trees to be plotted,

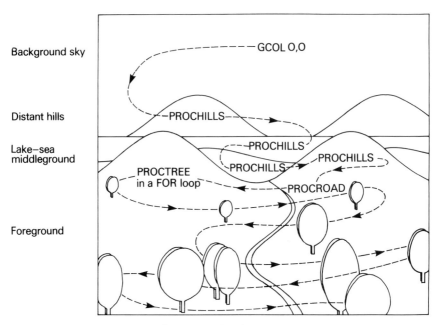

Fig. 4.2   Picture structure and program structure

anything between 3 and 152, is chosen and a parameter controlling whether or not the trees should be coloured or shaded is fixed in line 240. The trees are plotted in the FOR–NEXT loop bounded by lines 250 and 430. In lines 260 to 340, the height and width of the tree, its position relative to its temporal priority, the size of its stem and parameters which affect its colouring/shading are determined. In lines 350 to 380, the position of the tree is checked to avoid the road or the left edge of a previously plotted tree, using the POINT ($X\%,Y\%$) command which returns the colour of any given coordinate pair. If the position violates this constraint, the program returns to line 270 to recompute height, width, position etc. The tree is then called from line 390 (PROCTREE) and coloured (PROCTREE again) in line 410 or shaded (PROCTSHADE) in line 420.

PROCTREE in lines 860 to 1010 is a straightforward fast draw, centre fill ellipse plotting routine which uses only 16 ellipse circumference points, and puts a stem (trunk) on the ellipse in lines 980 to 1000. PROCTSHADE in lines 1040 to 1200 is trickier in that the circumference points of the ellipse have to be determined for horizontal pixel widths using the arcsine function in line 1100, and switching of colours in line 1120 is required to ensure that no adjacent pixels are coloured the same. The extent of the ellipse is computed in the FOR–NEXT loop between lines 1090 and 1150, and PROCLINE which uses the PLOT 21 command to fill a vertical line on each side of the ellipse is given in lines 1220 to 1260.

Program 4.3 Random landscapes

```
 10 REM Random Landscapes
 20 MODE1
 30 DIM YH%(64),CF%(1)
 40 VDU19,0,6;0;19,1,4;0;
 50 VDU19,2,2;0;19,3,7;0;
 60 VDU23,1,0;0;0;0;
 70 REM This Segment Plots the Far Hills,Lake,
 80 REM Middle and Foreground,then the Road
 90 K%=2-RND(3):N%=50
100 YS%=635+K%*RND(N%)
110 PROCHILLS(YS%,1,143,0,0)
120 YS%=YS%-(20+RND(N%))
130 PROCHILLS(YS%,1,0,0,1)
140 YS%=YS%-(20+RND(N%))
150 K%=2-RND(3):CK%=2-RND(2)
160 PROCHILLS(YS%,2,179,K%,CK%)
170 YS%=YS%-RND(N%/4)
180 K%=2-RND(3):CK%=2-RND(2)
190 PROCHILLS(YS%,2,0,K%,CK%)
200 PROCROAD(3,0)
210 REM This Segment Plots Various Sizes and
220 REM Shades of Tree from Back to Foreground
230 N%=100:INC%=0:M%=2+RND(150)
240 KZ%=INT(RND(1)+0.5)
250 FOR II%=1 TO M%
260   INC%=INC%+RND(1000/M%):VDU29,0;0;
270   XL%=RND(1279):IZ%=XL%/20:YL%=YH%(IZ%)-INC%+1
280   YT%=(((YH%(IZ%)-YL%)/YH%(IZ%))*N%+RND(20))*3
290   YH%=YT%/(2.0+RND(1)):XH%=YH%/(1.0+RND(1))
300   IF XH%<4 THEN GOTO 270
310   IF XH%/YH%<=1 THEN XB%=YH%*0.05 ELSE XB%=XH%*0.05
320   YT%=YT%/40:YB%=-YH%*1.4:ZC%=RND(3):TZ%=0
330   IF XL%-XH%<5 OR XL%+XH%>1275 THEN ZC%=1
340   IF YL%-YH%<5 THEN ZC%=1
350   FOR IL%=XL%-XH% TO XL%+XH% STEP 4
360     IF POINT(IL%,YL%)=3 OR POINT(IL%,YL%+YB%)=3 THEN TZ%=1
370     NEXT IL%
380   IF TZ%=1 THEN GOTO 270
390   PROCTREE(XH%,YH%,0,3)
400   XL%=XL%+YT%:YL%=YL%-YT%:T%=KZ%*ZC%
410   IF T%<=2 THEN PROCTREE(XH%,YH%,0,1)
420   IF T%>2 THEN PROCTSHADE(XH%,YH%)
430   NEXT II%
440 REM This Segment Switches the Colours,
450 REM thus Simulating the Four Seasons
460 FOR I%=1 TO 20
470   FOR II%=1 TO 5000:NEXT II%
480   READ COL0%,COL1%,COL2%,COL3%
490   VDU19,0,COL0%;0;19,1,COL1%;0;
500   VDU19,2,COL2%;0;19,3,COL3%;0;
510   NEXT I%:FOR II%=1 TO 15000:NEXTII%
520 RUN
530 END
540 :
550 REM Plots a Wave or Line of Colour
```

Program 4.3   continued

```
560 DEFPROCHILLS(YS%,COL%,J%,K%,CK%)
570 GCOL J%,COL%
580 DT=RAD(10):TH=RAD(RND(360))
590 S=SIN(DT):C=COS(DT):SS=SIN(TH):CC=COS(TH)
600 SI%=RND(100):YN%=CK%*YS%+(1-CK%)*(YS%+SI%*SS)
610 MOVE 0,0:MOVE 0,YN%:YH%(0)=YN%
620 FOR I%=20 TO 1280 STEP 20
630    SN=SS*CC+CC*S:CC=CC*C-SS*S:SS=SN
640    YN%=CK%*(YN%-K%*RND(5))+(1-CK%)*(YS%+I%*SS)
650    YH%(I%DIV20)=YN%
660    PLOT85,I%,0:PLOT85,I%,YN%
670    NEXT I%
680 ENDPROC
690 :
700 REM Plots a Twisting Road based on a Sine Wave
710 DEFPROCROAD(COL%,J%)
720 GCOLJ%,COL%
730 II%=26+RND(10):INC%=RND(2)
740 YR%=YH%(II%):IZ%=II%*20:SI%=60+RND(60)
750 DT=RAD(20):TH=RAD(0)
760 S=SIN(DT):C=COS(DT):SS=SIN(TH):CC=COS(TH)
770 II%=IZ%+SI%*SS:MOVE II%,YR%:MOVE II%+INC%,YR%
780 FOR IJ%=YR%-20 TO -20 STEP -20
790    INC%=INC%+RND(2)
800    SN=SS*C+CC*S:CC=CC*C-SS*S:SS=SN
810    II%=IZ%+SI%*SS:PLOT85,II%,IJ%
820    II%=II%+INC%:PLOT85,II%,IJ%
830    NEXT IJ%
840 ENDPROC
850 :
860 REM Plots a Solid Ellipsoid Tree
870 DEFPROCTREE(XX%,YY%,J%,COL%)
880 GCOL J%,COL%:VDU29,XL%;YL%;
890 IF COL%=1 AND RND(10)<=2 THEN GCOL J%,0
900 DT=2*PI/15:A=XX%/YY%
910 C=COS(DT):S=SIN(DT):SX=S/A:SY=S*A
920 XA=XX%:YA=0
930 MOVE 0,0:MOVE XA,0
940 FOR I%=1 TO 15
950    T=XA*C-YA*SY:YA=YA*C+XA*SX:XA=T
960    PLOT85,XA,YA:MOVE 0,0
970    NEXT I%
980 FOR I%=-XB% TO XB% STEP 4
990    MOVE I%,0:DRAW I%,YB%
1000   NEXT I%
1010 ENDPROC
1020 :
1030 REM Computes the Shaded Area of the Tree
1040 DEFPROCTSHADE(XX%,YY%)
1050 COL1%=INT(RND(1)+0.5)
1060 IF COL1%=0 THEN COL2%=1 ELSE COL2%=0
1070 CF%(0)=COL1%:CF%(1)=COL2%:VDU29,XL%;YL%;
1080 PROCLINE(0,YY%,0,1)
1090 FOR I%=4 TO XX% STEP 4
```

Program 4.3   continued

```
1100    J%=YY%*SIN(ACS(I%/XX%))
1110    K%=0:KK%=1
1120    IF POINT(I%-1,-J%)=CF%(0) THEN K%=1:KK%=0
1130    PROCLINE(I%,J%,K%,KK%)
1140    PROCLINE(-I%,J%,K%,KK%)
1150    NEXT I%
1160 GCOLO,1
1170 FOR I%=-XB% TO XB% STEP 4
1180    MOVE I%,-YY%:DRAW I%,YB%
1190    NEXT I%
1200 ENDPROC
1210 :
1220 REM Shades the Tree Line by Line
1230 DEFPROCLINE(X%,Y%,K%,KK%)
1240 GCOLO,CF%(K%):MOVE X%,-Y%:PLOT21,X%,Y%
1250 GCOLO,CF%(KK%):MOVE X%,-Y%+4:PLOT21,X%,Y%
1260 ENDPROC
1270 :
1280 REM This Data Holds Sets of Colour Numbers
1290 REM Defining Autumn,Winter,Spring and Summer
1300 DATA 3,4,2,7,6,4,3,7,6,1,3,7,4,1,3,7,6,4,1,5
1310 DATA 6,4,7,5,6,4,7,0,4,4,7,0,5,4,7,0,4,4,7,0
1320 DATA 5,4,7,0,6,4,7,0,6,5,7,0,6,5,2,0,6,4,2,3
1330 DATA 6,4,2,7,6,4,2,3,6,4,2,7,3,4,2,7,6,4,2,7
```

The last section of the main program is quite elementary. The FOR–NEXT loop between lines 460 and 510 involves reading in new colours (actual colour numbers) from DATA statements, switching the existing colours to these new colours and leaving these on the screen long enough for the viewer to appreciate the effect. Twenty such switches are made, using a sequence of colour numbers which reflect the seasons: the green, white and blues of summer switch to the red-yellow, red-purple of autumn and early winter, then to the white, blues and purple of deep winter, which turn to blue-green in spring and back to yellow, white, green and the blues of summer. The snow scenes of winter are particularly pleasing. A selection of these scenes is shown in Plate 5.

Many of the programs in this book and all the landscapes in this chapter will produce slightly different pictures each time they are run for many of their elements in terms of their number, form, size and position are randomly determined. The degree of difference between successive runs will depend upon the element in question and its importance to the scene. In fact in this program, the effect of random choice is extremely significant. The third and fourth calls to PROCHILLS for example can determine whether the scene is dominated by rolling hills, plains or gentle slopes. The number of trees is the other significant feature producing a few free standing specimens or dense forests. Landscapes which are hilly, flat, with little vegetation or covered in forests can result. The program can generate very different scenes each time and unlike our next program which simulates a hard landscape, this one continually generates aesthetic surprise.

At present, our trees whose dimensions are fixed in line 290 can vary from approximately round to elliptical ones whose height is twice their width. Clearly there is enormous room for experiment here by changing possible dimensions to give much more elongated trees, and such changes can dramatically alter the entire atmosphere of the landscape. It is also worth examining the decisions concerning the shading and colouring of trees. In each run, lines 330 and 340 fix a parameter value which ensures that any tree which overlaps the left, right and bottom edges of the screen will be coloured, not shaded, thus providing a more solid frame effect to the picture. Trees other than those around the frame are determined in terms of colour and shade as follows. In line 240, the variable $KZ\%$ is randomly set as 0 or 1. If 0, trees are coloured, *not* shaded; if 1, trees are coloured, *or* shaded. Thus on average in only half the program runs, shading is possible. In 320, a variable $ZC\%$ is randomly set as 1, 2, or 3. In line 400, $ZC\%$ and $KZ\%$ are combined, and the choice to colour or shade effectively made in lines 410 and 420. Within PROCTREE in line 890, a random choice ensures that $\frac{1}{5}$ of the trees will be coloured light blue, $\frac{4}{5}$ dark blue. This concatenation of randomly structured choices is presented in Fig. 4.3 where it is clear that in the case where shading is possible, on average $\frac{2}{15}$ of the trees will be light blue, $\frac{8}{15}$ dark blue and $\frac{5}{15}$ shaded. Finally a selection of random landscapes is shown in Fig. 4.4, demonstrating the possible range.

4.3 HARD LANDSCAPES

Hard landscapes in this chapter will inevitably be urban rather than rural, cityscapes rather than countryside, although in the next chapter we will concern ourselves with a geometry which is able to reproduce the harshness characteristic of the most severe mountainous scenes. In the meantime, we will content ourselves with generating images based on hard and clean regular geometries and appropriate colour. We will attempt to simulate that most urban of places, New York, which conjures up images of dark streets, and bright lights; in MODE1, our simulation will be based on yellow, black, dark blue and light blue. In terms of geometry, New York is composed of various layers of 20th century architecture – rectangular slab blocks and high rise, and we will thus build a city of rectangles, only at the end softening the scene with a more romantic image.

We will once again use temporal priority as the organizing device for our computer program. In essence we will paint three areas of colour across the screen on the dark blue background which comprises the night sky. The horizon ground will be light blue reflecting the lighter westward sky, then we will overplot a layer of black rectangles edged in light blue, and finally the

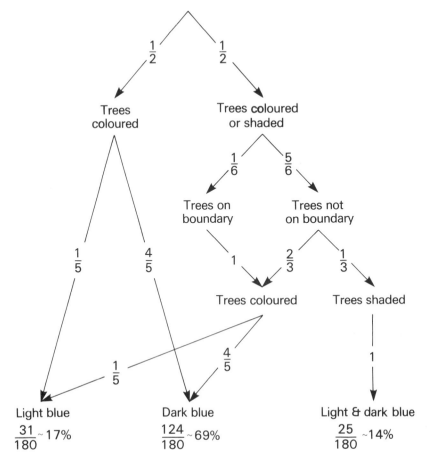

Fig. 4.3   Randomly-structured choice sequences

foreground will be composed of black blocks edged in yellow. On this canvas, we will paint some characteristic New York features based on early and late 20th century architecture. Early skyscrapers will be plotted, some with the classic stepped effect imposed to enable daylighting conditions to be met. Towering above these will be the later architecture of World Trade Center-like buildings, and softening the scene will be the Beaux Arts design of the tower of the Chrysler Building: all memorable features which generate 'New York', yet not quite New York.

The other feature which our program will contain is the contrast of different styles of modern architecture. The city will be built up in layers from horizon to foreground, increasing in height thus mirroring the classic rise in population densities as the centre is approached. Layer is built upon layer in much the

Fig. 4.4 Random landscapes

same way that the modern city evolved, and rising above it all is the late 20th century city which makes the traditional skyscraper appear dwarflike. Our program is not only good kinetic art but it is a crude simulation of modern city building and it contains all the features of recent architecture. Surprisingly perhaps, the profile generated finds parallels in smaller cities, in modern towns, even in places like Cardiff where the skyline also contrasts early and late 20th century tower building.

To generate an impression of city buildings as background, we need to generate hundreds of rectangular blocks, and to do this with any speed, we need to use the graphics window command VDU24. We can then colour and edge the windows to reflect the various backgrounds already indicated. The essence of the program is a procedure PROCTOWER which sets up a rectangular window of the appropriate size and position, colours and edges it. PROCTOWER is also used to set up the tall towers in the foreground and it also places 'real' windows in each of these blocks which are then randomly lit. Here we introduce for the first time a type of two-level pseudo-recursion in that for a real window to be reproduced VDU24 has to be called within the existing graphics window, although PROCTOWER is not recalled. In the last part of the program, the top of the Chrysler Building is drawn using ellipses to create the skyscraper's 'dome' in the elaborate Art Deco of America in the 1920s. This is achieved by a procedure called PROCDOME which also plots the radio mast.

The program is listed as Program 4.4. Initialization occurs up to line 60 which establishes the dark blue background on which is first set the light blue city horizon using a graphics window in line 70. Three FOR–NEXT loops control the way the back-, middle- and foregrounds are elaborated. The loop bounded by lines 110 and 250 enables the colours of each ground to be set in lines 120 and 130. The loop between lines 140 and 230 controls three layers of buildings which are drawn to fill each ground. The loop between lines 160 and 210 constructs a randomly chosen number of rectangular blocks which become lesser in number and slightly larger in size as the foreground is approached. Between 36 and 50 blocks are randomly positioned horizontally to form each layer in each ground. The number and size of each tower is fixed in line 150 and positioned in lines 170 to 190; the procedure PROCTOWER is called in line 200 with its window index fixed to plot real windows or not, with its colours and its position as its arguments. In line 220, the base level of each layer is progressively reduced reflecting the temporal priority of the algorithm.

PROCTOWER itself is listed in lines 500 to 670. The basic window is set in line 530 using the edge colour. This is then displaced and reset with the main colour in line 570 giving the same type of depth cue used previously in plotting trees in the Random Landscapes program (Program 4.3) and clouds in the Cloud Sculptures programs in Chapter 3 (Program 3.14 and extensions). Line 580 tests to see if windows are required in the tower. If so, parameters of a grid of windows are set in lines 590 and 600, and the FOR–NEXT loops

Program 4.4 Window on New York

```
 10 REM Window on New York
 20 MODE1
 30 VDU23,1,0;0;0;0;
 40 VDU19,0,4;0;19,1,0;0;
 50 VDU19,2,3;0;19,3,6;0;
 60 YY%=500+RND(100)
 70 VDU24,0;0;1279;YY%;
 80 GCOLO,131:CLG:C4%=3:C5%=1
 90 REM Plots Back,Middle and Foregrounds
100 REM of Windowless Tower Blocks
110 FOR LK%=1 TO 3
120   IF LK%=1 THEN C1%=129:C2%=131 ELSE C1%=131:C2%=129
130   IF LK%=3 THEN C1%=130:C2%=129:C4%=2:C5%=1
140   FOR KL%=1 TO 3
150     M%=30+RND(20)-7*(LK%-1):XY%=1279/M%
160     FOR L%=1 TO M%
170       XX%=RND(1279):VDU29,XX%;YY%;
180       XI%=XY%*(1.3+RND(1)):YI%=XI%/(1+RND(4))
190       IF RND(2)=1 THEN YX%=YI%:YI%=XI%:XI%=YX%
200       PROCTOWER(XI%,YI%,1,C1%,C2%,C3%,C4%,C5%)
210       NEXT L%
220     YY%=YY%-40-RND(30)
230     NEXT KL%:VDU26:GCOLO,129
240   IF LK%=2 THEN VDU24,0;0;1279;YY%;:CLG
250   NEXT LK%
260 REM Plots a Very High "Lit-up" Tower
270 C1%=131:C2%=129:C3%=130:C4%=3:C5%=1
280 XC%=200+RND(200):XCC%=XC%:VDU29,XC%;512;
290 XI%=40+RND(25):YI%=XI%*(7+RND(1)):MN%=300
300 PROCTOWER(XI%,YI%,0,C1%,C2%,C3%,C4%,C5%)
310 XC%=XC%*1.8:XINC%=(1279-XC%)/4:MN%=150
320 REM Plots Three Tall Towers,then the Chrysler Building
330 FOR LK%=1 TO 3
340   XC%=XC%+XINC%*(0.43+RND(1)):YC%=512
350   VDU29,XC%;YC%;
360   XI%=25+RND(35):YI%=XI%*(4+RND(1))
370   FOR KL%=1 TO RND(3)
380     PROCTOWER(XI%,YI%,0,C1%,C2%,C3%,C4%,C5%)
390     XI%=XI%*1.3:YC%=YC%*0.85
400     VDU29,XC%;YC%;:C3%=130
410     NEXT KL%
420   NEXT LK%
430 VDU26:XC%=XCC%*1.8:YC%=0
440 PROCDOME(XC%,YC%)
450 VDU26:GCOLO,0:MOVE 0,1023
460 DRAW 0,0:DRAW 1279,0:DRAW 1279,1023
470 AA=INKEY(1000):RUN
480 END
490 :
500 REM Colours and Edges a Graphics Window
510 REM Sometimes with Windows within
520 DEFPROCTOWER(X%,Y%,K%,C1%,C2%,C3%,C4%,C5%)
530 VDU24,-X%*1.25;-Y%;-X%;Y%;
540 GCOLO,C1%:CLG
550 GCOLO,C5%:MOVE -X%*1.25,-Y%:DRAW -X%*1.25,Y%
```

Program 4.4   continued

```
560 GCOLO,C4%:MOVE -X%-4,-Y%+4:DRAW -X%-4,Y%-4
570 VDU24,-X%;-Y%;X%;Y%;:GCOLO,C2%:CLG
580 IF K%=1 THEN GOTO 670
590 A=Y%/X%:NN%=3*A:GCOLO,C3%
600 YA%=Y%/(2*NN%):XA%=X%/NN%
610 FOR I%=-X%+XA% TO X%-2*XA% STEP XA%
620   FOR J%=-Y%+YA% TO Y%-2*YA% STEP YA%
630     II%=I%+XA%:JJ%=J%+YA%
640     IF RND(Y%)>MN% THEN VDU24,I%;J%;II%;JJ%;:CLG
650   NEXT J%
660   NEXT I%
670 ENDPROC
680 :
690 REM Plots Ellipsoid Design Resembling
700 REM the Top of the Chrysler Building
710 DEFPROCDOME(XC%,YC%)
720 CC%=32:ZZ%=XC%
730 FOR I%=1 TO 3
740   IF I%>1 THEN GCOL3,2 ELSE GCOLO,0
750   IF I%>1 THEN YE%=320:XE%=64 ELSE YE%=420:XE%=132
760   IF I%=2 THEN ZZ%=XC%-XE%
770   IF I%=3 THEN ZZ%=XC%+XE%
780   VDU29,ZZ%;YC%;
790   FOR YY%=16 TO YE% STEP CC%
800     FOR Y%=4 TO YY% STEP 4
810       X%=XE%/YY%*SQR(YY%*YY%-Y%*Y%)
820       MOVE X%,Y%:DRAW -X%,Y%
830     NEXT Y%
840   NEXT YY%
850   NEXT I%
860 VDU29,XC%;YC%;:GCOLO,2:S%=9
870 MOVE 0,0:DRAW 0,750
880 YY%=387:Y%=YY%/1.3:Y3%=490:J%=0
890 Y1%=(YY%-Y%)/S%:Y2%=(Y3%-YY%)/S%
900 FOR I%=4 TO S%*4 STEP 4
910   MOVE -I%,Y%:DRAW -I%,Y3%
920   MOVE I%,Y%:DRAW I%,Y3%
930   J%=J%+1:A=(S%+1-J%)/((S%+1)/2)
940   Y%=Y%+Y1%*A:Y3%=Y3%-Y2%*A
950   NEXT I%
960 GCOLO,2:MOVE 0,0:DRAW 0,750
970 ENDPROC
```

between lines 610 and 660 are used to set up and randomly light (in yellow) each window if a size threshold is met in line 640.

After the various 'grounds' have been established up to line 250, lines 260 to 300 use PROCTOWER again to draw a very tall, densely lit World Trade Center type of tower on the left of the picture. In lines 330 to 420, three slightly smaller but nevertheless significant skyscraper blocks are drawn each with up to three steps determined in the FOR–NEXT loop between lines 370 and 410. As the towers approach the foreground, the windows get considerably larger in these positions. The precise form depends on the arguments of PROCTOWER which is called in line 380. Finally, the dome of the Chrysler Building, for a brief period in 1930 the largest building in the world, is drawn using PROCDOME which is called in line 440 and listed in lines 690 to 970. The dome is based on the upper half of an ellipsoid within which two sets of smaller vertically orientated elipsoids give a depth cue. The FOR–NEXT loop between 730 and 850 establishes these three shapes whose sizes and colours are fixed in lines 740 to 770 and whose form is produced in the two loops between lines 790 and 840. In line 820, the extent of each ellipse is computed from coordinate, rather than polar form. Note that the two smaller sets of ellipses are over-plotted using GCOL3 operations which gives rise to an ornate form as well as an unusual kinetic effect. Finally the radio mast is plotted in lines 870 to 950.

We have called our program 'Window on New York', rather appropriately as it produces a landscape built almost entirely out of the use of graphics windows. But those who know David Juniper's beautiful picture 'Manhattan Window' will recognize from where I have drawn my inspiration. The program here is quite unashamedly a computer realization of Juniper's original which I dedicate to him, the artist. A typical picture from the program is produced in Plate 6. In fact, the randomness here hardly affects form at all, only size and position and thus the program produces very similar cityscapes each time it is run. The picture is full of contrast in terms of the tall and the small, the hard and the soft. The new city rising above the old is the dominant impression but the other sense is of more recent city building becoming harsher and more powerful. The blaze of light from the tall tower symbolizes both the extensive energy demands of the large city and/or the extensive use of mirror glass; it does not matter which for the impression is the same. Finally, the picture produces instantly recognizable forms which dominate the foreground. Detailed comparison with the reality reveals these forms are not quite right but sufficiently 'right' to impress the image. There is much exploration one can do with this program. PROCTOWER and PROCDOME could be used to generate cities of domes with occasional towers, low rise rather than high rise cities, cities like Florence rather than New York. All this is quite feasible and readers are encouraged to elaborate the building blocks provided here, and to compose them in different ways.

4.4 RECURSIVE STRUCTURES: TREES AND OTHER BRANCHING PROCESSES

Nature is never as clean cut or as simple in form as the processes implied in Random Landscapes. Nor are the artificial urban landscapes of our large cities as regular or ordered as that presented in Window on New York. Nevertheless, the central principle that complexity results from the repeated application of simpler processes and structures has characterized our landscapes so far. By repeating the same designs over and over again and generating forms of different size, position and even shape from the same function does appear to represent the way reality is structured. This kind of repetition or iteration might be said to generate *extensive complexity* where the overall composition of the picture is based on many parts. In contrast, we can generate forms of *intensive complexity* in which the parts reflect the whole and in which detail is produced by the same function which is used to organize the overall structure. A simple example of this operation, recursion as it is called, was demonstrated in Program 4.4 where a tower block was formed as a graphics window, and a real window or rectangular detail within the block was formed using another graphics window within the original one. The essence of recursion then is nesting a function within the same function, the sequence of nesting or hierarchy usually reflecting successive levels of detail.

Recursion is reflected in the idea of self-similarity, the notion that the whole has the same structure and form as the parts, albeit at a different scale. This concept is central to the ideas of this section and to the next chapter and also appears to be fundamental to the way natural complexity is produced. The classic example, to be elaborated here, is the tree. Twigs bear the same relation to one another and to the sub-branches which contain them as the sub-branches do to one another and the branches which root them to the trunk. A sub-branch and its twigs is thus a microcosm of the tree itself. It is no accident that such relationships which exist in hierarchical form are often described by logical or branching 'trees'.

Computationally, a recursive algorithm or procedure is one which is based on an operation at a given level of detail which depends on the same operation at a lower or higher level of detail. In programming terms then, a recursive procedure is one which calls itself. Extreme care is required in the design of recursive procedures for the recursion must be terminated at a level of detail appropriate both to the problem being solved and to the size of the computer available. However, recursive programming can be extremely elegant and economical, as we will see in the next section. Before we demonstrate such programs, we will digress a little to look at some of the properties of natural branching systems, particularly trees, because for realistic design, it is necessary to structure our recursion according to the known properties of the systems being modelled.

A wide range of branching processes in nature exhibit dichotomous or binary branching where a branch splits into two. The tree is again our classic example where a branch splits off from the trunk, a sub-branch from the branch and so on. Ternary or three-way branching does exist in some trees and plants but this is much less common. In river systems, for example, binary branching must occur because of the physical properties of the drainage basin which imply that two or more tributaries joining a main river at the same point is extremely unlikely. Branching in artificial phenomena is more likely to involve more than binary subdivision. Road systems for example may contain junctions with up to five ways while artificial hierarchies in which neighbourhoods, towns, cities, even regions, and nation-states might be organized, do not necessarily conform to dichotomous branching hierarchies (Woldenberg, 1971). However as Stevens (1974) so cogently shows, binary branching in natural systems probably embodies the most efficient organization through the law of least effort.

Tree forms are governed by regular relationships and it is essential to know these in order to generate realistic branching processes. Assume that the depth of the branching process D represents the level of the hierarchy reached after D such branch points have been encountered, starting from the root of the tree. D will also represent the level of recursion in the sequel, and its definition for a symmetrical binary branching tree is shown in Fig. 4.5(a). The number of branches N_D at any level D is then given by the following branch number formula:

$$N_D = b^D, \tag{4.2}$$

where b is the branch or bifurcation ratio, that is the number of branches at any one level emanating from a branch at the next level. For binary branching, $b = 2$, for ternary $b = 3$ and so on. Other branch number formulae are possible, some of greater generality (Woldenberg, 1971) but equation (4.2) is appropriate for any symmetric and complete branching tree.

Equation (4.2) is also useful in calculating the number of procedure calls in a recursive scheme where each branch requires a separate call. For example in a binary scheme where the maximum recursion is to the eighth level, that is $D_{max} = 8$, then at this level, equation (4.2) indicates there are 256 branches. The total number of branches at all levels in the hierarchy is given by evaluating equation (4.2) at each level D. Then the total number of branches N is

$$N = \sum_{D=1}^{D_{max}} N_D = \sum_{D=1}^{D_{max}} b^D \tag{4.3}$$

which gives $N = 510$ for an eight level binary branching hierarchy. What equations (4.2) and (4.3) really indicate however is that a recursive scheme based on branching is combinatorially explosive and must be stopped before its demands for machine memory make the scheme infeasible.

Various relationships between branch sizes in terms of length and width (diameter), angles of branching at each branch point and the relative sizes of each recursive level are quite widely known although there does not appear to be a complete set of formulae which tie all these relationships together. Here we will treat the size of branches and their relative position in the hierarchy separately from branching angles. First, the relationship between the widths or diameters of two branches at the bifurcation with the main branch has been

a

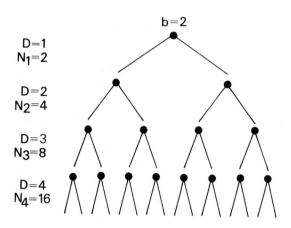

D=1
$N_1=2$

D=2
$N_2=4$

D=3
$N_3=8$

D=4
$N_4=16$

b=2

b

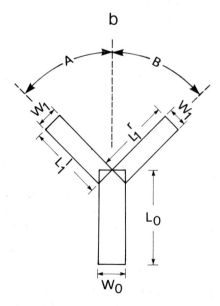

Fig. 4.5 Branching parameters

studied for several centuries. Indeed, Leonardo da Vinci quoted in Stevens (1974) and Mandelbrot (1982) recorded in one of his *Notebooks* (No. 394) that

> All the branches of a tree at every stage of its height when put together are equal in thickness to the trunk below them.

Formally, Leonardo's observation suggests that

$$W_0^\alpha = W_1^\alpha + W_2^\alpha \tag{4.4}$$

where $\alpha = 2$, and W_0 is the width or diameter of the trunk, W_1 and W_2 the widths of the two bifurcating branches. If we assume that $W_1 = W_2$, a not unreasonable assumption which implies a symmetrical tree, then the ratio of each bifurcating branch, now called W_1, to the trunk W_0 is given as

$$\frac{W_1}{W_0} = \frac{1}{\sqrt[\alpha]{2}} = 2^{-\frac{1}{\alpha}}. \tag{4.5}$$

In fact, it is more likely that $\alpha = 3$ in the case of volumes although empirical evidence shows α to be between 2.5 and 2.7, varying of course for different trees and other branching systems such as arteries.

The width of a branch in relation to its length for typical trees has been studied by McMahon (1975) amongst others. In general, he shows that width is proportional to length to the power $3/2$ thus deriving a relationship which appears elsewhere in nature (see Thompson, 1961; Mandelbrot, 1982). Formally then

$$W_0 = K(L_0)^{3/2} \quad \text{and} \quad W_1 = K(L_1)^{3/2} \tag{4.6}$$

where L_0 and L_1 are the lengths of the relevant branches and K is a constant of proportionality. From equation (4.6), the ratio of successive widths and lengths can be formed by dividing W_1 by W_0. Then

$$\frac{W_1}{W_0} = \left\{\frac{L_1}{L_0}\right\}^{\frac{3}{2}} \tag{4.7}$$

which is a contrasting form to equation (4.5). It is now possible from equations (4.5) and (4.7) to derive recursive relationships which relate successive branch widths and lengths. From equation (4.5), assuming that we index the successor branch W_1 by W_{n+1} and the predecessor branch by W_n, W_{n+1} can be derived from W_n as

$$W_{n+1} = 2^{-\frac{1}{\alpha}} W_n. \tag{4.8}$$

Substituting from the RHS of equation (4.5) for the LHS of (4.7), and then rearranging, but using the successor-predecessor indices $n+1$ and n for 1 and 0, leads to a recursive formula for branch lengths

$$L_{n+1} = 2^{-\frac{2}{3\alpha}} L_n. \tag{4.9}$$

Definitions of branch widths and lengths (as well as branch angles) are given in Fig. 4.5(b) for a typical binary bifurcation. To use equations (4.8) and (4.9) recursively, it would be necessary to input the first length and width, L_0 and W_0. If the ratio of these were known then one could be derived from a knowledge of the other but the literature on tree design is surprisingly deficient in this regard. Intuitively acceptable tree designs we have found are given by setting $W_0/L_0 \simeq 0.1$. We have already noted that the value of α has been empirically and theoretically derived as being between 2 and 3. For this range, the ratio $2^{-1/\alpha}$ varies from 0.707 (for $\alpha = 2$) to 0.794 (for $\alpha = 3$), and the ratio $2^{-2\alpha/3}$ varies from 0.794 (for $\alpha = 2$) to 0.857 (for $\alpha = 3$). These ranges are not very wide and any value within them will lead to acceptable tree designs. Finally, as Fig. 4.5(b) shows, the branching angles – A for the left branch, B for the right – determine the spread of the tree. Murray, quoted in Stevens (1974), has shown that the sum of these absolute angles is normally in the range $75° \leqslant |A| + |B| \leqslant 90°$. Branch angles seem to vary enormously for different trees and in fact length and width also relate to angles. In general, the nearer any one of these angles $|A|$ or $|B|$ is to 90°, the smaller that branch in terms of width and length, and Stevens (1974) shows how these relationships vary for a typical tree. Here however we will set our total branch angles at less than this range, usually between 30° and 75° in order to generate detailed trees with a manageable spread.

In the following section, we will thus have several parameters determining our trees: the branch angles $|A|$ and $|B|$ input in terms of the absolute deviation from the vertical, the left and right contraction ratios for branch lengths, that is the ratios L_{n+1}^l/L_n^l and L_{n+1}^r/L_n^r for left and right branches respectively, and the input length L_0 and width W_0 of the stem or trunk. We will keep these parameters within the ranges already specified but we have also been guided by the work of Aoni and Kunii (1984) who have shown that 'realistic' tree designs are generated when the contraction ratios are about 0.7, the total angles between 25° and 70°, when the recursion depth ($D_{\max}$) is between 7 and 9 and when the contraction ratio for branch widths W_1/W_0 is set at around 0.7.

4.5   THE ARCHITECTURE OF TREES

We have written a program to draw branching structures which are controlled by the above parameters and whose only limitation on depth of recursion is the memory of the machine and the size of number it can store. The program not only enables us to design trees but also other regular forms which involve branching and whose form is sensitive to the chosen parameters. As in previous programs, we will sketch the program outline first, then detail its listing, and finally illustrate its use and outputs.

Given a stem or trunk, the program generates dichotomous or binary branching to the stated depth of recursion. Branches are referred to as left or right and the essence of the program is two similarly structured procedures PROCLBRANCH and PROCRBRANCH which compute and draw the left and right branch positions respectively. The nature of the recursion is such that if a left or a right branch is taken, the operation then involves a node which defines a further branching in both left and right directions. PROCLBRANCH and PROCRBRANCH therefore call each other and this sets up a potentially infinite recursion. Every recursion of this kind requires a stopping rule which is simply a check on the depth of branching reached, and termination of the recursion when the prespecified depth has been reached. In the program, the depth D_{max} which is input is reduced at each branching thus giving the number of levels of each branching from the lowest (deepest) branching. When this number reaches zero, then the recursion is stopped. Although the program is for binary trees, it could easily be adapted for ternary, quaternary, quinary trees and so on by simply noting that every directional branch procedure must call every other directional branch procedure.

It is possible to call these procedures directly from one another although in these types of branching, values computed in the procedure from which other procedures are called, are usually required in all the others. In binary branching for example, variables associated with the branch on which the recursion finds itself are used in both left and right branching at the next level. If left is called before right, then it is necessary to ensure that the variable in question is specifically retained for eventual input to the right branch, and this would involve declaring such variables as LOCAL to the procedure. To avoid losing the values of such variables, Abelson and DiSessa (1980) argue that it is good practice where more than one procedure is called from another, to insert an intermediate procedure in whose arguments lie the variables in question common to every procedure using them. In this case, on any branch, the procedure PROCNODE is used to effect this. Its arguments are then common to PROCLBRANCH and PROCRBRANCH which are both called from PROCNODE. This procedure can also be used to effect tests common to the procedures it calls, such as those based on the stopping rule.

In general, the values of the variables which form the arguments of any procedure in BBC Basic are unique to that procedure. In any other case where variables need to be unique in this way, they should be declared as LOCAL to the procedure. The remaining variables will be altered in terms of the global operation of the program. One final point is to stress again that recursive procedures can gobble up memory as equations (4.2) and (4.3) indicate. Moreover these limits can only be worked out precisely if the memory requirements of the program and its recursive calls are known in detail, for the computer will reserve memory when it requires it, and this will occur only when such programs are run.

The program to draw branching trees is listed in Program 4.5. It is quite

Program 4.5   Branching structures: tree architecture

```
10 REM Branching Structures:Tree Architecture
20 MODE1:@%=&20103
30 VDU23,1,0;0;0;0;
40 VDU19,1,4;0;19,2,2;0;
50 VDU29,640;100;:VDU28,0,4,39,0
60 REPEAT
70   PRINT TAB(14)"SIZE OF STEM"
80   INPUT TAB(14)"HEIGHT = ",L%,TAB(15)"WIDTH = ",W%
90   PRINT TAB(7)"BRANCH CONTRACTION FACTORS"
100  INPUT TAB(16)"LEFT = ",CL,TAB(15)"RIGHT = ",CR
110  PRINT TAB(11)"ANGLES OF BRANCHES"
120  INPUT TAB(16)"LEFT = ",A,TAB(15)"RIGHT = ",B
130  INPUT TAB(4)"BALANCED TREE ? TYPE YES OR NO ",U$
140  INPUT TAB(8)"DEPTH OF RECURSION = ",D%
150  CLS:PRINT TAB(6)"STEM HEIGHT ";L%;" WIDTH ";W%
160  PRINT TAB(4)"CONTRACTIONS:LEFT ";CL;" RIGHT ";CR
170  PRINT TAB(3)"BRANCH ANGLES:LEFT ";A;" RIGHT ";B
180  PRINT TAB(6)"BALANCED__";U$;" TREE DEPTH ";D%
190  X%=0:Y%=0:Z=RAD(90+A):ZZ=RAD(90-B)
200  PROCDRAW(X%,Y%,L%,X%,Y%+L%,RAD(90),W%)
210  Y%=Y%+L%:A=RAD(A):B=RAD(B)
220  PROCRBRANCH(L%,D%,X%,Y%,Z,ZZ,0.75*W%,0)
230  PROCLBRANCH(L%,D%,X%,Y%,Z,ZZ,0.75*W%,1)
240  AA=GET:CLS:CLG
250  UNTIL FALSE
260 END
270 :
280 REM Left Branch Construction
290 DEFPROCLBRANCH(L%,D%,X%,Y%,Z,ZZ,W%,K%)
300 XX%=X%+CL*L%*COS(Z):YY%=Y%+CL*L%*SIN(Z)
310 PROCDRAW(X%,Y%,CL*L%,XX%,YY%,Z,W%)
320 S=Z:ZZ=Z-B:Z=Z+A
330 IF K%=1 AND LEFT$(U$,1)="Y" ZZ=S-A:Z=S+B
340 PROCNODE(CL*L%,D%,XX%,YY%,Z,ZZ,0.75*W%,K%,1)
350 MOVE X%,Y%
360 ENDPROC
370 :
380 REM Right Branch Construction
390 DEFPROCRBRANCH(L%,D%,X%,Y%,Z,ZZ,W%,K%)
400 XX%=X%+CR*L%*COS(ZZ):YY%=Y%+CR*L%*SIN(ZZ)
410 PROCDRAW(X%,Y%,CR*L%,XX%,YY%,ZZ,W%)
420 S=ZZ:Z=ZZ+A:ZZ=ZZ-B
430 IF K%=0 AND LEFT$(U$,1)="Y" ZZ=S-A:Z=S+B
440 PROCNODE(CR*L%,D%,XX%,YY%,Z,ZZ,0.75*W%,K%,0)
450 MOVE X%,Y%
460 ENDPROC
470 :
480 REM Dichotomous or Binary Branching
490 DEFPROCNODE(L%,D%,X%,Y%,Z,ZZ,W%,K%,Q%)
500 LOCAL K1%,K2%
510 IF D%=0 THEN ENDPROC
520 QZ%=K%+Q%:K1%=1:K2%=0
530 IF QZ%=1 THEN K1%=0:K2%=1
540 PROCRBRANCH(L%,D%-1,X%,Y%,Z,ZZ,W%,K1%)
550 PROCLBRANCH(L%,D%-1,X%,Y%,Z,ZZ,W%,K2%)
```

Program 4.5   continued

```
560 ENDPROC
570 :
580 REM Branch Drawing
590 DEFPROCDRAW(X%,Y%,L%,XX%,YY%,Z,W%)
600 GCOLO,1:Z=Z+RAD(90)
610 X1%=W%*COS(Z):Y1%=W%*SIN(Z)
620 MOVE X%-X1%,Y%-Y1%:MOVE XX%-X1%,YY%-Y1%
630 PLOT85,X%+X1%,Y%+Y1%:PLOT85,XX%+X1%,YY%+Y1%
640 GCOLO,2:MOVE X%+X1%,Y%+Y1%:DRAW XX%+X1%,YY%+Y1%
650 ENDPROC
```

straightforward. After initializations up to line 50, the REPEAT–UNTIL loop between lines 60 and 250 embodies the main program which involves inputting key parameter values and starting the process of recursive computation and plotting. The input parameters are requested from the user between lines 70 and 140: the height and width of the stem, left and right branch contraction ratios, left and right branch angles in absolute value from the predecessor branch direction, a response as to whether or not the tree should be 'balanced' which involves alternate switching of the left and right angles, and the depth of recursion, are all requested. Lines 150 to 180 print out these data so that a typical user can examine the tree generated in the light of these parameters. PROCDRAW which draws the stem (or any branch) is called in line 200 using length, width and position of each branch as inputs. The procedure is listed in lines 580 to 650. Essentially it computes the corners of the branch or stem, colours these in, using two triangle plot commands PLOT85, and edges the stem with a second colour to achieve a depth cue. If the width of the stem is zero, the second colour overplots the first, thus generating a 'matchstick' tree.

The branching and recursion is begun with calls to PROCRBRANCH and PROCLBRANCH in lines 220 and 230. The arguments to each of these procedures are, length, depth, x–y position, left and right branch angles at the given point of branching, a reduced width of the input branch set at $0.75W_n$ ($\alpha \simeq 2.5$), and the balance switch explained below. PROCLBRANCH is listed in lines 280 to 360, PROCRBRANCH in lines 380 to 460 and both have an identical structure. The midpoint position of the end of each branch is computed in line 300 for the left branch, in line 400 for the right branch. PROCDRAW to draw each branch is called in lines 310, and 410 respectively. New left and right branch angles for the next bifurcation are computed in lines 320, or 420, and the tree 'balanced' in lines 330, 430. PROCNODE which controls the bifurcation is called in lines 340, 440 and the position moved back to the start of the branch drawing in lines 350, or 450. PROCNODE itself is listed in lines 480 to 560. In 510, the stopping rule is invoked while lines 520 and 530 relate to balancing the tree. New right and left branches are called in lines 540 and 550 with the level of recursion reduced by 1.

We should say a little more about balancing the tree. If the left branch angle is greater than the right, the tree will lean to the left, and vice versa, thus implying an imbalance. Now in cases where, say the right branch angle were 0 and the left some positive value, branches only on the left of the tree would be generated for the right branches would just constitute a continuation of the previous branch – the trunk, the first left branch and so on. Such branching is referred to as monopodial, and is characteristic of many trees except that their non-zero branch angles do not all occur in one direction. To avoid this asymmetry but to retain the notion of the monopodial tree, the left and right angles can be switched alternately thus balancing the tree, but keeping long straight branches. We accomplish this in the program with a rather tricky system of switches which enables the program to know whether the branch it is generating has a left or right predecessor and whether this predecessor has been generated as a continuation branch (zero angle) or deviation branch (positive angle). Lines 330 and 430 in the left and right procedures and lines 520 and 530 in PROCNODE act to ensure that correct switching occurs.

The program can be used to generate very conventional looking trees. Try a value of 200 for the size of the stem, 20 (10% of 200) for its width, branch contraction ratios of 0.8, angles of bertween 10° and 30°, and a recursive depth anything over seven levels. Such trees can be balanced or unbalanced. Then try generating an unbalanced tree with one of the branch angles 0, and the same tree with the balancing switches in operation. Set $D_{max} = 7$ to generate the tree in a few seconds and to get a broad impression of its spread. If it is of the right proportions, set $D_{max} = 14$. A tree in full foliage is generated in this way but it can take up to three hours with the depth of recursion set at this level.

Clearly the program should be used experimentally. 'Matchstick' trees are generated if the width is set equal to zero. If the contraction ratios are too small, the tree will appear gnarled and old; if they are too large, the structure will be too undifferentiated. If the branch angles are too small, the program will generate too narrow a tree spread; if too large, the spread will be too great. In fact as the branch angles approach 90° each, the design generated resembles the plan of a tree rather than its cross section, and with such angles, town plan-like forms can easily be produced. This is not really surprising because there is a well-known correspondence between spatial organization and hierarchy. Indeed, there is even a famous paper in the design literature by Christopher Alexander (1966) entitled *'A City is Not a Tree'*, which seeks to show that simple hierarchies are too obvious a way of describing the spatial organization of neighbourhoods and districts. The point of all this is to emphasize that whether we generate a tree form or plan form depends critically upon the given parameters. Varying these shows their importance as generators of really quite different forms rather than variations on the design of a tree.

Figures 4.6(a) to (f) reveal several different types of form generated using Program 4.5 with different parameter values. Figures 4.6(a) and (b) show two rather different but nevertheless broadly similar tree forms and experimentation with the parameters around the given values does not lead to modifications implying different tree types. In Fig. 4.6(c), the plan-like form of a tree is generated by varying the branch angles showing how sensitive the program is to these parameters. Figures 4.6(d) to (f), however, reveal very different shapes. The program generates a hexagonal net in Fig. 4.6(d) when the branch angles are 60° and there is no contraction, i.e. the contraction ratios are unity. With the branch angles at 90°, squares are generated and triangles emerge when these angles are 120°. In Fig. 4.6(e), the branch angles are 90° but the contraction ratios are less than unity, and a plan form emerges. This looks like a special form of pedestrian access – road traffic segregation called the Radburn layout familiar to architects and town planners. The roads represent a network of culs-de-sac linked to a main feeder while pedestrians are free to reach any part of the layout without crossing a road. In Fig. 4.6(f), the left branch angle and contraction ratio are both zero, and this generates a spiral form. Finally, by setting $D_{max} = 13$, a tree in full foliage based on Fig. 4.6(a) is generated and this is shown in Plate 7.

The variations you can produce with this program are seemingly endless but there are nevertheless deep mathematical reasons as to why trees turn into hexagonal lattices, spirals and town plans. It is not possible to explore this further here but the ideas are central to the next chapter. In particular, it is clear that the branches will avoid one another (not touch – known as *self-avoidance*) with certain sets of parameters as in Fig. 4.6(c), while they will close in on each other exactly as in Fig. 4.6(d) with other parameters. These designs also fill space, that is they enclose space and sometimes are referred to as *space-filling*.

In Fig. 4.6(f), we see an example of the kind of geometry produced using the language LOGO which in turn is based on recursive ideas and programming (Papert, 1980). Finally, we also see how irregularity might be introduced recursively, especially in Figs 4.6(a) to (c), and in the next chapter, these ideas will be central when we introduce notions of fractal geometry which enable highly realistic patterns to be generated (Mandelbrot, 1982).

4.6 TREESCAPES: SAVANNAH AND VALE

All our more elaborate designs so far have been based on replicating simpler designs many times, thus generating extensively complex pictures. We can now build up pictures of this kind but using designs which also reveal intensive complexity. Program 4.5 can be used to draw woods and forests, treelines and scrubland, trees of different size, orientation and shape in the effort to capture reality a little more closely. Moreover, trees are often a central feature of the

STEM HEIGHT 200.0 WIDTH 20.0
CONTRACTIONS:LEFT 0.8 RIGHT 0.8
BRANCH ANGLES:LEFT 22.0 RIGHT 24.0
BALANCED__Y TREE DEPTH 5.0

STEM HEIGHT 200.0 WIDTH 20.0
CONTRACTIONS:LEFT 0.8 RIGHT 0.7
BRANCH ANGLES:LEFT 20.0 RIGHT 30.0
BALANCED__Y TREE DEPTH 10.0

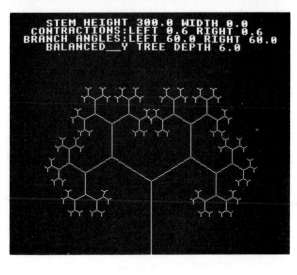

STEM HEIGHT 300.0 WIDTH 0.0
CONTRACTIONS:LEFT 0.6 RIGHT 0.6
BRANCH ANGLES:LEFT 60.0 RIGHT 60.0
BALANCED__Y TREE DEPTH 6.0

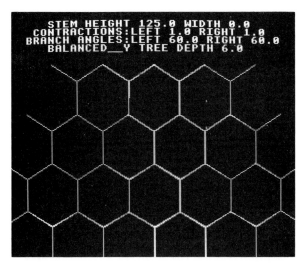

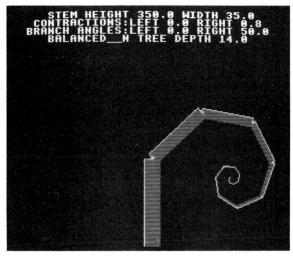

Fig. 4.6 'Tree' designs generated by branching

landscape; they are often focal points in landscape and certainly give the landscape form. Even in Random Landscapes, the softness of the pictures created is largely due to the rounded tree shapes which generate orchard-like scenes. There are in fact particular landscapes where the tree is all-important. This is true of flat plains where the horizon is very distant as on the Russian steppes or the plains of the mid-western USA. Towards the tropics, dry grasslands or Savannah where rather windswept umbrella-like trees grow, have characteristic form. We can generate such forms very easily and use trees to great advantage to focus the scene.

Our Savannah will be composed of a light blue sky, and a green grassland as foreground. On the horizon, a hint of dryness – of desert – is given by a yellow band of sand which extends to the middle distance. On this canvas, we will paint several black umbrella trees, with no width, but randomly located across the horizon and middle distance but no nearer to the foreground than this. The program is listed in Program 4.6 which differs from Program 4.5 only in terms of the main program. Lines 10 to 260 of 4.5 are replaced in 4.6 while lines 270 to 650 of Program 4.5 are also common to 4.6 and thus not repeated again. To run Program 4.6 then, readers must add lines 270 to 650 of Program 4.5, otherwise the tree generating procedures – PROCLBRANCH, PROCR-BRANCH, PROCNODE and PROCDRAW will be absent.

Program 4.6   Savannah landscapes

```
 10 REM Savannah Landscapes
 20 MODE1
 30 VDU23,1,0;0;0;0;
 40 VDU19,0,6;0;19,1,2;0;
 50 VDU19,2,0;0;19,3,3;0;
 60 W%=0:U$="YES"
 70 VDU24,0;0;1279;700;
 80 GCOL0,131:CLG
 90 VDU24,0;0;1279;600;
100 GCOL0,129:CLG
110 VDU26:Y0%=600+RND(100):D%=4+RND(2)
120 CL=0.7+(2*RND(1))/10
130 CR=0.7+(2*RND(1))/10
140 FOR IJ%=1 TO 5+RND(5)
150    X0%=100+RND(980)
160    Y0%=Y0%-10-RND(30)
170    VDU29,X0%;Y0%; :L%=100-(Y0%/10)
180    A=12+RND(18):B=12+RND(18)
190    X%=0:Y%=0:Z=RAD(90+A):ZZ=RAD(90-B)
200    PROCDRAW(X%,Y%,L%,X%,Y%+L%,RAD(90),W%)
210    Y%=Y%+L%:A=RAD(A):B=RAD(B)
220    PROCRBRANCH(L%,D%,X%,Y%,Z,ZZ,0.75*W%,0)
230    PROCLBRANCH(L%,D%,X%,Y%,Z,ZZ,0.75*W%,1)
240    NEXT IJ%
250 AA=GET:GOTO 20
260 END
```

Lines 10 to 50 in Program 4.6 initialize the program and set up the light blue (cyan) background. A yellow graphics window is fixed at line 70 and a green window plotted over this at line 90. The yellow horizon band is thus between 600 and 700 screen units up the picture and this division of green foreground from blue background lies astride the golden section subdivision of the vertical screen distance which is $0.618 \times 1023 = 632$ screen units in height. Throughout this book, our landscape designs will reflect this golden section ratio which is widely regarded as the ratio which gives the most pleasing contrast of styles, objects and areas (Ghyka, 1946). In line 60, we 'balance' each tree and set its width to zero, thus enabling 'matchstick' or frame trees to be generated. In lines 110 to 130, we fix the level of recursion and the contraction ratios for each tree in which $4 \leqslant D_{max} \leqslant 6$ and the ratios vary between 0.7 and 0.9.

Between five and ten trees are plotted in the FOR–NEXT loop in lines 140 to 240. In each case, the vertical position is reduced slightly (line 160) and the horizontal position fixed randomly (line 150). As the trees approach the foreground they get slightly larger (line 170) and their umbrella shape is determined by the branch angles fixed in line 180. Lines 200 to 230 which start the tree recursion are the same as those in Program 4.5. A typical landscape produced by this program is illustrated in Plate 8. In one sense, this is reminiscent of a David Hockney abstract and of some of the work of contemporary West Coast painters and illustrators. There is a hot, shimmering feel to the picture. Simplicity of form is of the essence illustrating the basic principle that a little is often better than a lot. Moreover, every medium creates its own limits on complexity and simplicity and I feel we have got it about right here. This is one of the hardest lessons to learn in art and it is as true of computer art as any other medium; perhaps it is truer for so much of computer art is the dreary kind of graphics associated with computer games. This is therefore a principle we will also use extensively and implicitly in this book. Note finally that our landscape is also generated using temporal priority which is invoked in line 160.

We are now in a position to put forward a much more realistic landscape using several of the programs presented so far. In Chapter 3, we introduced a program to sculpt cloud forms (Program 3.14), and earlier in this chapter, we developed Programs 4.2 and 4.3 to plot and overplot profiles of colour simulating hills from sinewaves. Combining these with our program to generate trees enables us to construct a landscape reminiscent of the wetter, western regions of the southern British Isles. As in Random Landscapes, the picture structure is almost entirely dictated by the program structure and vice versa due to the dominance of temporal priority in its generation. The structure of the program is obvious. PROCCLOUDS based exactly on lines 60 to 180 of Program 3.14 which is simply set up as a procedure now, is first called to elaborate the background. PROCHILLS from Program 4.2 is then called several times to generate the distant hills. We then plot several lines of trees on the green foreground using PROCTLINE which in turn calls PROCTREE several times. PROCTREE simply organizes the original calls to PROCDRAW, PROCRBRANCH and PROCLBRANCH which starts the recursive process. After five undulating lines of trees have been plotted, the picture is finished off by final calls to PROCTREE and PROCHILLS which produce a frame for the picture, illustrating another time-honoured principle of picture composition.

The program is listed as Program 4.7. Lines 10 to 80 effect the initialization and the rest of the main program follows the logic just sketched. PROCCLOUDS is called in line 90; the FOR–NEXT loop from 120 to 160 calls PROCHILLS six times using the sine wave option and generating a line of rolling hills based on a mix of black and blue colour with high order and zero GCOL operators. The FOR–NEXT loop bounded by lines 190 to 240 calls PROCTLINE five times while in line 290 PROCTREE plots a large tree framing the picture and PROCHILLS finishes the foreground in line 300. In lines 310 and 320, green is first switched to white and then cyan to dark blue, thus simulating the movement to winter but really just illustrating the superb colour contrasts of the BBC Microcomputer.

PROCCLOUDS in lines 370 to 510, and PROCHILLS in lines 530 to 650 need no discussion. PROCTLINE in lines 680 to 770 calls all the procedures used to plot a tree in PROCTREE but in fact, this procedure plots a wave of matchstick trees from left to right whose limits are set up in the main program and whose location depends on a sinewave fixed in line 720. This gives an impression of undulating topography in the far foreground. All PROCTREE does in lines 790 to 860 is simply make the first calls to PROCDRAW, PROCRBRANCH and PROCLBRANCH which in turn involve PROCNODE. These procedures, although the same as those in Programs 4.5 and 4.6, are repeated here in lines 880 to 1210. Note that the two colours in lines 1160 and 1200 of PROCDRAW are now fixed in the main program before each call to PROCTLINE and PROCTREE.

A typical picture from this program is presented in Fig. 4.7 and a winter scene produced by switching colours is shown in Plate 9. This is influenced by where I live in the beautiful Vale of Glamorgan whose gentle, green countryside I drive across on my way to work each day. There is one unanticipated feature which is not present in Random Landscapes where there are no clouds. When the high order GCOL statements involve generating a line of hills which overplot the clouds which they always do, the colour in the areas across the clouds darkens, giving the impression that the cloud is casting a shadow across the hill. The frame clearly sets off the picture in an attractive way, and lastly it is worth noting that the lines of trees take about one hour to plot thus illustrating another feature: intricate detail always takes time.

All these pictures in this chapter have begun to have a certain feel to them much must reflect the limits and potential of the hardware and software, my

Program 4.7 The Vale of Glamorgan

```
 10 REM The Vale of Glamorgan
 20 REM Plots Clouds,Distant Hills,Middle Ground and
 30 REM Line of Trees,then frames Picture with a Large
 40 REM Tree and finally Switches Colours to Winter
 50 MODE1
 60 VDU19,0,6;0;19,1,0;0;
 70 VDU19,2,7;0;19,3,2;0;
 80 VDU23,1,0;0;0;0;
 90 PROCCLOUDS
100 K%=0:N%=30:G%=0
110 VDU26:YS%=685+K%*RND(N%)
120 FOR H%=0 TO 5
130    READ COL%,G%
140    PROCHILLS(YS%,COL%,G%,K%,0)
150    YS%=YS%-(10+RND(N%)):K%=2-RND(3)
160    NEXT H%
170 YS%=YS%-(100+RND(30))
180 XI%=0:XE%=400+RND(200)
190 FOR H%=0 TO 4
200    PROCTLINE
210    YS%=YS%-30-RND(20)
220    XI%=XE%-250-RND(200):XE%=XE%+150+RND(150)
230    IF XE%>1250 THEN XE%=1250
240    NEXT H%
250 VDU26:L%=275:W%=33
260 CL=0.85:CR=0.78:A=12:B=23
270 U$="YES":D%=8:VDU29,200;35;
280 CS1%=1:CS2%=3
290 AA=GET:PROCTREE:VDU26
300 YS%=75+RND(50):PROCHILLS(YS%,1,0,0,0)
310 AA=GET:VDU19,3,7;0;
320 AA=GET:VDU19,0,4;0;
330 AA=GET:RESTORE:GOTO 50
340 END
350 :
360 REM Clouds based on Polar Plots
370 DEFPROCCLOUDS
380 FOR K%=1 TO 6+RND(10)
390    X0%=RND(1279):Y0%=700+RND(400)
400    A=60+RND(75):B=A/(3+RND(4))
410    H=A+B:G=H/B:F=A-B
420    FOR L%=1 TO 2
430       GCOL0,L%:VDU29,X0%;Y0%;:MOVE A,0
440       FOR I=0 TO 2*PI STEP 0.1
450          X%=H*COS(I)-B*COS(G*I)
460          Y%=F*SIN(I)-B*SIN(G*I)
470          MOVE0,0:PLOT85,X%,Y%
480          NEXT I
490       X0%=X0%+4+RND(4):Y0%=Y0%+4+RND(4)
500       NEXT L%:NEXT K%
510 ENDPROC
520 :
530 REM Hills based on Sine Waves
540 DEFPROCHILLS(YS%,COL%,J%,K%,CK%)
550 GCOL J%,COL%
```

Program 4.7 continued

```
560 DT=RAD(10):TH=RAD(RND(360))
570 S=SIN(DT):C=COS(DT):SS=SIN(TH):CC=COS(TH)
580 SI%=20+RND(30):YN%=CK%*YS%+(1-CK%)*(YS%+SI%*SS)
590 MOVE 0,0:MOVE 0,YN%
600 FOR I%=20 TO 1280 STEP 20
610     SN=SS*C+CC*S:CC=CC*C-SS*S:SS=SN
620     YN%=CK%*(YN%-K%*RND(5))+(1-CK%)*(YS%+SI%*SS)
630     PLOT85,I%,0:PLOT85,I%,YN%
640     NEXT I%
650 ENDPROC
660 :
670 REM Positions and Plots a Line of Trees
680 DEFPROCTLINE
690 W%=0:U$="YES":CS1%=1:CS2%=1
700 CL=0.78:CR=0.85:SI%=20+RND(25)
710 XI%=XI%+15+RND(65)
720 YN%=YS%+SI%*(SIN(XI%/80))
730 A=10+RND(15):B=10+RND(15):D%=3+RND(2)
740 L%=9000/YN%:VDU29,XI%;YN%;
750 PROCTREE:VDU26
760 IF XI%<XE% THEN GOTO 710
770 ENDPROC
780 :
790 REM Rest of Procedures deal with Branching Trees
800 DEFPROCTREE
810 X%=0:Y%=0:Z=RAD(90+A):ZZ=RAD(90-B)
820 PROCDRAW(X%,Y%,L%,X%,Y%+L%,RAD(90),W%)
830 Y%=Y%+L%:A=RAD(A):B=RAD(B)
840 PROCRBRANCH(L%,D%,X%,Y%,Z,ZZ,0.85*W%,0)
850 PROCLBRANCH(L%,D%,X%,Y%,Z,ZZ,0.85*W%,1)
860 ENDPROC
870 :
880 DEFPROCLBRANCH(L%,D%,X%,Y%,Z,ZZ,W%,K%)
890 XX%=X%+CL*L%*COS(Z):YY%=Y%+CL*L%*SIN(Z)
900 PROCDRAW(X%,Y%,CL*L%,XX%,YY%,Z,W%)
910 S=Z:ZZ=Z-B:Z=Z+A
920 IF K%=1 AND LEFT$(U$,1)="Y" ZZ=S-A:Z=S+B
930 PROCNODE(CL*L%,D%,XX%,YY%,Z,ZZ,0.75*W%,K%,1)
940 MOVE X%,Y%
950 ENDPROC
960 :
970 DEFPROCRBRANCH(L%,D%,X%,Y%,Z,ZZ,W%,K%)
980 XX%=X%+CR*L%*COS(ZZ):YY%=Y%+CR*L%*SIN(ZZ)
990 PROCDRAW(X%,Y%,CR*L%,XX%,YY%,ZZ,W%)
1000 S=ZZ:Z=ZZ+A:ZZ=ZZ-B
1010 IF K%=0 AND LEFT$(U$,1)="Y" ZZ=S-A:Z=S+B
1020 PROCNODE(CR*L%,D%,XX%,YY%,Z,ZZ,0.75*W%,K%,0)
1030 MOVE X%,Y%
1040 ENDPROC
1050 :
1060 DEFPROCNODE(L%,D%,X%,Y%,Z,ZZ,W%,K%,Q%)
1070 LOCAL K1%,K2%
1080 IF D%=0 THEN ENDPROC
1090 QZ%=K%+Q%:K1%=1:K2%=0
1100 IF QZ%=1 THEN K1%=0:K2%=1
```

Program 4.7   continued

```
1110 PROCRBRANCH(L%,D%-1,X%,Y%,Z,ZZ,W%,K1%)
1120 PROCLBRANCH(L%,D%-1,X%,Y%,Z,ZZ,W%,K2%)
1130 ENDPROC
1140 :
1150 DEFPROCDRAW(X%,Y%,L%,XX%,YY%,Z,W%)
1160 GCOL0,CS1%:Z=Z+RAD(90)
1170 X1%=W%*COS(Z):Y1%=W%*SIN(Z)
1180 MOVE X%-X1%,Y%-Y1%:MOVE XX%-X1%,YY%-Y1%
1190 PLOT85,X%+X1%,Y%+Y1%:PLOT85,XX%+X1%,YY%+Y1%
1200 GCOL0,CS2%:MOVE X%+X1%,Y%+Y1%:DRAW XX%+X1%,YY%+Y1%
1210 ENDPROC
1220 :
1230 DATA 1,143,1,0,1,143,0,179,1,70,3,0
```

style of programming, my intuitive ability to dissect and analyse a scene and much else besides which I can barely begin to articulate. I would be very surprised if others wrote programs in exactly the same way as myself or visualized scenes in quite the same way either. I guess the pictures in this book bear my stamp in some way which reinforces my belief that art cannot be legislated for. This is what makes any book about art and certainly a book

Fig. 4.7   The Vale of Glamorgan

about computer art so precocious. But what I hope to impress here is that computer art, like all art, is as much an affair of the heart as of the mind, although, as in other forms of art, technique, intuition, experience, intelligence and imagination are all mixed together.

4.7   NON-RECURSIVE TREES: PALM BEACH AND VERMILION SANDS

One of the most interesting features of Program 4.5 involves the sensitivity of the tree parameters to the resulting form. Indeed, in that program, it is rather hard to vary the values of these parameters significantly without producing very different forms, generating grids, spirals, lattices and suchlike rather than trees. Indeed, it is clear that some of the parameters in Program 4.5 are not particularly relevant to the kind of detail needed to generate various types of natural tree, while the recursive method of generation in itself may not be suitable for some trees. It is this latter point we will explore here. An excellent example of a 'non-recursive' tree is the palm tree which we will construct here and use to populate some subtropical landscapes.

There are many different types of palms but essentially, most are based on a very tall trunk without branches and a bunch of palms spiralling out in all directions from the top of the trunk. The actual design of the tree is straightforward. The trunk is composed of *segments* which resemble upside-down plant pots embedded into one another; the trunk is usually bent in the direction of the prevailing wind but is normally vertical or upright at its top. The palms are composed of spiralling branches with the ends of the leaves following the line of the spirals on each side of the branch but with the leaves at an angle away from the trunk on both sides of the branch. The palms droop and bunch around the trunk's top in a loose fashion. The essence of our program is based on two procedures: PROCSEGMENT generates and plots each segment of the trunk while PROCPALM is used to construct and draw each palm in the bunch. The number of segments and palms and their size is closely controlled in relation to the height of the tree which is an input variable here. Both these procedures are called from a third procedure PROCPTREE which collects all the necessary data to draw the complete tree.

The program is listed in Program 4.8. The main program in lines 10 to 140 simply initializes the set-up and requests the user to input the position of the palm on the screen (lines 80 and 90) and its height (line 100). The tree is then called from PROCPTREE in line 110 and in lines 120 and 130 the user requested to finish with the current screen of palms or plot another in another position. The background is set as yellow, the palm segments are black, edged in green, and the palms black. The user can thus use the program to compose a grove or oasis of palm trees, or even a forest if this is felt appropriate. PROCPTREE is listed in lines 160 to 350. In line 180, the number of segments is fixed and the average size of each segment relative to height determined in

Program 4.8 Palm tree architecture

```
 10 REM Palm Tree Architecture
 20 MODE2
 30 VDU23,1,0;0;0;0;
 40 VDU19,0,3;0;19,1,0;0;19,7,2;0;
 50 VDU28,0,5,19,1
 60 RESTORE:CLS:COLOUR1
 70 PRINT TAB(3)"TREE POSITION"
 80 INPUT TAB(6)"X = ",XO%
 90 INPUT TAB(6)"Y = ",YO%
100 INPUT TAB(3)"HEIGHT = ",H%
110 PROCPTREE(XO%,YO%,H%):AA=GET:CLS
120 AA=GET:INPUT TAB(4)"FINISHED",U$
130 IF LEFT$(U$,1)="Y" THEN GOTO 20 ELSE GOTO 60
140 END
150 :
160 REM Sets up Structure of a Palm Tree
170 DEFPROCPTREE(XQ%,YQ%,H%)
180 VDU29,XQ%;YQ%;:N%=6+RND(4)
190 S%=H%/N%:A=RAD(60+RND(15)):AI=(PI/2-A)/N%
200 X1%=0:Y1%=0:MOVE X1%,Y1%
210 FOR I%=1 TO N%
220    X2%=X1%+S%*COS(A):Y2%=Y1%+S%*SIN(A)
230    PROCSEGMENT
240    A=A+AI:S%=S%-RND(0.1*S%)
250    X1%=X2%:Y1%=Y2%
260    NEXT I%
270 VDU29,XQ%+X1%;YQ%+Y1%;
280 Z=1.01:RX=0.9:RY=1.1
290 XO%=0:YO%=0:READ LL%
300 FOR L%=1 TO LL%
310    READ J%,R%,ST%:RD=H%/500:R%=RD*R%
320    M%=300-1.35*(R%/RD)+RND(30)
330    PROCPALM(XO%,YO%,R%,Z,J%,ST%,RX,RY,M%)
340    NEXT L%
350 ENDPROC
360 :
370 REM Constructs and Plots Segment of the Trunk
380 DEFPROCSEGMENT
390 AZ=0.35:BZ=0.28:CZ=0.22:DZ=0.16
400 AA=A+PI/2:CA=COS(AA):SA=SIN(AA)
410 GCOLO,1:XX%=S%*CA:YY%=S%*SA
420 XA%=X1%+XX%*AZ:YA%=Y1%+YY%*AZ
430 XB%=X1%-XX%*BZ:YB%=Y1%-YY%*BZ
440 XC%=X2%-XX%*CZ:YC%=Y2%-YY%*CZ
450 XD%=X2%+XX%*DZ:YD%=Y2%+YY%*DZ
460 MOVE XA%,YA%:MOVE XB%,YB%
470 PLOT85,XD%,YD%:PLOT85,XC%,YC%:GCOLO,7
480 MOVE XD%,YD%:DRAW XA%,YA%:DRAW XB%,YB%
490 ENDPROC
500 :
510 REM Constructs and Plots a Palm
520 DEFPROCPALM(X%,Y%,R%,Z,J%,T%,RX,RY,M%)
530 RR%=R%:MOVE X%,Y%:XC%=X%:YC%=Y%:RJ%=J%*RR%
540 IF J%=-1 THEN TB%=180-T%:TE%=180-M% ELSE TB%=T%:TE%=M%
550 FOR I%=TB% TO TE% STEP J%*T%
```

Program 4.8   continued

```
560    GCOLO,1:R1%=RX*R%:R2%=RY*R%
570    CZ=COS(RAD(I%)):SZ=SIN(RAD(I%))
580    X1%=XC%+R1%*CZ-RJ%:Y1%=YC%+R1%*SZ
590    DRAW X1%,Y1%:MOVE X%,Y%
600    X1%=XC%+R2%*CZ-RJ%:Y1%=YC%+R2%*SZ
610    DRAW X1%,Y1%:MOVE X%,Y%
620    X%=XC%+R%*CZ-RJ%:Y%=YC%+R%*SZ
630    GCOLO,1:DRAW X%,Y%:R%=Z*R%
640     NEXT I%
650  ENDPROC
660  :
670  DATA 17,1,150,5,1,125,6,1,100,7,1,70,8,1,50,12,1,30,25
680  DATA -1,135,6,-1,110,7,-1,90,8,-1,65,10,-1,40,20
690  DATA 1,92,8,1,43,13,-1,75,9,-1,48,20,1,180,5,-1,180,5
```

line 190 where the angles of incline of the tree due to the wind are fixed. These are determined so that the tree trunk will be ultimately upright after all the segments have been plotted. The FOR–NEXT loop between lines 210 and 260 fixes the midpoint base coordinates of each segment, calls PROCSEGMENT in line 230, and increments the angle of slope and reduces the segment size a little in line 240.

Before we go further in this procedure, we will look at PROCSEGMENT which is listed in lines 370 to 490. Lines 420 to 450 fix the coordinates of each corner of the segment, and then in lines 460 and 470, two PLOT85 commands are used to fill the area as two adjacent triangles. Line 480 edges the left of the segment and its base in green to provide the usual depth cue or three-dimensional effect. Back in PROCPTREE at line 270 and on, the palms are computed and plotted in the FOR–NEXT loop between lines 300 and 340. In line 310, data on the orientation (left or right side of the trunk) of each palm, its initial radius at the top of the trunk and the step size for each leaf are read from DATA statements (listed at the end of the program in lines 670 to 690). The ultimate angular extent of each palm is computed in line 320, and the palm itself called from PROCPALM in line 330.

Lines 510 to 650 list PROCPALM. Its position and orientation (left or right of the trunk) is fixed in lines 530 and 540, and the FOR–NEXT loop between lines 550 and 640 plots the palm spiral at given steps where two leaves are drawn on either side of the branch. In the jargon of a previous section, this involves ternary, monopodial branching to one level only with respect to leaves but to many levels with respect to each palm branch. The spiral is fixed using polar coordinates in line 570, each leaf is drawn in lines 580 and 590, and 600 and 610, and the branch extended in lines 620 and 630. In line 630, the radius of each spiral is compounded to enable spiral divergence to be built in.

We will not show an oasis of palms produced from this program but we can alter the main program of Program 4.8 to produce a more typical landscape. Program 4.9 simply replaces the main program lines of 4.8 (lines 10 to 140)

Program 4.9 Palm beach

```
 10 REM Palm Beach
 20 MODE2
 30 VDU23,1,0;0;0;0;
 40 VDU19,0,3;0;19,1,0;0;19,7,2;0;19,3,4;0;
 50 VDU24,0;660;1279;1023;
 60 GCOL0,131:CLG:VDU26
 70 YF%=650:YG%=YF%
 80 XG%=RND(1279):YG%=YG%-30-RND(25)
 90 H%=200+(YF%-YG%)
100 RESTORE
110 PROCPTREE(XG%,YG%,H%)
120 IF YG%>450 THEN VDU26:GOTO 80
130 AA=GET:GOTO 20
140 END
```

with instructions which enable us to plot 'Palm Beach'. In exactly the same spirit and using a very similar structure to Savannah (Program 4.6), we have plotted a dark blue sky, a yellow beach and occasional palms on the horizon. The horizon is 650 screen units high, near the golden section and the palms provide the classic focal effect. In Program 4.9, a graphics window establishes the beach in line 50, the vertical start point is fixed in line 70, and both horizontal and vertical base locations for each palm are determined in line 80. Height is fixed in line 90, the palm called using PROCPTREE in line 110 and a check made to see that no palms are generated any nearer the foreground than 450 screen units, in line 120. If they are nearer, the program finishes and another scene begins. No more than seven palms are plotted in this structure. A typical landscape is shown as Plate 10.

As with our tree program, we can use our palm tree to form many other subtropical pictures, in the same way we generalized the tree program to 'Vale'. In fact, the reason why the palm is constructed using MODE2, the lowest resolution, is that for the picture we have in mind, we will require six colours: light blue, black, dark blue, red, green and yellow. We have called this landscape 'Vermilion Sands'. It is a mixture of mainly reds and yellows, organized as 'strata' of colour, interspersed with dark blue sea–lake, and black fringes. It is framed by three palms in the same manner as Vale. It is inspired by J. G. Ballard's (1975) brilliant collection of short stories *Vermilion Sands* which conjure up to me a mythical, magical paradise: California without the smog, America without the 'dream'. In fact my original inspiration for Cloud Sculptures (Program 3.14) came from one of Ballard's short stories in this book and I originally intended to use these clouds as background to Vermilion Sands. But my clouds are not those of hot climes although you could easily use them here and see what *you* think.

The program is listed as Program 4.10. Like Random Landscapes, and Vale, it makes extensive use of temporal priority but plotting blocks or 'strata' of overlapping colour, not hills, using PROCSTRATA. These blocks are randomly

Program 4.10　Vermilion Sands

```
 10 REM Vermilion Sands
 20 REM Plots Blocks or 'Strata' of Colour forming
 30 REM Sub-Tropical Scene framed by a Palm Grove
 40 MODE2
 50 VDU23,1,0;0;0;0;
 60 VDU19,0,6;0;19,1,0;0;19,2,7;0;19,3,4;0;
 70 VDU19,4,1;0;19,5,3;0;19,6,5;0;19,7,2;0;
 80 S%=100:STT=0.07:Q=0.2:YI%=730
 90 STI=0.005:YII%=15:QI=0.02:LK%=0
100 FOR J%=3 TO 11
110   STT=STT+STI:Q=Q+QI:YI%=YI%-YII%
120   GCOLO,4+J%MOD2
130   PROCSTRATA:NEXT J%
140 S%=0:STT=1.0:Q=0.1
150 YI%=645:GCOLO,1:PROCSTRATA
160 YI%=642:GCOLO,3:PROCSTRATA
170 S%=75:STT=0.05:Q=0.2
180 YI%=550:GCOLO,5:PROCSTRATA
190 YI%=535:GCOLO,3:PROCSTRATA
200 YI%=505:GCOLO,1:PROCSTRATA
210 YI%=500:GCOLO,3:PROCSTRATA
220 S%=120:STT=0.07:YI%=480:Q=0.1:QI=0.0:STI=0.0015
230 FOR J%=0 TO 20
240   YI%=YI%-10:Q=Q+QI:STT=STT-STI
250   GCOLO,2+RND(3):PROCSTRATA:NEXT J%
260 S%=0:STT=1.0
270 YI%=450:GCOLO,5:PROCSTRATA
280 FOR J%=450 TO 0 STEP-4
290   FOR K%=0 TO 1279 STEP 8
300     IF RND(1279)<(1279-K%) THEN GCOLO,4 ELSE GCOLO,5
310     PLOT69,K%,J%
320     NEXT K%:NEXT J%
330 PROCPTREE(100,120,300)
340 RESTORE:PROCPTREE(400,100,400)
350 RESTORE:PROCPTREE(200,100,750)
360 S%=100:STT=0.06:Q=0.15:LK%=1
370 YI%=150:GCOLO,1:VDU29,0;0;:PROCSTRATA
380 AA=GET:GOTO 40
390 END
400 :
410 REM Plots a Randomly Perturbed Block of Colour
420 DEFPROCSTRATA
430 ST%=1279*STT:Y1%=YI%+RND(S%):Y2%=YI%+RND(S%)
440 IF LK%=1 THEN Y1%=YI%:Y2%=0.4*YI%
450 YY%=Y1%:MOVE 0,0:MOVE 0,YY%
460 Y%=Y2%-Y1%:Z%=ABS(Y%)*Q
470 FOR I%=ST% TO 1279+ST% STEP ST%
480   YZ=I%/1279:YY%=Y1%+Y%*YZ
490   IF RND(2)=1 THEN YY%=YY%+RND(Z%) ELSE YY%=YY%-RND(Z%)
500   PLOT85,I%,0:PLOT85,I%,YY%:NEXT I%
510 ENDPROC
520 :
530 REM Sets up Structure of a Palm Tree
540 DEFPROCPTREE(XQ%,YQ%,H%)
550 VDU29,XQ%;YQ%;:N%=6+RND(4)
```

Program 4.10 continued

```
560 S%=H%/N%:A=RAD(60+RND(15)):AI=(PI/2-A)/N%
570 X1%=0:Y1%=0:MOVE X1%,Y1%
580 FOR I%=1 TO N%
590    X2%=X1%+S%*COS(A):Y2%=Y1%+S%*SIN(A)
600    PROCSEGMENT
610    A=A+AI:S%=S%-RND(0.1*S%)
620    X1%=X2%:Y1%=Y2%
630    NEXT I%
640 VDU29,XQ%+X1%;YQ%+Y1%;
650 Z=1.01:RX=0.9:RY=1.1
660 X0%=0:Y0%=0:READ LL%
670 FOR L%=1 TO LL%
680    READ J%,R%,ST%:RD=H%/500:R%=RD*R%
690    M%=300-1.35*(R%/RD)+RND(30)
700    PROCPALM(X0%,Y0%,R%,Z,J%,ST%,RX,RY,M%)
710    NEXT L%
720 ENDPROC
730 :
740 REM Constructs and Plots Segment of the Trunk
750 DEFPROCSEGMENT
760 AZ=0.35:BZ=0.28:CZ=0.22:DZ=0.16
770 AA=A+PI/2:CA=COS(AA):SA=SIN(AA)
780 GCOLO,1:XX%=S%*CA:YY%=S%*SA
790 XA%=X1%+XX%*AZ:YA%=Y1%+YY%*AZ
800 XB%=X1%-XX%*BZ:YB%=Y1%-YY%*BZ
810 XC%=X2%-XX%*CZ:YC%=Y2%-YY%*CZ
820 XD%=X2%+XX%*DZ:YD%=Y2%+YY%*DZ
830 MOVE XA%,YA%:MOVE XB%,YB%
840 PLOT85,XD%,YD%:PLOT85,XC%,YC%:GCOLO,7
850 MOVE XD%,YD%:DRAW XA%,YA%:DRAW XB%,YB%
860 ENDPROC
870 :
880 REM Constructs and Plots a Palm
890 DEFPROCPALM(X%,Y%,R%,Z,J%,T%,RX,RY,M%)
900 RR%=R%:MOVE X%,Y%:XC%=X%:YC%=Y%:RJ%=J%*R R%
910 IF J%=-1 THEN TB%=180-T%:TE%=180-M% ELSE TB%=T%:TE%=M%
920 FOR I%=TB% TO TE% STEP J%*T%
930    GCOLO,1:R1%=RX*R%:R2%=RY*R%
940    CZ=COS(RAD(I%)):SZ=SIN(RAD(I%))
950    X1%=XC%+R1%*CZ-RJ%:Y1%=YC%+R1%*SZ
960    DRAW X1%,Y1%:MOVE X%,Y%
970    X1%=XC%+R2%*CZ-RJ%:Y1%=YC%+R2%*SZ
980    DRAW X1%,Y1%:MOVE X%,Y%
990    X%=XC%+R%*CZ-RJ%:Y%=YC%+R%*SZ
1000   GCOLO,1:DRAW X%,Y%:R%=Z*R%
1010   NEXT I%
1020 ENDPROC
1030 :
1040 DATA 17,1,150,5,1,125,6,1,100,7,1,70,8,1,50,12,1,30,25
1050 DATA -1,135,6,-1,110,7,-1,90,8,-1,65,10,-1,40,20
1060 DATA 1,92,8,1,43,13,-1,75,9,-1,48,20,1,180,5,-1,180,5
```

perturbed in the horizontal plane, but once the picture reaches the foreground the dot shading technique used in one of the Cloud Sculptures programs in Chapter 3, is used to produce a 'vermillion' effect and the picture is then framed by the palms which call PROCPTREE and related procedures.

Initialization and the light blue sky are established up to line 70. In the FOR–NEXT loop bounded by lines 100 to 130, PROCSTRATA is called nine times with the step size, and incline of the strata varying each time, and the colour fixed in line 120 alternating between red and yellow. Between lines 140 and 210, PROCSTRATA is called again, six times. First the upper edge of the middle ground is established in black, and a lake or sea established in dark blue (lines 150 and 160). Yellow, red, blue and black strata then progressively block-in the middle ground moving down the screen to the foreground. In the FOR–NEXT loop between lines 230 to 250, PROCSTRATA is called 21 times, with increasing random perturbations of the horizontal or sloping line and with reducing step sizes which give a more jagged effect. This too is a kind of depth cue with more detail appearing as the foreground is approached.

Taking lines 270 to 320, the foreground is coloured yellow, and red dots increasing in density to the left of the picture, giving the vermilion effect referred to above, are plotted. Finally in lines 330 to 370, three calls to PROCPTREE are made, and then a final call to PROCSTRATA which produces the black foreground frame. PROCSTRATA itself is listed in lines 410 to 510. In line 430, the step size and incline of the strata are fixed while line 440 fixes the direction of incline. The FOR–NEXT loop between 470 and 500 increases the height according to step size and incline direction, determines a random perturbation around this and plots a block of colour from the last position using two PLOT85 commands in line 500. In watching the program run, note how the step size STT and the random perturbation factor Z affect the speed and shape of the resultant plotting. The completed picture is shown in colour on the cover of the book and in black and white in Fig. 4.8. If you have read Ballard, is this your image of Vermilion Sands? How can you modify this to capture his reality more closely?

And so another long chapter reaches its conclusion but compared with the end of Chapter 3, we have now really broached computer art based on the mathematical modelling of picture structure. A number of issues stand out here and it is worth noting them before proceeding. The correspondence between picture structure and program structure in terms of temporal priority is all important and basic to much of our picture processing. Such overplotting combined with 'depth cues' based on edging give impressions of three dimensions without their complexity of construction. Softness and hardness, colour balance and randomly-structured choice have been shown to be significant as well as spatial effects such as focusing on objects, and framing them. As yet however, we have avoided techniques for the production of more natural textures, although we have broached the subject of generating detail

Fig. 4.8   Vermilion Sands

at different scales in some considerable depth. Without getting into three-dimensional representations, we can still improve our landscapes in this regard, and in the next chapter we will combine recursion with randomness in the attempt to introduce greater realism. Our quest will be to explore the fascinating world of fractal geometry, the world where dimensions other than two or three predominate, and the world which offers so much hope to the fields of computer graphics and computer art.

5

Randomness and recursion: fractal landscapes

> It is widely held that minimal art is restricted to limited
> combinations of standard shapes; lines, circles, spirals
> and the like. But such need not be the case. The fractals
> used in scientific models are also very simple (because
> science puts a premium on simplicity). And I agree that
> many may be viewed as a new form of minimal
> geometric art.
>
> (Benoit B. Mandelbrot, *The Fractal Geometry of Nature*, 1982)

Our designs so far have been based on constructing pictures using regular geometry. Landscapes based on sinewaves, clouds based on polar coordinate plots and suchlike have been the norm although some sense of the irregular was introduced in the tree designs developed in Chapter 4. In this chapter, we will broach the subject of irregularity and how to model it visually in a comprehensive manner, exploring ideas involving randomness and the degree to which structure and form emerge from random simulation subject to geometric constraints. This is entirely consistent with the plan of this book in which more realistic visual modelling is gradually built up, and this chapter will demonstrate the power of randomness and recursion in enabling this quest for visual realism.

To the uninitiated, randomness might imply chaos and with such a view, it is hard to see how it can have a major use in anything as definite as computer graphics. In fact, randomness is a construct of our imagination, invented to enable us to handle situations where we are uncertain about true explanation. Albert Einstein once said that: "God does not play with dice!" in expressing his disquiet with the idea that scientists believed the world to be intrinsically random in certain ways. Even if nature appears irregular, it must be explicable, yet to reconstruct it, we will never achieve a complete description. Hence randomness can be useful to us in approximating such a description. What this chapter will illustrate however is that to use the concept of randomness intelligently, it must always be used within some framework which constrains it in some way. The real trick in using the concept to its best advantage, is to recognize the kinds of constraints which 'contain' randomness, within which random motion and random geometry are allowed to 'roam free'. This chapter is all about the realism which can be visually generated in this way.

There is an immediate, obvious and perhaps trivial example of constrained randomness. Most computers have a random number generator which in the case of a typical microcomputer such as the BBC machine, generates a number randomly within a prespecified range. It is this range which acts as a trivial kind of constraint. For example, the statement $M\% = RND(N\%)$ selects a number between 1 and $N\%$ at random which implies that the greater the number of times the random number function is called in the case of this expression, the more likely a particular number will have occurred in proportion to $1/N\%$. In other words, the generator is so constituted as to give any number within the range an equal chance of selection. Thus the value of $N\%$ constrains the range and can be used to structure the degree of randomness.

A new idea of structure emerges from this which might crudely be thought of as 'Structure = Randomness + Constraint'. There are a variety of constraints which are worth listing. Range has already been mentioned but in a geometric context, such constraints relate generally to the *position* and *size* of any object on the two-dimensional screen. These two factors interact although position is usually influenced by screen limits, boundaries, windows, angular variation about the coordinate axes and suchlike while size relates to constraints on the magnitude of line, area, shape etc. As a simple example of positional constraint which incorporates range, consider the following one line program which plots dots randomly on the screen:

```
MODE0:REPEAT:PLOT69,RND(1279),RND(1023):UNTIL FALSE
```

This will fill the screen in a few minutes but increase the range of the horizontal and vertical limits by ten times, and then ten again and keep running it. Clearly the density of the plot is affected directly by these changes.

Several other types of constraint will be introduced here but a major concept will involve the idea that objects have the property of *self-similarity*. Objects which are self-similar, show the same level of detail or irregularity at different scales. There are some celebrated natural examples. Coastlines for example show the same level of irregularity over smaller and smaller areas as you get nearer and nearer to them. A rock fragment broken from a mountain seems to have the same level of detail in that in looking at the fragment, you can see the mountain 'in it' and vice versa. We have already seen a classic example of such self-similarity in the tree designs of Chapter 4 where trunk and branches have the same structure and form as twigs and leaf ends. Such objects are called by Mandelbrot (1982) *fractals.* We will have a lot to say about these later in this chapter and the fractal geometry which we outline will become central to the simulation of realistic irregularities through constrained randomness.

This chapter is organized into four broad sections. First, we will begin with least-constrained random designs which are called random walks. Entirely irregular walks and walks on predetermined grids serve to introduce several ideas, for example, modelling form as cellular automata. Then the degree of constraint will be increased to reflect walks on highly constrained shapes, in fact on and within circular forms. The next broad area of simulation takes these ideas and applies them to the graphical modelling of city systems and river systems, showing how artificial and natural constraints which reflect our knowledge of cities and rivers, can be used to structure randomness. We will then introduce self-similarity and fractal geometry, illustrating so-called non-random fractals first, that is designs based on systematic irregularity at different scales involving a variety of mathematical curves and tessellations. Finally random fractals will be explored, particularly in the context of fractal landscapes which will be illustrated using mountain range and coastline–continental–planet-like pictures.

5.1 RECTANGULAR RANDOM WALKS

If you substitute the command 'DRAW' for 'PLOT69', in the above one line program, you introduce connectivity into the random dot program which indicates the trail or trace of the random number generator on the screen. After two minutes or so the screen is filled and it is then clear that the program has little structure and accords to our intuitive notions of randomness as chaos. The picture lacks structure because it is only constrained in the most trivial way. We can however give much more structure to this program by constraining the distance between randomly generated dots, that is, by constraining the position of new dots relative to previous ones, which is equivalent to constraining the length or size of the lines which mark the trail of the random generator. Thus the following constraints will characterize the algorithm: the initial point will be on the screen, no point will be outside the screen limits, each point will be connected by a line to the point previously generated, and what gives most structure to the picture, each subsequent point will be randomly chosen within a predetermined distance of the previous point. This point will be within a square with sides of $S\%$ units which marks any of the four quadrants centred on the previous point. Thus the maximum distance of the new from the old point will be $\sqrt{2}\ S\%$. The trace given by this algorithm is reminiscent of Perrin's classic diagrams of Brownian motion in the plane (illustrated in Mandelbrot, 1982), a point we will return to later.

The program listed as Program 5.1 follows this structure which is also the basis for the subsequent programs in this section. Assignments are made up to line 50 involving MODE, colour and cursor. In line 60, the start position of the

Program 5.1   Classical random walk

```
10 REM Classical Random Walk
20 MODE1
30 VDU23,1,0;0;0;0;
40 VDU19,0,4;0;19,1,6;0;
50 VDU19,2,0;0;19,3,5;0;
60 X%=RND(1279):Y%=RND(1023):MOVE X%,Y%
70 REPEAT
80    X1%=X%:Y1%=Y%
90    K%=RND(4):S%=100:GCOLO,1
100   IF K%=1 THEN X%=X1%+RND(S%):Y%=Y1%+RND(S%)
110   IF K%=2 THEN X%=X1%+RND(S%):Y%=Y1%-RND(S%)
120   IF K%=3 THEN X%=X1%-RND(S%):Y%=Y1%+RND(S%)
130   IF K%=4 THEN X%=X1%-RND(S%):Y%=Y1%-RND(S%)
140   IF X%>1279 OR X%<0 OR Y%>1023 OR Y%<0 THEN GOTO 90
150   DRAW X%,Y%
160   UNTIL FALSE
170 END
```

walk is fixed on the screen and new positions are generated randomly in the REPEAT–UNTIL loop bounded by lines 70 and 160. New points are generated randomly in any of the four quadrants whose origin is the existing point, the quadrant chosen and its maximum horizontal–vertical direction $S\%$ determined in line 90. Lines 100 to 130 apply to the particular quadrant chosen and randomly fix the new point RND $(S\%)$ units in the appropriate x and RND$(S\%)$ units in the appropriate y directions. Line 140 represents the boundary constraint, fixed as the screen limits which represent a reflecting barrier in that any point generated outside these limits is 'bounced back' onto the screen. Finally, connectivity of the points is ensured in the use of the DRAW command in line 150. This program takes about five minutes to cover the screen and Fig. 5.1(a) shows the result of the output after one minute, demonstrating the 'wire wool' texture which results from this technique. When the program is left to run, all points on the plane are eventually (in the limit) visited and we begin to see the conundrum of how a one-dimensional line defines a two-dimensional plane. There is little point in exploring this further now but later we will return to it as an example of fractal geometry.

We will now introduce further constraints into our standard program. In Program 5.2, we have constrained the walk to the extreme limits of the four quadrants from each existing point, that is to any one of the four positions defined in terms of the original point x, y as $(x+s,y+s)$, $(x+s,y-s)$, $(x-s,y+s)$ and $(x-s,y-s)$ where s is now a fixed increment. This simulates a walk on a diagonal grid. The only changes in Program 5.1 are in the step size to $S\% = 20$ in line 90 and in the deletion of the random functions of step size to fixed sizes in lines 100 to 130. In fact, we have repeated Program 5.1 entirely with these changes as Program 5.2 because it is this latter program to which we will now make several minor extensions and changes. This program takes

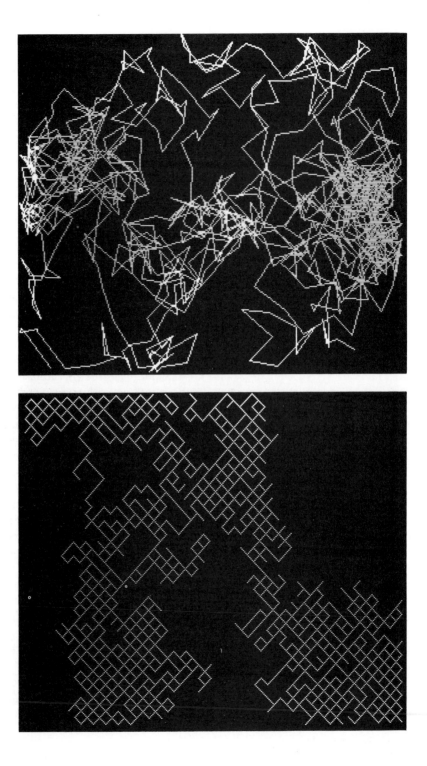

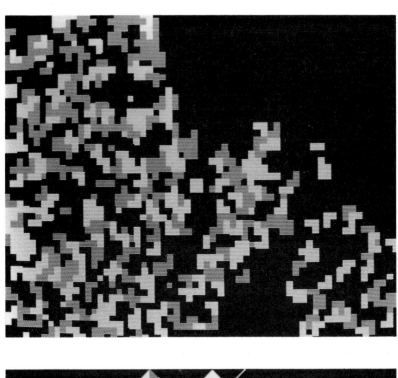

Fig. 5.1 Random walks

Program 5.2   Random walk on a diagonal grid

```
 10 REM Random Walk on a Diagonal Grid
 20 MODE1
 30 VDU23,1,0;0;0;0;
 40 VDU19,0,4;0;19,1,6;0;
 50 VDU19,2,0;0;19,3,5;0;
 60 X%=RND(1279):Y%=RND(1023):MOVE X%,Y%
 70 REPEAT
 80    X1%=X%:Y1%=Y%
 90    K%=RND(4):S%=20:GCOL0,1
100    IF K%=1 THEN X%=X1%+S%:Y%=Y1%+S%
110    IF K%=2 THEN X%=X1%+S%:Y%=Y1%-S%
120    IF K%=3 THEN X%=X1%-S%:Y%=Y1%+S%
130    IF K%=4 THEN X%=X1%-S%:Y%=Y1%-S%
140    IF X%>1279 OR X%<0 OR Y%>1023 OR Y%<0 THEN GOTO 90
150    DRAW X%,Y%
160    UNTIL FALSE
170 END
```

about two minutes to fill the plane with a diagonal, lattice-like grid which is illustrated after about one minute in Fig. 5.1(b).

One obvious variant of Program 5.2 is to a horizontal–vertical grid rather than a diagonal one which would be achieved by altering the movements in lines 100 to 130 to $(x+s,y)$ $(x,y-s)$, $(x,y+s)$ and $(x-s,y)$ respectively. The use of such techniques in shading however has much promise. By keeping the horizontal–vertical motion the same but randomly choosing the 'distance' of this motion, it is possible to simulate the effect of pencil colouring. To do this, we have changed the start position and screen limits in Program 5.2 and chosen the step size and colour randomly replacing lines 60, 90 and 140 by

     60 X%=400:Y%=450:MOVE X%,Y%
     90 K%=RND(4):S%=RND(20):GCOL0,RND(3)
    140 IF X%>600 OR X%<300 OR Y%>800 OR Y%<300 THEN GOTO 90

The shading of the box which results from this program gives the impression of slate in that the direction is diagonal and the form strata-like.

Two other examples of rectangular random walks introduce the idea of evolution, of growth and decay, and the idea of cell-space models or cellular automata. Using the diagonal grid program listed as Program 5.2, the drawn trace of the random generator is replaced by a cell which in turn is defined by a graphics window. The only change to the program is to line 150 which becomes

    150 VDU24,X%−S%;Y%−S%;X%+S%;Y%+S%;:GCOL0,127+RND(4):CLG

Note that if the background colour represents the pre-evolutionary state, the colour definition in line 150 uses all four colours of MODE1, one of which is the background colour which can represent the death of a cell. Once the screen is full after about three minutes – that is after the system has evolved – about a quarter of the cells continue to 'die' and this represents the system's steady state. A typical picture is shown in Fig. 5.1(c).

Finally, we can define a triangular rather than a rectangular cell and the following changes to Program 5.2 accomplish this

```
 90 K%=RND(4):S%=50:GCOL0,RND(3)
150 PLOT85,X%,Y%
```

In this automata, we see the effect of single line extensions as well as triangles due to the way the random generator works. Changing line 20 to MODE2 and the colour definition in line 90 to GCOL0,RND(7) produces a very pleasant cell-like design which is illustrated in Fig. 5.1(d).

These last two examples of cell-space models demonstrate how randomness can be constrained to produce simulations of almost realistic spatial or geographical phenomena (Tobler, 1979). The extensions and applications are many. A famous example of such a process involving life, death and evolution is John Conway's Game of Life which is characteristic of many cell-space models which generate fanciful and intriguing patterns (see Eigen and Winkler, 1983). A three-dimensional version of the Game of Life extending these ideas has been proposed using BBC Basic (Banthorpe, 1984), and these ideas will make their appearance again a little later when we examine the simulation of cities.

5.2 CIRCULAR RANDOM WALKS

A greater degree of constraint can be introduced into a random walk by restricting the orientation of the walk to stricter limits and directions. For example, a walk in which the subsequent move relative to an existing position is always in a certain (relative) direction is likely to generate circular motion. There are many real systems which might display this kind of behaviour. An insect responding to a fixed point of light but repelled by the immediate heat of the light is a typical example. The local property of such behaviour is always to turn in the general direction of the source but far enough from it to protect the system from actually reaching the source. The global property of such behaviour is that the motion generates circular patterns whose precise form is randomly determined. Such behaviour is akin to that of the Brownian motion given by Program 5.1 but more strictly constrained.

This type of walk is displayed by running Program 5.3. This program calculates movement randomly within angular and directional limits which are consistent with a circle of a predetermined radius r. For such a circle, it would take n movements of length $2\pi r/n$ with an increment in angle between each move of $2\pi/n$ to draw the circle, where n is large. These angles and lengths provide the limits which are used to generate random changes in

Program 5.3   Random circular walk

```
 10 REM Random Circular Walk
 20 MODE1
 30 VDU23,1,0;0;0;0;
 40 VDU29,640;312;
 50 GCOL0,1:DT=5:R%=200
 60 N%=360/(DT+5):AV%=2*PI*R%/N%
 70 A=0:X%=0:Y%=0:MOVE X%,Y%
 80 REPEAT
 90    A=A+RAD(4÷RND(DT))
100    D%=(0.25+RND(1))*AV%
110    X%=X%+D%*COS(A):Y%=Y%+D%*SIN(A)
120    DRAW X%,Y%
130    UNTIL FALSE
140 END
```

direction. In Program 5.3, after initializations to line 50, the average angular increment and segment of the circle are computed in line 60 while in line 70 a move is made to the start of the walk at the base of the circle. The REPEAT–UNTIL loop between 80 and 130 generates the circular motion. The angular increment is fixed randomly in line 90, the length of this increment in line 100 and the coordinates of the next point in line 110. In line 120, the segment is drawn. Running the program generates a continuous circular form which after about one minute resembles a ball of wool whose centre is easy to approximate. The program can easily be modified to produce a spiral by reducing or increasing the distance travelled $D\%$ in line 100 systematically as the walk proceeds. In fact, this type of relative motion is the basis of the educational language LOGO which has been developed to enable a variety of problems to be modelled in relative terms (Abelson and DiSessa, 1980).

A model of a circular random walk in which the circular geometry is entirely predetermined involves random movement to fixed points on the circumference or within the limits of the circle itself. The circle is defined by a series of coordinates which represent the order of points on its circumference and all motion is then computed in relation to these positions. Thus the resolution of the circular form can be increased by increasing the number of points up to the resolution of the screen itself. The first program provides a structure for the subsequent circular walks in this section and in this case, the circle is defined by 40 equally spaced points on its circumference which are selected and coloured randomly. The program itself yields a pattern of random 'lighting' which is reminiscent of twinkling stars in the night sky, or perhaps a distant Ferris wheel. It provides a beautiful example of randomness under constraint in that the geometry is entirely regular and determined but the 'signalling' of the form is entirely random, hence stochastic.

This program is listed in Program 5.4 which provides the structure for subsequent variants. The points of the circle are stored in coordinate arrays $X\%(40)$ and $Y\%(40)$ defined in line 30. Angular increments, radius and

Program 5.4   Random walk on a circle

```
10 REM Random Walk on a Circle
20 MODE2
30 DIM X%(40),Y%(40)
40 VDU23,1,0;0;0;0;
50 VDU29,640;512;
60 N%=40:DT=2*PI/N%:R%=300
70 C=SIN(DT):S=COS(DT):X=R%:Y=0
80 FOR I%=0 TO N%
90    T=X*C-Y*S:Y=Y*C+X*S:X=T
100   X%(I%)=X:Y%(I%)=Y:NEXT I%
110 MOVE 0,R%:MOVE R%,0
120 REPEAT
130   I%=RND(N%):GCOLO,RND(7)
140   PLOT69,X%(I%),Y%(I%)
150   UNTIL FALSE
160 END
```

trigonometric functions, and start coordinates are defined in lines 60 and 70, while the FOR–NEXT loop between lines 80 and 100 computes the coordinates of the circle's circumference using the recursive formulation given by equations (2.15) and (2.16) in Chapter 2. The essence of the program lies between the REPEAT–UNTIL loop from lines 120 to 150 where each point and its colour are selected randomly in line 130, and 'lit' using PLOT69, in line 140. Using other graphics primitives instead of PLOT69, in line 140 gives rise to a variety of forms but with the same random structure. For example, use of the DRAW command or the PLOT21, function fills the circle with multicoloured lines, solid or dotted, while the use of PLOT85, fills the circle with randomly positioned solid triangles. In fact in Program 5.4, two more commands are made before the random process begins to enable commands such as PLOT85, to be used, although for several graphics primitives only one such initial command is required. A typical form from this last variant of Program 5.4 is shown in Fig. 5.2(a). The real attraction of these walks as art forms however lies in the random generation process itself which can provide fascinating visual sequences although the stroboscopic effect can sometimes be disturbing.

Finally, let us imagine that the points defining the circumference of the circle mark a circular graphics window within which plotting is to take place. The example shown here will involve plotting dots randomly positioned within the circle but the technique of ensuring that the plotting takes place *within* the circle is considerably more general in its import. It is a mathematical fact that for any line connecting one point on the circumference to any other, the line lies entirely within the circle. The circle is said to have the property of convexity and a straight line connecting circumferential points is one test of this convexity. Let us take any two such points i and j defined by coordinate pairs (X_i, Y_i) and (X_j, Y_j). Then any point k lying on the straight line connecting

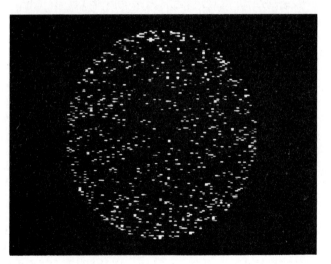

Fig. 5.2   Circular random walks

these two points is defined by the coordinates

$$\left.\begin{array}{l} X_k = \alpha X_i + (1-\alpha)X_j \\ Y_k = \alpha Y_i + (1-\alpha)Y_j \end{array}\right\} \tag{5.1}$$

where $0 \leqslant \alpha \leqslant 1$. When $\alpha = 0$, the point (X_k, Y_k) is (X_j, Y_j) while when $\alpha = 1$, the point is (X_i, Y_i).

To fill a circular window with randomly positioned dots, it suffices to select i

and *j* randomly from the set of circumferential points and then to select α randomly within the 0–1 range, thus determining the point by equations (5.1). In Program 5.4, lines 130 and 140 should be replaced by

```
130 I%=RND(N%):J%=RND(N%):Z=RND(1):GCOL0,RND(7)
140 PLOT69,Z*X%(I%)+(1−Z)*X%(J%),Z*Y%(I%)+(1−Z)*Y%(J%)
```

Note that the function RND(1) returns a real value between 0 and 1 in contrast to RND(N%) where N% > 1 returns an integral value between 1 and N%. This modification to Program 5.4 will fill the circle within five minutes and it is then clear from Fig. 5.2(b) that the program could be modified to provide a suitable model for forming new shades of colour based on random mixing. If the program is to be adapted in this way, some stopping rule must be invoked which recognizes that a steady state distribution has been approached. In fact this could be done empirically, after the program has run for a prespecified time for example. A rigorous analysis of the random walks in this and the previous section is of course possible and would aid the definition of stopping rules. Such analysis which uses Markov chain theory is beyond the scope of this book but it is explored in most books on elementary probability theory.

5.3 RANDOM SIMULATIONS: CITY SYSTEMS AND RIVER SYSTEMS

The random walks introduced so far represent spontaneous motion in that structure is automatically reproduced once the process has begun. Yet strictly speaking, automata are more than this in that such systems usually represent mechanisms with more complex, concealed motive power. The cell-space models of an earlier section represented the simplest examples of such automata, and it is now appropriate to elaborate their complexity by developing much more realistic models of cellular automata based on known behaviours. Our first example combines the simple cell-space model of the rectangular walk with the circular constraints of the previous section and in so doing, leads to a spatial simulation of the evolution of a city system.

Activity or land use types in cities are quite systematically distributed and are usually ordered with respect to their distance from the city centre relative to their economic profitability. For example, commercial uses usually occupy space at the centre, industrial uses mainly locate in the inner city (at least in the case of cities of the industrial era), open space such as parks characterize inner city land uses developed in the late Victorian era, and the outer city is composed mainly of the residential suburbs. Here we will simulate the spatial location of three land uses – commercial/industrial, public open space and residential – whose respective locational foci are the core, the inner city and the suburbs.

If you examine a cross-section of these three land uses in a typical city from the centre to the outer suburbs, the probability of finding any site chosen at random as being occupied by the three land uses in question, is given by the profiles in Fig. 5.3. Rings marking the inner and outer limits of the land uses in question – the so-called Von Thunen rings (see Haggett, Cliff and Frey, 1977) – are also shown in Fig. 5.3. This profile and its abstracted ring plan are typical of most large cities, although their form here is much simplified. From the profiles which schematically give the probability of location at any distance from the centre, it is possible to hypothesize computable relationships. Defining the commercial/industrial, open space and residential land uses by the index $l = 1, 2, 3$ respectively, and the particular site in question by its distance D_i from the city centre, the probability of locating land use l at i is defined as p_i^l. If the distance from the centre where the land use l is most probable is Z^l and the absolute distance from the most probable location over which the land use in question occurs R^l, the probability of locating l at i is given by

$$p_i^l = 1 - \{|D_i - Z^l|/R^l\}. \tag{5.2}$$

The term $|D_i - Z^l|$ measures the absolute distance from the location in question i to the most probable location of l. When this distance is 0, that is when the location is at its most probable, $p_i^l = 1$. When the distance is equal to the range R^l, that is when the location in question is at the outer range of the location of l, the probability $p_i^l = 0$. If the distance is beyond (greater than) this range, equation (5.2) gives $p_i^l < 0$ and the program is so organized to ensure that p_i^l is effectively zero. Lastly, the program is structured to ensure that land use 1 (commercial/industrial) is considered two out of ten times, land use 2 (open space) three times in ten and residential land use 3, five times in ten; thus reflecting the frequency of occurrence of these activities in a typical city.

Program 5.5 provides an algorithm which implements these ideas. Line 30 defines arrays $Z\%(3)$ and $R\%(3)$ for the most probable distance and range for each of three land uses as defined in equation (5.2). Line 60 positions the centre (origin) of the city at the centre of the screen while line 70 defines its maximum radius and the maximum dimension of a typical site in the city. Lines 80 and 90 set up the distance and range data for each of the three land uses. The essence of the city simulation is contained in the REPEAT–UNTIL loop bounded by lines 100 and 190. Each pass through this loop chooses a location within the city limits, randomly computes the type of land use to be considered, computes its probability of occurrence, determines the size of site and then checks to see if it meets the requirement for existence. If so, the site is plotted and another site is then considered. Location is fixed in lines 110 and 120 through angular variation, distance and its conversion to coordinates. The type of land use is randomly determined according to its frequency of occurrence in the city in lines 120, 130 and 140. Its probability of occurrence at that location is computed using equation (5.2) in line 150 and its size randomly determined in lines 160 and 170. In line 180, if the random number chosen is less than its probability number, the site passes the final test for

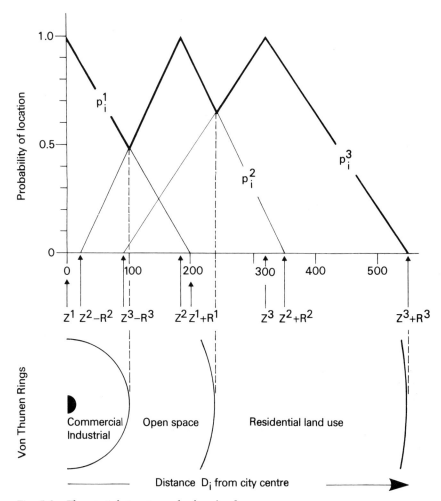

Fig. 5.3 The spatial structure of urban land use

existence and is plotted as a graphics window. This is done in PROCPLOT defined between lines 220 and 250.

    After running the program for about ten minutes, a reasonably complete looking city has evolved where the spatial organization mirrored by the colour of sites (blue for $l = 1$, green $l = 2$ and red $l = 3$) has clearly been determined as a function of distance from the city centre. No stopping rule is embodied in the algorithm and if the program is run for several hours a steady state based largely on the distance, not frequency, profiles emerges. A typical simulation is

Program 5.5   City simulation

```
10 REM City Simulation
20 MODE1
30 DIM Z%(3),R%(3)
40 VDU23,1,0;0;0;0;
50 VDU19,1,4;0;19,2,2;0;19,3,1;0;
60 VDU29,640;512;
70 RS%=400:S%=12
80 Z%(1)=0:Z%(2)=185:Z%(3)=320
90 R%(1)=200:R%(2)=165:R%(3)=230
100 REPEAT
110    A=RAD(RND(360)):D%=RND(RS%)
120    K%=RND(10):X%=D%*COS(A):Y%=D%*SIN(A)
130    IF K%<=2 THEN L%=1 ELSE L%=2
140    IF K%>5 THEN L%=3
150    ZZ=(ABS(D%-Z%(L%)))/R%(L%):P%=100*(1-ZZ)
160    S1%=RND(S%):S2%=RND(S%)
170    S3%=RND(S%):S4%=RND(S%)
180    IF RND(100)<P% THEN PROCPLOT
190    UNTIL FALSE
200 END
210 :
220 DEFPROCPLOT
230 VDU24,X%-S1%;Y%-S2%;X%+S3%;Y%+S4%;
240 GCOL0,128+L%:CLG
250 ENDPROC
```

shown in Plate 11. In fact, as in several of the previously specified circular random walks, this program provides an excellent model for shading and mixing colours. Consider the profiles in Fig. 5.3 to be perfectly symmetrical and evenly spaced, the frequencies of the occurrence of uses to be identical, and the graphics window to be replaced with the PLOT69, command. The colours used to plot different uses should be ordered as white, light blue, dark blue or some such gradation, and if this is done, the program will produce a circular design in which blue gradually changes to white at its centre. This is a straightforward modification of Program 5.5 and is left as an exercise for the reader. However, as a hint in achieving the required effect, colours in line 50, limits in lines 80 and 90, the range of $K\%$ and its spacing in lines 120, 130 and 140, and the plotting in line 230 should be altered.

Random walks have been quite widely used to simulate physical systems which exhibit direction such as river and road networks (Haggett and Chorley, 1969). Here we will develop a simulation of a river system whose characteristic is that each adjacent small area of the system forms a drainage basin (or several such basins) each area draining into another, the whole resembling a set of tree structures based on dichotomous branching as displayed in Chapter 4. However the way such systems are constructed is quite different from the earlier tree forms which were 'grown' from the trunk up. Here the morphology results from starting with the branch ends and connecting or draining according to given rules of direction. The starting point, its position and the order in which drainage areas are considered are thus critical to the resulting form.

As this simulation is one of the most complex in this book, it is worth beginning by outlining the rules which govern the simulation before examining the computer program. In essence, the system of areas to be drained (the drainage basins) is the screen which is divided up into $n \times m$ small areas in the x-y directions respectively, each of which is required to be drained. Each area can drain in any of the four directions, north, south, east or west but the actual direction although chosen randomly, is constrained by several rules. The predominant drainage direction is assumed to be from north to south, and from west to east. This is achieved by starting the construction with the cell at the top left of the screen, moving horizontally and then vertically down to finish at the bottom right. Thus the neighbours to the north and west of each cell have already been drained at any point in the simulation and thus constrain the choice of directions. According to this logic, the longest rivers will run from the north-west of the screen to the south-east.

Each time a cell is examined, it is subject to the following rules:

(1) The cell is abandoned and the next considered, if it has already been linked into the drainage system by a prior construction.
(2) A virgin cell is drained by a random choice over any of the four directions, north, south, east or west.
(3) The out-direction of drainage cannot be the same as the in-direction.
(4) If more than 30 attempts at a random choice of the out-direction have failed, the cell is abandoned and the next considered.
(5) If the new cell into which the old cell is drained, has already been drained, a test is carried out to see if this cell is part of the present river system being constructed or part of a previously constructed system. If part of the present system, it represents a cycle in the system which is illegal and this necessitates a new choice. If it is a previously constructed system, the present river system is deemed to be a tributary of the older one.
(6) The usual limits on direction imposed by the screen boundary are observed.

A flow chart of this process is illustrated in Fig 5.4, and the program itself is listed as Program 5.6. The program operates in MODE1 and draws a blue river system on the black background. In line 30, the arrays $X\%(200)$ and $Y\%(200)$ contain enough storage for the coordinates of the links in the river system under construction which are necessary to implement the test which rejects the possibility of cycling in the network. Lines 50 and 60 set up the cell sizes and limits on the screen. The essence of the simulation is contained in the two nested FOR–NEXT loops between lines 70 and 80, and line 270 which control the order in which cells of the system are considered, from top-left to bottom-

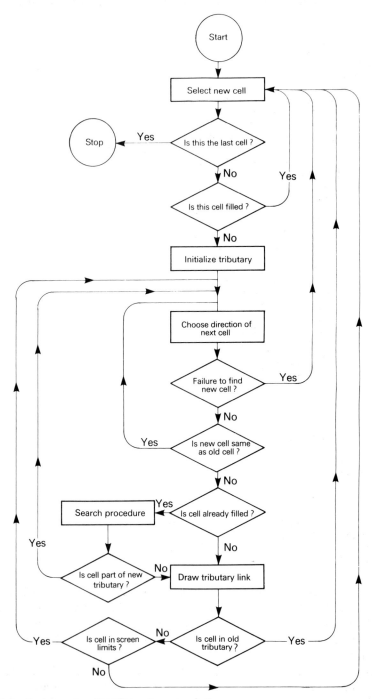

Fig. 5.4 Decision structure for a river simulation

Program 5.6   River simulation

```
10 REM River Simulation
20 MODE1
30 DIM X%(200),Y%(200)
40 VDU19,1,4;0;:VDU23,1,0;0;0;0;
50 COL1%=1:GCOL0,COL1%:YS%=30:XS%=30
60 Y1%=-1:Y2%=1024:X1%=-1:X2%=1280
70 FOR I%=Y2% TO Y1% STEP -YS%
80    FOR J%=X1% TO X2% STEP XS%
90       N%=0:IP%=-10:JP%=-10:IY%=I%:JX%=J%:MOVE JX%,IY%
100      IF POINT(J%,I%)=COL1% THEN GOTO 270
110      KD%=0:X%(N%)=JX%:Y%(N%)=IY%
120      KD%=KD%+1:K%=RND(4):KP%=-1
130      IF K%=1 THEN XA%=XS%:YA%=0
140      IF K%=2 THEN XA%=0:YA%=-YS%
150      IF K%=3 THEN XA%=-XS%:YA%=0
160      IF K%=4 THEN XA%=0:YA%=YS%
170      IYY%=IY%+YA%:JXX%=JX%+XA%
180      IF KD%>30 THEN GOTO 270
190      IF IYY%=IP% AND JXX%=JP% THEN GOTO 120
200      IF POINT(JXX%,IYY%)=COL1% THEN PROCSEARCH
210      IF KP%=0 THEN GOTO 120
220      IP%=IY%:JP%=JX%:IY%=IYY%:JX%=JXX%
230      PROCDRAW
240      IF KP%=1 THEN GOTO 270
250      IF JX%<0 OR JX%>1279 OR IY%<0 OR IY%>1023 THEN GOTO 270
260      N%=N%+1:GOTO 110
270      NEXT J%:NEXT I%
280 AA=GET:MODE7
290 END
300 :
310 DEFPROCSEARCH
320 KP%=1
330 FOR L%=0 TO N%
340    IF X%(L%)=JXX% AND Y%(L%)=IYY% THEN KP%=0
350    NEXT L%
360 ENDPROC
370 :
380 DEFPROCDRAW
390 Z=N%*0.0
400 IF JP%=JX% THEN ZX=Z:ZY=0 ELSE ZX=0:ZY=Z
410 MOVE JP%-ZX,IP%-ZY:MOVE JP%+ZX,IP%+ZY
420 PLOT85,JX%-ZX,IY%-ZY:PLOT85,JX%+ZX,IY%+ZY
430 ENDPROC
```

right. In line 90, a move is made to the appropriate cell, and if it is already drained, it is abandoned in line 100 where the POINT($X\%,Y\%$) command is used to see whether it has already been coloured blue. Note how this hardware type test is used to enable a search over all previously considered cells to be circumvented.

Line 110 sets up the start position of a new river system and between lines 120 and 170 a random choice of out-direction and its coordinate position is made. If more than 30 such choices have been made, this cell is abandoned in line 180. If the out-direction is the same as the in-direction, line 190 enables a new choice to be made. If these tests are passed, then the new cell to which the old is to be drained is examined in line 200 and using the POINT command, if it is already drained, a procedure to see whether or not the cell is part of the current river system is initiated. This procedure PROCSEARCH is defined in lines 310 to 360 and simply enables a counter to be set indicating the status of the new cell. Line 210 enables a new choice to be made if this test reveals a cycle; if not, the link is drawn by a call to PROCDRAW, itself defined in lines 380 to 430. This procedure enables the link in question to be drawn in proportion to the number of links ('amount of water') in the current system. In fact in line 390, this possibility is not used in this listing: it will be elaborated below. Finally, once the link is drawn, the system is abandoned if the new cell is part of an old river system (line 240) or if the cell is outside screen limits (line 250). If not, a new link in the current system is considered (line 260), and so on. All cells on the screen are ultimately examined using these rules.

As programmed, the typical length of river is rather short and the drainage pattern is only loosely constrained in direction. The output is more like the drainage patterns you would find on a large flattish plain: rivers going nowhere in particular. However if the north direction given in line 160 is deleted (thus implying a steeply inclined north to south plain) and if the random choice of direction in line 120 is set as $K\% = RND(3)$ then a much more characteristic set of river systems emerges, with two or three long rivers draining north to south across the entire screen. Making these changes and also setting the thickness of the river link in proportion to discharge (number of links so far) by changing line 390 to 390 $Z = N\%*0.17$, results in the morphology shown in Fig. 5.5 which appears a reasonably realistic structure.

There are a number of points to note. Notice how previous decisions in the order of cell consideration increasingly constrain the randomness of choice as the simulation proceeds, until no choice remains when the last cell is considered. This is a classic example of reducing the degrees of freedom of the system as the simulation evolves. Also note how the use of the POINT command reduces both the need for search over and the need for storage of the whole system constructed so far. Finally, the manner of construction here is quite different from the space-filling curves we are about to see and the way trees were constructed in Chapter 4. Nevertheless, river systems have a strong relationship to fractal geometry in that on examining their form in the small, this is similar to that in the large. It is to such considerations that we will now turn.

5.4   FRACTAL GEOMETRY: THE STUDY OF SELF-SIMILAR, IRREGULAR FORM

Randomness is a form of irregularity which has no intrinsic structure, for the

Fig. 5.5   A simulated river morphology

structures which emerge from the simulations already developed in this chapter reflect external constraints. Although quite elaborate and highly distinct designs can be generated by blending randomness with constraint, there is another deeper form of irregularity which does have intrinsic structure. This is the type of irregularity in an object which has the same form at different levels of detail, at different scales, and in such phenomena, the recurrence of this type of similarity at different scales imposes its own constraints on form. We have already mentioned typical objects such as coastlines, rock formations and trees. These and many other natural forms have this property best summarized by Mandelbrot (1982): "When each piece of the shape is geometrically similar to the whole, both the shape and the cascade that generates it are called *self-similar*".

Such shapes engender real problems in their formal study. For example in examining coastlines, Mandelbrot (1967) observed that their length seemed to depend on the yardstick used to measure them; that is, their length varied with scale. As scale became finer, more and more detailed features, bays and promontories, nooks and crannies, emerged which increased their length. Mandelbrot was thus led to conclude that to all intents and purposes, their length might be considered "infinite, or rather, undefinable". Secondly, such curves exhibit an irregularity which is not smooth, hence cannot be studied using the calculus. Such curves though are continuous but non-rectifiable (that is, crudely speaking, cannot be differentiated). Thirdly, such irregularities which form the basis of curves of 'infinite' length lead to patterns which seem to span space. But curves are one-dimensional and space is two. How can it thus be both one- and two-dimensional? In Program 5.1, the random walk or Brownian motion manifests all the properties of this kind of phenomenon which poses such basic mathematical conundrums.

These types of object which are not bound by scale but are referred to as scaling (Mandelbrot, 1981) thus seem to lie between dimensions. Brownian motion in the plane and coastlines seem to be more than one-dimensional but not quite two. They appear to be of fractional or non-integral dimension which is defined when their actual dimension seems different from their topological dimension. Such objects are called *fractals* by Mandelbrot (1982) (from the Latin *fractus* meaning irregular) and their study has initiated a new branch of mathematics of major relevance to computer graphics called fractal geometry (Batty, 1985).

Although it is not possible to derive the concept of fractal dimension with any degree of rigour here, it is worth saying something about the subject and providing an intuitive justification for the idea of non-integral (fractional) dimension. In the geometry of Euclid, we define a line by its length, a plane by its area, a cube by its volume and so on. We associate dimension 1 with lines, 2 with planes, 3 with cubes and we derive masses of higher dimension by taking the basic element of length in 1 dimension and raising it to its dimensional constant as a power. Thus a line of length L is of length L^1, a plane defined by lengths L in both its dimensions is of area L^2, a cube of lengths L in each of its 3 dimensions has a volume of L^3 and so on. These lengths, areas or volumes are independent of the measure used which is clearly related to the regularity of the geometry. The basic idea of the fractal dimension is now easy to state. A fractal is a shape whose dimensional mass is given by L^D where D is the fractal or fractional dimension which is non-integral. It is this mass which is invariant under measurement by different yardsticks.

The question then emerges as to how can we calculate the fractal dimension if we are considering a shape like a coastline which is manifestly self-similar. First of all, consider a line of length $L = 1$, the unit length, which can be divided into N equal parts. We can generate each of these N parts by applying a ratio $1/n$ to the line L where n is the number of elements into which the line is divided. Then we have the trivial relationship that the length of the line is given by $L^1 = N(L/n)^1 = 1$ and clearly in this case $N = n$. However for a plane defined by length L in each of its two dimensions, its volume L^2 is also 1. Assume the square is divided up in N subsquares each with sides of L/n, then the area of the plane is $N(L/n)^2 = 1$. Now let us define the ratio L/n as $r(n)$ and thus the area relationship becomes

$$Nr(n)^2 = 1. \tag{5.3}$$

Equation (5.3) implies the following: if you divide a square into N subsquares, and apply the area of each subsquare given by $r(n)^2$ to this, the result will be the area. The same relationship exists in any dimension where N is number of parts the mass is divided into and the power reflects the dimensional constant. Now by analogy to equation (5.3), the relationship for a fractal is given by

$$Nr(n)^D = 1 \tag{5.4}$$

where D is the fractal dimension. Equation (5.4) can be first manipulated to solve for D as

$$D = -\log N/\log r(n) = \log N/\log n \tag{5.5}$$

where $r(n) = 1/n$. Other relations which may be useful are

$$r(n) = N^{-1/D} \quad \text{and} \quad N = r(n)^{-D}.$$

Clearly from equation (5.5), it is necessary to know the partitioning process at different scales in terms of N and $r(n)$ to compute the fractal dimension.

5.5 NON-RANDOM FRACTALS: SPACE-FILLING CURVES

The easiest way to illustrate these ideas is by example, and we will first build up a simple model of a coastline involving non-random fractals. To generate a fractal shape, we begin with an *initiator* which is the form of the shape at the first scale and then generate a new shape at the next scale down using a *generator*. We can cascade down the scales, in hierarchical fashion, by applying the generator recursively to each detail of the previously generated shape, thus constructing the fractal to any scale desired. Now our first fractal is an approximation to the coastline. The initiator is a straight line and the generator is based on dividing the line into three parts but perturbing its regularity over the centre part by constructing two parts – two lines of the same length as the centre part, thus forming an equilateral triangle at the centre. Thus the new perturbed line is 4/3 times the length of the first straight line, the initiator. We can apply the generator recursively to each of the four new parts of the line and so on cascading down the scales but increasing the length of the overall line by 4/3 each time. In this way, the curve tends to infinite length but the effect of this is soon lost to the naked eye when viewed from a fixed scale.

The initiator, generator and cascade are shown in Fig. 5.6(a) where it is clear that $N = 4$, the number of parts created by the subdivision, and the ratio $r(n) = 1/3$. From equation (5.5), the dimension $D = \log 4/\log 3 \sim 1.2618$. In fact, measurements of the fractal dimension of real coastlines give values of the

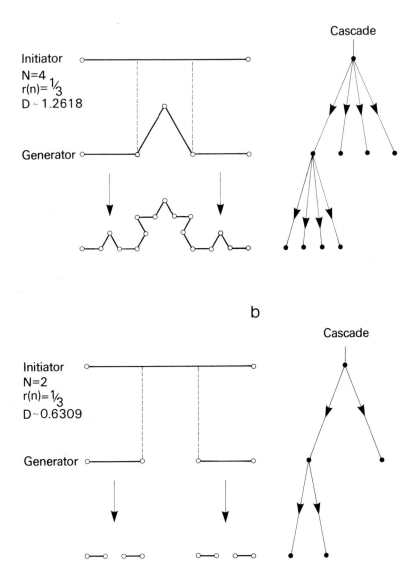

Fig. 5.6 Initiators, generators and cascades

same order (Mandelbrot, 1967) and clearly such a shape has a dimension greater than 1 but nearer to 1 than to 2. Fractals with dimensions less than 1 can also be constructed. Examine Fig. 5.6(b) where the initiator is the same as in (a) but the generator omits the central displacement, subdividing the initiator into two not four parts. Equation (5.5) yields a dimension of $D = \log 2/\log 3 \sim 0.6309$, and the cascade applied to this process yields lines which in total sum to 2/3 the length of the lines at the previous scale. Mandelbrot (1982) refers to this process of cascading in which holes or 'tremas' are introduced into the shape as 'curdling' and the resultant shapes he calls 'Cantor Dusts'. There are strong affinities here to the generation of the branching trees presented in Chapter 4 which are fractals of this variety.

Perhaps the most intriguing example of fractals is the class of space-filling curves which like any curve are of topological dimension 1, but are continuous and span or fill two-dimensional space. A particular example of such a curve is due to Peano and the form of the initiator, its generator and the resulting cascade are shown in Fig. 5.7. Essentially the initiator is the plane, in this case a square which is divided into $3 \times 3 = 9$ subsquares. The generator is a non-rectifiable curve which spans the larger square by twisting its way across using the smaller squares in the manner shown in Fig. 5.7(b). The corners of the spanning curve have been cut off to indicate the direction and continuity of the span. The cascade process involved uses the same spanning pattern across each of the subsquares and so on down the hierarchy. It is intuitively obvious that the cascade generates a continuous curve which 'fills' the space. Equation (5.5) gives a fractal dimension of $D = \log 9/\log 3 = 2$ which justifies the assertion of space-filling.

A computer program to draw the Peano curve to any level of recursion is listed in Program 5.7. This is based on an extremely straightforward structure which mirrors the cascade illustrated in Fig. 5.7(c). The essence of the program is the procedure PROCSPACE whose arguments are the size of square, its depth of recursion, its angular position in the bigger picture, and its orientation relative to its immediate successor squares in the cascade. PROCSPACE calls itself nine times to effect the cascade, and when the recursion is stopped at the lowest level required, a call to PROCDRAW effects the plotting. The program assumes an original square tipped on one edge as in Fig. 5.7. The size of one of its edges is input in line 30, a factor reflecting its edge cutoff, called a distortion factor is required in line 40, and the user inputs the depth of recursion required in line 50. Typical input values might be 800 units for the square size, 0.3 for the distortion factor and any level of recursion up to about four or five above which the level of screen resolution dominates.

Assignments are made in lines 60 to 80 and colours and standard angles fixed in lines 90 and 100. A move is made to the bottom corner of the square and a call to PROCSPACE initiates the recursion in line 110. This procedure is defined in lines 150 to 260. Line 160 invokes the stopping rule at the lowest

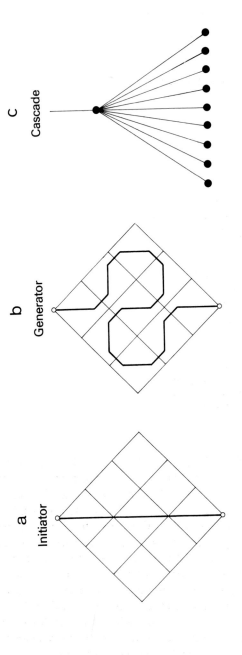

a
Initiator

b
Generator

c
Cascade

$N=9:r(n)=1/3:D=2$

Fig. 5.7 Initiator, generator and cascade for the Peano space-filling curve

Program 5.7 The Peano space-filling curve

```
 10 REM The Peano Space-Filling Curve
 20 CLS
 30 INPUT TAB(11)"SIZE OF EDGE = ",S
 40 INPUT TAB(10)"DISTORTION FACTOR = ",DS
 50 INPUT TAB(9)"DEPTH OF RECURSION = ",D%
 60 MODE1
 70 VDU23,1,0;0;0;0;
 80 VDU29,640;25;
 90 GCOL0,1:P=PI/2:X=0:Y=0
100 DT=1-DS:TH=P/2:MOVE X,Y
110 PROCSPACE(S,D%,P,1)
120 AA=GET:MODE7
130 END
140 :
150 DEFPROCSPACE(S,D%,A,Z%)
160 IF D%=0 THEN PROCDRAW(A,Z%):ENDPROC
170 PROCSPACE(S/3,D%-1,A,1)
180 PROCSPACE(S/3,D%-1,A+P,-1)
190 PROCSPACE(S/3,D%-1,A,-1)
200 PROCSPACE(S/3,D%-1,A-P,-1)
210 PROCSPACE(S/3,D%-1,A-2*P,1)
220 PROCSPACE(S/3,D%-1,A-P,1)
230 PROCSPACE(S/3,D%-1,A,1)
240 PROCSPACE(S/3,D%-1,A+P,-1)
250 PROCSPACE(S/3,D%-1,A,Z%)
260 ENDPROC
270 :
280 DEFPROCDRAW(A,Z%)
290 X1=S*COS(A):Y1=S*SIN(A)
300 X2=X+DT*X1:Y2=Y+DT*Y1:AA=A+Z%*TH
310 DRAW X2,Y2:ZZ=DS*SQR(2)*S
320 DRAW X2+ZZ*COS(AA),Y2+ZZ*SIN(AA)
330 X=X+X1:Y=Y+Y1
340 ENDPROC
```

level with a call to PROCDRAW and an ENDPROC. In fact, the structure of this procedure is a perfect illustration of fractal structure in that nine calls to itself are made in lines 170 to 250 ($N=9$) and in each call the similarity ratio $r(n) = 1/3$ is applied to the side of the square $S\%$ to reduce its size to $S\%/3$. The second argument in each procedure call reduces the level of recursion, the third positions the starting angle of the subsquare, and the final argument is an orientation parameter, a switch which enables a change in plotting direction to occur. This last parameter is crucial for it enables the subsquares to be 'glued' to each other in the proper way; note that in the last call in line 250, this parameter must be the same as that which is passed in the higher level procedure call. Finally, the procedure PROCDRAW in lines 280 to 340 computes the span of the subsquare in terms of these sets of coordinates which are used to draw the relevant portions of the Peano curve.

The Peano curve at recursive level 3 is illustrated in Fig. 5.8(a). If you experiment by running the program with different depth levels, you soon see

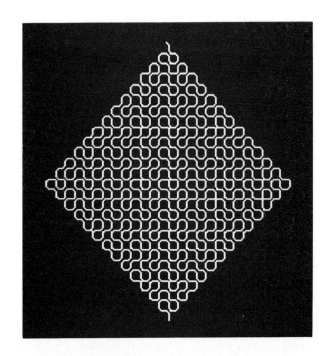

Fig. 5.8 Peano-type curves

how it fills the plane. Moreover the regularity and symmetry of the space-filling design suggests that more elaborate variations in the detailed shape of the spanning curve could lead to rather intriguing pictures. For example, if you leave out line 320, Fig. 5.8(b) results at depth 3 and this is suggestive of the art of Maurits Escher. In this way, the program can be interpreted as a way of filling the plane, of forming regular tessellations of standard shapes. In fact Escher's own pictures all entitled 'Study of the Regular Division of the Plane . . .', each with a different object (with Reptiles, with Birds, with Horsemen, and so on) can be reproduced by modifying the drawing commands in PROCDRAW but by keeping the same overall program structure. There is a whole new world of computer graphics to explore here and many immediate exercises suggest themselves. Other space-filling curves such as those suggested by David Hilbert and Wraclaw Sierpinski (see Abelson and DiSessa, 1980) follow the same structure as the program presented here. Other programs have been published (Cownie, 1982; McGregor and Watt, 1984) and readers are recommended to follow these up.

5.6 KOCH RECURSION

The process of constructing continuous, non-rectifiable curves with fractal dimensions between 1 and 2 such as the coastline curve in Fig. 5.6(a) involves a process of recursion as the cascade structure implies. This process and its algorithm was first presented by Helge von Koch in 1904 in terms of the initiator and generator shown in Fig. 5.6(a) and henceforth, it will be referred to as Koch recursion; that is, the same recursive process can be used to generate a variety of curves different from Koch's original curve. This section will elaborate the ways in which this process can be applied and each curve generated will be specified in terms of its initiator, generator, cascade and geometric form which is the result of running the associated program.

To introduce the standard program for Koch recursion, we will use the original Koch or 'snowflake' curve which is in fact based on the components shown in Fig. 5.6(a). In this first case, the initiator is an equilateral triangle and the generator (which does itself incorporate a smaller similar triangle) is applied recursively to each of the sides of the previous triangle. The ultimate form is a snowflake-like structure. The essence of our computer program involves a program segment or procedure PROCGEN which when applied to any straight line effects the displacement – the irregularity – consistent with the given level of recursion. The parameters of this procedure are the end points of the line specified by coordinates (x_i, y_i) and (x_j, y_j) and the level of recursion. The displacement at any level is specified by scaling constants which are applicable to any scale. Three such constants are required by the program: a midpoint ratio R, a width ratio W and a height ratio H and these are applied in the following way.

First the length of the line is computed as $L = \{(x_i - x_j)^2 + (y_i - y_j)^2\}^{\frac{1}{2}}$. The midpoint of the line is taken as $R*L$, the displacement widths either side of this point as $(R - W)*L$ and $(R + W)*L$, and the height of the perturbation above $R*L$ as $H*L$. Clearly $0 \leqslant R, W, H \leqslant 1$. New coordinates defining the points on the line and above it are computed using these distances measured from the given points (x_i, y_i) and (x_j, y_j). These points are shown in Fig. 5.9 which also demonstrates the basic idea of introducing irregularity through midpoint displacement. The Koch curve is produced from the program listed in Program 5.8. In this listing, there is the standard procedure PROCGEN in lines 1000 to 1120 which is used in this and the next four programs. The arguments of PROCGEN are the endpoints X1%, Y1%, X2%, Y2% of the line being displaced and the depth of recursion D%. The length of the line and its angular slope are computed in lines 1010 and 1020, and lines 1030 to 1050 locate this angle in its appropriate quadrant. Line 1060 computes the appropriate trigonometric functions and right angle displacement which are used in determining the midpoint coordinates (X3%, Y3%) in line 1070, width coordinates (XA%, YA%) and (XB%, YB%) in lines 1080 and 1090, and height coordinates (XC%, YC%) in line 1100. These coordinates define four parts of the displaced line, each part of which is subject to further displacement which is controlled by the call to PROCNODE in line 1110.

The Koch snowflake itself is initiated in the main program, in lines 10 to 190 in Program 5.8. The program requests the user to input the midpoint ratio (line ratio) R, height ratio H, width ratio W, the initial line length and the level of recursion required, in lines 30 to 70. The initiator, in this case a solid triangle, is centred and plotted in lines 110 to 140 and the recursion is begun in lines 150 to 170 where the three calls to PROCGEN are applied to the three

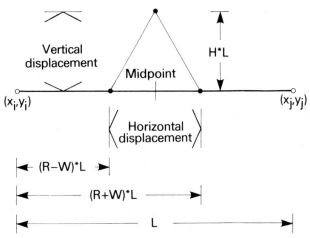

Fig. 5.9   Systematic linear irregularity through midpoint displacement

Program 5.8 The Koch snowflake

```
  10 REM Koch Snowflake
  20 CLS
  30 INPUT TAB(12)"LINE RATIO = ",R
  40 INPUT TAB(11)"HEIGHT RATIO = ",H
  50 INPUT TAB(12)"WIDTH RATIO = ",W
  60 INPUT TAB(12)"LINE LENGTH = ",X%
  70 INPUT TAB(9)"DEPTH OF RECURSION = ",D%
  80 MODE1
  90 VDU23,1,0;0;0;0;
 100 VDU19,0,4;0;19,1,6;0;
 110 GCOL0,1:XZ%=X%*COS(RAD(60)):YZ%=X%*SIN(RAD(60))
 120 X0%=(1279-X%)/2:Y0%=512-(H*X%+YZ%)/2+H*X%
 130 VDU29,X0%;Y0%;:X1%=0:X2%=X%:Y1%=0:Y2%=0
 140 MOVE X1%,Y1%:MOVE X2%,Y2%:PLOT85,XZ%,YZ%
 150 PROCGEN(X1%,Y1%,XZ%,YZ%,D%)
 160 PROCGEN(XZ%,YZ%,X2%,Y2%,D%)
 170 PROCGEN(X2%,Y2%,X1%,Y1%,D%)
 180 AA=GET:MODE7
 190 END
 200 :
 210 DEFPROCNODE(A1%,B1%,AA%,BA%,AB%,BB%,AC%,BC%,A2%,B2%,D%)
 220 MOVE AA%,BA%:MOVE AB%,BB%:PLOT85,AC%,BC%
 230 IF D%=0 THEN ENDPROC
 240 PROCGEN(A1%,B1%,AA%,BA%,D%-1)
 250 PROCGEN(AA%,BA%,AC%,BC%,D%-1)
 260 PROCGEN(AC%,BC%,AB%,BB%,D%-1)
 270 PROCGEN(AB%,BB%,A2%,B2%,D%-1)
 280 ENDPROC
 290 :
1000 DEFPROCGEN(X1%,Y1%,X2%,Y2%,D%)
1010 X=X2%-X1%:Y=Y2%-Y1%
1020 L=SQR(X^2+Y^2):Z=ABS(Y)/L:A=ASN(Z)
1030 IF X<0 AND Y>=0 THEN A=PI-A
1040 IF X<=0 AND Y<0 THEN A=PI+A
1050 IF X>0 AND Y<0 THEN A=2*PI-A
1060 C=COS(A):S=SIN(A):A=A+(PI/2)
1070 X3%=X1%+R*L*C:Y3%=Y1%+R*L*S
1080 XA%=X1%+(R-W)*L*C:YA%=Y1%+(R-W)*L*S
1090 XB%=X1%+(R+W)*L*C:YB%=Y1%+(R+W)*L*S
1100 XC%=X3%+H*L*COS(A):YC%=Y3%+H*L*SIN(A)
1110 PROCNODE(X1%,Y1%,XA%,YA%,XB%,YB%,XC%,YC%,X2%,Y2%,D%)
1120 ENDPROC
```

respective sides of the initial triangle. The procedure PROCNODE in lines 210
to 280 is critical in that it controls the cascade structure, the level of recursion
and the plotting. In this case, line 220 enables the displacement to be plotted as
a triangle, line 230 is the stopping rule, while lines 240 to 270 involve four
calls to PROCGEN which reflect the next level of displacement applied to the
four segments of the currently displaced line.

A typical Koch snowflake curve is shown in Fig. 5.10 at a recursive depth of
$D\% = 3$ and the full recursion to $D\% = 3$ is shown in Plate 12; after that, any
further recursion provides detail below the screen resolution in MODE1. To

Initiator

Generator

Cascade

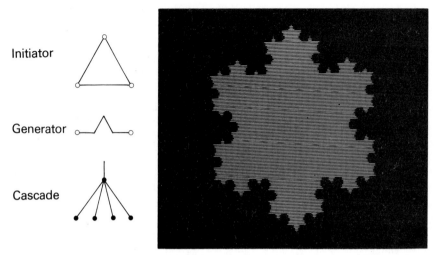

Fig. 5.10   The Koch snowflake curve

generate a perfect snowflake, the original triangle must be equilateral as must each displacement, thus the parameters must be: $R = 0.5$; $W = 0.1666$ which implies the division of the line into three equal parts at $0.3333*L$ and $0.6666*L$; and $H = 0.2866$. A typical length of initiating line (side of the triangle) would be 600 screen units, and different levels of recursion up to $D\% = 4$ should be tried. Different initiators could easily be programmed here (such as squares, hexagons etc.) but it is instructive to explore the effects of varying R, W and H. For example when $W = 0$, the recursion generates 'telegraph poles' on each side of the triangle. When $W = R$, the recursion can be made to generate circular forms although this program will crash due to distances becoming too small to handle. Readers should speculate on and attempt such investigations.

Our first variant on this theme involves the construction of a Koch landscape or a Koch forest. The triangle will no longer be used as initiator; instead, we will revert to a straight (horizontal) line which will be drawn as a slab, thus providing a 'base' for the 'forest'. Here we will just list the changes we need to make to Program 5.8. Lines 110 to 170 of this program should be replaced by the following new lines

```
110 GCOL0,1
120 X0%=(1279−X%)/2
130 VDU29,X0%;300;
140 X1%=0:X2%=X%:Y1%=0:Y2%=0
150 MOVE X1%,Y1%:MOVE X2%,Y2%
160 PLOT85,X1%,−X%*W*2.5:PLOT85,X2%,−X%*W*2.5
170 PROCGEN(X1%,Y1%,X2%,Y2%,D%)
```

which essentially change the form of the initiator and the first call to the generator. This program can be made to generate a forest-like landscape if the following parameters are used: $R = 0.333$; $H = 0.42$; $W = 0.034$; $X\%$ (line length) $= 1200$; and $D\% = 4$. The output is shown in Fig. 5.11 where it is clear that the recursion generates spike-like branches. The design is also *self-avoiding*, that is, the branches do not intersect or overlap which is due to the choice of parameters. This is very much a matter of trial and error but it can be an important matter in generating visually acceptable fractals such as the tree designs already explored in Chapter 4. What the Koch landscape does reinforce is the visual meaning of self-similarity and the importance of recursion in generating detail. There is no way an artist could develop the kind of detail which we see in fractal geometry and this illustrates a recurrent theme in this book: that the mathematical modelling of picture structure is likely to become recognized as the true basis of computer art.

The second variant on the Koch curve involves sweeping around the plane and generating a design in which the Koch forest results as the complement of the two-dimensional sweep. In this case, the initiator is two sides of a triangle whose angle subtended by the sides is about 96°, sufficient to make the triangle a little 'flatter' than right-angled. The generator is based on the same shape as the initiator, applied to each line of the initiator, and applied to its interior. Each time the generator is applied, it is applied to the interior of the previous shape and this results in a flip-flop action whose first stages are illustrated in Fig. 5.12. The recursion clearly succeeds in filling the plane and examination of initiator and generator clearly reveals the fractal dimension to be $D = 2$. The

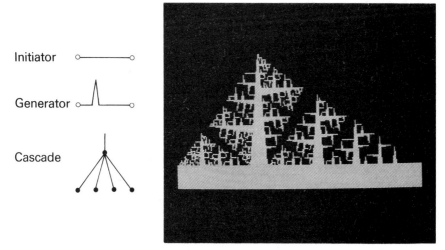

Fig. 5.11 A Koch landscape

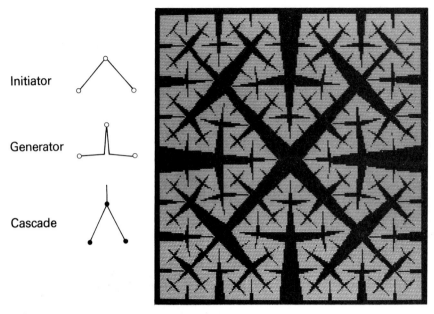

Fig. 5.12   The Peano–Cesaro triangle sweep

design which is constructed here is based on sweeping the plane with four initiators arranged as a square. The generator is called for each of the two sides of the initiator and the cascade is as shown in Fig. 5.12.

The structure of the program is similar to Program 5.8 but the initiators, cascade and plotting are sufficiently different to warrant a separate listing of the main program and PROCNODE which is given as Program 5.9. Note that to run this program, lines 1000 to 1120 (PROCGEN) of Program 5.8 must be added. We have called the resulting design in Fig. 5.12 the Peano–Cesaro Triangle Sweep (after Mandelbrot, 1982). The program needs little comment except to say that the plotting in PROCNODE occurs only once at the lowest level of recursion, and that as previously this procedure clearly illustrates the cascade at all levels below the initiator. To avoid self-intersection as in the fern-like design of Fig. 5.12, the following parameters should be used: $R = 0.5$; $H = 0.45$; $W = 0.5$: $X\% = 800$; and $4 \leqslant D\% \leqslant 7$.

The third variant on the Koch curve is known as the Dragon curve. This involves the same initiator and generator as the Peano–Cesaro Triangle Sweep but one generator is now applied to the exterior, the other to the interior of the initiator in the manner shown in Fig. 5.13. The cascade structure below the first initiating level is the same as in Program 5.9 although the order of the points defining the line segments is different. However, as the program which is listed as Program 5.10 shows, the initiator is not in fact the two-sided

Program 5.9   The Peano–Cesaro triangle sweep

```
10 REM Peano-Cesaro Triangle Sweep
20 CLS
30 INPUT TAB(12)"LINE RATIO = ",R
40 INPUT TAB(11)"HEIGHT RATIO = ",H
50 INPUT TAB(12)"WIDTH RATIO = ",W
60 INPUT TAB(12)"LINE LENGTH = ",X%
70 INPUT TAB(9)"DEPTH OF RECURSION = ",D%
80 MODE1
90 VDU23,1,0;0;0;0;
100 VDU19,0,4;0;19,1,6;0;
110 X0%=(1279-X%)/2:Y0%=(1023-X%)/2
120 GCOL0,1:VDU29,X0%;Y0%;
130 X1%=0:X2%=X%:Y1%=0:Y2%=0
140 PROCGEN(X1%,Y1%,X2%,Y2%,D%)
150 PROCGEN(X2%,Y2%,X2%,Y2%+X%,D%)
160 PROCGEN(X2%,Y2%+X%,X2%-X%,Y2%+X%,D%)
170 PROCGEN(X2%-X%,Y2%+X%,X2%-X%,Y2%,D%)
180 AA=GET:MODE7
190 END
200 :
210 DEFPROCNODE(A1%,B1%,AA%,BA%,AB%,BB%,AC%,BC%,A2%,B2%,D%)
220 IF D%=0 THEN MOVE A1%,B1%:MOVE AC%,BC%:PLOT85,A2%,B2%
230 IF D%=0 THEN ENDPROC
240 :
250 :
260 PROCGEN(AC%,BC%,A1%,B1%,D%-1)
270 PROCGEN(A2%,B2%,AC%,BC%,D%-1)
280 ENDPROC
290 :
```

triangle, but the base of this, the straight line to which the two-sided triangle generator is first applied. The result is of course the same as the cascade shown in Fig. 5.13, which in effect initiates the process from the second level of recursion. Note that in Program 5.10, PROCNODE is the same as in Program 5.9 except that the order of parameters in line 270 is changed. The initiator in the main program is of course different, but as in Program 5.9, PROCGEN in lines 1000 to 1120 of Program 5.8 is also required to generate the Dragon curve. The parameters used to generate the curve shown in Fig. 5.13(a) are: $R = 0.5$; $H = 0.5$; $W = 0.5$; $X\% = 500$; and $D\% \geqslant 6$. The curve is a closed design of finite extent and as the level of recursion increases, the detail becomes greater and the curve is effectively filled in at the level of screen resolution used by MODE1.

Two variants on the Dragon curve itself can be easily developed. The first involves embedding two Dragon curves into one another. Examining the single curve in Fig. 5.13(a), it is quite clear that self-similarity characterizes both the curve and its edges in their entirety. New curves can be 'glued' to existing ones to provide a jig-saw fit; in fact the plane could be tiled, Escher-like, with Dragon curves. Figure 5.13(b) shows how two such Dragons can be

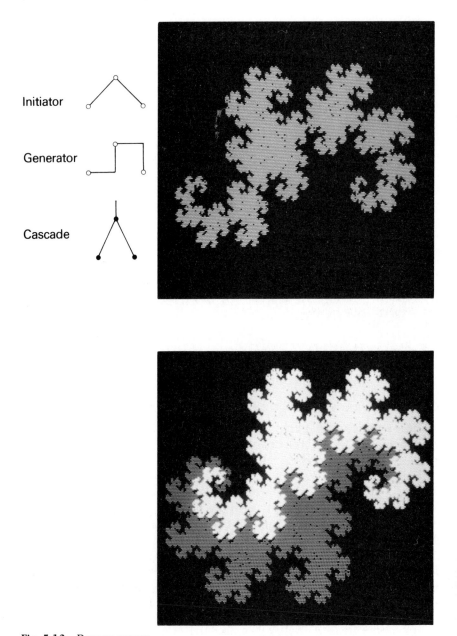

Initiator

Generator

Cascade

Fig. 5.13 Dragon curves

Program 5.10 The dragon curve

```
10 REM Dragon Curve
20 CLS
30 INPUT TAB(12)"LINE RATIO = ",R
40 INPUT TAB(11)"HEIGHT RATIO = ",H
50 INPUT TAB(12)"WIDTH RATIO = ",W
60 INPUT TAB(12)"LINE LENGTH = ",X%
70 INPUT TAB(9)"DEPTH OF RECURSION = ",D%
80 MODE1
90 VDU23,1,0;0;0;0;
100 VDU19,0,4;0;19,1,6;0;
110 X0%=(1279-X%)/2:Y0%=(1023-X%)/2
120 GCOLO,1:VDU29,X0%;Y0%;
130 X1%=0:X2%=X%:Y1%=Y0%:Y2%=Y0%
140 PROCGEN(X1%,Y1%,X2%,Y2%,D%)
150 :
160 :
170 :
180 AA=GET:MODE7
190 END
200 :
210 DEFPROCNODE(A1%,B1%,AA%,BA%,AB%,BB%,AC%,BC%,A2%,B2%,D%)
220 IF D%=0 THEN MOVE A1%,B1%:MOVE AC%,BC%:PLOT85,A2%,B2%
230 IF D%=0 THEN ENDPROC
240 :
250 :
260 PROCGEN(AC%,BC%,A1%,B1%,D%-1)
270 PROCGEN(AC%,BC%,A2%,B2%,D%-1)
280 ENDPROC
290 :
```

fitted together using the following modification to Program 5.10

```
    100  VDU19,1,1;0;19,2,3;0;
    110  X0%=(1279−X%)/2:Y0%=(1023−X%)/2
    120  GCOL0,1:VDU29,X0%;Y0%;
    130  X1%=0:X2%=X%:Y1%=Y0%:Y2%=Y0%:DD%=D%
    140  PROCGEN(X1%,Y1%,X2%,Y2%,D%)
    150  GCOL0,2
    160  X1%=X%:X2%=0:Y1%=X%/2:Y2%=X%/2:D%=DD%
    170  PROCGEN(X1%,Y1%,X2%,Y2%,D%)
```

which involves the addition of a new initiator in lines 150 to 170, and a colour change. The second change simply involves a change in the exterior-interior generator of the Dragon curve to both arms of the generator always being exterior. This requires changing line 260 in Program 5.9 to

    260 PROCGEN(A1%,B1%,AC%,BC%,D%−1)

and the resulting design, its initiator, generator and cascade are shown in Fig. 5.14. This is called a C-curve because the closed shape resembles a large C on its edge, as do its self-similar parts.

Finally in this section, we will introduce a non-random fractal design which

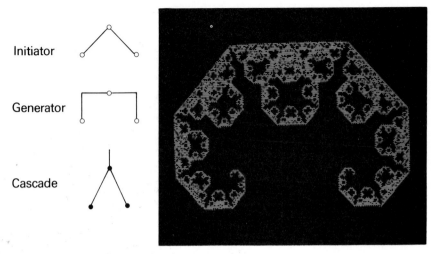

Initiator

Generator

Cascade

Fig. 5.14   The C-curve

is generated using a Koch cascade but using a simpler structure than that contained in Program 5.8. This structure is curious in that at first sight it looks two-dimensional but recursion introduces 'holes' into the initiator and the resulting design is clearly of a fractal dimension between 1 and 2. In fact, the process of cascade is reminiscent of percolation and can be considered as the two-dimensional equivalent to the curdling process introduced earlier to generate a Cantor Dust. Mandelbrot (1982) calls the design a Sierpinski Gasket, after the Polish mathematician of that name; its initiator, generator, cascade and resulting design to recursive depth 4 are shown in Fig. 5.15.

The program to generate the Gasket is listed as Program 5.11. Its structure is similar to those developed earlier in this section: main program to set up the initiator, PROCNODE to control the recursive process and plotting, PROCTRI which has the same function as PROCGEN above in that it computes positional information relating to the level of cascade. Lines 30 and 40 prompt the user to input the length of the side of the triangle which initiates the process, and the depth of recursion. Lines 70 to 120 involve plotting the triangle initiator while PROCTRI in line 130 begins the process of recursive subdivision. The original initiator is a solid triangle but the process of recursion introduces the 'holes' which are themselves triangles symmetrically located at the corners of the higher level triangle. PROCNODE in lines 170 to 230 has a familiar structure: plotting in line 180, stopping in line 190 and three calls to PROCTRI which divide the higher level triangle into three empty, leaving one solid triangle, in lines 200 to 220. PROCTRI itself simply computes the midpoint of the side of the triangle whose positions it is passed, and computes the remaining interior vertex, information which it then passes to PROCNODE in line 290. The design

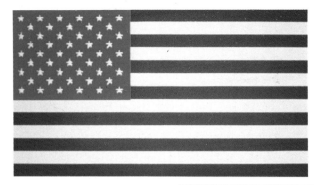

Plate 1   The US national flag

Plate 2   The Welsh flag

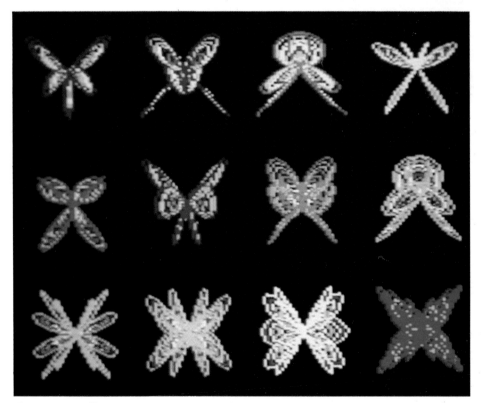

Plate 3   Butterflies

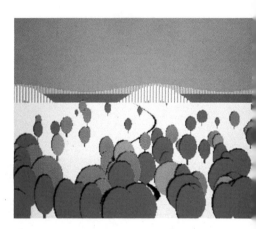

Plate 4   Cloud sculptures

Plate 5   The seasons

Plate 7   A tree in full foliage

Plate 6   Window on New York

Plate 9   The vale in winter

Plate 10   Palm beach

Plate 8   Savannah

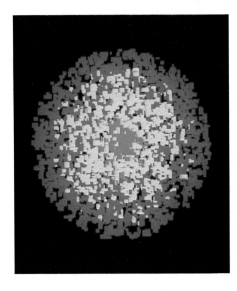

Plate 11   City simulation

Plate 12   Koch snowflake curves

Plate 13   A simulated Alpine range

Plate 14   Planetrise over Labelgraph Hill

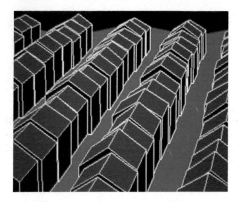

Plate 16   The valleyscape of New Tredegar

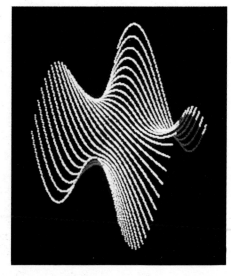

Plate 15   The saddle surface with underside shading

Plate 17 Off Moon Base Alpha, prior to animation

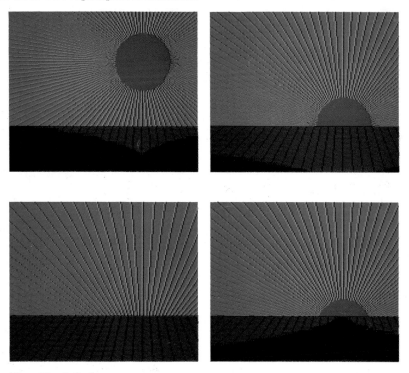

Plate 18 Stills from sunrise, sunset

Plate 19   Mickey mice © 1987 The Walt Disney Company

Plate 20   Mickey on a skate board © 1987 The Walt Disney Company

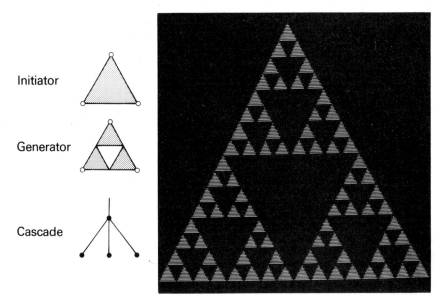

Initiator

Generator

Cascade

Fig. 5.15   Sierpinski's gasket

in Fig. 5.15 is the result of running this program which shows how a two-dimensional structure is 'reduced' to one whose fractal dimension is clearly $D = \log 3/\log 2 \sim 1.5849$.

Readers who wish to explore these ideas further should look at Cownie's (1982) little book, and at the more elaborate treatment by McGregor and Watt (1984). Those familiar with Seymour Papert's (1980) LOGO language will recognize that recursion is central to its use, and the connection between the ideas here and LOGO through recursive designs is clearly and cogently spelt out in Thornburg's (1983) magnificent book.

5.7   THE CONSTRUCTION OF FRACTAL LANDSCAPES

The non-random fractals introduced in previous sections led to several intriguing and beautiful designs, but they were presented as examples of recreational graphics, of ornamentation and abstract art rather than as aids to generating realism. Nevertheless, contained in those concepts, were notions involving recursion, cascade, dimension, self-avoidance and of course self-similarity which are essential to the generation of detail. In fact, the point was made several times that the kind of detail generated could only be produced using fractals, and in this section, we will equate detail with realism, extending these ideas and using them to much greater effect in the study and application of random fractals.

Program 5.11   Sierpinski's gasket

```
 10 REM Sierpinski's Gasket
 20 CLS
 30 INPUT TAB(11)"SIZE OF SIDE = ",L%
 40 INPUT TAB(9)"DEPTH OF RECURSION = ",D%
 50 MODE1
 60 VDU23,1,0;0;0;0;
 70 C=COS(RAD(60)):S=SIN(RAD(60))
 80 H%=SQR(L%^2-(0.5*L%)^2)
 90 VDU29,640-L%/2;512-H%/2;
100 X1%=0:X2%=L%:Y1%=0:Y2%=0
110 X3%=L%*C:Y3%=L%*S:GCOLO,1
120 MOVE X1%,Y1%:MOVE X2%,Y2%:PLOT85,X3%,Y3%:GCOLO,0
130 PROCTRI(X1%,Y1%,X2%,Y2%,X3%,Y3%,D%,L%)
140 AA=GET:MODE7
150 END
160 :
170 DEFPROCNODE(X1%,Y1%,X2%,Y2%,X3%,Y3%,X4%,Y4%,X5%,Y5%,X6%,Y6%,D%,L%)
180 MOVE X4%,Y4%:MOVE X5%,Y5%:PLOT85,X6%,Y6%
190 IF D%=0 THEN ENDPROC
200 PROCTRI(X1%,Y1%,X4%,Y4%,X5%,Y5%,D%-1,L%)
210 PROCTRI(X4%,Y4%,X2%,Y2%,X6%,Y6%,D%-1,L%)
220 PROCTRI(X5%,Y5%,X6%,Y6%,X3%,Y3%,D%-1,L%)
230 ENDPROC
240 :
250 DEFPROCTRI(XA%,YA%,XB%,YB%,XC%,YC%,D%,L%)
260 LL%=L%/2:XD%=XA%+LL%:YD%=YA%
270 XE%=XA%+LL%*C:YE%=YA%+LL%*S
280 XF%=XE%+LL%:YF%=YE%
290 PROCNODE(XA%,YA%,XB%,YB%,XC%,YC%,XD%,YD%,XE%,YE%,XF%,YF%,D%,LL%)
300 ENDPROC
```

Random fractals have already been introduced, albeit indirectly. The random walk in Program 5.1 is an example of Brownian motion in the plane which Mandelbrot (1982) shows is a fractal concept. In fact, the trail of the walk in Program 5.1 was not generated as a cascade but was simply produced at a fixed scale. That is, the fractal characteristic of such motion is that if you examine it at the next level down, the irregularity of the walk has the same detail as that of higher levels. Brownian motion is thus scaling, not scale-bound, and thus to turn Program 5.1 into a fractal form would require the trail of the walk to be randomly determined at all levels of the cascade to that level at or just below the level of screen resolution.

A feature of a random fractal is that it generates detail and irregularity which cannot be described in any deterministic way. Mountains and coastlines are clearly of this type, and this is why we have to turn to ideas of random self-similarity; not because of any metaphysical notion that the world is an intrinsically random place but because such detail can only be generated in this way. As Mandelbrot (1982) says, objects which we wish to model are "... moulded throughout the ages by multiple influences that are not recorded and cannot be reconstituted in any detail. The goal of achieving a full description is hopeless, and should not even be entertained." Thus random fractals are necessary to approximate unexplained and unexplainable detail.

In this section, we will introduce techniques which enable two-dimensional detail to be built up. This will lead to fractal landscapes which are 'flat' in the sense of Chapter 4 but the fact that such detail can be generated will make such landscapes more than flat: fractals, it will be recognized, enable subtle depth cues to be established in what are essentially two-dimensional constructions of three-dimensional scenes. The technique we will use involves perturbing a line a random distance and in random direction about its midpoint, thus constructing two line segments from one. Embedding this algorithm in a Koch cascade leads to a random Koch recursion on the line, and results in self-similarity which is random. To extend the algorithm to the plane, the plane is tiled with triangles whose sides are perturbed in the stated manner although other polygonal packings could be used.

This technique of midpoint displacement has been widely used in the construction of fractal landscapes (Fournier, Fussell and Carpenter, 1982), although it only leads to an approximation of random self-similarity as illustrated by Brownian motion. Mandelbrot (1982) himself is not entirely happy with it but he implicitly endorses it as a way of approaching random fractals when he says: ". . . it suffices to deform the different portions of the curve and to modify their sizes, all at random, and string them together in random order. Such an *invocation* of chance is allowable in preliminary investigations . . .". Nevertheless, the technique is only an approximation, necessary in this context where the machine's capacity is so limited. But as we shall see the problems of midpoint displacement either do not appear because the screen resolution is too coarse to detect them or have to be resolved in an *ad hoc* way. To take these ideas further, does require one to harness Mandelbrot's mathematical theory especially in the construction of fractals which exist in dimensions higher than two (Norton, 1982).

The easiest way to explain the technique of generating random fractals is through the diagrammatic sequence shown in Fig. 5.16. We have already seen in Fig. 5.9 how a line is perturbed – subdivided into four segments about its midpoint – in the process of Koch recursion. The process used here is similar except that the displacement is random but within certain limits of the midpoint in terms of its orientation and magnitude. Fig. 5.16(a) shows the area about the midpoint of a line within which the random choice is made and Fig. 5.16(b) shows typical displacements in which the original line is subdivided into two segments. The same process of displacement is then applied to each of these line segments and in this way, detail is generated down to the required level of recursion.

To generate random fractals in two-dimensions using this technique, the space must first be spanned using some method of continuous subdivision. It is widely recognized that triangles are the most efficient and parsimonious way

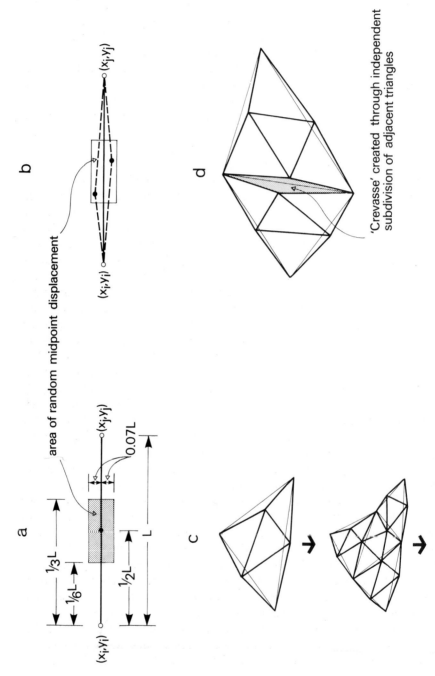

a

b

area of random midpoint displacement

(x_i, y_i) (x_j, y_j)

$\frac{1}{3}L$ $\frac{1}{6}L$

(x_i, y_i) (x_j, y_j)

0.07L

$\frac{1}{2}L$

L

c

d

'Crevasse' created through independent subdivision of adjacent triangles

Fig. 5.16 The construction of random fractals

of spanning space. If the subdivision process is thus applied to each side of a triangle, the triangle can be divided into four smaller triangles by linking the new points into a central triangle. This is the same type of recursion as in the construction of the Sierpinski Gasket earlier and it is illustrated in Fig. 5.16(c). Further subdivision of the newly created triangles results in a recursion which generates more and more detail in the manner shown. Useful examples of the process and its application to mountain scenes are shown in Smith (1983) and Van Dam (1984), and I have applied the ideas to city simulation (Batty, 1985).

There is however a major problem with this technique. To keep all the points of the subdivided triangles at all levels in store as they are generated, it is necessary to ensure that the ultimate pattern of polygons remains continuous, that is, that overlaps and holes between polygons are avoided. If a triangle is subdivided without reference to its adjacent triangles, in general the subdivided triangles will not be adjacent to those which result when the subdivision is applied to the original adjacent shapes. This problem is illustrated in Fig. 5.16(d). To overcome it, polygon points have to be stored, matched and averaged to ensure continuity and adjacency of shapes. This would require the creation of dynamic store and considerable computation involving sorting and matching. It is simply not possible to develop such techniques here for the program involved would be too long and elaborate, although it must be noted that it is possible even on machines with the capacity of the BBC computer. To circumvent the worst excesses of the problem of ensuring that the triangles are 'glued' together correctly, we will plot the triangles as they are created from the first to the last level of recursion. This might appear to defeat the purpose of the recursion and obscure all detail but what we will do is plot a triangle which is a reduced form of the triangle in question, the reduction giving enough flexibility at each level to enable lower levels to represent the appropriate fractal detail. In short, we will compute a *minimal* version of each triangle which reduces the holes and overlaps between triangles when they are glued together to a minimum.

The first program in which this technique is applied involves the construction of an Alpine range and is listed in Program 5.12. In fact, in the rest of this section, we will only examine those sections of this program which involve the technique of random midpoint displacement and which involve the procedures from line 1000 to 1400: the procedures in these lines are standard and could be used for any shape which had been triangulated and required rendering in terms of fractal detail. For example, these are used in the Planetrise sequence which is developed in the next section. First then, PROCNODE in lines 1010 to 1080 has the same function as previous procedures of that name. Its arguments are the coordinates of the four subdivided triangles which result from PROCGEN and which are passed in their correct order back to PROCGEN four times in lines 1040 to 1070. This procedure also contains the stopping rule in line 1030. PROCGEN in lines

1100 to 1250 is implemented four times at each level of the cascade and in essence, it controls subdivision of a triangle (whose coordinates form its arguments) into four as shown in Fig. 5.16(c). The midpoint displacement itself is determined for each side of the triangle by the procedure PROCPOINT which is called in lines 1120, 1140 and 1160. The coordinates determining the displacements and those relating to the minimal triangles are fixed in lines 1130, 1150 and 1170. In line 1190, there is a control which enables the plotting of the subdivided triangles to be missed. In fact, the plotting and rendering of the triangles is controlled by PROCCOLOUR which is always specific to the problem in hand and will be detailed in the next section. Four calls are made to PROCCOLOUR in lines 1200 to 1240, one for each subdivided triangle.

Random midpoint displacement of each side of a triangle is effected in PROCPOINT in lines 1270 to 1400. This has a similar structure to PROCGEN in earlier programs in this chapter, and this procedure follows the logic shown in Fig. 5.16(a). The length of the side is computed in line 1290, and its angle determined in lines 1290 to 1320. The trigonometry of the displacement is computed in lines 1330 and 1340. In line 1350, a random choice, right or left of the midpoint, is made and in line 1360 a random choice up or down from the point is made. The actual position is randomly computed within its limits in line 1380 in terms of coordinates, and the coordinates of the minimal triangle are fixed in line 1390. These procedures can be used to render any filled area which can be subdivided into triangles. The algorithm is entirely general apart from the calls to PROCCOLOUR which are specific to the landscape or object in question. We will now explore how these techniques can be used to their greatest effect.

5.8   THE ALPINE RANGE AND THE PLANETRISE SEQUENCE

In Program 5.12, this method of triangular subdivision is used to create the kind of detail characteristic of a mountain range. The structure of the range is a predetermined input to the program; each mountain is defined as a triangle whose coordinates are read from DATA statements. The program essentially generates the fractal detail from this global starting point and appropriately renders the resulting scene to reflect the colours associated with Alpine vistas. The input structure to the program is drawn in Fig. 5.17 and this makes clear that the program is simply one of fractal rendering on a picture structure which is imposed from outside.

The structure of the main program in Program 5.12 involves the input of the coordinates defining the various grounds characterizing the picture and various calls to the fractal routines already outlined which generate the ultimate picture to the required level of detail. The two nested FOR–NEXT loops between lines 50 and 150 deal with the background and foreground

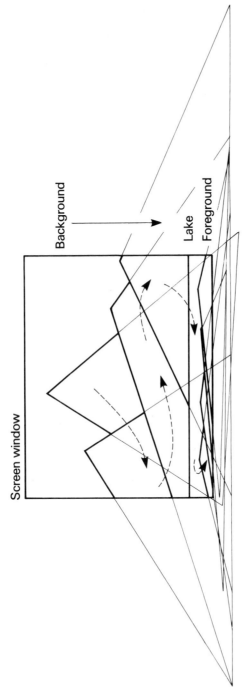

Fig. 5.17   The input structure of the Alpine range

Program 5.12   Alpine range

```
10 REM Alpine Range
20 CLS:MODE1
30 VDU23,1,0;0;0;0;
40 VDU19,0,4;0;19,1,0;0;19,2,6;0;19,3,7;0;
50 FOR L%=1 TO 2
60   READ NUM%,YT%,KW%
70   FOR KL%=1 TO NUM%
80     READ D%,X1%,Y1%,X2%,Y2%,X3%,Y3%
90     PROCGEN(X1%,Y1%,X2%,Y2%,X3%,Y3%,D%)
100    NEXT KL%
110  IF L%=2 GOTO 150
120  GCOLO,2:MOVE 0,0:MOVE 0,150:PLOT85,1300,150
130  MOVE 1300,0:PLOT85,0,0:GCOLO,1:MOVE 0,100:MOVE 0,0
140  PLOT85,1300,100:MOVE 1300,0:PLOT85,0,0
150  NEXT L%
160 AA=GET:MODE7
170 END
180 :
190 REM Plots and Colours each Triangle
200 DEFPROCCOLOUR(WX%,WY%,XX%,XY%,ZX%,ZY%)
210 IF WY%>XY% THEN YTT%=WY% ELSE YTT%=XY%
220 IF YTT%<ZY% THEN YTT%=ZY%
230 G%=2:BQ%=0.35*YT%:BE%=0.8*YT%:ZT%=YT%*(1-(YTT%/YT%)^G%)
240 IF RND(YT%)<=ZT% THEN GCOLO,1 ELSE GCOLO,3
250 IF YTT%<BQ% THEN GCOLO,1:IF YTT%>BE% THEN GCOLO,3
260 MOVE WX%,WY%:MOVE XX%,XY%:PLOT85,ZX%,ZY%
270 ENDPROC
280 :
290 REM Data Defining Outlines of Mountains and Foregrounds
300 DATA 4,900,0,6,-50,-50,1400,-150,550,900
310 DATA 5,-1000,-100,750,-100,250,700
320 DATA 5,-1000,-100,1900,-100,1000,550
330 DATA 5,0,-100,2600,-100,1250,500
340 DATA 4,90,0,2,-500,-100,1500,-100,100,80
350 DATA 2,-700,-100,1850,-100,500,65
360 DATA 2,-500,-50,1200,-80,890,57
370 DATA 2,0,-30,1800,-100,1100,85
1000 :
1010 REM Controls the Hierarchical Subdivision Process
1020 DEFPROCNODE(A1%,B1%,A2%,B2%,A3%,B3%,AA%,BA%,AB%,BB%,AC%,BC%,D%)
1030 IF D%=0 THEN ENDPROC
1040 PROCGEN(A1%,B1%,AA%,BA%,AC%,BC%,D%-1)
1050 PROCGEN(AC%,BC%,AB%,BB%,A3%,B3%,D%-1)
1060 PROCGEN(AA%,BA%,A2%,B2%,AB%,BB%,D%-1)
1070 PROCGEN(AA%,BA%,AB%,BB%,AC%,BC%,D%-1)
1080 ENDPROC
1090 :
1100 REM Subdivides a Triangle into Four by Midpoint Displacement
1110 DEFPROCGEN(X1%,Y1%,X2%,Y2%,X3%,Y3%,D%)
1120 X=X2%-X1%:Y=Y2%-Y1%:PROCPOINT
1130 XA%=X1%+XZ%:YA%=Y1%+YZ%:AX%=-XP%:AY%=-YP%
1140 X=X3%-X1%:Y=Y3%-Y1%:PROCPOINT
1150 XC%=X1%+XZ%:YC%=Y1%+YZ%:CX%=XP%:CY%=YP%
1160 X=X3%-X2%:Y=Y3%-Y2%:PROCPOINT
1170 XB%=X2%+XZ%:YB%=Y2%+YZ%:BX%=-XP%:BY%=-YP%
```

Program 5.12 continued

```
1180 IF D%=0 THEN AX%=0:AY%=0:BX%=0:BY%=0:CX%=0:CY%=0
1190 IF D%<>0 AND KW%=1 THEN GOTO 1240
1200 PROC COLOUR(X1%,Y1%,XA%+AX%,YA%+AY%,XC%+CX%,YC%+CY%)
1210 PROC COLOUR(XC%+CX%,YC%+CY%,XB%+BX%,YB%+BY%,X3%,Y3%)
1220 PROC COLOUR(XA%+AX%,YA%+AY%,XB%+BX%,YB%+BY%,XC%+CX%,YC%+CY%)
1230 PROC COLOUR(XA%+AX%,YA%+AY%,X2%,Y2%,XB%+BX%,YB%+BY%)
1240 PROC NODE(X1%,Y1%,X2%,Y2%,X3%,Y3%,XA%,YA%,XB%,YB%,XC%,YC%,D%)
1250 END PROC
1260 :
1270 REM Computes the Midpoint Displacement
1280 DEF PROC POINT
1290 L=SQR(X^2+Y^2):Z=ABS(Y)/L:A=ASN(Z)
1300 IF X<0 AND Y>=0 THEN A=PI-A
1310 IF X<=0 AND Y<0 THEN A=PI+A
1320 IF X>0 AND Y<0 THEN A=2*PI-A
1330 C=COS(A):S=SIN(A):A=A+(PI/2)
1340 CC=COS(A):SS=SIN(A)
1350 IF RND(2)=1 THEN K%=1 ELSE K%=-1
1360 IF RND(2)=1 THEN KK%=1 ELSE KK%=-1
1370 R=0.5+(K%*RND(1)/6):W=KK%*(0.03+RND(1)/25)
1380 XZ%=R*L*C+W*L*CC:YZ%=R*L*S+W*L*SS
1390 WW=-0.05:XP%=WW*L*CC:YP%=WW*L*SS
1400 END PROC
```

respectively reflecting a simple form of temporal priority. The background consists of the range itself which is composed of four very high mountains and their peaks which in turn dominate the picture. The foreground consists of four very flat but jagged surfaces which are reminiscent of a glacier. The back- and fore-grounds are separated by a thin blue lake. This is the structure presented in Fig. 5.17 which is read from DATA statements (lines 290 to 370) accessed from line 80 at the heart of the nested loops. In line 60 which is between the loops, the number of surfaces, a maximum height parameter $YT\%$ which we will refer to as y_{max}, and the dummy parameter $KW\%$ which enables detail to be filled solid (as here) or in outline, is read in from DATA. A surface (triangles) is read in in line 80 and the fractal rendering is started by a call to PROCGEN in line 90. After the number of objects forming the 'ground' have been rendered, the blue lake is plotted in lines 110 to 140. Control is then returned to the outer loop in line 150 which enables the foreground to be constructed.

We have already outlined the fractal procedures in lines 1000 to 1400 and all that remains is to describe the plotting and colouring for this particular picture which is given in PROCCOLOUR defined between lines 190 and 270. In lines 210 and 220, the maximum vertical height of the triangle whose coordinates have been passed as the arguments of this procedure is determined and in line 230 the probability of the triangle being coloured one shade or another is computed. This is computed as a function of the actual triangle height y and the input maximum triangle height y_{max} as

$$z = y_{max}\{1 - (y/y_{max})^2\}, \quad 0 \leqslant y \leqslant y_{max}. \tag{5.6}$$

From equation (5.6), $0 \leqslant z \leqslant y_{max}$, and in line 240 if a random number chosen with the limit of y_{max} is less than z, one colour is used; if not the other. In this case, the closer y to y_{max}, or the nearer z to 0, the more likely the colour chosen be white reflecting the mountain peaks. Finally in line 250 limits above and below which the mountain should be coloured white or black are fixed and in line 260, the detail is appropriately plotted and rendered.

The picture produced by a run of this program is illustrated in Plate 13 and comparison must be immediately made with Fig. 5.17. No gaps appear between adjacent triangles and the fractal detail generated gives the effect of a classic Alpine scene. This is based on some experimentation with the overlapping of mountain structures and the recursive depth used. Readers should change the colours of the various components of the picture using the VDU19 command but generally I have found the colours used here to be the most appropriate. The Alpine Range picture illustrates once again the message of this book that mathematical modelling of picture structure and detail is essential in computer graphics. It would be extremely difficult, if not impossible, to generate scenes such as that in Plate 13 using a drawing package and light pen. As Glassner's (1984) book illustrates: "In the hands of talented programmers and artists, fractals can be used to create computer generated pictures that were previously impossible". Readers are referred to Mandelbrot's (1982) book and the articles by McDermott (1983) and Sorensen (1984b) for further examples.

One of the most dramatic computer pictures of all time appears on the cover and within Mandelbrot's (1982) book. This is the picture which looks like the Earth viewed from the Moon, entitled 'Planetrise over Labelgraph Hill' and generated by Richard Voss. This is a brilliant example of both what is possible with fractals and what would be impossible without them. In fact, Voss's picture was constructed using three-dimensional Brownian motion but we can approximate this using our midpoint displacement technique in two-dimensions. This provides a useful conclusion to this chapter and in my view the best computer picture ever is the best in this book and the best yet on the BBC machine. A grand claim perhaps but one which returns us to the reality that the best computer art and graphics will always be based on the best theories of modelling and simulation.

The program to compute the 'Planetrise' picture is listed as Program 5.13 but note that the listing in lines 10 to 830 excludes PROCNODE, PROCGEN and PROCPOINT in Program 5.12 and these lines (1000 to 1400) *must* be added in order to run the program. The picture structure is straightforward: a blue circular planet is centred, plotted and filled on the screen and it is covered with continents and islands reminiscent of those you might see on Earth around the Pacific Rim – East Asia, Oceania and the Americas. These continents read from DATA are then fractally rendered in such a way that their centres are coloured yellow – hills and mountains, their peripheral areas

Program 5.13   Planetrise over Labelgraph Hill

```
 10 REM Planetrise over Labelgraph Hill
 20 REM With Apologies to Dr.Richard Voss
 30 CLS:MODE1
 40 VDU23,1,0;0;0;0;
 50 VDU19,0,0;0;19,1,2;0;19,2,3;0;19,3,4;0;
 60 X0%=640:Y0%=600:GCOLO,3:RZ%=350
 70 MOVE X0%,Y0%:MOVE X0%+RZ%,Y0%
 80 PROCCIRCLE(X0%,Y0%,RZ%,RZ%,1,0,85,4)
 90 READ NUM%
100 FOR I%=1 TO NUM%
110   READ D%,X1%,Y1%,X2%,Y2%,X3%,Y3%
120   KW%=0:XQ%=X3%:YQ%=Y3%
130   X4%=ABS(X1%-X2%):Y4%=ABS(Y1%-Y2%)
140   IF X2%>X1% THEN X4%=X1%+X4% ELSE X4%=X2%+X4%
150   IF Y2%>Y1% THEN Y4%=Y1%+Y4% ELSE Y4%=Y2%+Y4%
160   YT%=SQR((X4%-X3%)^2+(Y4%-Y3%)^2)
170   PROCGEN(X1%,Y1%,X2%,Y2%,X3%,Y3%,D%)
180   NEXT I%
190 GCOLO,0:RR%=1500:RZ%=RZ%+2
200 MOVE X0%+RR%,Y0%:MOVE X0%+RZ%,Y0%
210 PROCCIRCLE(X0%,Y0%,RZ%,RR%/RZ%,1,85,85)
220 FOR I%=Y0%-RZ% TO Y0%+RZ% STEP 4
230   TH=ACS(ABS(I%-Y0%)/RZ%):X=RZ%*SIN(TH)
240   FOR J%=0 TO 2*X STEP 4
250     KS%=RND(2*X-J%):IF KS%>=J% THEN GCOLO,0 ELSE GOTO 270
260     PLOT69,X0%+X-J%,I%
270     NEXT J%:NEXT I%
280 READ NUM%
290 FOR I%=1 TO NUM%
300   READ D%,X1%,Y1%,X2%,Y2%,X3%,Y3%
310   GCOLO,2:KW%=1
320   PROCGEN(X1%,Y1%,X2%,Y2%,X3%,Y3%,D%)
330   NEXT I%
340 GCOLO,0:READ NUM%
350 FOR I%=1 TO NUM%
360   READ X0%,Y0%,RY%,RX%
370   MOVE X0%,Y0%:MOVE X0%+RX%,Y0%
380   PROCCIRCLE(X0%,Y0%,RX%,RY%,1,0,85,4)
390   NEXT I%
400 AA=GET:MODE7
410 END
420 :
430 REM Draws an Interior-Exterior Circle-Ellipse
440 DEFPROCCIRCLE(X0%,Y0%,RX%,RY%,RA,RB,TA%,TB%)
450 FOR ANG=0 TO 360 STEP 4
460   X=RX%*COS(RAD(ANG)):Y=RY%*SIN(RAD(ANG))
470   XX=RA*X:YY=RA*Y:X=RB*X:Y=RB*Y
480   PLOTTA%,X0%+XX,Y0%+YY:PLOTTB%,X0%+X,Y0%+Y
490   NEXT ANG
500 ENDPROC
510 :
520 REM Plots and Colours Each Triangle
530 DEFPROCCOLOUR(WX%,WY%,XX%,XY%,ZX%,ZY%)
540 IF KW%=0 THEN GOTO 560
550 MOVE WX%,WY%:DRAW XX%,XY%:DRAW ZX%,ZY%:DRAW WX%,WY%:ENDPROC
```

Program 5.13   continued

```
560 IF WY%>XY% THEN Y4%=WY% ELSE Y4%=XY%
570 IF Y4%<ZY% THEN Y4%=ZY%
580 IF WX%>XX% THEN X4%=WX% ELSE X4%=XX%
590 IF X4%<ZX% THEN X4%=ZX%
600 YTT%=SQR((X4%-XQ%)^2+(Y4%-YQ%)^2):YTT%=ABS(YT%-YTT%)
610 G%=2:BQ%=0.20*YT%:BE%=0.68*YT%:ZT%=YT%*(1-(YTT%/YT%)^G%)
620 IF RND(YT%)<=ZT% THEN GCOLO,1 ELSE GCOLO,2
630 IF YTT%<BQ% THEN GCOLO,3:IF YTT%>BE% THEN GCOLO,2
640 MOVE WX%,WY%:MOVE XX%,XY%:PLOT85,ZX%,ZY%
650 ENDPROC
660 :
670 REM Data Defining Outlines of Land Masses and Moon's Surface
680 DATA 21,3,630,660,680,750,540,750
690 DATA 3,680,750,690,850,540,750,3,690,850,540,1000,540,750
700 DATA 3,690,850,660,880,1080,980,3,540,1000,410,970,540,750
710 DATA 3,410,970,330,790,540,750,3,330,790,360,700,540,750
720 DATA 3,360,700,490,630,540,750,3,490,630,590,670,540,750
730 DATA 3,650,530,690,550,540,750,3,650,530,740,550,690,450
740 DATA 3,650,530,480,400,690,450,3,500,360,610,280,690,450
750 DATA 3,610,280,770,430,690,450,3,770,430,740,550,690,450
760 DATA 3,990,440,800,690,1190,650,3,800,690,840,790,1190,650
770 DATA 3,840,790,1080,880,1190,650,3,330,500,390,550,440,500
780 DATA 3,330,500,440,500,390,460,3,400,480,390,250,440,500
790 DATA 6,3,-100,130,1300,130,1300,-800,3,-100,130,1300,130,-100,-800
800 DATA 3,100,0,1300,160,1300,0,3,-100,180,1300,0,0,0
810 DATA 3,100,100,1300,100,-100,-100,3,0,100,1300,100,640,-400
820 DATA 5,500,30,18,60,800,40,15,40
830 DATA 300,50,16,45,1100,60,22,80,100,40,18,60
```

green – coastal plains and flat agricultural regions. A light source is then introduced from the left of the scene which leaves the right-side of the planet in darkness; this is achieved using the random dot technique first explored in the Cloud Sculpture scenes in Program 3.14 and also used in Program 4.10. Finally, a lunar-like landscape is constructed as a foreground in which triangles are subdivided but *not* filled, and finally craters are introduced as elliptical holes in the yellowish lunar sand.

Another feature of the program involves the way in which the continents are wrapped around the globe. In fact, what we do is simply plot the continents as though they are erupting into space and then simply clean them off to ensure the resulting shape is spherical. We lay the continents flat across the globe as if we were laying pastry strips over the edge of a pie, and we then sculpt off the overlaps as if we are trimming around the pie dish. The way we introduce the depth cues in this picture largely consists of the way the right-side of the planet is shaded, and the way the predetermined continental structure is configured in the DATA statements. If the continents were to be set up randomly – an obvious extension of the program – more attention would have to be paid to continental structure to ensure ridiculous-looking land masses did not emerge.

Examining Program 5.13, the first significant action is the construction of the solid blue globe which is accomplished by a call to PROCCIRCLE in line 80. This procedure defined in lines 430 to 500 enables a filled ellipse of any dimension to be plotted in which the origin of the ellipse itself may be an ellipse: that is, if the origin is 0, a conventional ellipse is drawn but if the origin is a positive and non-zero distance, the filled ellipse will be bounded by this smaller ellipse centred on the origin. In this way, we can draw circles or ellipses with circular or elliptical holes in. We can use this facility to trim the edges of an already plotted circle or as a technique of masking the continental overlaps on our Earth-like planet. The procedure is based on the conventional trigonometric form for an ellipse and the simplest fill procedure.

The FOR–NEXT loop between lines 100 and 180 controls the construction and fractal rendering of the continents. In line 110, their coordinate data are read from DATA statements located in lines 670 to 830, and between lines 130 and 160, the height/distance value YT% is computed which is used in determining the colour of the piece of continent relative to position. Fractal rendering begins in line 170 with a call to PROCGEN. Once all the continents have been constructed, it is necessary to trim the overlaps (see Fig. 5.18) and

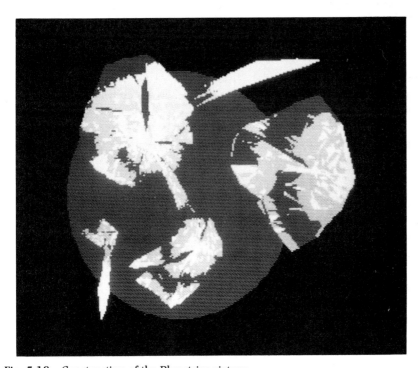

Fig. 5.18   Construction of the Planetrise picture

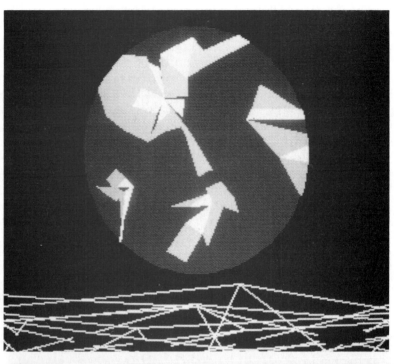

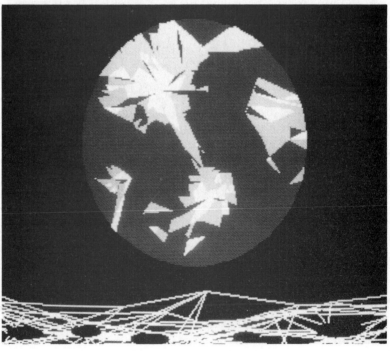

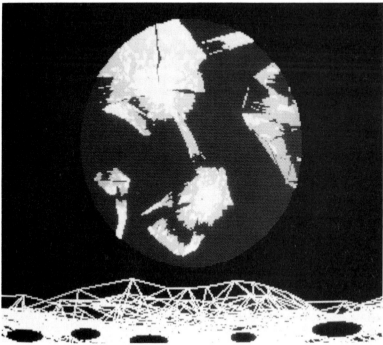

Fig. 5.19 Planetrise at different levels of fractal rendering

thus in lines 190 to 210, parameters are fixed which enable a very large black circle with a hole the size of the planet to be plotted, thus reestablishing the background. The light source based on random shading of the planet is controlled by the FOR–NEXT loop between lines 220 and 270, and then in the rest of the program – lines 290 to 390, the lunarscape is constructed. This is straightforward: a FOR–NEXT loop in lines 290 to 330 reads in triangular coordinate data (line 300) from DATA statements and renders these with a call to PROCGEN in line 320. Note here that in line 310, $KW\%$ is set as 1 which ensures that the rendering is only of the triangle outlines. In fact, this does generate a foreground which is partly filled because of the level of recursion and screen resolution but the appearance achieved is an irregular mix of black (unfilled) and yellow. Onto this surface, between lines 350 and 390, a FOR–NEXT loop reads data relating to the size and positioning of five black craters which are plotted with a call to PROCCIRCLE in line 380. Finally, PROCCOLOUR which is listed in lines 520 to 650 has a broadly similar structure to the same procedure defined in Program 5.12 except that lines 540 and 550 enable the plotting to be in outline only, if $KW\% = 1$.

Figure 5.18 shows the intermediate stage of construction of the Planetrise picture to the depths of recursion specified in the DATA statements ($D\% > 3$) and the final picture is shown in Plate 14. The intermediate picture without the shading and the lunarscape prior to the continental masking, is that illustrated in Fig. 5.18 and is that reached by running the program to line 180. Plate 14 reflects the rest of the program actions but note that these two pictures differ slightly because they reflect different runs of the program (that is, the final picture is *not* the ultimate completion of the intermediate one). In Fig. 5.19, we show the effect of varying the level of recursion on the picture. We have omitted the shading in lines 220 to 270 and then overridden the level of recursion in the DATA statements so that Fig. 5.19(a) reflects fractal detail for the continents and lunarscape to $D\% = 0$, Fig. 5.19(b) to $D\% = 1$, Fig. 5.19(c) to $D\% = 2$ and Fig. 5.19(d) to $D\% = 3$. The pictures speak for themselves as an example of fractal geometry. Many extensions suggest themselves. Superlative effects can be achieved using other colours: try a red planet with white and light blue for continents and white for lunar sand. The program can be made more general by omitting the DATA statements and introducing procedures to generate continents and foregrounds which in turn might use PROCCIRCLE to enable realistic-looking land masses to be generated. Try to do this in no more than the number of lines used for the DATA statements: it should be possible.

Chapters such as this one do not warrant drawn-out conclusions but here more so than at any point previously, we are in a position to argue the case that good computer graphics and art must be based on the powerful mathematical modelling of picture structure. Indeed in the construction of fractal landscapes, it is hard to see how the human hand could produce the same level of detail as the type of geometrical recursion invoked here, although good art will always remain much more than good programming: a strong visual imagination combined with the imaginative, ingenious use of programming and modelling continue to be essential. Nevertheless, what fractal geometry does illustrate is that new art forms will arise through computer simulation using such techniques, different from conventional art and in this sense computer and conventional art are non-comparable.

Throughout this book, we have been developing art in which the third dimension has been grossly and sometimes coarsely approximated through a variety of depth cues involving temporal priority, light source shading and so on. But it is now time to move on and to generate more realistic three-dimensional images. This we will do in the next chapter but to do so, we must take one step back to make a step forward. In Chapter 6, we will treat simple objects which are initially measured in three-dimensions but transformed into two-dimensions for purposes of graphic representation. We will return to some of the ideas introduced in Chapter 3 in extending our knowledge of spatial mathematics to embrace the third dimension, and we will then gradually build up more complicated pictures. The third dimension is essential to developing realistic images but so is the fourth – time – and in the last substantive chapter of this book, we will explore the modelling of motion and the making of elementary computer movies.

its coordinates and their system as *screen coordinates* and the *screen coordinate system*. Strictly speaking, the two-dimensional image is generated in coordinates whose magnitude reflects the scale of the original three-dimensional scene, that is the scale of the world space in which the object and viewpoint exists. Thus a further scaling may be necessary to establish actual screen coordinates. In what follows, the original world coordinates will be consistent with the screen units and thus no further transformations are required. There is however no loss of generality in this assumption.

The picture generation process at whose heart lies these transformations, has been elaborated by Greenberg (1982) as a five-fold process whose stages are listed as follows:

(1) A mathematical description of the object or scene is first required in terms of its world coordinates. This must be generated by the computer mathematically or input to the computer using any of the available peripheral devices, the keyboard or set up as DATA statements in the program.

(2) This three-dimensional description must then be transformed into its two-dimensional image using appropriate mathematical transformations and projections with respect to a predetermined viewpoint.

(3) Lines and/or surfaces hidden from the viewpoint must be determined so that these can be removed or obscured when the image is plotted.

(4) Various types of light falling on the object's surfaces must be determined with respect to known light sources and the given viewpoint.

(5) Finally, appropriate RGB intensities must be selected from the computations at stage 4, and the object can then be plotted and rendered on the appropriate display device.

It is worth elaborating these stages in a little more detail so that the types of technique to be developed in the sequel can be anticipated, and so that the various parts of the process which are difficult to implement on microcomputers of the type assumed here, are identified. In the first stage, the object or scene is described mathematically as a set of points, lines and surfaces whose position and orientation are given by the set of world coordinate vectors $[x^w y^w z^w]$. Depending upon the algorithm used at later stages of the process, these data must be organized efficiently and thus it is necessary to code them in the most appropriate data structure. In this chapter as indeed throughout this book, we will not have recourse to worry very much about the efficiency of this coding – our pictures are not complex or elaborate enough – although a hint of these considerations will be given here a little later.

There are basically three sorts of object or scene introduced in this chapter which require similar data structures for their easy access and processing but are each generated quite differently. There are objects which cannot be generated using any general mathematical function in contrast to objects which can. This first sort of object is often irregular, but need not be so, and is usually coded by the user outside the program, thus input as data to the program. With the second type of object which can be generated mathematically, there are two cases. There are simple objects such as cylinders or spheres which have a mathematical form based on trigonometric functions, while there are surfaces which are defined everywhere using a single function. To summarize, we can think of these three objects as objects requiring external coding by the user hence inputting to the program, objects defined as solids of rotation, and objects defined as surfaces. In fact, the object we will code outside the program is quite regular geometrically – it is a simple house (a box with a pitched roof) – although there is no simple mathematical form to describe it. Nevertheless, this illustrates the more important point that the way objects are generated is not of major importance to the techniques which follow although their regularity can often be exploited to aid their processing and programming.

The second stage of the process involves most of the formal mathematics to be introduced here. Normally the transformation from world to screen coordinates can be separated into two operations. First, there is the *viewing transformation* which involves moving the coordinate system (and object) from its actual position in world space to the viewpoint position and rotating the system in the direction of viewing. Second, the operation which follows this involves *projection* of the object onto a flat plane – the screen – which is usually placed some distance from the viewpoint but perpendicular to the viewing direction. There are several possible projections but those treated here are planar geometric, that is, projections onto a plane not a sphere or some other nonlinear shape. Of these planar projections we will mainly deal with *perspective projections* which involve regular distortion of lines and angles due to the effect of perspective. However we will also examine the simpler class of projections – the so-called *parallel projections* – where parallel lines in three-dimensions remain parallel in projection.

The third stage involves the identification and possible removal of lines and/or surfaces which are hidden from the viewpoint. Algorithms to achieve this are of two types – those that work on the object itself in world space, and those that work on the already transformed image in the display or screen space. In this context, these image space algorithms, one of which will be introduced in the next section, are simpler than their world space counterparts. Clearly, world space hidden line algorithms may work simultaneously with the three-dimensional transformation sequence, while in the case of the image space algorithms, these can only begin once the transformation from three- to two-dimensions is complete. In fact, we will discuss a simple image space algorithm in the next section but in the rest of this chapter, we will concentrate on world space techniques.

Two such techniques will be explored. First we will present an appropriately modified form of the painter's algorithm, based on sorting the object's surfaces with respect to distance from the viewpoint. This is the so-called depth sort or z-buffer algorithm (Newman and Sproull, 1979; Foley and Van Dam, 1982). The essence of this technique is that the surfaces furthest from the viewpoint are plotted first and then nearer surfaces are plotted, hence painted over the more distant ones. The technique is clearly only of use with raster scan technology. The second and more general technique is referred to as backsurface elimination (Myers, 1982). This involves determining those surfaces of the object which face away from the viewing, noting these and eliminating them when the object is ultimately plotted in screen space. This technique will be introduced after the depth sort, and used in the construction of the major picture of this chapter – the space picture which is presented in the last section.

The last two stages of the picture generation process involve questions of colour and lighting, and the consequent rendering of the object depends very largely on the available palette of colours. In BBC Basic, only eight absolute colours are available, and these are generally insufficient for anything other than the most rudimentary application of a lighting model. Moreover, the level of screen resolution also limits the ability to realistically render the object. Nevertheless in the next section where we illustrate all five stages in the process, a simple lighting model will be used which determines the probability of any point on the surface of the object being light or dark. In more advanced graphics and art, these last two stages are among the most important in generating pictures with a high degree of realism. In a sense, they begin when one can get no further with transformation, and although more could be done here with the available hardware, this would involve questions of colour mixing beyond the scope of this book as well as lighting models whose mathematics and physics is also beyond the level intended here. Interested readers are referred to the book by Greenberg, Marcus, Schmidt and Gorter (1982) for an excellent introduction as well as to the standard texts for technical details.

We will introduce the picture generation process at three levels of complexity and sophistication. In the next section we will present all the stages of the process using the simplest possible model – a transformation from three- to two-dimensions involving parallel projection and an image space hidden line/point/surface algorithm which both involve recognizing certain properties of the screen space in advance and effecting an appropriate transformation to exploit these. This will give us an idea of the process without much additional mathematics at this stage and at the same time, will provide us with a quick, robust and effective technique for plotting three-dimensional surfaces. After that we will introduce the mathematics of three-dimensional transformations in preparation for programs which will enable us to reproduce three-dimensional scenes on two-dimensional display devices.

6.2 GENERATING SURFACES THROUGH PARALLEL PROJECTION

The most difficult stage of the picture generation process involves transformations from three-dimensional world to two-dimensional screen coordinates for this will involve us in mathematical operations involving vector algebra in three-space, yet to be introduced. However we can simplify the process if we assume first that the xy plane of the object occupies a predetermined position on the two-dimensional screen and the z coordinates are all measured vertically in the y direction on the screen from appropriate points on the given xy plane. Thus the z dimension in world space is the y dimension in screen space, each z direction from xy being parallel and having the same measured value as in the world coordinate system. It is easiest to visualize this construction graphically as follows.

Imagine we are dealing with a function $z = f(x,y)$ where the value of z exists for every value of x and y. Thus the function is continuous in x and y although it may not be single-valued and there may be discontinuities in z. It is possible to visualize such functions as continuous surfaces whose height is given by z for every combination of the values x and y in the xy plane. Consider the xy world coordinates as being equivalent to the xy screen coordinates as in Fig. 6.1(a). If we were to plot the value of z for each point xy in the y screen direction, we would produce a projection whose lines were parallel but the y world coordinate direction would be obscured by the surface. One way of resolving this would be to rotate the xy plane and to plot z in a similar way, that is parallel to the y screen direction and such a projection is shown in Fig. 6.1(b). This projection shows how the x,y and z world coordinates can be plotted on the two-dimensional screen by effectively reducing a three-dimensional system to two-dimensions.

By associating each of the three world coordinates with the two screen coordinates in a predetermined way, we only require the two-dimensional transformations already introduced in Chapter 3, to construct the projection.

We can proceed as follows. The world coordinate system is represented by vectors of the form $[x^w y^w z^w]$ and from Fig. 6.1(a), it is clear that we are associating $[x^w y^w]$ with the screen coordinates $[x^s y^s]$. However the first step in our construction is to rotate $[x^w y^w]$ as in Fig. 6.1(b) and this is achieved using the two-dimensional counter-clockwise rotation whose non-homogeneous form was presented earlier as equation (3.12). Then for a rotation of angle θ

$$[x^s y^s] = [x^w y^w] \begin{bmatrix} \cos(\theta) & \sin(\theta) \\ -\sin(\theta) & \cos(\theta) \end{bmatrix}. \qquad (6.1)$$

Equation (6.1) has the matrix form

$$p^s = p^w A \qquad (6.2)$$

where p^s, p^w are 1×2 row vectors of screen and world coordinates respectively and A is a 2×2 rotation matrix.

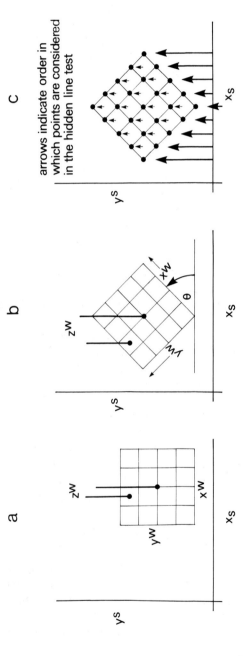

Fig. 6.1 Approximating three-dimensions with two-dimensions

The essence of the technique can now be stated. We know that the xy plane on the screen will be the rotated set of $[x^w y^w]$ vectors from equation (6.1) and we assume that the limits of this plane as seen on the screen in Fig. 6.1(b) are known. Within the limits of the rotated xy plane, it is possible from any set of screen coordinates $[x^s y^s]$ to compute the original world coordinates $[x^w y^w]$ by manipulating equation (6.2) as

$$p^s A^{-1} = p^w. \tag{6.3}$$

Equation (6.3) has the form

$$[x^s y^s] \begin{bmatrix} \cos(\theta) & -\sin(\theta) \\ \sin(\theta) & \cos(\theta) \end{bmatrix} = [x^w y^w] \tag{6.4}$$

where it is clear that the inverse of A has a simple form. Writing out equation (6.4) fully leads to

$$\left. \begin{array}{l} x^w = x^s \cos(\theta) + y^s \sin(\theta) \\ y^w = -x^s \sin(\theta) + y^s \cos(\theta) \end{array} \right\} \tag{6.5}$$

which is the transformation back from screen to world coordinates (for the xy plane) for this particular projection.

The surface based on $z^w = f(x^w, y^w)$ is plotted as follows. In the area of the xy plane on the screen, the screen coordinates $[x^s y^s]$ are systematically considered and their original world coordinates $[x^w y^w]$ computed from equations (6.5). The z^w coordinate is then calculated from $z^w = f(x^w, y^w)$ and the height of the z value on the screen is calculated by adding z^w to the value of its associated screen y^s. That is, $z^s = z^w + y^s$, which for every point $x^s y^s$ on the screen shows that the surface lies z^w units vertically above the point in question. In this way, the projection is said to be parallel because each z^s direction is parallel to the y^s direction. There is a further simplification that can be made. If we assume that the rotation of the $x^w y^w$ plane is symmetrical, that is that the rectangular area over which the surface is plotted is 'balanced' on one of its ends, this means that the angle of rotation $\theta = 45° = \pi/4$. Then $\sin(45°) = \cos(45°) = 1/\sqrt{2} = \sqrt{2}/2$. Equations (6.5) can now be simplified as

$$x^w = \frac{2}{\sqrt{2}} (x^s + y^s), \quad \text{and} \quad y^w = \frac{2}{\sqrt{2}} (y^s - x^s),$$

which leads to marginally simpler but much faster computations.

In terms of the process so far, no data structure as such is required at the first stage for the surface is defined mathematically and its points generated as we proceed. The second stage of transforming these points to those actually plotted on the screen has just been explained, and we now encounter the process of removing parts of the surface which are hidden. We have already anticipated the mechanism to do this by rotating the xy plane $45°$.

Figure 6.1(c) shows the points considered as a grid on the rotated xy plane and it is clear that these grid points are also aligned with the horizontal grid of the screen itself which in turn corresponds to the screen's pixels. Now each point on the surface is z^w units above its xy grid point. Consider the case where a grid point $x_A y_A$ generates a function value which is z_A units above the point. Examine another grid point, say $x_A y_B$, which is in the same vertical alignment but above the point $x_A y_A$. This point gives a value of z_B which is less than the value z_A. But when plotted on the screen, this point is obscured by z_A because the associated screen value of z_A is $y_A + z_A$ which is greater than $y_B + z_B$. In this sense, the point $[x_A y_A z_A]$ 'hides' the point $[x_A y_B z_B]$. This is also shown in Fig. 6.1(c).

The hidden point algorithm works as follows. Each of the x^s values which occur within the limits of the xy plane is examined at a level of resolution appropriate to the number of pixels across the screen. Then for each x, all points xy are examined which lie vertically within the screen limits of the xy plane, starting with the point which has the smallest y^s value and proceeding until the largest y^s value is reached. These points will lie on the xy grid which in this direction, is at a level of resolution larger than the vertical pixel resolution, thus creating the impression of lines running in one direction across the surface (in this case in the horizontal direction). For each point in the vertical direction, we compute its world coordinates and z^s value; as we consider points in a vertical direction up the screen, we plot any point which is greater than the largest z^s_{max} so far and any point which is less than the smallest z^s_{min} so far. Points which fall inside these limits are hidden from view and as the algorithm proceeds, the values of z^s_{max} and z^s_{min} are successively updated. A moment's reflection shows that this is a hidden point algorithm which works on the image space, defining the surface by continuous lines if the x resolution is always less than or equal to the horizontal pixel size.

We will examine this method in a little more detail when we look at its program but first we must examine how the last two stages of the picture generation process can be operationalized. In fact we will treat these two stages as one using a simple lighting model which is based on the obvious principle that the amount of light falling on an object varies inversely with the distance of the object from the light source. Thus the greater the distance from the source, the 'darker' the object. Usually in computer graphics, light sources are so far distant as to have little effect on any scene and thus the characteristics of illumination relate to ambience, the reflectivity of materials and suchlike. These issues are too tricky to broach here, so we will assume that the inverse distance model applies by assuming our surfaces exist in a dark space which is illuminated by a light source in one corner.

A point on the surface is located at point $[x^s z^s]$ and let us assume that the distance from $x^s z^s$ to the light source located at point $x^L y^L$ is defined by d_{sL}. Then the luminance of the object $l(x^s, z^s)$ is given as

$$l(x^s, z^s) \propto \frac{1}{d_{sL}}$$

where

$$d_{sL} = \{(x^s - x^L)^2 + (z^s - y^L)^2\}^{\frac{1}{2}}.$$

The way we can implement this idea is to compute the distance between a point on the surface and the light source as above, and to check whether this distance is less than a randomly chosen distance which is computed by selecting a random number over the maximum known distance range. As the distance between the source and the point on the object increases, it becomes increasingly likely that this distance will be greater than the randomly chosen one. If the surface is then coloured dark or light according to whether this test is true or false, the surface will get lighter in colour as the light source is approached. This is of course none other than the random shading technique used earlier to shade the sea in Chapter 3 and several of the landscapes in Chapters 4 and 5. It is of course necessary to choose two colours which best reflect the notions of 'dark' and 'light': blue and cyan are those used in the programs which follow.

We are now in a position to present a program which incorporates these ideas for a variety of mathematical functions in which the value z^w is computed as some function of the Euclidean distance from a fixed origin point. These functions have the general form

$$z^w = f\{[(x^w)^2 + (y^w)^2]^{\frac{1}{2}}\},$$

where the x^w and y^w coordinates in any quadrant are measured from the origin, here the centre of the xy plane $(0,0)$. The general program is listed as Program 6.1 where the form used is based on the sine function. In the sequel, other functions will be used and these can be easily inserted into the program's last line.

The program is structured according to the five stages of the picture generation process. Initializations are made up to line 60 which involve the selection of dark and light blue as the two colours used to plot the surface at the screen resolution associated with MODE1. The essence of the program is two nested FOR–NEXT loops, the first between lines 90 and 180 controlling the selection of the horizontal dimension, the second between lines 110 and 180 controlling the vertical dimension. Before the selection of xy coordinates begins, line 70 sets the light source at point $LX\%$, $LY\%$ and centres the origin of the surface plot to the centre of the screen. The sine and cosine functions associated with $\theta = 45°$ are set in line 80, as well as the horizontal limits of the surface (T) and the vertical scale factor $(H\%)$.

Now for each pixel step based on an increment in the horizontal screen unit of 0.05, the lower and upper vertical bounds of the xy plane are set in line 100.

Program 6.1   Surface plot with image space transformation and light source shading

```
10 REM 3-D Mathematical Surface Plot
20 REM Based on Image Space Transformation
30 REM With Light Source Shading
40 MODE1
50 VDU23,1,0;0;0;0;
60 VDU19,1,4;0;19,2,6;0;
70 LX%=300:LY%=-300:VDU29,640;512;
80 S=SQR(2)/2:T=6*PI*S:H%=30
90 FOR A=-T TO T STEP 0.05
100    MAX%=-1000:BB=-T-A:BE=T-ABS(A)
110    FOR B=BB TO BE
120       IF B<-BE THEN GOTO 180
130       X=S*(A+B):Y=S*(B-A)
140       Z%=FNZ(X,Y)+H%*B:GCOLO,2
150       IF Z%<MAX% THEN GOTO 180
160       IF RND(300)<FND(H%*A,Z%) THEN GCOLO,1
170       MAX%=Z%:PLOT69,H%*A,Z%
180       NEXT B:NEXT A
190 AA=GET:MODE7
200 END
210 :
220 DEFFND(X%,Y%)
230 =SQR((X%-LX%)^2+(Y%-LY%)^2)-300
240 :
250 DEFFNZ(X,Y)
260 R=SQR(X*X+Y*Y):=300*SIN(R)/R
```

However as the *xy* plane is square, the vertical plot bounds must be within this and line 120 ensures that this is the case. Note that the reason why the FOR–NEXT loop controlling the vertical dimension takes the surface outside its bounds is for measurement of the appropriate pixel plot only and line 120 ensures that the surface only appears for the appropriate square *xy* plane. The inverse transformation from screen coordinates A, B to world coordinates X, Y is made in line 130 and the function z and its screen location z^s are computed by the function call in line 140. The function itself is defined for any world coordinates x, y in lines 250 and 260. The third stage of the process involves testing whether or not the computed z^s is hidden in terms of the maximum value of z^s so far. This is tested in line 150 while the last stages of the process are handled in line 160. There the randomly chosen distance is compared to the actual distance between the pixel point and light source and its colour appropriately determined. Note that the distance from the surface point to the light source is computed by the function in lines 220 and 230. If the point has passed the hidden surface test in line 150, it is plotted in line 170 and the maximum value updated. Note that this program only plots the top surface; any part underneath which may be seen is not plotted.

This program is extremely versatile and we have used it not only to plot the sine function as a three-dimensional surface in Program 6.1 but to plot exponential, normal and saddle functions. The sine function produces the familiar jelly-like surface shown in Fig. 6.2(a) while replacing line 260 in the program by

260 R=SQR(X*X+Y*Y):=500*EXP(−0.3*R)

gives a negative exponential surface, the familiar model for population densities in cities, whose three-dimensional form is shown in Fig. 6.2(b). The bell-shaped curve which is found in statistics is generated if line 260 becomes

260 R=SQR(X*X+Y*Y):=300*EXP(−0.035*R*R)

The surface is shown in Fig. 6.2(c) while a more intricate 'saddle' function surface is produced if line 260 is replaced with

260 R=SQR(X*X+Y*Y):=X*Y*(X−Y)*(X+Y)/(1.5*R)

We will not show this saddle function yet but readers are encouraged to modify the program by moving the light source, using other, perhaps more intricate functions, and plotting the lines describing the function's surface in the other direction. This latter possibility could be easily achieved by reiterating lines 90 to 180 but controlling the direction with respect to these iterations. In this way, the surface would appear as though it had a net laid upon it.

Program 6.1 plots only the top side of the surface because the hidden point algorithm only works with respect to the maximum values of the surface. Sometimes however the underside of the surface can be seen and if this is so, minimum values of z for any given x need to be calculated. We have modified Program 6.1 in the listing in Program 6.2. There we have introduced three visibility tests in lines 150, 160 and 170 which respectively detect a point on the surface which is invisible, a point on the surface visible from above, and a point visible from below. Note in this listing that we have coloured the top surface dark blue, and the underside light blue. The lighting model has thus been excluded from the listing and the output for the saddle function is shown in Plate 15.

6.3 THE THREE-DIMENSIONAL REALITY: REPRESENTATIONS AND TRANSFORMATIONS

The method of representing a three-dimensional object or scene is an integral component of the various techniques used to move and transform the object in three-dimensional space. As mentioned earlier, an object in three dimensions is represented as a set of points or vertices which in turn define the object's edges and surfaces. Each point is represented as an ordered triple $[x^w y^w z^w]$ where the w superscript indicates that we are dealing with the world coordinate system. The way the three dimensions x, y and z are arranged with respect to each other is arbitrary but certain conventions have emerged and

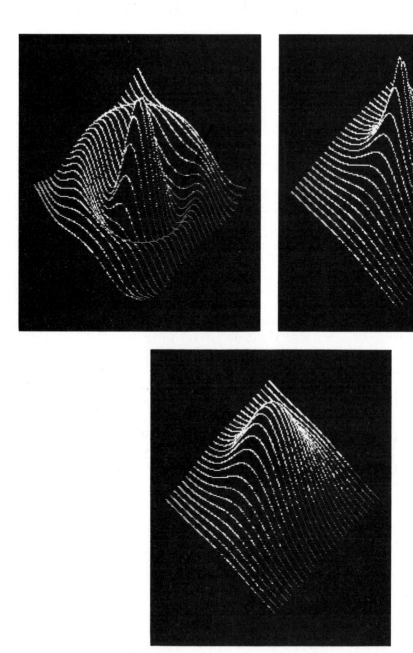

Fig. 6.2   Surface plots

Program 6.2   Surface plot with underside shading

```
10 REM 3-D Mathematical Surface Plot
20 REM Based on Image Space Transformation
30 REM With Under-Surface Shading
40 MODE1
50 VDU23,1,0;0;0;0;
60 VDU19,1,4;0;19,2,6;0;
70 LX%=300:LY%=-300:VDU29,640;512;
80 S=SQR(2)/2:T=6*PI*S:H%=30
90 FOR A=-T TO T STEP 0.05
100    MIN%=1000:MAX%=-1000:BB=-T-A:BE=T-ABS(A)
110    FOR B=BB TO BE
120       IF B<-BE THEN GOTO 190
130       X=S*(A+B):Y=S*(B-A)
140       Z%=FNZ(X,Y)+H%*B
150       IF Z%<MAX% AND Z%>MIN% THEN GOTO 190
160       IF Z%<MIN% THEN MIN%=Z%:GCOL0,2
170       IF Z%>MAX% THEN MAX%=Z%:GCOL0,1
180       PLOT69,H%*A,Z%
190       NEXT B:NEXT A
200 AA=GET:MODE7
210 END
220 :
230 DEFFNZ(X,Y)
240 R=SQR(X*X+Y*Y):=X*Y*(X-Y)*(X+Y)/(1.5*R)
```

we will adhere to these. Basically there are two ways of defining these dimensions as axes of the three-dimensional coordinate system and these are best appreciated visually in Figs 6.3(a) and (b).

Figure 6.3(a) defines a right hand (RH) coordinate system, Fig. 6.3(b) a left hand (LH) system. These are so-called because their axes can be twisted without destroying their adjacency to mirror the relationship of the thumb, fore-finger and middle finger of the left hand and right hand respectively. This

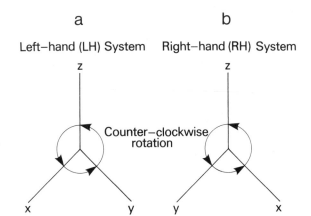

Fig. 6.3   Three-dimensional coordinate systems

convention is of little importance in the sequel but we need to note it because we will represent three-dimensional data in the right hand system to begin with as in Fig. 6.3(a), transforming this to a left hand system as in Fig. 6.3(b) prior to projection on the screen. For the moment, simply note that for the RH system the data are represented with the xy coordinates defining points in the plane while the vertical dimension is given as the z dimension in Fig. 6.3(a).

Three-dimensional transformations can be formally defined as straightforward extensions to the two-dimensional transformations introduced in Chapter 3. We will work in homogeneous coordinates so that we can represent the standard operations of translation, scaling and rotation in matrix form. Thus for any vector of world coordinates expressed in homogeneous form as $[x_n y_n z_n 1]$, we can manipulate these using the standard matrix transform analogous to the two-dimensional form in equation (3.13). This is given as

$$[x_{n+1} y_{n+1} z_{n+1} \ 1] = [x_n y_n z_n \ 1] \begin{bmatrix} a_{11} & a_{12} & a_{13} & 0 \\ a_{21} & a_{22} & a_{23} & 0 \\ a_{31} & a_{32} & a_{33} & 0 \\ \hdashline a_{41} & a_{42} & a_{43} & 1 \end{bmatrix} \tag{6.6}$$

A very distinct interpretation of the structure of this 4×4 matrix in equation (6.6) exists in terms of the blocks of elements defined within the broken-line partitions. Figure 6.4 shows the structure of this matrix as

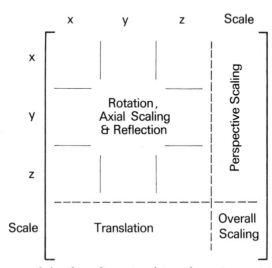

Fig. 6.4 Structure of the three-dimensional transformation matrix (after Harris, 1984)

portrayed by Harris (1984) in which the actions of its various elements are made clear. Note that the upper right hand column of zeros in equation (6.6) can be made to effect the perspective transformation which is described in the next section. Note also in equation (6.6) that the overall scaling controlled by the last cell in the matrix transform has no effective action when set to unity.

The standard transformations of three-dimensional coordinates can now be presented using equation (6.6) in analogy to the transformations introduced for the two-dimensional case in Chapter 3. First translation is effected using the matrix

$$T = \begin{bmatrix} 1 & 0 & 0 & 0 \\ 0 & 1 & 0 & 0 \\ 0 & 0 & 1 & 0 \\ T_1 & T_2 & T_3 & 1 \end{bmatrix} \tag{6.7}$$

which if applied to the vector $[x_n y_n z_n\ 1]$ produces a positive displacement of the point to $[x_n + T_1\ y_n + T_2\ z_n + T_3\ 1]$. Axial scaling is accomplished by the matrix

$$S = \begin{bmatrix} S_1 & 0 & 0 & 0 \\ 0 & S_2 & 0 & 0 \\ 0 & 0 & S_3 & 0 \\ 0 & 0 & 0 & 1 \end{bmatrix} \tag{6.8}$$

which scales the original vector to $[S_1 x_n\ S_2 y_n\ S_3 z_n\ 1]$. A special case of axial scaling is called reflection which is quite literally the reflection of a point about one or more of its axes. This is accomplished by a negative unit scaling, that is by setting $S_1 = -1$, $S_2 = -1$ and/or $S_3 = -1$ dependent upon the axis or axes about which reflection is required.

Rotation, however, is a little trickier than in the two-dimensional case. Rotating a point in three-dimensions is always defined in a counter-clockwise direction with respect to two of the dimensions, holding the 3rd constant. That is, rotation is about the axis which is fixed or constant. This is quite clear from Fig. 6.3(a) where the arrows show the direction of rotation in each of the three planes defining the coordinate system. From this we can define the following rotation matrices for an angular rotation of θ degrees or radians. First with respect to the xy plane, rotation about z is given by

$$R_z = \begin{bmatrix} \cos(\theta) & \sin(\theta) & 0 & 0 \\ -\sin(\theta) & \cos(\theta) & 0 & 0 \\ 0 & 0 & 1 & 0 \\ 0 & 0 & 0 & 1 \end{bmatrix} \tag{6.9}$$

while with respect to the yz plane, rotation about x is defined by

$$R_x = \begin{bmatrix} 1 & 0 & 0 & 0 \\ 0 & \cos(\theta) & \sin(\theta) & 0 \\ 0 & -\sin(\theta) & \cos(\theta) & 0 \\ 0 & 0 & 0 & 1 \end{bmatrix}. \tag{6.10}$$

Finally with respect to the xz plane, rotation about y in a counter-clockwise direction is effected by

$$R_y = \begin{bmatrix} \cos(\theta) & 0 & -\sin(\theta) & 0 \\ 0 & 1 & 0 & 0 \\ \sin(\theta) & 0 & \cos(\theta) & 0 \\ 0 & 0 & 0 & 1 \end{bmatrix}. \tag{6.11}$$

The inverses of all these transformations have a particularly simple form. In the case of T, T^{-1} involves negative displacements $-T_1$, $-T_2$ and $-T_3$; for S, the inverse S^{-1} consists of inverse scaling factors $1/S_1$, $1/S_2$ and $1/S_3$. And for the rotation matrices, the off-diagonal elements – the sine functions – simply involve a reversal of sign. These inverses are essential as the transformation of a coordinate system is always the inverse of the transformation of a point and vice versa (Foley and Van Dam, 1982). We now have all the elements necessary to explore the viewing and perspective transformations which are required to turn a three-dimensional object into a two-dimensional screen image.

6.4   THE VIEWING AND PERSPECTIVE TRANSFORMATIONS

It is convenient both for purposes of presentation and for program organization to separate the three- to two-dimensional transformation process into two stages – the *viewing transformation* which establishes the correct orientation of the object in world coordinates with respect to the viewpoint and the *perspective transformation* which involves projecting the world coordinates onto the two-dimensional plane. The simplest way to appreciate these operations is diagrammatically for this enables a quick impression of the techniques to be gained prior to their formal presentation. In Fig. 6.5(a), the world coordinates are shown for a RH system as in Fig. 6.3(a) and a viewpoint – the viewer's eye position – is also shown in the world space.

At the viewpoint, another coordinate system is shown which with a little thought, is clearly seen to be a transformation of the world coordinate system itself. The coordinate system at the viewpoint has the obvious feature that the z dimension is pointing along the line of sight from the viewpoint to the origin of

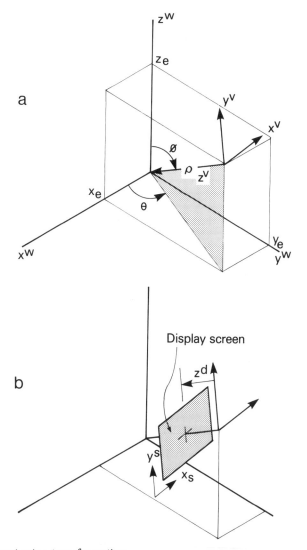

Fig. 6.5   The viewing transformation

the world coordinate system, and that the xy plane is at right-angles to this line of sight. What effectively this means is that the xy plane is equivalent to the two-dimensional screen placed at the viewpoint with the z direction directly 'into' the screen.

Transforming the world coordinate system from its origin to the viewpoint in Fig. 6.5(a) will involve translation and rotation of axes but because the screen coordinate system is LH, will also involve a reflection about its y axis at some stage. But before we present these transformations, we should say a little more about the nature and location of the viewpoint. The viewpoint is located using world coordinates $[x_e y_e z_e]$ but when viewing an object, it is often more convenient and intuitively acceptable to describe the viewpoint in terms of its distance from and its orientation about the object. In Fig. 6.5(a), we show how the three Cartesian coordinates which fix the viewpoint at $[x_e y_e z_e]$ can be replaced by three angular distance measures which are sometimes referred to as spherical (or polar) coordinates. The distance to the object is measured as the distance from the viewpoint to the origin of the world coordinate system and is defined as ρ. It is assumed that the origin is 'near' the object in question, often within it, thus it locates the viewpoint quite unambiguously with respect to the object.

To enable panning around the object, θ is defined as the angular variation from the x axis which is in a counter-clockwise direction in the xy plane. In terms of the world space, this angle measures the orientation on the 'ground'. The height of the viewpoint is controlled by the angle ϕ which varies in a clockwise direction from the z axis in the zy plane. Thus an angle of $\phi = 0°$ implies a vertical viewpoint above the object, $\phi = 90°$ a ground level view and so on. These three measures are sufficient to describe the viewpoint and an examination of Fig. 6.5(a) leads to the Cartesian coordinates of the point $[x_e y_e z_e]$ being defined in spherical form as

$$\left. \begin{aligned} x_e &= \rho \, \sin(\phi)\cos(\theta) \\ y_e &= \rho \, \sin(\phi)\sin(\theta) \quad \text{and} \\ z_e &= \rho \, \cos(\phi). \end{aligned} \right\} \tag{6.12}$$

There are several ways in which the world coordinate system can be transformed to the viewpoint as in Fig. 6.5(a). The sequence of operations adopted here however is that used by Myers (1982); it is straightforward and readers are referred to his account for a more detailed algebraic and diagrammatic presentation. The first stage involves *translating* the origin of the coordinate system to the viewpoint using the spherical coordinates in equation (6.12). Noting that the translation of the coordinate system is the inverse of the operation of translating a point shown earlier as T in equation (6.7), this operation defined in matrix terms as T^c, is given as

$$T^c = \begin{bmatrix} 1 & 0 & 0 & 0 \\ 0 & 1 & 0 & 0 \\ 0 & 0 & 1 & 0 \\ -\rho \sin(\phi)\cos(\theta) & -\rho \sin(\phi)\sin(\theta) & -\cos(\phi) & 1 \end{bmatrix}.$$

The second operation involves rotating the xy dimensions (the xy plane) in a counter-clockwise direction $(90-\theta)$ degrees about the z axis. Using equation (6.10) and simplifying the functions $\sin(90-\theta)$ and $\cos(90-\theta)$ gives the matrix R_z^c defined as

$$R_z^c = \begin{bmatrix} \sin(\theta) & \cos(\theta) & 0 & 0 \\ -\cos(\theta) & \sin(\theta) & 0 & 0 \\ 0 & 0 & 1 & 0 \\ 0 & 0 & 0 & 1 \end{bmatrix}.$$

The final rotation involves a counter-clockwise movement of the yz plane $(180-\phi)$ degrees about the x coordinate axis, so that the z axis ultimately points along the direction of the line of sight from the viewpoint to the initial origin of the world coordinate system. The inverse of equation (6.9) gives

$$R_x^c = \begin{bmatrix} 1 & 0 & 0 & 0 \\ 0 & -\cos(\phi) & -\sin(\phi) & 0 \\ 0 & \sin(\phi) & -\cos(\phi) & 0 \\ 0 & 0 & 0 & 1 \end{bmatrix}.$$

At this point, we still have a RH system and to turn this into a conventional display system parallel to the viewing direction, we must reflect the x axis using the scaling transformation in equation (6.8) as

$$S_x^c = \begin{bmatrix} -1 & 0 & 0 & 0 \\ 0 & 1 & 0 & 0 \\ 0 & 0 & 1 & 0 \\ 0 & 0 & 0 & 1 \end{bmatrix}.$$

This gives a LH coordinate system.

Combining these transformations in the order in which we have introduced them, we can derive the simplified transformation matrix V as

$$V = T^c R_z^c R_x^c S_x^c = \begin{bmatrix} -\sin(\theta) & -\cos(\theta)\cos(\phi) & -\cos(\theta)\sin(\phi) & 0 \\ \cos(\theta) & -\sin(\theta)\cos(\phi) & -\sin(\theta)\sin(\phi) & 0 \\ 0 & \sin(\phi) & -\cos(\phi) & 0 \\ 0 & 0 & \rho & 1 \end{bmatrix}. \quad (6.13)$$

Matrix equation (6.13) transforms a vector of world coordinates $[x^w y^w z^w\ 1]$ into another vector of world coordinates but located in a different orientation from the initial system at the viewpoint. This vector is defined as $[x^v y^v z^v 1]$.

The $x^v y^v$ coordinates represent the object on the plane which is perpendicular to the line of sight which in turn is now represented by the z^v coordinate direction. As such the z^v direction is not 'seen' by the viewer but this coordinate is still essential to the transformation from three- to two-dimensions as it affects the projection which we now present. Imagine that the display screen is placed at distance z^d from the viewpoint, between this viewpoint and the origin of the initial world coordinate system. This is shown in Fig. 6.5(b) and comparison with Fig. 6.5(a) shows that the screen is parallel to the transformed xy plane. If this screen were to be placed at the viewpoint – at the viewer's eye – the projection of the object would be infinitely small and thus as we move the screen away from the eye the object is scaled proportionately by the ratio of the distance from screen to eye, to origin to eye, that is in the ratio z^d/z^v.

The object is scaled by this ratio in both its x and y directions and this achieves the required foreshortening when the screen is between the viewpoint and origin. Thus the screen coordinates x^s and y^s are given as

$$x^s = \frac{z^d}{z^v} x^v \quad \text{and} \quad y^s = \frac{z^d}{z^v} y^v. \tag{6.14}$$

In matrix form, the transformation which leads to equation (6.14) can be written first as

$$[x^v y^v \ 0 \ \frac{z^v}{z^d}] = [x^v y^v z^v \ 1] \begin{bmatrix} 1 & 0 & 0 & 0 \\ 0 & 1 & 0 & 0 \\ 0 & 0 & 0 & \frac{1}{z^d} \\ 0 & 0 & 0 & 0 \end{bmatrix}. \tag{6.15}$$

The screen coordinates can be derived by normalizing equation (6.15) with respect to the overall scaling factor. In vector form, this is

$$[x^s y^s \ 0 \ 1] = \frac{z^d}{z^v} [x^v y^v \ 0 \ \frac{z^v}{z^d}]. \tag{6.16}$$

Equation (6.16) gives a three point perspective image in which the original $x^w y^w z^w$ coordinates when projected on the screen all converge towards vanishing points at increasing distances from the viewer. This is the most complex of the class of perspective projections for some retain the parallelism of the original z dimension, thus involving only two vanishing points. A fuller treatment is given in Foley and Van Dam (1982).

We can now collect the various results in equations (6.13) and (6.16) together and show how a typical set of world coordinates $x^w y^w z^w$ can be transformed to screen coordinates $x^s y^s$. Assuming the viewpoint is defined by ϕ, θ and ρ, and that the distance of the screen from the viewpoint is given as z^d, the screen coordinates are calculated as

$$x^s = -\frac{z^d}{z^v}(x^w \sin(\theta) - y^w \cos(\theta))$$

$$y^s = -\frac{z^d}{z^v}(x^w \cos(\theta)\cos(\phi) + y^w \sin(\theta)\cos(\phi) + z^w \sin(\phi)) \qquad (6.17)$$

where

$$z^v = -x^w \cos(\theta)\sin(\phi) - y^w \sin(\theta)\sin(\phi) - z^w \cos(\phi) + \rho$$

Equations (6.17) are those which will form the procedure used to effect the transformations in the programs now to be presented.

6.5 WIRE FRAME AND SIMPLE HIDDEN SURFACE MODELS

We are now in a position to develop a set of programs which completely reflect the formal mathematics used in the first three stages of the picture generation process but before we do this, some comments on program development are in order. So far in this book, we have listed entire programs, making minor modifications to them so that different effects can be achieved. Only at the end of the last chapter when developing fractal rendering did we form programs by combining elements from earlier programs leaving the reader to piece together the programs in question. This process of building programs by combining segments associated with other programs will be continued in this chapter. Such segments represent program modules which can be merged together systematically to produce quite different scenes. These modules will be based on sets of procedures and one practice will be first to list the full but simplest version of the program, and to then add more detail to it by adding new segments. The programs which build on the original version will not be fully listed but readers will be continually advised how to merge new listings with earlier ones to make up the program under discussion.

The transformations in equations (6.17) enable us to consistently perform the second stage of the picture generation process. These equations provide accurate and effective representations of three-dimensional objects on the two-dimensional screen but without any lines hidden from the viewer being removed. Such objects are referred to as *wire frames*; it is possible to 'see through' them although they can still be effective despite the presence of visual illusion. We will begin our programming by representing a simple object – a house based on a square box with a pitched roof – as a wire frame. The program is listed as Program 6.3 and it is structured in three main sections. First there is a main program from lines 10 to 210 in which initializations, input data, transformations and screen plotting are all controlled by calls to procedures. Second from lines 1000 to 1480, the procedures enabling input,

Program 6.3   Wire frame perspectives

```
  10 REM Wire Frame Perspectives
  20 MODE1
  30 DIM W%(10,3),S%(10,2),P%(7,5),NP%(7),V%(7),Q%(7)
  40 VDU23,1,0;0;0;0;
  50 VDU19,0,1;0;19,1,4;0;19,2,0;0;
  60 VDU28,0,5,39,0:VDU24,0;0;1279;830;
  70 N%=10:M%=7:ZZ=200:VDU29,640;400;
  80 COLOUR 128:GCOL0,129
  90 CLS:CLG:COLOUR 2
 100 PROCINPUT
 110 INPUT TAB(1,1)"DISTANCE FROM VIEW",RHO%
 120 INPUT TAB(1,2)"DISTANCE FROM SCREEN",DIS%
 130 INPUT TAB(1,3)"HORIZONTAL ANGLE",TH
 140 INPUT TAB(1,4)"VERTICAL ANGLE",PH
 150 TH=RAD(TH):PH=RAD(PH)
 160 PROCSETUP
 170 FOR I%=1 TO N%
 180    PROCTRANS(I%):NEXT I%
 190 PROCSCREEN
 200 AA=GET:CLS:CLG:GOTO 110
 210 END
1000 :
1010 REM Reads Coordinate & Surface Arrays from DATA
1020 DEFPROCINPUT
1030 FOR I%=1 TO N%
1040    FOR J%=1 TO 3
1050       READ W%(I%,J%)
1060       NEXT J%:NEXT I%
1070 FOR I%=1 TO M%
1080    READ NP%(I%)
1090    FOR J%=1 TO NP%(I%)
1100       READ P%(I%,J%)
1110       NEXT J%:NEXT I%
1120 ENDPROC
1130 :
1140 REM Sets Up Trigonometric Functions
1150 DEFPROCSETUP
1160 S1=SIN(TH):C1=COS(TH):S2=SIN(PH):C2=COS(PH)
1170 XR%=RHO%*S2*C1:YR%=RHO%*S2*S1:ZR%=RHO%*C2
1180 ENDPROC
1190 :
1200 REM Transform World to Screen Coordinates
1210 DEFPROCTRANS(I%)
1220 X%=W%(I%,1):Y%=W%(I%,2):Z%=W%(I%,3)
1230 X1=-X%*S1+Y%*C1
1240 Y1=-X%*C1*C2-Y%*S1*C2+Z%*S2
1250 Z1=-X%*S2*C1-Y%*S2*S1-Z%*C2+RHO%
1260 D=DIS%/Z1:S%(I%,1)=D*X1:S%(I%,2)=D*Y1
1270 ENDPROC
1280 :
1290 REM Plots Edges of Each Surface of the Object
1300 DEFPROCFRAME(I%)
1310 PROCMOVE(I%,1)
1320 FOR J%=2 TO NP%(I%)
1330    K%=P%(I%,J%):DRAW S%(K%,1),S%(K%,2)
```

Program 6.3 continued

```
1340    NEXT J%
1350 K%=P%(I%,1):DRAW S%(K%,1),S%(K%,2)
1360 ENDPROC
1370 :
1380 REM Moves to the Plotting Position
1390 DEFPROCMOVE(I%,J%)
1400 K%=P%(I%,J%):MOVE S%(K%,1),S%(K%,2)
1410 ENDPROC
1420 :
1430 REM Coordinate & Surface Data for the House
1440 DATA 200,-200,-200,200,-200,200,200,200,200
1450 DATA 200,200,-200,-200,200,-200,-200,200,200
1460 DATA -200,-200,200,-200,-200,-200,0,200,300,0,-200,300
1470 DATA 4,1,2,3,4,4,1,8,5,4,4,5,6,7,8,5,4,3,9,6,5
1480 DATA 5,1,2,10,7,8,4,2,10,9,3,4,7,10,9,6
2000 :
2010 REM Controls Type of Plotting of the Object
2020 DEFPROCSCREEN
2030 FOR I%=1 TO M%
2040    PROCFRAME(I%):NEXT I%
2050 ENDPROC
```

transformation and plotting to be achieved are listed while the third section from lines 2000 to 2050 is a simple procedure controlling the screen plotting. The program is sectionalized in this way, in modules from line 10 upwards, from line 1000 upwards, and from line 2000 upwards. Thus changes to any of these sections can be made without disturbing the other sections and this also enables the changes to be easily and unambiguously located. We will make such changes and extensions later but first we must explore Program 6.3.

In the main program, line 30 dimensions a number of important arrays. $W\%$ is the three-dimensional array of world coordinates, there being ten such ordered triples defining the house; $S\%$ is the equivalent two-dimensional array of screen coordinates; $P\%$ is the so-called surface array which in this case consists of seven surfaces or faces of the house, each surface being located by up to five coordinate points or vertices; and $NP\%$ is the number of such vertices for each surface. Various initializations involving colour, origin, text and graphics windows are made in lines 40 to 90 and then in line 100, PROCINPUT is called. This procedure lies in the second section from lines 1010 to 1120. It reads ten sets of world coordinates, and then the vertices defining the surface array from DATA statements located at lines 1430 to 1480. This point coordinate data is that associated with the corners of the square house with the pitched roof.

Back in the main program, the location of the viewpoint and the display screen relative to this viewpoint in terms of the parameters ρ, z^d, θ and ϕ involve the statements in lines 110 to 140. In line 150, θ and ϕ are converted from degrees to radians and line 160 calls PROCSETUP which in turn computes the standard trigonometric functions used in equations (6.17) in lines 1140 to 1180. Note also that in line 1170, the Cartesian coordinates of the viewpoint are calculated using equations (6.12). At this point in the main program, we are in a position to effect the transformations and initiate the display. The transformations are done for each vertex in the FOR–NEXT loop in lines 170 and 180 which calls PROCTRANS. This procedure at lines 1200 to 1270 essentially computes the screen coordinates x^s and y^s using equations (6.17). Finally in line 190, a call to PROCSCREEN enables the object to be plotted.

PROCSCREEN is located from lines 2010 to 2050. The FOR–NEXT loop in lines 2030 and 2040 calls PROCFRAME for each surface of the object which examines each surface and draws the frame of this surface as lines between its ordered vertices. PROCFRAME itself which is listed from lines 1290 to 1360 calls a standard move procedure PROCMOVE for the first vertex, and then initiates the drawing operations in the FOR–NEXT loop from lines 1320 to 1340. In line 1350, the polygon framing the surface in question is closed. Note also that the vertices are identified from the $P\%$ array and then plotted using the screen coordinate array $S\%$. This easy access to the data structure does have the disadvantage that adjacent surfaces contain edges which are drawn more than once but the extra time involved is not enough to offset the benefits of simpler program structure.

There are several more detailed points to note. The world coordinates are set to the same magnitude as the screen units, and are measured about the origin of the world coordinate system. Thus no screen scaling transformations are required. This program works well with ρ set as 1000, z^d between 700 and 900, while ϕ and θ can take on any values between $0°$ and $360°$. When $\phi = 0°$, this gives a vertical view of the house; when $\phi = 90°$, this gives a ground level view. When $\theta = 0°$, the house is viewed side on; when $\theta = 45°$, corner on, and so forth. It is essential that readers explore the effect of varying all these parameters so that they gain a feel for such perspective transformations by moving towards, even into and away from the house, and by moving the screen position to different locations. A typical example of the wire frame produced is shown in Fig. 6.6.

The wire frame is visually ambiguous and for many purposes unacceptable, hence the existence of the third stage of the picture generation process which involves eliminating lines hidden from the viewpoint. The algorithm we will develop and add to Program 6.3 works on the object or scene in world space by finding the distance of each flat surface from the viewpoint, sorting these distances from largest to smallest, and then plotting the surfaces in this order. As we plot these surfaces at greatest distances from the viewpoint first, the nearer surfaces may overlap the more distant ones. To hide surfaces which are obscured in this way, it is necessary to implement the algorithm on a raster scan device because when a surface is plotted, it must be completely filled in

```
DISTANCE FROM VIEW?1000
DISTANCE FROM SCREEN?800
HORIZONTAL ANGLE?35
VERTICAL ANGLE?65
```

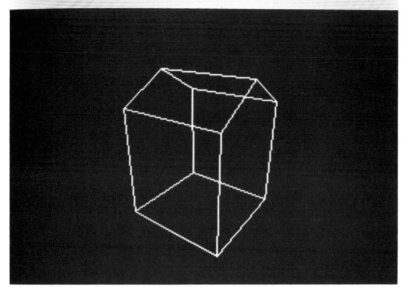

Fig. 6.6   The wire frame house

order to entirely obscure, hence hide those surfaces which lie behind it. To adapt the algorithm to deal with hidden lines, each surface can be plotted in the background colour and then framed or edged by the visible lines. Essentially this algorithm is the hidden surface method referred to as the z-buffer or depth sort algorithm (Foley and Van Dam, 1982) which is the three-dimensional formal equivalent of the painter's algorithm introduced in Chapter 4 to construct 'flat' landscapes.

Program 6.3 can be extended by replacing lines upwards from 2000 by the segment listed in Program 6.4. This segment adds the depth sort and hidden surface plotting to the wireframe program. Up to the call to PROCSCREEN in line 190 of Program 6.3, it is the same as Program 6.3 and all the changes are thus additional procedure calls from PROCSCREEN which are listed thereafter. PROCSCREEN itself in lines 2010 to 2070 first establishes the distances from viewpoint to surface in PROCDEPTH and sorts these from largest to smallest in PROCSORT. This gives the order of plotting which is controlled by a call to PROCFILL which fills the surface in question, and then by a call to the existing procedure PROCFRAME which edges the surface.

PROCDEPTH in lines 2090 to 2230 begins by examining each surface in

Program 6.4   Hidden surface based on depth sort

```
2000 :
2010 REM Controls Type of Plotting of the Object
2020 DEFPROCSCREEN
2030 PROCDEPTH:PROCSORT
2040 FOR I%=1 TO M%
2050    PROCFILL(Q%(I%))
2060    AA=INKEY(ZZ):NEXT I%
2070 ENDPROC
2080 :
2090 REM Computes Average Surface Depth from Viewpoint
2100 DEFPROCDEPTH
2110 FOR I%=1 TO M%
2120    V%(I%)=-EXP(20):Q%(I%)=EXP(20)
2130    FOR J%=1 TO NP%(I%)
2140      K%=P%(I%,J%)
2150      D1%=(W%(K%,1)-XR%)^2:D2%=(W%(K%,2)-YR%)^2
2160      D3%=(W%(K%,3)-ZR%)^2:D%=SQR(D1%+D2%+D3%)
2170      IF D%>=V%(I%) THEN V%(I%)=D%
2180      IF D%<=Q%(I%) THEN Q%(I%)=D%
2190      NEXT J%:NEXT I%
2200 FOR I%=1 TO M%
2210    V%(I%)=(V%(I%)+Q%(I%))/2:Q%(I%)=I%
2220    NEXT I%
2230 ENDPROC
2240 :
2250 REM Bubble Sort on the Depth Values
2260 DEFPROCSORT
2270 FOR I%=2 TO M%
2280    FOR J%=I% TO 2 STEP -1
2290      IF V%(J%)<=V%(J%-1) THEN GOTO 2330
2300      T%=V%(J%):F%=Q%(J%)
2310      V%(J%)=V%(J%-1):Q%(J%)=Q%(J%-1)
2320      V%(J%-1)=T%:Q%(J%-1)=F%:NEXT J%
2330    NEXT I%
2340 ENDPROC
2350 :
2360 REM Fills Each Surface In Order of Depth Sort
2370 DEFPROCFILL(I%)
2380 COL%=2:IF I%>=6 THEN COL%=0
2390 GCOLO,COL%:PROCMOVE(I%,1):PROCMOVE(I%,2)
2400 K%=P%(I%,3):PLOT85,S%(K%,1),S%(K%,2):PROCMOVE(I%,1)
2410 K%=P%(I%,4):PLOT85,S%(K%,1),S%(K%,2)
2420 IF NP%(I%)=5 THEN K%=P%(I%,5):PLOT85,S%(K%,1),S%(K%,2)
2430 GCOLO,3:PROCFRAME(I%)
2440 ENDPROC
```

the FOR–NEXT loop between lines 2110 and 2190. Each vertex of a given surface is examined in the loop between lines 2130 and 2190 and the distance to the point computed in lines 2150 and 2160. For each surface, the smallest and largest distances associated with its vertices are required and the tests to determine this are given in lines 2170 and 2180. After all surfaces have been examined, the FOR–NEXT loop between lines 2200 and 2220 computes the average of the smallest and largest distances to the vertices of each surface, and stores this as the distance to be sorted by PROCSORT. The sorting is accomplished in PROCSORT which is listed between lines 2250 and 2340. The algorithm used is a standard 'bubble' sort which involves moving the largest distances encountered so far in the sort up the stack until no further reordering is encountered. The logic of this sort should be explored by readers who have not seen it before. Note that the arrays $V\%$ and $Q\%$ dimensioned in Program 6.3 but not used there, are used in this depth sort.

Finally PROCFILL is listed in lines 2360 to 2440. This is a standard set of commands which fill the surface in question with a given colour using appropriate combinations of MOVE and PLOT85 commands depending upon whether the surface is four- or five-sided. Finally in line 2430, a call to PROCFRAME edges the surface in a different colour. If the algorithm is to be adapted to hidden lines only, then changing $COL\%$ variable in line 2380 to $COL\% = 1$ in both cases will enable this. To put Program 6.4 into 6.3 which is of course necessary to run the depth sort algorithm, Program 6.4 must either be typed onto the end of 6.3, or a new file created just for Program 6.4 which is then merged with 6.3 using the method outlined in Chapter 37 of the User Guide. This involves the creation of a *SPOOL "Filename" file which is then merged with the original program using the *EXEC "Filename" Command. It will be assumed that readers who are developing these programs alongside this text will be using this procedure.

Running Programs 6.3 and 6.4 together produces a solid black house with red roof whose edges are outlined in white. From the run, it is quite clear how the depth sort achieves this. We can illustrate the whole process graphically by merging the code listed in Program 6.5 into the Program (6.3 + 6.4). This simply plots all the different surfaces of the house up to the order they are considered at different locations on the screen. To achieve a reasonable demonstration, set $\rho = 1000$, $z^d = 450$, $\theta = 35$ and $\phi = 65$. The result is presented in Fig. 6.7 which clearly illustrates how the depth sort considers the

Program 6.5   Stages in the depth sort

```
2000 :
2010 REM Controls Type of Plotting of the Object
2020 DEFPROCSCREEN
2030 PROCDEPTH:PROCSORT
2031 FOR L%=1 TO M%
2032   IF L%=1 THEN DA%=86:INC%=328
2033   IF L%=5 THEN DA%=220:INC%=420
2034   IF L%<=4 THEN DB%=600 ELSE DB%=220
2035   VDU29,DA%;DB%;
2040   FOR I%=1 TO L%
2050     PROCFILL(Q%(I%))
2060     AA=INKEY(ZZ):NEXT I%
2061   DA%=DA%+INC%:NEXT L%
2070 ENDPROC
```

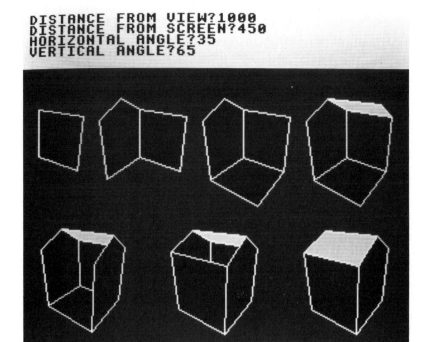

Fig. 6.7   A 'solid' house based on depth sorting

'inside' of the house first, and how the transformations used give a clear three point perspective display. The other simple modification we have introduced here is some code which enables the viewpoint to be shifted around the house, thus simulating the effect of panning. This is listed in Program 6.6 which replaces lines 100 to 210 in the main program of the merged Program

Program 6.6   Panning and zooming around the house

```
100 PROCINPUT
102 RHO%=1000:DIS%=800:H=0:PHH=0:ZZ=0
104 REPEAT
106   H=H+RND(30):PHH=PHH+RND(30)
110   PRINT TAB(1,1)"DISTANCE FROM VIEW",RHO%
120   PRINT TAB(1,2)"DISTANCE FROM SCREEN",DIS%
130   PRINT TAB(1,3)"HORIZONTAL ANGLE",PHH
140   PRINT TAB(1,4)"VERTICAL ANGLE",H
150   TH=RAD(H):PH=RAD(PHH)
160   PROCSETUP
170   FOR I%=1 TO N%
180     PROCTRANS(I%):NEXT I%
190   PROCSCREEN
200   AA=INKEY(700):CLG:CLS:UNTIL FALSE
210 END
```

$(6.3 + 6.4)$. ρ and z^d are set at 1000 and 800 respectively while θ and ϕ are continually increased by a random amount thus enabling the viewpoint to be shifted around, over and under the house. This iteration is embedded in a REPEAT–UNTIL loop located between lines 104 and 200 which continually updates the view parameters. As the angular parameters are always increased, the program will eventually crash but by then its use in exploring the panning operation will have been long exhausted.

As in all our programs so far, as soon as we have introduced a technique of graphical modelling, we must use it to create some computer art. The program segment which is listed as Program 6.7 when merged with Programs 6.3 and 6.4, creates an urban landscape by replicating the standard house many times in long lines of terraces splayed across the screen. Program 6.7 which is a modified main program with new procedures, uses the standard depth sort on each house outlined in Program 6.4 above but also uses a coarser depth sort to enable the terraces to be viewed from one general direction; in short then Program 6.7 represents a combination of the depth sort with the painter's algorithm which plots lines of terraces from the background to the foreground of the picture. After the usual initializations, the program first prompts the user to input viewpoint data in lines 80 to 110, and then in line 150 calls PROCSETUP. Also in line 150, there is a procedure call to PROCBACK which plots a solid blue background as a sinewave in the manner used in Chapter 4 to create the Random Landscapes, and Vale of Glamorgan pictures. This gives the impression of a low gently rolling horizon of distant hills. The procedure which is defined in lines 290 to 400 computes a random wave within given limits of frequency and amplitude and also determines the minimum y coordinate on the screen where the terraces should begin to be plotted.

The main program itself determines the number of rows of terraces dependent upon the viewpoint but there are always at least five rows. Each row is plotted within the FOR–NEXT loop between lines 170 and 250 within which is a REPEAT–UNTIL loop which plots additional houses in any terrrace until the current house is outside the screen limits. The house is computed using the depth sort algorithm while PROCPLACE, called in line 200, places the new house being plotted in front of but abutting the last house. The plotting is so controlled as to enable the screen to be entirely filled with terraces, thus ensuring a complete picture. The essence of the terrace plotting is contained in PROCPLACE which is listed in lines 420 to 620. This procedure positions the house in such a way that it touches the previous house (lines 440 to 470) and then makes a random perturbation to the standard house size in setting all the other coordinates in the rest of the procedure. The REPEAT–UNTIL loops in lines 490 to 520 and 540 to 600 represent as efficient a way to set up the data structure as I have been able to find. Ten sets of three-dimensional coordinates giving 30 values in all are set up here and readers are challenged to try and improve the efficiency of this coding.

Program 6.7   The valleyscape of New Tredegar

```
 10 REM The Valleyscape of New Tredegar
 20 MODE1
 30 DIM W%(10,3),S%(10,2),P%(7,5),NP%(7),V%(7),Q%(7)
 40 VDU23,1,0;0;0;0;
 50 VDU19,0,1;0;19,1,4;0;19,2,0;0;
 60 N%=10:M%=7:ZZ=0:COLOUR 2
 70 PROCINPUT
 80 INPUT TAB(1,1)"DISTANCE FROM VIEW",RHO%
 90 INPUT TAB(1,2)"DISTANCE FROM SCREEN",DIS%
100 INPUT TAB(1,3)"HORIZONTAL ANGLE",TH
110 INPUT TAB(1,4)"VERTICAL ANGLE",PH
120 GCOL0,130:CLG:VDU29,0;0;
130 XB%=1200:INC%=500:ZBASE%=-200:START%=-200
140 TH=RAD(TH):PH=RAD(PH)
150 PROCSETUP:PROCBACK
160 VDU29,640;MAX%;
170 FOR JI%=1 TO 5+INT(RHO%/DIS%)
180    W%(4,2)=START%
190    REPEAT
200      PROCPLACE
210      FOR I%=1 TO N%
220        PROCTRANS(I%):NEXT I%
230      PROCSCREEN
240    UNTIL S%(5,1)<-900 OR S%(4,1)>900 OR S%(8,2)<-1100
250    XB%=XB%-INC%-RND(200):NEXT JI%
260 AA=GET:GCOL0,128:CLG:COLOUR 2:GOTO 80
270 END
280 :
290 REM Plots the Background as a Sine Wave
300 DEFPROCBACK
310 GCOL0,1:YS%=900:DT=RAD(10):A=RAD(RND(360))
320 S=SIN(DT):C=COS(DT):SS=SIN(A):CC=COS(A)
330 SI=25+RND(25):YN%=YS%+SI*SS
340 MOVE 0,0:MOVE 0,YN%:MAX%=100000
350 FOR I%=20 TO 1280 STEP 20
360    SN=SS*C+CC*S:CC=CC*C-SS*S:SS=SN
370    YN%=YS%+SI*SS:IF YN%<=MAX% THEN MAX%=YN%
380    PLOT85,I%,0:PLOT85,I%,YN%
390    NEXT I%
400 ENDPROC
410 :
420 REM Computes the Coordinates of the Next House
430 DEFPROCPLACE
440 X1%=XB%-150-RND(50):X2%=XB%+150+RND(50)
450 X3%=(X1%+X2%)/2:Y1%=W%(4,2)
460 Y2%=Y1%+350+RND(50):Z1%=ZBASE%
470 Z2%=Z1%+250+RND(50):Z3%=Z2%+100+RND(25)
480 K1%=0:K2%=4:K3%=2
490 REPEAT
500    K1%=K1%+1:K2%=K2%+1:K3%=K3%+1
510    W%(K1%,1)=X1%:W%(K2%,1)=X2%:W%(K3%,2)=Y2%
520    UNTIL K1%=4
530 K1%=8:K2%=0:K3%=6:K4%=1:K5%=3:K6%=5
540 REPEAT
550    K1%=K1%+1:K2%=K2%+1:K3%=K3%+1
```

Program 6.7   continued

```
560    K4%=K4%+1:K5%=K5%+1:K6%=K6%+1
570    W%(K1%,1)=X3%:W%(K2%,2)=Y1%:W%(K3%,2)=Y1%
580    W%(K4%,3)=Z2%:W%(K5%,3)=Z1%
590    W%(K6%,3)=Z2%:W%(K1%,3)=Z3%
600    UNTIL K2%=2
610    W%(9,2)=Y2%:W%(10,2)=Y1%:W%(1,3)=Z1%:W%(8,3)=Z1%
620    ENDPROC
```

Running the program with $\rho = 10000$, $z^d = 5000$, $\theta = 100$ and $\phi = 80$ produces a picture of long lines of bleak terraces, looking across the rooftops; this is shown in Plate 16. The scene could be anywhere in industrial Britain, but the rolling horizon reminds one of the Welsh Valleys. We have called the scene New Tredegar after that place where line upon line of terraces cover the valleyside. This landscape provokes strong reactions, it has an evocative imagery, and in this case the computer picture is almost a kind of urban sculpture. It is essential that you explore this program by changing the viewpoint parameters. You will find that with quite small variations in θ, the temporal priority merged with depth sort will break down and this provides an excellent illustration of the point that there is no feasible three-dimensional hidden surface procedure to date which enables the general case to be treated. All such algorithms are to some extent tailored to the problem in hand and their limitations become especially clear when they are used to create scenes more complicated than those for which they were first demonstrated. Nevertheless more general procedures than those of this section are available and to these we will now turn.

6.6 BACKSURFACE ELIMINATION: A MORE GENERAL HIDDEN LINE AND SURFACE ALGORITHM

There are several problems with the depth sort hidden surface algorithm introduced above. It only works on raster graphics devices because it achieves an appropriate display not by eliminating what is hidden but by overplotting. As such it cannot be implemented on a vector display. Secondly, as it plots all the surfaces, it is wasteful in terms of computer time and this can become a problem with very complex pictures. But the most severe problem involves the inability of the algorithm itself to handle complex but nevertheless convex shapes. The algorithm can simply break down because the average depth/distance calculations become ambiguous. In short, although the algorithm works satisfactorily on reasonably square convex shapes, it can break down when confronted with shapes composed of many smaller surfaces. For example, consider the case of a long rectangular object whose backface is a complete plane but whose front faces are much smaller adjacent crenellated planes. It is easy to envisage a situation where the 'average' distance to the long back surface is smaller than the 'average' to one of the shorter front surfaces facing the viewer. What in fact is required is not simply the *distance* which to any surface is an average, but the *orientation* of the surface with respect to the viewpoint.

The algorithm we are about to propose works by computing the orientation of each surface and then eliminating those which face away from the viewpoint. The technique will still only work on convex objects for on nonconvex objects, it is possible for a face to point towards the viewpoint but be hidden by another face which points away from the viewpoint but is nearer. Thus distance can still be important and this suggests that an even more general algorithm might be composed from the earlier depth sort and the backsurface elimination technique which we will present in a moment. We will not do this here but it should be possible for the careful reader who has absorbed and understood all the material presented so far to compose such an algorithm for him or herself. More elaborate and general algorithms are given in Newman and Sproull (1979) and Foley and Van Dam (1982), and interested readers are referred to the excellent survey article by Sutherland, Sproull and Schumacker (1974) which despite its age, is still relevant.

The algorithm can be presented in two stages. First, the surfaces of the object must be coded in the order in which their vertices are contiguous so that the direction of the surface – facing towards the interior or exterior of the object – can be easily and directly determined. This is essential so that the direction of the vector which is *perpendicular* or *normal* to any surface can be calculated. Second, when these normal vectors have been computed, their direction is compared to that of the line of sight from the viewer to the surface in question. From this comparison, it is a simple matter to determine whether or not the surface points towards the viewer, and such a test is used to include or eliminate the surface from the plotting routine. Clearly, the algorithm works in the world space of the object, not its image space.

Figures 6.8(a) and (b) present a diagrammatic exposition of these two stages and we will now complement this by a formal presentation. As implied above whenever a normal vector is computed for a surface, we must know the direction in which the vector points and this is achieved externally in the data structure used to encode the object. This means that when the vertices describing the end points of the lines which define the surface, are placed in the surface array $P\%$ (already introduced in all the Programs from 6.3 on), the order of these vertices must consistently reflect the direction of the surface related to the interior/exterior of the object. These vertices must be ordered in a clockwise or counter-clockwise direction around the surface in question. In Fig. 6.8(a) and in the programs that follow, the vertices are ordered counter-clockwise and the following equations used to compute normals etc. apply directly. If however the vertices are ordered clockwise, the signs of the equations must be reversed. The important point to note is that these vertices

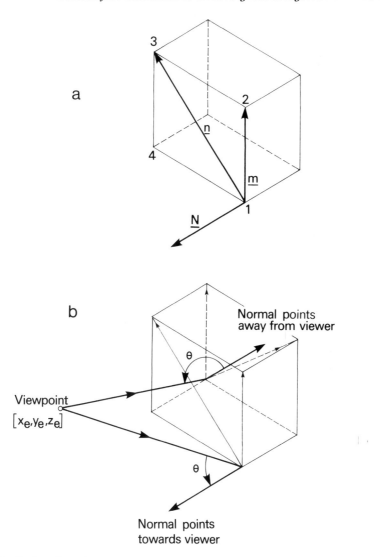

Fig. 6.8 Backsurface elimination

must not be placed randomly in the surface array but ordered in one direction or the other.

To compute the vector normal for the surface shown in Fig. 6.8(a) as the vector $N = [x_n y_n z_n]$, it is necessary to compute the vectors from any fixed vertex on the surface to any two successively ordered vertices on the same surface, and to then compute their cross product. The two vectors in question are referred to as $m = [x_m y_m z_m]$ and $n = [x_n y_n z_n]$ where n and m relate to the vectors formed which link surface vertices l and m, and l and n respectively. Note that $l < m < n$. Let us assume that the fixed vertex l in question is vertex 1, vertex m is 2 and vertex n is 3 as shown in Fig. 6.8(a). Then the two vectors m and n are computed as

$$m = [x_m y_m z_m] = [x_2 - x_1 \ y_2 - y_1 \ z_2 - z_1]$$

and

$$n = [x_n y_n z_n] = [x_3 - x_1 \ y_3 - y_1 \ z_3 - z_1].$$

The cross product of these two vectors given as

$$N = [x_n \ y_n \ z_n] = m \times n,$$

produces the vector normal N which can be derived as

$$N = [y_m z_n - y_n z_m \ z_m x_n - z_n x_m \ x_m y_n - x_n y_m]. \tag{6.18}$$

Equation (6.18) gives the vector which is normal to the vertex l on the surface in question, but is also normal to any point on the surface which is true because the surface is a flat plane. The orientation of this vector is to the outside of the object if the vertices are coded counter-clockwise, to the inside if the coding is the opposite of this. Thus the normal points towards a viewer who is facing the surface as Fig. 6.8(a) makes clear.

It is now necessary to compare this normal vector N with the line of sight vector e describing the direction of the sight line from the eye coordinates $[x_e y_e z_e]$ to the point on the surface at which the normal has been computed. This point is $[x_l y_l z_l]$ where in the example in Fig. 6.8(a) $l = 1$. Then e is defined as

$$e = [x_e - x_1 \ y_e - y_1 \ z_e - z_1].$$

In relation to the normal N, this vector e is shown in Fig. 6.8(b). It is quite clear from this illustration that if the normal points towards the viewer, implying that the surface is visible, then the angle between the vectors N and e is between $0°$ and $90°$. If the surface points away from the viewer, this angle is between $90°$ and $180°$. This is shown for two such surfaces in Fig. 6.8(b) and thus the second stage of this algorithm involves computing the angle at which the two vectors intersect. This computation involves the dot product between the vectors N and e which is formally defined as

$$e \cdot N = |e||N|\cos(\theta). \tag{6.19}$$

$|e|$ and $|N|$ are absolute value vectors associated with e and N while θ is the angle formed by their intersection. From equation (6.19) we get

$$\cos(\theta) = \frac{e \cdot N}{|e||N|}, \tag{6.20}$$

from which it is obvious that if $0 \leqslant \theta < 90°$, equation (6.20) will be positive whereas if $90° < \theta < 180°$, the equation value will be negative. As the denominator $|e\|N|$ is by definition positive, the sign of (6.20) is thus determined by $e . N$. Thus the absolute value vectors do not need to be computed. The dot product $e . N$ is calculated as

$$\delta = e . N = x_e x_n + y_e y_n + z_e z_n, \qquad (6.21)$$

and if δ is negative, the normal points away from the viewer and the surface is thus hidden. The surface is visible only when δ is positive. When δ is zero, the surface can either be eliminated or included because the screen plotting will resolve its form. Of course, the test can also be applied to hidden lines which in our examples here are always subsets of the surfaces in question.

The algebra of this method is explained in a little more detail in Myers (1982) and it is developed in depth in the standard texts such as Foley and Van Dam (1982). If the reader requires a deeper understanding of vector algebra which is not strictly necessary for these purposes but would be essential for taking these ideas further, it is necessary to examine the appropriate sections of any text on linear, vector or matrix algebra such as Hadley (1961).

6.7   SOLIDS OF ROTATION: CONSTRUCTING AND PLOTTING CYLINDERS, CONES AND SPHERES

We now have considerably more technique at our disposal and can begin to construct more elaborate solid objects than the house we initially explored. Indeed in this section, we will make use of all the techniques in this chapter to construct regular man-made objects whose geometry is easily defined. Although highly organized in spatial terms, the vertices and surfaces which define a house cannot be generated using a geometric model whose algebraic form is entirely general. On the other hand, objects such as cylinders, cones and spheres amongst others can be quickly and easily generated by tracing out their surface structure using standard trigonometric functions. Such objects are frequently called *solids of rotation*, a term which implies that their form is traced out by rotating a set of points or surfaces around some fixed point. In the sequel we will explore such solids and show how they can be plotted using the algorithms of previous sections.

The easiest object to begin with is the cylinder which as Fig. 6.9(a) shows, can be defined as two end surfaces – *circular plates*, joined together by a number of *rectangular panels*. Clearly the greater the number of points which trace out each plate, the greater the number of panels, and the closer the object approximates the 'true' cylindrical form. The object is easy to generate for its vertices are all determined in terms of the two end plates which in turn are made up of regularly spaced points on the circumference of a circle. One of the attractions of setting up three-dimensional objects as solids of rotation is that

a

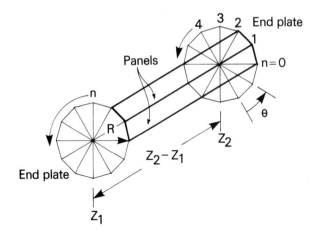

b

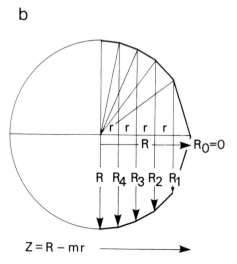

Fig. 6.9   Solids of rotation

the dimensions describing the world coordinates are directly related to each other trigonometrically.

Consider the cylinder in Fig. 6.9(a). The vertices of each end plate are given by the coordinate vector

$$[x_n y_n z_k], \quad n = 0, 1, \ldots, N; \ k = 1,2$$

where the elements are computed as

$$x_n = R\,\cos(n\theta)$$
$$y_n = R\,\sin(n\theta)$$

and

$$z_k = z_1 \text{ or } z_2.$$

(6.22)

The points traced out on each end plate are equally spaced at angular increments of θ and centred on the cylindrical axis where the cylinder has radius R. As there are N such increments making up the rotation, $N\theta = 360°$. The plates are located at z_1 and z_2 in the z_k dimension, thus the length of the cylinder and each of its panels is $[z_2 - z_1]$. The four vertices which define a typical panel are thus formed from two adjacent vertices of each of the end plates, that is from $[x_n y_n z_1]$, $[x_n y_n z_2]$, $[x_{n-1} y_{n-1} z_2]$ and $[x_{n-1} y_{n-1} z_1]$. Starting from the points where $\theta = 0$ and assuming the rotation is a full circular sweep back to the same points now defined by $N\theta$, this generates end plates with N segments, defined by $N+1$ vertices where the first and last vertices, $n = 0$ and $n = N$ are the same. The cylinder would thus be composed of N panels.

We will first introduce a standard program to plot such a solid of rotation and this is listed as Program 6.8. This program has a similar structure to Program 6.3 with the main program controlling inputs, transformations and screen plotting through procedure calls from line 10 upwards, the data structures, transformations and plotting being located from line 1000 upwards, and the screen plotting itself being given from line 2000 upwards. The program is the strict equivalent of Program 6.3 in that it generates a wire frame of a cylinder, and will be used as the basis for a hidden surface algorithm using backsurface elimination. As set up, the program assumes that the cylinder is composed of 15 panels, each end plate being based on circles with 15 segments defined by 16 sets of coordinates. In lines 30 and 40, the arrays are dimensioned. $W\%$ is the three-dimensional world coordinate array in which elements 0–15 represent the first end plate coordinates, 16–31 the second end plate coordinates. $S\%$ is the associated two-dimensional screen array while $P\%$ is the surface array for the two end plates which each have 16 vertices. $PP\%$ is the surface array for 15 panels, each having five vertices. $NE\%$ and $NS\%$ are arrays used for the backsurface elimination in the next program. Note that $N\%$ defined in line 80 is the number of panels computed as $N\% = 360/\theta$ where $\theta = 24$, the angular increment used in the rotational sweep.

In line 110 instead of the call to PROCINPUT, there is a call to PROCSOLID which sets up the solid of rotation. This procedure is listed in lines 1010 to 1180. Two nested FOR–NEXT loops between lines 1040 and 1100 generate the two end plates using equations (6.22) where the z_1 and z_2 values are reflected about the centre point of the cylinder which acts as the origin of the world coordinate system. From these coordinates, the two surface arrays are

Program 6.8   A wire cylinder as a solid of rotation

```
  10 REM Wire Cylinder:Solid of Rotation
  20 MODE1
  30 DIM W%(31,2),S%(31,1),P%(1,15)
  40 DIM PP%(14,4),NE%(1,2),NS%(14,2)
  50 VDU23,1,0;0;0;0;
  60 VDU19,0,1;0;19,1,4;0;19,2,0;0;
  70 VDU28,0,5,39,0:VDU24,0;0;1279;830;
  80 ST%=24:N%=360/ST%:ZZ=200:VDU29,640;512;
  90 COLOUR 128:GCOL0,129
 100 CLS:CLG:COLOUR 2
 110 PROCSOLID
 120 INPUT TAB(1,1)"DISTANCE FROM VIEW",RHO%
 130 INPUT TAB(1,2)"DISTANCE FROM SCREEN",DIS%
 140 INPUT TAB(1,3)"HORIZONTAL ANGLE",TH
 150 INPUT TAB(1,4)"VERTICAL ANGLE",PH
 160 TH=RAD(TH):PH=RAD(PH)
 170 PROCSETUP
 180 FOR I%=0 TO 2*N%+1
 190   PROCTRANS(I%):NEXT I%
 200 PROCSCREEN
 210 AA=GET:CLS:CLG:GOTO 120
 220 END
1000 :
1010 REM Sets Up Coordinate & Surface Arrays
1020 DEFPROCSOLID
1030 XX%=350:R%=200:K%=0
1040 FOR L%=1 TO 2
1050   FOR I%=0 TO 360 STEP ST%
1060     W%(K%,0)=XX%
1070     W%(K%,1)=R%*COS(RAD(I%))
1080     W%(K%,2)=R%*SIN(RAD(I%))
1090     K%=K%+1:NEXT I%
1100   XX%=-XX%:NEXT L%
1110 FOR I%=0 TO N%
1120   P%(0,I%)=I%:K%=N%+I%+1
1130   P%(1,I%)=K%:NEXT I%
1140 FOR I%=0 TO N%-1
1150   PP%(I%,4)=P%(0,I%):PP%(I%,0)=P%(0,I%)
1160   PP%(I%,1)=P%(0,I%+1):PP%(I%,2)=P%(1,I%+1)
1170   PP%(I%,3)=P%(1,I%):NEXT I%
1180 ENDPROC
1190 :
1200 REM Sets Up Trigonometric Functions
1210 DEFPROCSETUP
1220 S1=SIN(TH):C1=COS(TH):S2=SIN(PH):C2=COS(PH)
1230 XR%=RHO%*S2*C1:YR%=RHO%*S2*S1:ZR%=RHO%*C2
1240 ENDPROC
1250 :
1260 REM Transform World to Screen Coordinates
1270 DEFPROCTRANS(I%)
1280 X%=W%(I%,0):Y%=W%(I%,1):Z%=W%(I%,2)
1290 X1=-X%*S1+Y%*C1
1300 Y1=-X%*C1*C2-Y%*S1*C2+Z%*S2
1310 Z1=-X%*S2*C1-Y%*S2*S1-Z%*C2+RHO%
```

Program 6.8   continued

```
1320 D=DIS%/Z1:S%(I%,0)=D*X1:S%(I%,1)=D*Y1
1330 ENDPROC
1340 :
1350 REM Plots Edges of End Surfaces of the Object
1360 DEFPROCFRAME1(I%)
1370 K%=P%(I%,0):MOVE S%(K%,0),S%(K%,1)
1380 FOR J%=1 TO N%
1390    K%=P%(I%,J%):DRAW S%(K%,0),S%(K%,1)
1400    NEXT J%
1410 ENDPROC
1420 :
1430 REM Plots Edges of Side Surfaces of the Object
1440 DEFPROCFRAME2(I%)
1450 K%=PP%(I%,0):MOVE S%(K%,0),S%(K%,1)
1460 FOR J%=1 TO 4
1470    K%=PP%(I%,J%):DRAW S%(K%,0),S%(K%,1)
1480    NEXT J%
1490 ENDPROC
2000 :
2010 REM Controls Type of Plotting of the Object
2020 DEFPROCSCREEN
2030 FOR I%=0 TO 1
2040    PROCFRAME1(I%):NEXT I%
2050 FOR I%=0 TO N%-1
2060    PROCFRAME2(I%):NEXT I%
2070 ENDPROC
```

set up in a straightforward manner in the two FOR–NEXT loops between lines 1110 and 1130, and 1140 and 1170. This provides a reasonably efficient method of generating the data structure.

The rest of the program is very similar to Program 6.3. Back in the main program, the viewpoint is read in from the keyboard (lines 120 to 150), the trigonometric functions determined by PROCSETUP while the FOR–NEXT loop in lines 180 to 190 calls PROCTRANS which transforms the world coordinates to the screen display. These procedures are identical to those already introduced. The call to PROCSCREEN which in turn is listed in lines 2010 to 2070 is slightly different from Program 6.3 in that the end plate surfaces are plotted in lines 2030 to 2040 by a call to PROCFRAME1 while the panels are plotted by a call to PROCFRAME2 in lines 2050 and 2060. These two procedures listed at lines 1350 to 1410 and 1430 to 1490 respectively simply access the two surface arrays individually. It is quite straightforward to generalize these procedures to one single procedure and this would be a useful exercise for the reader. But here we have kept them separate purely for pedagogic purposes as it clarifies the structure of the object being displayed.

To run the program, select ρ as 1000, z^d as 800, θ as $45°$ and ϕ as $65°$. This generates Fig. 6.10. The same range of values as that used earlier for the house is applicable. Pan around the cylinder and zoom in by increasing the screen

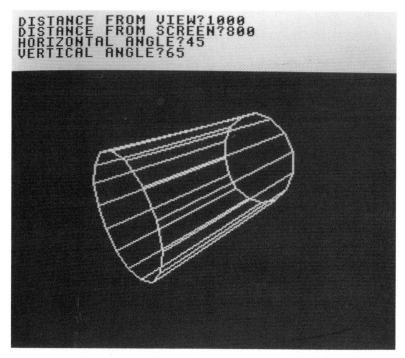

```
DISTANCE FROM VIEW?1000
DISTANCE FROM SCREEN?800
HORIZONTAL ANGLE?45
VERTICAL ANGLE?65
```

Fig. 6.10   The wire frame cylinder

distance z^d. Note that the radius and length of the cylinder are fixed in line 1030 as $R\% = 200$ and $XX\% = 350$ (which implies a length of 700). Try generating a Ferris wheel with $XX\%$ reduced to 50 and $R\%$ at 350. This will be the basis of the sphere we introduce a little later which will be composed of thin tapering cylindrical slices.

We can immediately extend the wire frame program to incorporate the backsurface elimination technique developed in the previous section. The logic of this has already been explained and in essence, it involves computing the surface normals, in this case for each end plate and panel, and then comparing each of these vectors with the appropriate line of sight vectors, thus enabling surfaces pointing away from the viewer to be eliminated. We can augment Program 6.8 by adding all these operations to the screen plotting segment from line 2000 upwards. These additions are listed in Program 6.9 which must be merged with Program 6.8 to enable solid objects with hidden lines and surfaces to be plotted. Note that this merged program (6.8 + 6.9) will be the basis for the rest of the programs introduced in this chapter.

In Program 6.9, PROCSCREEN which is defined between lines 2010 and 2200, is divided into two operations – the computation of the surface normals

Program 6.9   Backsurface elimination

```
2000 :
2010 REM Controls Type of Plotting of the Object
2020 DEFPROCSCREEN
2030 PROCNORMAL
2040 FOR I%=0 TO 1
2050   K%=P%(I%,0):DX%=XR%-W%(K%,0)
2060   DY%=YR%-W%(K%,1):DZ%=ZR%-W%(K%,2)
2070   Q=NE%(I%,0)*DX%+NE%(I%,1)*DY%+NE%(I%,2)*DZ%
2080   IF Q<0 THEN GOTO 2110
2090   GCOL0,2:PROCFILL1(I%)
2100   GCOL0,3:PROCFRAME1(I%)
2110   NEXT I%
2120 FOR I%=0 TO N%-1
2130   K%=PP%(I%,0):DX%=XR%-W%(K%,0)
2140   DY%=YR%-W%(K%,1):DZ%=ZR%-W%(K%,2)
2150   Q=NS%(I%,0)*DX%+NS%(I%,1)*DY%+NS%(I%,2)*DZ%
2160   IF Q<0 THEN GOTO 2190
2170   GCOL0,2:PROCFILL2(I%)
2180   GCOL0,3:PROCFRAME2(I%)
2190   NEXT I%
2200 ENDPROC
2210 :
2220 REM Computes the Vectors Normal to the Object's Surfaces
2230 DEFPROCNORMAL
2240 M1%=2:M2%=1:M3%=0
2250 FOR I%=0 TO 1
2260   PROCVECTOR(M1%,M2%,M3%)
2270   NE%(I%,0)=BV%*FV%-CV%*EV%
2280   NE%(I%,1)=CV%*DV%-AV%*FV%
2290   NE%(I%,2)=AV%*EV%-BV%*DV%
2300   M1%=N%+1:M2%=N%+2:M3%=N%+3:NEXT I%
2310 FOR I%=0 TO N%-1
2320   K%=PP%(I%,0):L%=PP%(I%,1):M%=PP%(I%,2)
2330   PROCVECTOR(K%,L%,M%)
2340   NS%(I%,0)=BV%*FV%-CV%*EV%
2350   NS%(I%,1)=CV%*DV%-AV%*FV%
2360   NS%(I%,2)=AV%*EV%-BV%*DV%
2370   NEXT I%
2380 ENDPROC
2390 :
2400 REM Computes Direction Vector
2410 DEFPROCVECTOR(L%,K%,M%)
2420 AV%=W%(L%,0)-W%(K%,0):BV%=W%(L%,1)-W%(K%,1)
2430 CV%=W%(L%,2)-W%(K%,2):DV%=W%(M%,0)-W%(K%,0)
2440 EV%=W%(M%,1)-W%(K%,1):FV%=W%(M%,2)-W%(K%,2)
2450 ENDPROC
2460 :
2470 REM Fills an End Surface
2480 DEFPROCFILL1(I%)
2490 K%=P%(I%,0):MOVE S%(K%,0),S%(K%,1)
2500 K%=P%(I%,1):MOVE S%(K%,0),S%(K%,1)
2510 FOR J%=2 TO N%
2520   K%=P%(I%,J%):PLOT85,S%(K%,0),S%(K%,1)
2530   K%=P%(I%,0):MOVE S%(K%,0),S%(K%,1)
```

Program 6.9   continued

```
2540   NEXT J%
2550 ENDPROC
2560 :
2570 REM Fills a Side Surface
2580 DEFPROCFILL2(I%)
2590 K%=PP%(I%,0):MOVE S%(K%,0),S%(K%,1)
2600 K%=PP%(I%,1):MOVE S%(K%,0),S%(K%,1)
2610 K%=PP%(I%,3):PLOT85,S%(K%,0),S%(K%,1)
2620 K%=PP%(I%,2):PLOT85,S%(K%,0),S%(K%,1)
2630 ENDPROC
```

and the test for visibility and subsequent plotting or elimination. In line 2030, PROCNORMAL is called to effect the first operation. This procedure is defined between lines 2220 and 2380, and computes the normals for the two end plates first in the FOR–NEXT loop bounded by lines 2250 and 2300, and the normals for each panel in the FOR–NEXT loop between lines 2310 and 2370. In these loops, PROCVECTOR is called for each surface, and this is listed in lines 2400 to 2450. Effectively this computes the components of the two sequential surface vectors from the first vertex in each surface which in turn are used to compute the components of the normal vector given in equation (6.18).

Back in PROCSCREEN, the FOR–NEXT loop between lines 2040 and 2110 deals with the visibility test and plotting/elimination of the end plates. The cross product of the surface normal and line of sight vector is computed between lines 2050 and 2070, and the test to see whether or not the surface in question is to be plotted or eliminated is made in line 2080. If the surface is to be plotted, line 2090 calls PROCFILL1 which fills the end plate in solid colour using an appropriate combination of PLOT85 and MOVE commands listed in lines 2470 to 2550. Then the surface is edged in a different colour by a call to PROCFRAME1 in line 2100. The FOR–NEXT loop between lines 2120 and 2190 does the same for the cylinder's panels: the cross product is computed between lines 2130 and 2150, the test for visibility made in line 2160, and plotting and edging accomplished by calls to PROCFILL2 and PROCFRAME2 in lines 2170 and 2180. Note that PROCFILL2 defined by lines 2570 to 2630 is an appropriately organized fill routine for the panels.

Program 6.9 must be merged with Program 6.8 to achieve the backsurface elimination either by typing from line 2000 on or using the appropriate *SPOOL procedure (see Chapter 37: User Guide). The same viewpoint parameter values as used earlier lead to pictures such as that shown in Fig. 6.11(a). Explore this program by panning and zooming, and note that by removing the two calls to PROCFILL1 and PROCFILL2 in lines 2090 and 2170, the method reverts from a hidden surface to hidden line program. Simply type 2090: and 2170: to achieve this; the hidden line picture is shown in Fig. 6.11(b).

We now have an entirely general purpose program which we can quickly

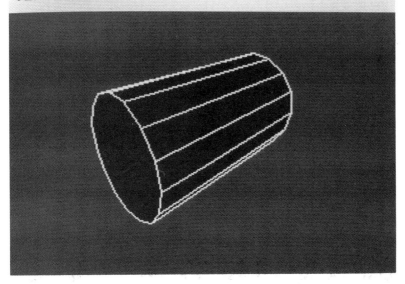

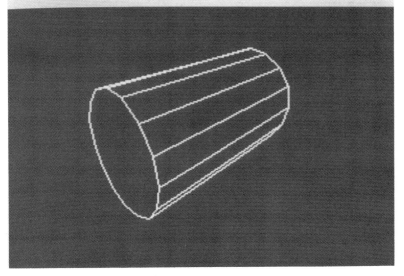

Fig. 6.11 The 'solid' cylinder

adapt to generate a variety of shapes. The two key variables which can be changed in the cylinder rotation relate to the radius of the cylinder and the number of segments or panels used to approximate its limiting circular form. If the number of segments were fixed at $N\% = 3$, this would imply $\theta = 120°$ and a triangular beam would be the result. Changing line 80 to

    80 ST%=120:N%=360/ST%:ZZ=200:VDU29,640;512;

will achieve this. A rectangular beam or box can be formed by setting $N\% = 4$ and $\theta = 90°$ as in

    80 ST%=90:N%=360/ST%:ZZ=200:VDU29,640;512;

while a hexagonal solid results using $N\% = 6$ and $\theta = 60°$ with a change in line 80 to

    80 ST%=60:N%=360/ST%:ZZ=200:VDU29,640;512;

By changing the radius of one of the end plates, the cylinder can be made to taper to a point in one of its directions. A cone can be created by setting one end plate to a radius of 0 and this is done by changing line 1100 to

    1100 XX%= −XX%:R%=0:NEXT L%

Quite clearly by combining radius and segment number changes, pyramids and cones of various shapes and sizes can be directly and easily constructed using the same program. The possibilities are endless and some of these will be used a little later.

We are now in a position to define a much more complex shape by constructing the shape from systematic positioning of cylinders. This shape is the sphere or globe. Looking back at Fig. 6.9(b), it is possible to visualize a sphere as being made up of a number of tapering cylinders which act as slices through the sphere. The end plates of such cylinders will vary with the radius of the cross section through the sphere at the point where they are defined. Essentially the sphere can be viewed as a series of conical sections whose general coordinate structure can be determined by the following formulae. We will first assume that the radius of the sphere is R and that the sphere is composed of M slices with equal width r, so that its diameter is $Mr = 2R$. The origin of the world coordinate system is also taken to be the centre of the sphere.

Then the value of the z coordinate for the mth segment or slice is given by

$$z^m = R - mr, \quad m = 0, 1, \ldots, M \tag{6.23}$$

and the radius of the segment or slice associated with the point z^m is defined as

$$R_m = \{R^2 - (z^m)^2\}^{\frac{1}{2}} \tag{6.24}$$

by Pythagoras's theorem. This is clearly illustrated in Fig. 6.9(b). The xy

coordinates of the plate or circular slice associated with z^m, called x_n^m and y_n^m respectively follow equations (6.22) and are computed as

$$x_n^m = R_m \cos(n\theta)$$

and

$$y_n^m = R_m \sin(n\theta)$$

(6.25)

From equations (6.23) and (6.25), a typical cylindrical segment of the sphere of width r with end plates located at z^m and z^{m+1} is given by the vectors

$$[x_n^m \ y_n^m \ z^m] \text{ and } [x_n^{m+1} \ y_n^{m+1} \ z^{m+1}], \quad n=0,1,\ldots, M$$

Note that at each end of the sphere where $m=0$ and $m=M$, $z^0 = R$, and from equation (6.24), $R_0 = 0$ and $z^m = -R$ so $R_M = 0$, thus implying that the end segments are cones.

Our basic program in this section and the rest of this chapter involves the merger of Programs 6.8 and 6.9 and a switch to MODE2 to enable more colours to be introduced. We must now merge into this composite the listing in Program 6.10 which involves fairly extensive changes to the main program and the addition of two new procedures PROCSPHERE and PROCDIST which reflect the computation of cylindrical segments and their ordering to form a sphere. The major change lies between lines 10 and 300 in the main program and involves the addition of two arrays XX% and R% each with two elements which store the positions of the segment end plates (in XX%) and the radii in R%. The program is general enough to enable the number of segments defining the level of resolution of the sphere to be read in from the keyboard. We have assumed the number of such segments to be $NUM\% = 10$. But if $NUM\% = 2$, we are able to approximate the sphere by a square box, and by varying $NUM\%$ between 2 and 10, we can generate a variety of shapes which in the limit approach a true sphere.

Normal viewpoint and setup arrangements are made in the main program but in lines 190 and 200, the size of the sphere in the z direction is read in from a DATA statement (itself given in line 470). In line 210 the procedure PROCDIST is called and this effectively calculates the nearest and furthest locations on the sphere relative to the viewpoint. This is necessary for ordering the segments and the procedure is defined in lines 400 to 460. Back in the main program, the FOR–NEXT loop between lines 220 and 280 controls the number of cylindrical segments of the sphere. PROCSPHERE listed in lines 320 to 380 computes the radius from equation (6.24) and orders the z values associated with the segments. Some changes are also required in PROCSOLID in lines 1060 to 1090 which involve taking account of the variables XX% and R% which have now been declared as arrays: the FOR–NEXT loop between lines 250 and 260 transforms world to screen coordinates and the call to PROCSCREEN in line 270 activates the hidden surface plotting for the segment in question.

Program 6.10   A sphere as a composition of cylindrical segments

```
 10 REM Solid Sphere:Hidden Surface Elimination
 20 MODE2
 30 DIM W%(31,2),S%(31,1),P%(1,15),PP%(14,4)
 40 DIM NE%(1,2),NS%(14,2),XX%(1),R%(1)
 50 VDU23,1,0;0;0;0;
 60 VDU19,0,1;0;19,1,4;0;19,2,0;0;19,3,7;0;
 70 VDU28,0,5,39,0:VDU24,0;0;1279;830;
 80 ST%=24:N%=360/ST%:ZZ=200:VDU29,640;400;
 90 COLOUR 128:GCOLO,129
100 CLS:CLG:COLOUR 2
110 INPUT TAB(1,1)"NO.OF SEGMENTS",NUM%
120 NUM%=NUM%-1:CLS:CLG
130 INPUT TAB(1,1)"VIEW DISTANCE",RHO%
140 INPUT TAB(1,2)"SCREEN DISTANCE",DIS%
150 INPUT TAB(1,3)"HORIZONTAL ANG",TH
160 INPUT TAB(1,4)"VERTICAL ANGLE",PH
170 TH=RAD(TH):PH=RAD(PH)
180 PROCSETUP
190 READ XN%,XF%:XZ%=0:RR%=ABS(XF%-XN%)
200 SH%=RR%/(NUM%+1):RR%=(RR%/2)^2
210 PROCDIST
220 FOR LL%=0 TO NUM%
230    PROCSPHERE
240    PROCSOLID
250    FOR I%=0 TO 2*N%+1
260      PROCTRANS(I%):NEXT I%
270    PROCSCREEN
280    NEXT LL%
290 AA=GET:CLS:CLG:RESTORE:GOTO 130
300 END
310 :
320 REM Defines a Segment in Appropriate Order
330 DEFPROCSPHERE
340 XX%(1)=XZ%:XZ%=XZ%+SH%:XX%(0)=XZ%
350 RO%=RR%-XX%(0)^2:R1%=RR%-XX%(1)^2
360 IF RO%<=0 THEN R%(0)=5 ELSE R%(0)=SQR(RO%)
370 IF R1%<=0 THEN R%(1)=5 ELSE R%(1)=SQR(R1%)
380 ENDPROC
390 :
400 REM Computes Nearest & Farthest Distances
410 DEFPROCDIST
420 D1%=(XN%-XR%)^2:D2%=YR%^2
430 D3%=ZR%^2:DA%=SQR(D1%+D2%+D3%)
440 D1%=(XF%-XR%)^2:DB%=SQR(D1%+D2%+D3%)
450 IF DA%<DB% THEN XZ%=XF%:SH%=-SH% ELSE XZ%=XN%
460 ENDPROC
470 DATA -400,400
1000 :
1020 DEFPROCSOLID
1030 K%=0
1040 FOR L%=1 TO 2
```

Program 6.10   continued

```
1050    FOR I%=0 TO 360 STEP ST%
1060      W%(K%,0)=XX%(L%-1)
1070      W%(K%,1)=R%(L%-1)*COS(RAD(I%))
1080      W%(K%,2)=R%(L%-1)*SIN(RAD(I%))
1090      K%=K%+1:NEXT I%
1100    NEXT L%
2000 :
2090 GCOL0,0:PROCFILL1(I%)
```

This program plots each end plate of the cylinder which faces the viewer in building up the sphere: viewed from a horizontal angle of θ set at $45°$ say, nearer segments overplot further ones and there is no problem. But viewed side on with the horizontal at $90°$, the temporal priority of cylindrical segment plotting breaks down and the end plates of the segment which are orientated towards the viewer but hidden anyway are plotted. To avoid this problem, all one needs to do is remove the end plate plotting from the algorithm. Setting lines 2090 and 2100 to 2090: and 2100: achieves this and the sphere can now be viewed from any direction. Try panning and zooming around the object as in previous programs. Examine the typical oblique view with $\rho = 1000$, $z^d = 700$, $\theta = 45°$ and $\phi = 45°$, then the end view with $\theta = 0$ and $\phi = 90°$, and the side-on view with $\theta = 90°$ and $\phi = 90°$. These three views are displayed in Figs 6.12(a) to (c) for the program without lines 2090 and 2100. But also try these views with these lines inserted to understand the limits of building up complex objects by achieving depth sort through simple distance calculations.

6.8   ROTATION AND ANIMATION: ELEMENTARY COMPUTER MOVIES

At this point, it is worthwhile summarizing the program structures which we introduced in the last section, and those to come so that we are clear about the various listings which need to be combined. Figures 6.13 (a) to (c) present the composite programs introduced in the last (6.13(a)), this (6.13(b)) and the next (6.13(c)) sections. In Fig. 6.13(a), we show how the wire frame (Program 6.8), the hidden surface (Programs 6.8 + 6.9) and the sphere (Programs 6.8 + 6.9 + 6.10) are formed. Figure 6.13(b) shows how the programs in this section are merged with Programs 6.8 and 6.9, and Fig. 6.13(c) shows how the space picture which is the most complicated design in the book is built up from the various program modules which will be outlined in the next and final section.

One of the basic ideas of computer animation is based on simulating motion, not by moving the object itself or its elements on the screen, but by utilizing some regular geometric property of the object, colouring the object's parts according to this regularity, and then switching the colours in a sequence

```
VIEW DISTANCE?1000
SCREEN DISTANCE?700
HORIZONTAL ANG?45
VERTICAL ANGLE?45
```

```
VIEW DISTANCE?1000
SCREEN DISTANCE?700
HORIZONTAL ANG?70
VERTICAL ANGLE?90
```

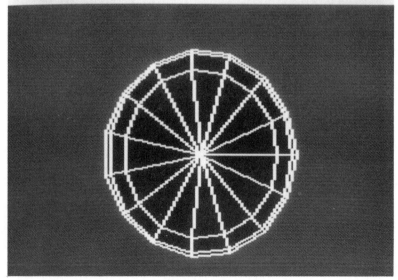

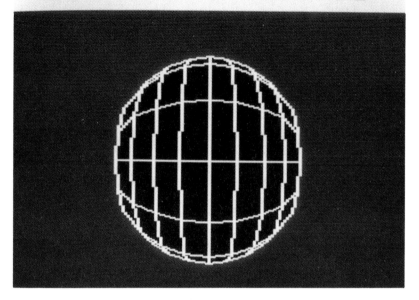

Fig. 6.12 Views of a sphere

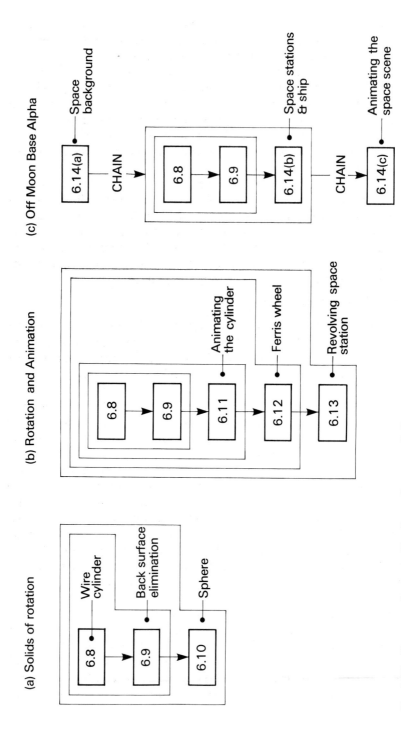

(a) Solids of rotation

(b) Rotation and Animation

(c) Off Moon Base Alpha

Fig. 6.13 Programs from combinations of program listings

which matches the geometric pattern. A cylinder is the ideal object on which to develop this technique. The cylinder in the previous section was itself generated by rotating a point around its end plates and using the points produced to define the cylinder's sides as distinct panels. It is thus possible to simulate actual rotation, motion of the cylinder, by colouring the panels in a regular progression according to their position in the rotation, and then switching these colours in a particular direction, thus simulating movement. This of course is only a very limited kind of animation but it does have great potential in computer movie-making, and can be used to great effect as we will see in the next chapter.

Before we present an extension to Program 6.8 + 6.9 enabling the cylinder to rotate, we must review the way colours are assigned in BBC Basic. In Chapter 2, we showed how colour in any graphics mode is referred to as logical colour and that the number of such colours is limited in each mode. Logical colours are selected from the palette of 16 actual colours, 8 of which are absolute, 8 of which are alternating absolutes or flashing. Any logical colour can be assigned as an actual colour using the command

   VDU19, logical colour, actual colour;0;

The notation of colour switching in any mode simply involves changing the actual colour assigned to a given logical colour. For example, a flashing red and yellow light can be simulated in MODE1 say, by colouring the light with the background colour, say black, using logical colour number 1, and then switching this logical colour to actual colours 1 and 3 repeatedly.

We have adapted the hidden surface program given in Programs 6.8 and 6.9 to deal with up to 10 different logical colours in MODE2; these can be systematically switched to any from a palette of 10 absolute colours. We could of course use up to 16 logical colours in this MODE but we will use less than 5 for any more than this would lead to confused animation of the object we are dealing with. The new listing is given as Program 6.11 and this must be merged with Program 6.8 and 6.9 to achieve the animation as Fig. 6.13(b) indicates. In Program 6.11, the main program differs from that in 6.8 in that it operates in MODE2; the cylinder panels, their frames and the frames of the end plates are coloured systematically using three colours which are set up in PROCSETCOL which is called in line 30. All else is the same as in previous programs except that the rotation of the cylinder is effected by a call to PROCMOTION in line 220.

PROCSETCOL is listed between lines 250 and 310. This procedure assigns three actual colours – magenta, cyan and white to the three logical colour numbers 4, 5 and 6 through the arrays $CL\%$ and $CA\%$ respectively. This is achieved in the FOR–NEXT loop from 270 to 300 in which the colours are fixed in line 280 and assigned in 290. When the cylinder is plotted, the frame of the end plate is drawn using the MOD command to generate the appropriate

Program 6.11   Animating the cylinder

```
   10 REM Filled Cylinder,Hidden Line & Simple Motion
   20 DIM CA%(10),CL%(10)
   30 MODE2:K%=0:NC%=3:COL%=1:PROCSETCOL
   40 DIM W%(31,2),S%(31,1),P%(1,15)
   50 DIM PP%(14,4),NE%(1,2),NS%(14,2)
   60 VDU23,1,0;0;0;0;
   70 VDU19,0,1;0;19,1,4;0;19,2,0;0;
   80 VDU28,0,5,39,0:VDU24,0;0;1279;830;
   90 ST%=24:N%=360/ST%:ZZ=200:VDU29,640;512;
  100 COLOUR 128:GCOLO,129
  110 CLS:CLG:COLOUR 2
  120 PROCSOLID
  130 INPUT TAB(1,1)"VIEW DISTANCE",RHO%
  140 INPUT TAB(1,2)"SCREEN DISTANCE",DIS%
  150 INPUT TAB(1,3)"HORIZONTAL ANG",TH
  160 INPUT TAB(1,4)"VERTICAL ANGLE",PH
  170 TH=RAD(TH):PH=RAD(PH)
  180 PROCSETUP
  190 FOR I%=0 TO 2*N%+1
  200   PROCTRANS(I%):NEXT I%
  210 PROCSCREEN
  220 PROCMOTION
  230 END
  240 :
  250 REM Sets up the Colour Palette for Motion
  260 DEFPROCSETCOL
  270 FOR I%=5 TO 5+NC%-1
  280   CA%(K%)=I%:CL%(K%)=I%-1
  290   VDU19,CL%(K%),CA%(K%);0;
  300   K%=K%+1:NEXT I%
  310 ENDPROC
  320 :
  330 REM Generates Motion By Switching the Colours
  340 DEFPROCMOTION
  350 REPEAT
  360   COL%=CA%(0)
  370   FOR I%=1 TO NC%-1
  380     CA%(I%-1)=CA%(I%):NEXT I%
  390   CA%(NC%-1)=COL%
  400   FOR J%=0 TO NC%-1
  410     VDU19,CL%(J%),CA%(J%);0;:NEXT J%
  420   AA=INKEY(20)
  430   UNTIL FALSE
  440 ENDPROC
 1000 :
 1385 GCOLO,CL%((J%+2)MODNC%)
 2000 :
 2165 COL%=CL%((I%+3)MODNC%)
 2170 GCOLO,COL%:PROCFILL2(I%)
 2180 GCOLO,COL%:PROCFRAME2(I%)
```

position in the colour sequence in line 1385 while the same is done for the filling and framing of the panels in lines 2165, 2170 and 2180. PROCMOTION defined in lines 330 to 440 simply switches these colours in a repetitive way. In lines 360 to 390, the three actual colours in the array *CA%* are reordered in such a way that the new first colour is the old last one, the new second one the old first one, and the new third the old second. The colour switching on the screen is determined in lines 400 and 410 and a delay to enable the switch to be detected introduced using the INKEY (20) command in line 420. This whole sequence is embedded in a REPEAT–UNTIL loop which controls the successive reassignment and switching, enabling the cylinder to appear as if it is rotating.

There are a couple of very important points to note. For successful rotation, the number of colours used must be a divisor of the number of segments of the shape. As there are fifteen panels, three colours produces five sequences of magenta, cyan and white. Two colours would not suffice as the first and the last panels would have the same colour. In this case only three or five (or fifteen) colours can form appropriate sequences. Readers are encouraged to extend the program to five colours but note that if fifteen were used, the text or background colours would have to switch. Second, the motion is structured so that the cylinder appears to revolve forwards; this is due to the way the new actual colours are assigned. If this assignment in lines 360 to 390 is reversed, the cylinder would then appear to revolve backwards. Try this change.

We now have the basis for a very effective animation which involves the listing given in Program 6.12. This should be merged with Programs 6.8, 6.9 and 6.11 as Fig. 6.13(b) shows. Here PROCSETCOL is changed so that the actual colours used are now black, black and blue, noting that blue is the background colour. The size of the cylinder is changed in line 1030 to a much narrower width and larger radius, and the end plates are no longer plotted, lines 2090 and 2100 being cleared. The hidden surface test is removed and this enables an open cylinder whose segments are broken to be plotted. Rotation of this structure is reminiscent of a Ferris wheel.

Program 6.12 A Ferris wheel

```
 250 REM Sets up the Colour Palette for Motion
 260 DEFPROCSETCOL
 270 CA%(0)=0:CA%(1)=0:CA%(2)=4
 280 FOR I%=5 TO 5+NC%-1
 290    CL%(K%)=I%-1:VDU19,CL%(K%),CA%(K%);0;
 300    K%=K%+1:NEXT I%
 310 ENDPROC
1000 :
1030 XX%=50:R%=300:K%=0
2090 :
2100 :
2160 :
```

Finally we can modify this program further to generate an impression of a revolving space station. The listing in Program 6.13 which must be added to Programs 6.8, 6.9, 6.11 and 6.12 essentially removes the solid fill plot for each panel, thus giving a broken wire frame (line 2170 is cleared). Line 120 which calls PROCSOLID once is removed and embedded in a FOR–NEXT loop between lines 184 and 215. In this loop, the radius of the Ferris wheel is reduced each time by ten units, and the resulting shape plotted six times. This gives the impression of a space structure with a blurred edge which when rotated is amazingly realistic. This motion blur is sometimes referred to as temporal-antialiasing (Fox and Waite, 1984). It is not possible to view the motion but a static picture of the object is shown in Fig. 6.14. All these changes are summarized in Fig. 6.13(b) and the ideas of this section will be taken forward in the next chapter. There are many possible elaborations to these programs. Readers are encouraged to explore different ways of framing and filling shapes with different colour sequences, using different line types. In this area of animation, effective computer art depends very much on knowing the limits and potential of the machine on which you are working but even given this, imaginative use of the machine's hardware through software is all important.

6.9 CONSTRUCTING COMPLEX PICTURES: OFF MOON BASE ALPHA

We are now in a position to construct a much more complex picture using many of the techniques of this chapter and some of those in previous ones. This will provide us with an illustration of not only how we can combine a whole range of three-dimensional modelling techniques in an effective way but will

Program 6.13   A space station in motion

```
110 CLS:CLG:COLOUR 2
120 :
130 INPUT TAB(1,1)"VIEW DISTANCE",RHO%
140 INPUT TAB(1,2)"SCREEN DISTANCE",DIS%
150 INPUT TAB(1,3)"HORIZONTAL ANG",TH
160 INPUT TAB(1,4)"VERTICAL ANGLE",PH
170 TH=RAD(TH):PH=RAD(PH)
180 PROCSETUP
183 RR%=300
184 FOR KL%=1 TO 6
185   PROCSOLID
190   FOR I%=0 TO 2*N%+1
200     PROCTRANS(I%):NEXT I%
210   PROCSCREEN
215   RR%=RR%-10:NEXT KL%
220 PROCMOTION
230 END
1000 :
1030 XX%=50:R%=RR%:K%=0
2170 :
```

Fig. 6.14   A space station prior to animation

also impress the point that the best computer art depends on using such combinations in a single picture. Here we will construct a picture of a space ship in near space, 'floating' off the moon, about to dock at one of two revolving space stations. The moon, the distant planet Earth and twinkling stars will form the background to the ship and stations, and we will use the techniques of the last section to make the ship and space stations revolve once the picture has been constructed. Our picture will be composed of three programs: first a program creating a backcloth of moon, Earth and stars using the techniques of 'flat' landscapes; second a program utilizing the techniques of solid modelling and backsurface elimination introduced earlier to produce spheres and cylinders which when joined together produce the objects of space; and finally a short program to enable animation of the objects using the ideas of the last section.

These programs are too long and large to be collapsed into one for this would exhaust the requirements of the machine's memory. But as the picture is built up of segments – background, foreground of ship and stations, and then motion – it is possible to set up three separate programs referred to as SPACE, SHIP and MOTION. The way these programs are chained together and the way they relate to previous ones is illustrated in Fig. 6.13(c). The additional listings involved here will be referred to as Programs 6.14(a), 6.14(b) and 6.14(c), 6.14(b) being merged with 6.8 and 6.9, and all these programs requiring to be run in the given sequence of (a), (b) then (c). We are introducing another important principle of picture structure here through separating the picture content into separate programs. The programs in question are essentially independent, and they simply create visual material in the MODE2 frame buffer. As each program is chained from the previous one, the frame buffer is not cleared and in principle there is no limit to the amount of detail in a picture which can be created in this way. In this case, the MODE is fixed in Program 6.14(a) which produces the background, and chains Program 6.14(b) (+6.8+6.9) called SHIP which in turn creates the ship and revolving stations. This program then chains the colour switching to enable motion (Program 6.14(c)). Note that such chaining could be used to build up great visual complexity if the picture can be easily separated into several relatively independent segments.

The first program in the sequence is the most straightforward and this is listed as Program 6.14(a). In the main program between lines 10 and 150, a background of twinkling stars, some coloured white, some flashing black and white are plotted at random positions on the screen in the FOR–NEXT loop between lines 70 and 90. Between 20 and 40 such stars are plotted. In line 100, the call to PROCWORLD plots the distant Earth, located over some of the stars in the bottom left hand corner of the screen. In line 120, the call to PROCMOON plots a section of the moon in the top right hand corner of the screen, while (line) 130 CHAIN "SHIP" loads and runs the file called SHIP which should exist on the filespace. This file contains the program which plots the space ship and space stations (Program 6.14(b)).

In lines 180 to 270, PROCWORLD is defined. This first calls PROCCIRCLE in line 200 which in turn is defined in lines 290 to 360: this plots a solid blue circle using the traditional polar coordinate method, with its centre off screen, thus allowing only the top right quadrant of the 'Earth' to be seen. Then in the FOR–NEXT loops between lines 210 and 260, and 240 and 260, four sets of coordinates describing the location of the Earth's continents are read from DATA statements. These continents are recognizable as North and Central America when plotted after they are read in line 250. The continents are constructed by an appropriate sequence of MOVE and PLOT85 commands, and filled in green. The DATA statements are located in lines 500 to 670; these coordinates have already been transformed to the appropriate projection onto the globe for the shapes have been taken from an existing spherical projection reproduced in a school atlas, thus illustrating that part of the background is created using the least general of all three-dimensional projections, that fixed externally to the program in the data.

Next the underside of the moon is plotted using an entirely different three-dimensional effect. The random shading technique is used here as if there were a light source on the left of the picture; this is consistent with the Earth light. It has been used earlier in this chapter on the surface plots and was used to great effect in the Planetrise sequence in Chapter 5. PROCMOON which enables the plotting is listed in lines 380 to 480. The edge of the moon is plotted between vertical screen units 700 and above. Lines 410 and 420 fix the radius of the moon and the screen limits in terms of the new origin, which is off the screen. The FOR–NEXT loop between 430 and 470 controls the vertical direction of plotting in pixel units (four screen units) while the FOR–NEXT loop between 450 and 470 controls the horizontal direction also in the appropriate pixel units. To establish the x coordinate marking the edge of the moon, the angle of rotation with respect to the origin is calculated first using the arcsine function in line 440 which also computes the coordinate. The plot then occurs left to right across the screen from this x position for a given y, and line 460 establishes whether or not the pixel in question is coloured white or black dependent upon its distance from the right-hand side of the screen. In this way, the surface of the moon combines the features of both a light source to the left and the characteristic surface texture known through observation.

Once this background has been created, the second program which creates the space ship and space stations and is referred to as "SHIP", is chained in line 130. This program is formed by merging the listing in Program 6.14(b) with Programs 6.8 and 6.9. The listing in Program 6.14(b) deals with the main program, and additional procedures which control the solids of rotation which are transformed and plotted using the standard procedures of Programs 6.8 and 6.9 located at lines 1000 onwards. The main program is in two parts. The FOR–NEXT loop between lines 90 and 210 reads data from the DATA statements with respect to two spheres which are plotted as space stations resembling artificial moons. The second part resides in the FOR–NEXT loop between lines 270 and 310 and this controls the plotting of the space ship whose cylindrical and conical sections are also read from coordinates given as DATA statements. These DATA statements are located at line 5010 upwards.

All the components used to determine the plotting of a sphere have already been introduced in Program 6.10 apart from small changes involving the logical colour plotting necessary to the later animation. From line 220 however there are substantial changes. In line 220, the front and rear ends of the space craft in terms of their z dimension and the viewpoint are read from data and PROCDIST is called in line 240 to set up the orientation of the ship relative to the viewpoint. Now as the segments of the ship are also read from DATA statements located between lines 5050 and 5120 ordered from the front to the rear of the ship, these statements must be read in an order which is associated with the position of the viewpoint. If the front of the ship is nearer the viewpoint for example, PROCDIST has already established that the plotting of the ship should proceed from its rear to the front. In this case, the segments of the ship should be read in reverse order from lines 5120 to 5050. In lines 250

Program 6.14(a)   Off Moon Base Alpha

```
 10 REM Off Moon Base Alpha
 20 REM A Backcloth of Earth,Moon & Stars
 30 MODE2
 40 VDU23,1,0;0;0;0;
 50 VDU19,1,7;0;19,2,4;0;19,3,2;0;
 60 VDU19,4,15;0;19,5,7;0;
 70 FOR I%=1 TO 20+RND(20)
 80   GCOL0,3+RND(2):PLOT69,RND(1279),RND(1023)
 90   NEXT I%
100 PROCWORLD
110 X0%=1500:Y0%=3000:YY%=700
120 PROCMOON(X0%,Y0%,YY%)
130 CHAIN"SHIP"
140 AA=GET:MODE7
150 END
160 :
170 REM Computes and Draws the Earth
180 DEFPROCWORLD
190 S%=2:R%=161*S%:GCOL0,2
200 PROCCIRCLE(R%,0,-30*S%):GCOL0,3
210 FOR I%=1 TO 4
220   READ N%:READ Y%,X%:READ YY%,XX%
230   MOVE X%*S%,Y%*S%:MOVE XX%*S%,YY%*S%
240   FOR J%=3 TO N%
250     READ Y%,X%:PLOT85,X%*S%,Y%*S%
260     NEXT J%:NEXT I%
270 ENDPROC
280 :
290 REM Computes and Fills a Standard Circle
300 DEFPROCCIRCLE(R%,XA%,YA%)
310 MOVE XA%,YA%:MOVE XA%,R%+YA%
320 FOR I%=0 TO 360 STEP 6
330   XX%=R%*COS(RAD(I%)):YY%=R%*SIN(RAD(I%))
340   PLOT85,XX%,YY%+YA%:MOVE XA%,YA%
350   NEXT I%
360 ENDPROC
370 :
380 REM Shades the Moon Using Random-Dot Technique
390 DEFPROCMOON(X0%,Y0%,YY%)
400 VDU29,X0%;Y0%;
410 R%=SQR((Y0%-YY%)^2+(X0%-1280)^2)
420 YB%=1024-Y0%:XL%=1280-X0%
430 FOR I%=YB% TO (YY%-Y0%) STEP -4
440   A=ASN(I%/R%):J%=-R%*COS(A):XE%=XL%-J%
450   FOR K%=J% TO XL% STEP 8
460     IF RND(XE%)<(XL%-K%) THEN GCOL0,1 ELSE GCOL0,0
470     PLOT69,K%,I%:NEXT K%:NEXT I%
480 ENDPROC
490 :
500 REM Coordinate Data for Earth's Continents
510 DATA 27,130,0,105,0,129,15,98,11,126,34,93
520 DATA 13,122,50,79,13,107,50,71,16,102,62
530 DATA 64,21,97,68,59,32,88,84,58,42,78
540 DATA 89,54,46,72,89,66,83,68,89,62,86
550 DATA 63,91,58,89,59,93,56,91,56,93
```

Program 6.14(a) continued

```
560 DATA 10,59,32,63,39,57,36,58,42,52,40
570 DATA 53,45,45,46,46,50,42,49,40,52
580 DATA 7,118,60,97,68,112,72,88,84,106,84,93
590 DATA 88,103,89,47,54,46,62,65,45,56,56,65,39
600 DATA 58,49,66,37,66,45,67,35,73,43,72,35,79
610 DATA 44,78,36,85,44,84,38,87,45,86,33
620 DATA 89,50,88,33,92,52,93,32,95,40,96
630 DATA 31,97,38,99,25,100,40,105,27,105
640 DATA 29,107,26,107,26,109,22,107,22,110,20
650 DATA 110,23,114,20,114,21,118,17,117,29
660 DATA 127,13,119,27,130,8,117,26,138,0
670 DATA 113,24,151,0,142,13,154,0,157
```

and 260, this order is determined relative to viewpoint and the FOR–NEXT loop between lines 270 and 310 which controls the plotting of the ship sections, is indexed by $JL\%$ which varies in increments of 10 or -10 over the range of line numbers associated with the relevant DATA statements. The operations in this loop are similar to earlier transformations and screen plotting but the procedure call to PROCCYLIN is new at line 280. This procedure is listed between lines 510 and 560 and essentially reads the appropriate DATA statement associated with the section of the ship being plotted and works out its positioning. Note the use of the RESTORE command in line 530 and the line number $JL\%$ which is the index of the FOR–NEXT loop in the main program.

Animation of this picture – the space ship and space stations – is effected in the same way the cylinder was rotated in the last section. Line 320 chains Program 6.14(c) which is called 'MOTION' on the filespace. This listing has a similar structure to PROCMOTION in Program 6.11 except that the spheres are rotated three times faster than the ship. This is achieved by switching the colours of the ship in the REPEAT–UNTIL loop between lines 70 and 150, but embedding within this a FOR–NEXT loop which switches the colours of the spheres three times between lines 100 and 140. Such techniques of differential motion have great potential and readers are encouraged to explore how the present picture can be further enhanced through such switchings. Prior to motion, a still of the picture is shown in Plate 17. Press any key to start the motion. Finally, note that by changing the viewpoint data with respect to the ship and spheres quite different views of the same scene can be generated, thus enabling a much slower but nevertheless effective way of 'animating' the picture to be guided by the user.

If you run this program, Program 6.14(a) will produce the background but the program 'SHIP' which is composed of Programs 6.14(b), 6.8 and 6.9 will fail with the error message 'No room' (unless a 6502 Second Processor is attached or unless you are using a 64K or 128K BBC Micro). To get enough space to run the program SHIP, it is necessary to compact Programs 6.8 and

Program 6.14(b)   Off Moon Base Alpha

```
10 REM Off Moon Base Alpha
20 REM Space Stations & Space-Ship
30 DIM W%(31,2),S%(31,1),P%(1,15),PP%(14,4)
40 DIM NE%(1,2),NS%(14,2),XX%(1),R%(1),O(2)
50 VDU23,1,0;0;0;0;
60 VDU19,6,4;0;19,7,6;0;19,8,6;0;
70 VDU19,9,4;0;19,10,4;0;19,11,6;0;
80 ST%=24:N%=360/ST%:O(0)=6:O(1)=7:O(2)=8:CL%=0
90 FOR JL%=1 TO 2
100   READ NUM%,XN%,RN%,XF%,RF%
110   READ RHO%,DIS%,TH,PH,XO%,YO%
120   TH=RAD(TH):PH=RAD(PH):VDU29,XO%;YO%;
130   XZ%=0:RR%=ABS(XF%-XN%)
140   SH%=RR%/(NUM%+1):RR%=(RR%/2)^2
150   PROCSETUP:PROCDIST
160   FOR LL%=0 TO NUM%
170     PROCSPHERE:PROCSOLID
180     FOR I%=0 TO 2*N%+1
190       PROCTRANS(I%):NEXT I%
200     PROCSCREEN
210     NEXT LL%:NEXT JL%
220 READ XN%,XF%,RHO%,DIS%,TH,PH,XO%,YO%
230 TH=RAD(TH):PH=RAD(PH):VDU29,XO%;YO%;
240 PROCSETUP:PROCDIST
250 O(0)=9:O(1)=10:O(2)=11:CL%=1:LB%=5120:LS%=-10
260 IF XZ%=XF% THEN LB%=5050:LS%=10
270 FOR JL%=LB% TO LB%+LS%*7 STEP LS%
280   PROCCYLIN:PROCSOLID
290   FOR I%=0 TO 2*N%+1
300     PROCTRANS(I%):NEXT I%
310   PROCSCREEN:NEXT JL%
320 CHAIN"MOTION"
330 END
340 :
350 REM Defines a Segment in Appropriate Order
360 DEFPROCSPHERE
370 XX%(1)=XZ%:XZ%=XZ%+SH%:XX%(0)=XZ%
380 R0%=RR%-XX%(0)^2:R1%=RR%-XX%(1)^2
390 IF R0%<=0 THEN R%(0)=5 ELSE R%(0)=SQR(R0%)
400 IF R1%<=0 THEN R%(1)=5 ELSE R%(1)=SQR(R1%)
410 ENDPROC
420 :
430 REM Computes Nearest & Farthest Distances
440 DEFPROCDIST
450 D1%=(XN%-XR%)^2:D2%=YR%^2
460 D3%=ZR%^2:DA%=SQR(D1%+D2%+D3%)
470 D1%=(XF%-XR%)^2:DB%=SQR(D1%+D2%+D3%)
480 IF DA%<DB% THEN XZ%=XF%:SH%=-SH% ELSE XZ%=XN%
490 ENDPROC
500 :
510 REM Reads Coordinates of Ship Segments
520 DEFPROCCYLIN
530 RESTORE JL%:READ XN%,RN%,XF%,RF%
540 XX%(0)=XN%:R%(0)=RN%:XX%(1)=XF%:R%(1)=RF%
550 IF LS%<0 THEN XX%(1)=XN%:R%(1)=RN%:XX%(0)=XF%:R%(0)=RF%
```

Program 6.14(b)   continued

```
560 ENDPROC
570 :
1010 REM Sets Up Coordinate & Surface Arrays
1020 DEFPROCSOLID
1030 K%=0
1040 FOR L%=1 TO 2
1050   FOR I%=0 TO 360 STEP ST%
1060     W%(K%,0)=XX%(L%-1)
1070     W%(K%,1)=R%(L%-1)*COS(RAD(I%))
1080     W%(K%,2)=R%(L%-1)*SIN(RAD(I%))
1090     K%=K%+1:NEXT I%
1100   NEXT L%
1190 :
1385 GCOLO,O((J%+2)MOD3)
2090 GCOLO,O:PROCFILL1(I%)
2100 GCOLO,4:PROCFRAME1(I%)
2165 COL%=O((I%+3)MOD3)
2170 GCOLO,COL%*CL%:PROCFILL2(I%)
2180 GCOLO,COL%:PROCFRAME2(I%)
5000 :
5010 REM Coordinate Data for Spheres & Ship
5020 DATA 9,-400,0,400,0,1000,300,12,110,550,850
5030 DATA 9,-400,0,400,0,1000,250,45,45,1100,500
5040 DATA -850,450,1000,500,45,120,640,420
5050 DATA 200,50,450,250
5060 DATA 150,150,200,150
5070 DATA 100,250,150,250
5080 DATA -100,200,100,200
5090 DATA -400,150,-100,170
5100 DATA -700,120,-400,120
5110 DATA -800,100,-700,120
5120 DATA -850,70,-800,100
```

Program 6.14(c)   Off Moon Base Alpha

```
10 REM Off Moon Base Alpha
20 REM Generates Motion By Switching Colours
30 DIM G%(2),S%(2)
40 G%(0)=4:G%(1)=4:G%(2)=6
50 S%(0)=4:S%(1)=6:S%(2)=6
60 AA=GET
70 REPEAT
80   C%=S%(0):S%(0)=S%(1):S%(1)=S%(2):S%(2)=C%
90   VDU19,9,S%(0);0;19,10,S%(1);0;19,11,S%(2);0;
100  FOR I%=1 TO 3
110    C%=G%(0):G%(0)=G%(1):G%(1)=G%(2):G%(2)=C%
120    VDU19,6,G%(0);0;19,7,G%(1);0;19,8,G%(2);0;
130    AA=INKEY(10)
140  NEXT I%
150  UNTIL FALSE
160 END
```

6.9 by removing all the dummy lines and REM statements, or by stringing lines together using the colon separator. In Program 6.14(b) the following lines should be removed

```
 10  REM Off Moon Base Alpha
 20  REM Space Stations & Space-Ship
340  :
350  REM Defines a Segment in Appropriate Order
420  :
430  REM Computes Nearest & Farthest Distances
500  :
510  REM Reads Coordinates of Ship Segments
570  :
5000 :
5010 REM Coordinate Data for Spheres & Ship
```

If this is done the program will fit into the space available. Consult Chapter 32 of the User Guide for ways of compacting programs if in doubt. Chaining 'Motion' provides no problems in terms of space for it is the memory requirements of the program 'SHIP' which touch the memory limits.

Before we conclude this chapter, there are a couple of issues relating to this last set of programs which are worth reflecting upon. The first point to note relates to the way the frame buffer is elaborated by a series of independent programs which build up segments of the picture. Although Program 6.14(a) clears the buffer with the MODE2 command, later programs leave the frame buffer unaltered and simply elaborate it. In this way, a picture can be continually embellished and it is perhaps one of the greatest features of the raster scan graphics device in the microcomputer, that although memory space for programs may be limited, if the picture can be decomposed into segments, it can be built up in layers by running program after program. In short, this is often the way paintings are produced: the painter paints over what has been produced according to logic or whim. Indeed, many of the great masters used canvases once worked upon by others on which to create their great art, and there are many accounts of how artists spent, indeed spend, months on the same picture, overpainting, embellishing, removing and restoring their art. Enormous potential exists with raster scan graphics to follow this example.

Another issue relates to the way structure can be introduced in data but altered through the results of computation. In Program 6.14(b), the data relating to the sections of the space ship are ordered externally and located sequentially in line numbers from front to rear. But as a result of computation, this data may be required from rear to front. The RESTORE command enables us to access the data in any order we require although its exact positioning within the program must be coded so that the program can recognize a particular position. This provides yet another technique of introducing a flexible order into the picture through a fixed order in the data. The technique has great potential.

To conclude this chapter, it is worth listing the kinds of technique we now have at our disposal to construct complex pictures. Clearly structure can be fixed in the data, either through predetermined graphical ordering or through the more flexible technique outlined in this last section. The full formal transformation of three- to two-dimensions, and the associated techniques of hidden line/surface elimination represent the other extreme in that the user has total control over the orientation and projection of the picture on the screen. Between these lie a variety of methods which enable the user to partially control the structure of the picture: temporal priority in the form of the painter's algorithm represents an obvious way in which to hide objects and build up realism, while a variety of depth cues involving edging, shading and approximate perspective have been introduced in this and in previous chapters. Finally the most promising approach to realistic computer art on small computers must involve simulating the artist's own activity through segmenting the picture, devising specific programs for each segment, and building up the picture in the frame buffer by running these programs in a predetermined order.

Once again the message of this book has been emphasized in this chapter and it bears repeating. Although computers may be excellent mediums for painting, the replacement of the artist's canvas and paint brush by the computer is not 'true' computer art but art on computers. A fine distinction perhaps but here 'true' computer art involves simulation, it involves modelling picture structure, it involves recognizing the limits of the machine and software and devising ingenious and imaginative programs which in turn lead to beautiful pictures. As yet such art is quite primitive as we have barely begun to understand the process of picture modelling but as machines get ever more powerful, this field is set to take off. In the next and last substantive chapter, we will move from graphics, formal art and abstract art to popular art where we will introduce animation and cartooning. We have already had a taste of this here but the essence of the next chapter is twofold: to show how movement can be 'simulated' on a computer and to show how computers can transform real time to computer time as well as world space to display space.

7

Animation, cartooning and simple computer movies

A painting, regardless of implicit dynamics, still exists
passively fixed in time. But a new art might pattern
action in time with all elements in motion at all times.
The graphic problem, then, will be how to manipulate a
field of visual elements so that all parts will contribute
purposely to some temporal (time-structured) design.

(John Whitney, *Digital Harmony:
On the Complementarity of Music and Visual Art*, 1980)

Almost as soon as computers began to display pictures, the idea of computer movies captured the imagination of both scientists and film-makers alike. For over twenty years now, computers have been used to assist movie-making, and some of the most pioneering computer graphics is presently being developed in the commercial sector at places such as Lucasfilms where the emphasis is not only on reducing the expense of film-making but on generating scenes that would hitherto have been impossible (Booth, Kochanek and Wein, 1983). Although techniques for moving pictures have been widely anticipated in earlier chapters, the whole subject of animation is worthy of separate treatment for the problems encountered are among the most challenging in computer graphics. Moreover, a discussion of computer motion, of time, of dynamics, provides a nice sense of closure to a book which has been largely about space for it serves to illustrate the important philosophical point that space and time are so inextricably linked together that time represents the natural fourth dimension.

Strictly speaking, animation means 'bringing an object to life' and the term has come to refer to that process of making cartoon films in which sequences of still frames drawn by hand or interpolated between key-frames, represent motion when displayed (Smith, 1983). In this chapter, we will be concerned with more than just animation in this sense, for we will explore how a sense of movement or motion can be given to any object which is displayed on the two-dimensional computer screen. We will thus refer to this movement as 'computer motion' but with the understanding that animation represents the same as this. All the pictures generated in this book could be subjected to animation, although the usual distinction between two- and three-dimensional representations also exists in this area (Crow, 1978). In movie-making, animation has usually been restricted to two-dimensions with the emphasis on creating the very large number of still frames (usually 24 per second of film) which compose the movie. Occasionally three-dimensional cartooning and movie-making have been developed in real time but this has proved considerably more difficult due to the limitations posed by computer time and memory.

With respect to computer animation, the process of constructing key-frames and those in-between can be accomplished in two- or three-dimensions. Clearly three-dimensions is more demanding but smooth motion is possible through precise control of the object's position in space. Many computer films are now being made using the traditional process of generating stills by computer, not by hand, and filming these in sequence. It does not usually matter that such frames are displayed in real time on the computer itself, for the emphasis is still on using the traditional film medium for display. A good example of this type of computer film-making might involve generating many frames of the space ship picture in Chapter 6 with each frame representing a point on a smooth trajectory of motion involving the ship. For example the trajectory used in docking the ship could be worked out, the sequence of frames representing a smooth transition along this path then generated, and the sequence then filmed using conventional means. This is the way sequences of film were made in the motion pictures *Tron* and *The Last Starfighter* (Jankel and Morton, 1984).

Quite clearly, various ideas in this book, especially those in Chapters 3 and 6 dealing with two- and three-dimensional graphics, could be exploited in this fashion if you had conventional film-making equipment. But computer animation and motion in this chapter is a little different in that the computer itself will act as the display device for the film. In short, the computer is the medium in which the film is both constructed and displayed and although it is possible to illustrate all the principles of computer movie-making in this way, such displays will be largely restricted to two- rather than three-dimensional scenes, due to the need to display objects quickly enough to give the impression of motion. Much larger computers would be needed to demonstrate three-dimensional motion in computer time although there do exist rudimentary examples on home-computers where three-dimensional real-time animation has been programmed in assembly language.

There is inevitably greater hardware dependence in this chapter than in previous ones, and the kind of computer movie-making you can engage in using the BBC micro is likely to be somewhat different from other similarly priced machines. Indeed in the film industry, special purpose computers are being built at places like Lucasfilms to handle particular graphics techniques such as fractal rendering, hidden line/surface elimination through ray tracing and suchlike, which can be implemented speedily and efficiently. Yet there are still many principles of computer movie-making to be presented which are independent of the hardware and this will be the emphasis in this chapter. Finally the programs here are less easy to demonstrate than those in previous chapters; what is gained through motion is traded-off in terms of the elaborateness of the pictures generated, and the pictures produced do not really lend themselves to animation through flick-book style presentation, always a possibility in showing computer animation without a computer! A particularly good example of this is in the book *Computer Animation Primer* by Fox and Waite (1984). Readers will have to suffice with static screen shots (stills) here and it is therefore even more essential in this chapter to key the programs into the machine and see them running for yourself.

7.1 VARIETIES OF COMPUTER MOTION

If you have already worked through a handful of the programs in this book you cannot fail to have been struck by the fact that computer graphics and art is essentially a dynamic activity. Designs and pictures are constructed in computer time and their process of construction represents the execution of some logically ordered sequence of instructions or rules which generate the object in some efficient way. Very few of our pictures in this book are generated instantaneously, and we have not bothered to hide the process of graphical computation. Thus the process of computation itself is a kind of animation although rarely do the rules in question reflect any notion of real time. Usually the rules are based on questions of efficiency and involve many approximations, short cuts and tricks which generate the final object. Just occasionally do such rules approximate real-time processes. For example, the construction of landscapes and trees often contains rules which mirror natural growth processes while the construction and rendering of architectural and mechanical artifacts sometimes resembles the order in which such objects are constructed in reality.

As pointed out several times in earlier chapters, the process of graphical computation usually reflects the picture structure in some way, and thus the execution of the process can often be visually quite pleasing. However, there is sometimes a stronger link to temporal motion and dynamics in an object's geometry which can be exploited to enable an efficient dynamics of construction. In Chapter 5, the successful application of both random and recursive techniques depended upon intrinsic properties of the object's structure. In Chapter 6, objects with rotational symmetry displayed an even stronger relationship to time. Cylinders and spheres generated by rotating a point lent themselves quite naturally to motion by using spatial structure as a way of exploiting temporal structure. Yet in all previous chapters except the last, time was regarded as implicit, hence arbitrary, despite the idea that spatial structure involves a process of structuring and restructuring which is essentially dynamic, hence temporal. In this chapter however, motion and time are essential to the objects modelled. Time will be explicit, often based on exploiting the implicit temporal properties which reside in the object's spatial structure as in the case of the rotating cylinders and spheres of the last chapter.

We can classify the varieties of computer motion introduced here into four types which we will discuss in turn: *kinetic* motion, *simulated* motion, *real-time* motion, and *frame* motion. The first of these – kinetic motion – has already been liberally illustrated throughout this book for this is the motion which results from graphical computation, and it usually serves to show the essential correspondence between picture and program structure. The clearest examples of such kinetic art occur in the landscapes introduced in Chapter 4 and to a lesser extent in Chapter 5, where the painter's algorithm was used to construct scenes by 'overpainting' from background to foreground. This type of animation essentially reflects the way a landscape painter sets about work, the technique used being sometimes referred to as one of 'temporal' priority. Many varieties of kinetic motion have been introduced from the most abstract in which picture construction is essentially arbitrary to more realistic constructions in which the process of graphical computation reflects some real process. For example in Chapter 5, the models simulating city and river structure essentially match computer time to the real time of city growth and river evolution, while the various random walks introduced also mirror the way particles are 'observed' in real time at the microscopic level. Even in the process of three-dimensional construction of architectural and mechanical objects in Chapter 6, the graphical computation sometimes reflects the real method of construction.

We will not explore these ideas of kinetic motion further here but they form an essential backcloth to all computer graphics and art. We will concentrate on the other three techniques which are all involved in simulating the actual motion of an object on the computer display. The first of these – simulated motion – does not involve actually moving the object on the screen but simulating motion and deceiving the eye through merging colour switching with the persistence of vision. We have already seen examples of this in previous chapters. For example in Chapter 6, cylinders, globes and a space station were 'rotated' (or rather the impression of rotation was created) by systematically switching the colours defined in the circular properties of the objects in question. In Chapter 4, we also showed how very long term change could be simulated in landscapes – reflecting seasonal change – by colour switching. In this chapter, we will take these ideas further by showing how objects plotted in different screen positions or frames, can be switched 'on' and 'off' in various sequences reflecting motion.

With simulated motion, objects may be plotted in different positions on the screen to reflect movement, but the actual animation begins once this plotting is complete, and is entirely organized through colour switching. Such animation can be extremely fast but it is limited by the number of colours encoded in the colour registers, which in turn is a function of the computer's hardware. The second type of animation to be explored here is called real-time motion, and this is usually slower but considerably more flexible. Essentially it involves plotting an object in one position, then erasing it, plotting it in another position, erasing it and so on. To avoid the discontinuity which results from the time taken to erase between subsequent plots, what is usually done is to combine this process with colour switching. The object is plotted visibly in a first position, and then invisibly in a second. Then the visible object is made invisible, the invisible visible by colour switching, and a third object is plotted invisibly in a third position while the first , now invisible, object is being erased. The process continues in this fashion, and thus one can generate motion of indefinite length but the process is slow and is only suitable for certain types of animation when programmed in Basic.

The last technique to be presented is referred to as frame motion. It is possible to move an object around the screen display by moving the screen memory containing the object through the computer's Random Access Memory. This is effectively what scrolling the screen is all about. There is a useful sideways scroll facility in the BBC Micro as well as the usual vertical scrolls but these are limited for they cannot be used together to generate diagonal movements. We have already seen an example of such scrolling in Chapter 3 in the Cloudscape program where the screen was scrolled down to reflect increasing cloud cover. It is however possible to achieve good animation in this way by plotting different frames of an object in different screen positions, using colour switching to display them, and using scrolling to position them in the movie. This leads to very fast animation but with much less flexibility than real-time motion.

Before we explore these various techniques and demonstrate them in programs, it is worth emphasizing the need to adapt the technique of animation to the problem in hand. Different picture structures and sequences imply different techniques. Speed of animation, detail of the picture and complexity of the scene are all issues which have to be taken into account in selecting an appropriate technique. And as in other areas of art, a strong sense of intuition and much ingenuity is required to develop good animation. The rules for computer animation have hardly been developed as yet. In writing this chapter, I could find little or nothing to guide me apart from the most obvious techniques with the exception of the excellent book by Fox and Waite (1984). And as you would expect from an open-ended introduction such as this one it is in this area that the most progress is likely to be made in the next decade.

In what follows, we will first examine colour switching in switching frames, and then move on to real-time motion in which frames are successively plotted and erased. This will involve us in exploring the way colours are coded in binary form and the way these colours can be changed using the bit map/bit plane structure of the screen memory. Our programs will be simple designs like windmills and space ship cartoons, thus reflecting the inevitable trade-off between the elaborateness of the picture and the detail of the motion. We will also present examples of very slow animation – sunrise, sunset, and very fast animation – a low flying aircraft. Finally, we will collect these ideas together in a simple computer movie of Mickey Mouse.

7.2   SIMULATING MOTION THROUGH COLOUR SWITCHING

We will introduce these techniques with designs based on the four colours defined in MODE1 although the ideas of this section can be extended to the 16 colours in the lower resolution MODE2 in a straightforward way. The essence of the technique involves assigning mutually exclusive subsets of colours from the logical colour set to distinct frames of the object plotted at different positions on the screen. To illustrate the idea, consider a pendulum with two positions on the screen, these positions defining the left- and right-most locations of the range over which the pendulum can swing. The first position – the first frame – is plotted using logical colour 1 and the second position, logical colour 2 say. Let us assume the background colour 0 is black. When we first plot each frame, we will assume each logical colour is set to red, thus showing the two positions which define the limits over which the pendulum can 'swing'. Now to deceive the eye into perceiving a swinging pendulum, we need to alternate the visibility/invisibility of each frame in a sequence so that while frame 1 is visible frame 2 is invisible and vice versa. To do this we would reassign logical colour registers 1 and 2 in the following way:

VDU19,log1,viscol;0;19,log2,inviscol;0;
VDU19,log1,inviscol;0;19,log2,viscol;0;

and embed these instructions in a loop with some possible delay between the VDU19 statements so that the motion of swinging reflects that of a typical clock.

These ideas are incorporated into the program listed as Program 7.1. In this listing, after initial setups in lines 20 and 30, both logical colours are assigned to red in line 40 while the right-hand pendulum is plotted using GCOL0,1 in lines 70 and 80. C1% is assigned the visible colour red (1) and C2% the invisible colour black (0) in line 90. These colours are then successively switched between lines 100 and 130 with the delay between switching controlled by the user from the keyboard. The pendulum itself is plotted in the procedure PROCLOCATE defined between lines 160 and 280. The pendulum

268   *Animation, cartooning and simple computer movies*

Program 7.1   Pendulum motion through colour switching

```
 10 REM Motion Through Colour Switching
 20 MODE1
 30 VDU23,1,0;0;0;0;29,640;512;
 40 VDU19,1,1;0;19,2,1;0;
 50 GCOLO,1:MOVE 0,0
 60 PROCLOCATE(300,350,80,80)
 70 GCOLO,2:MOVE 0,0
 80 PROCLOCATE(240,350,80,80)
 90 C1%=1:C2%=0
100 REPEAT
110    AA=GET:VDU19,1,C2%;0;19,2,C1%;0;
120    AA=GET:VDU19,1,C1%;0;19,2,C2%;0;
130    UNTIL FALSE
140 END
150 :
160 REM Locates and Plots a Pendulum
170 DEFPROCLOCATE(ANG,R%,XS%,YS%)
180 ANG=RAD(ANG):XO%=R%*COS(ANG):YO%=R%*SIN(ANG)
190 A=ATN(XS%/YS%):Z=SQR(XS%^2+YS%^2)
200 A1=ANG+PI+A:XA%=Z*COS(A1):YA%=Z*SIN(A1)
210 A2=ANG+2*PI-A:XB%=Z*COS(A2):YB%=Z*SIN(A2)
220 X1%=XO%+XA%:Y1%=YO%+YA%
230 X2%=XO%+XB%:Y2%=YO%+YB%
240 X3%=XO%-XA%:Y3%=YO%-YA%
250 X4%=XO%-XB%:Y4%=YO%-YB%
260 DRAW XO%,YO%:MOVE X2%,Y2%:MOVE X1%,Y1%
270 PLOT85,X3%,Y3%:PLOT85,X4%,Y4%
280 ENDPROC
```

block is fixed to a rod of length $R\%$ and is a rectangle with sides of length $2*XS\%$ and $2*YS\%$. In lines 180 to 210, the coordinates of the block are calculated with respect to the origin of the pendulum and size of the block. These are fixed in lines 220 to 250, and the rod and block finally drawn and filled in in lines 260 and 270.

This program is effective as long as the pendulum blocks do not overlap. In fact in MODE1, there is still one colour available and thus a third frame position could be plotted in logical colour 3. Thus the swinging could be enhanced into more effective motion if required. But if the frames overlap which is likely in many instances, this leads to problems. To see this alter the size of the block from 160×160 to 600×60 units replacing lines 50 to 80 of Program 7.1 with

```
50 GCOLO,1:MOVE 0,0
60 PROCLOCATE(300,350,300,30)
70 GCOLO,2:MOVE 0,0
80 PROCLOCATE(240,350,300,30)
```

Figure 7.1 shows the overlap which occurs. Because the left-hand block is plotted after the right-hand block, the left-hand overplots the right-hand.

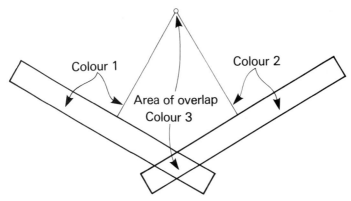

Fig. 7.1   Overlapping pendulums and overlapping colours

When colour switching occurs, the left-hand block remains complete, but the right-hand block is broken, thus reflecting the priority of plotting. To solve this problem, we must associate another colour with the area of overlap shown in Fig. 7.1 and when switching the colours, ensure that this third colour remains switched on at all times. However as we rarely know in advance where the overlap will occur, it is necessary to plot each block in such a way that the third colour emerges directly from the overlap of the first two assigned colours. To enable such an operation, we must digress into the way colours are coded as part of the screen memory, for the operations which effect their manipulation depend upon this.

In MODE1, the four colours given by logical colour numbers 0,1,2 and 3 are represented in the screen memory by the following 2 bit words: 00(0), 01(1), 10(2) and 11(3). Associated with these colours are a set of logical plotting operations controlled by the GCOL statements which enable colours to be manipulated according to their binary representation. These manipulations are based on simple Boolean or logical operations involving binary numbers. In essence, using a particular Boolean operation given the logical GCOL operator, enables one colour to 'combine' with another colour to produce a third which may or may not be the same as the original two. These logical operators are numbered as op-codes 0 to 4. GCOL0 is the usual one which simply enables the colour in question to overplot anything which is on the screen. However GCOL1 involves the disjunction of colours (the OR operation) in which the binary code of the colour being plotted is ORed with the binary code of the colour on the screen. GCOL2 represents the conjunction of colours (the binary AND operation) while GCOL3 is the exclusive OR and GCOL4 the NOT or inverse operation.

In most of this chapter, all that will concern us are the OR and AND operations. These operations work as follows: the OR operation (GCOL1) applies the Boolean OR operation to each pair of bits associated with the two colours being compared, while the AND operation (GCOL2) similarly applies the Boolean AND operation. The following results are possible for each bit comparison:

GCOL1: Boolean OR	GCOL2: Boolean AND
0 OR 0 = 0	0 AND 0 = 0
0 OR 1 = 1	0 AND 1 = 0
1 OR 0 = 1	1 AND 0 = 0
1 OR 1 = 1	1 AND 1 = 1

Another way of looking at these Boolean operations is in terms of truth tables; if 1 is true and 0 is false, then the OR operation makes a comparison involving any true value true while the AND operation makes a comparison involving any false value false.

We are now in a position using the standard Boolean operations to see what happens when a logical colour is plotted over another using the OR and AND operations. Table 7.1 shows these two sets of operations for the four logical

Table 7.1   Boolean operations associated with MODE1 colour plotting.

(a) *GCOL1 (OR) OPERATIONS*

Overplotted colour numbers

		BINARY					DECENARY		
OR	00	01	10	11		OR	0	1	2	3
00	00	01	10	11		0	0	1	2	3
Colour on 01	01	01	11	11		1	1	1	3	3
screen 10	10	11	10	11		2	2	3	2	3
11	11	11	11	11		3	3	3	3	3

(b) *GCOL2 (AND) OPERATIONS*

Overplotted colour numbers

		BINARY					DECENARY		
AND	00	01	10	11		AND	0	1	2	3
00	00	00	00	00		0	0	0	0	0
Colour on 01	00	01	00	01		1	0	1	0	1
screen 10	00	00	10	10		2	0	0	2	2
11	00	01	10	11		3	0	1	2	3

colours in MODE1 in terms of all possible overplots. The effect of these operations is shown in both the binary and decenary number systems. Both sets of operations are clearly symmetrical in that one colour overplotting another acts the same as the reverse: Boolean operations do not discriminate with respect to order. The second point worthy of note is that the OR operation always leads to numbers (of colours) which are the same or greater than the numbers of the two being compared. This is a result of the disjunction being inclusive but it is useful because it helps in assigning colours to the logical registers. In contrast, the AND operation leads to colour numbers the same or less than the numbers of those being compared.

We can now solve the problem posed earlier. If we plot the two overlapping blocks of our pendulum using the GCOL1 operation, not GCOL0, logical colour 1 (01) will combine with logical colour 2 (10) to yield logical colour 3 (11); from Table 7.1(a), 01 OR 10 = 11. The default colour of logical 3 is white and thus if lines 50 to 80 of Program 7.1 are now changed to

```
50 GCOL1,1:MOVE 0,0
60 PROCLOCATE(300,350,300,30)
70 GCOL1,2:MOVE 0,0
80 PROCLOCATE(240,350,300,30)
```

the overlap is shown as white. When the colours are now switched, the overlap remains but as white. Also note that the origin of the rods (the pivot) defining each pendulum is an area of overlap and this is also white. The final stage is to reassign logical colour 3 to red and when the switching now takes place, it appears as though the pendulum is swinging. This is done by including the changes immediately above in Program 7.1 and also changing line 40 to:

```
40 VDU19,1,1;0;19,2,1;0;19,3,1;0;
```

To summarize then, overlapping frames can be easily dealt with using GCOL1 but this requires additional colours given as the appropriate colour numbers defined by the ORing operation. If three objects all overlapping were required, the above logic would generate four overlaps which together with the background colour define eight colours. If four objects are defined this would generate sixteen colours which is the maximum available in MODE2 and this represents the limit for this type of colour switching. The number of colours required is thus given by the formula 2^n where n is the number of distinct objects which may overlap. With sixteen colours defined in MODE2 by a 4 bit word, four objects are possible and the appropriate way to assign each object its initial logical colour involves giving each object a separate bit. Then the colours 0001(1), 0010(2), 0100(4) and 1000(8) are appropriate, these sometimes being referred to as the 4 bit planes which make up the colours in the MODE2 screen memory (McGregor and Watt, 1984).

To conclude this section, and to demonstrate the effectiveness of colour switching, we have designed a program to simulate a ballet dancer in MODE1 based on two frames. The first frame pictures the dancer on one leg with arms outstretched while the second frame pictures the dancer having jumped from the ground with arms lower down. Together the pictures represent two suitable stills from the dance routine shown in Deken (1983). The dancer's body is divided into six parts – head, torso, two arms and two legs, each part being described by a succession of triangles used in filling the shape. The coordinates describing the dancer in each frame are given in DATA statements.

The program listed as Program 7.2 is particularly straightforward. Each part of the dancer is described by no more than 27 pairs of *xy* coordinates which are dimensioned in line 30. In line 50, the background colour 0 is set to cyan, the logical colour 1 associated with the first frame set to dark blue, the logical colour 2 associated with the second frame to the background colour cyan, and the area of overlap of the dance frames – logical colour 3 to dark blue. Positive transformations of the *xy* coordinates are set in lines 60 and 70, and two calls to PROCFIGURE in lines 80 and 90 read the data and plot the appropriate frames. As in Program 7.1, a REPEAT–UNTIL loop between lines 100 and 130 controls the colour switching using a fixed delay of $\frac{1}{2}$ second. Pressing the space bar continuously results in speeding up the animation; to slow it down, set DEL in line 70 to a higher value.

PROCFIGURE defined in lines 160 to 270, positions the dancer (line 180) while the FOR–NEXT loops between lines 190 and 260, and lines 210 and 240 read the logical GCOL operators and colours for each part of the figure, read the associated coordinate pairs (line 220), transform them (line 230) and plot the part in a call to PROCPLOTPART in line 250. PROCPLOTPART which is defined in lines 290 to 340, simply fills the appropriate part using the usual sequence of PLOT85 commands. In fact the first frame is plotted using GCOL op-code 0 not 1 while the second frame uses GCOL1 which still enables the area of overlap between the two frames to be given in logical colour 3. As Table 7.1(a) shows, GCOL0 or GCOL1 could have been used for the first frame which is plotted on the background colour. It is not possible to indicate the dance but the frames which are the two stills used are shown side by side in Fig. 7.2.

A simple extension to the program enables more than one dancer to be plotted. Essentially this involves constructing a frame which contains more than one dancer in the first position, and a similar frame for the second position. Three dancers are included. In this case, it is necessary to plot the figure three times in different positions of each frame, and use the RESTORE command to access the DATA statements in the correct order. The listing which must be merged with Program 7.2 is given as Program 7.3. There are plenty of possible extensions to this based on scaling the figures differentially and forming the first and second frames from different combinations of the

Program 7.2   Ballet dancer

```
 10 REM Ballet Dancer
 20 MODE1
 30 DIM X%(27),Y%(27)
 40 VDU23,1,0;0;0;0;
 50 VDU19,0,6;0;19,1,4;0;19,2,6;0;19,3,4;0;
 60 X0%=640:Y0%=512:S=5
 70 XC%=60:YC%=55:DEL=50
 80 PROCFIGURE(X0%,Y0%)
 90 PROCFIGURE(X0%,Y0%)
100 REPEAT
110   AA=INKEY(DEL):VDU19,1,6;0;19,2,4;0;
120   AA=INKEY(DEL):VDU19,1,4;0;19,2,6;0;
130   UNTIL FALSE
140 END
150 :
160 REM Reads Coordinates & Controls Plotting
170 DEFPROCFIGURE(X0%,Y0%)
180 VDU29,X0%;Y0%;
190 FOR L%=1 TO 6
200   READ K%,OP%,COL%
210   FOR J%=1 TO K%
220     READ Y%(J%),X%(J%)
230     X%(J%)=X%(J%)-XC%:Y%(J%)=Y%(J%)-YC%
240     NEXT J%
250   GCOL OP%,COL%:PROCPLOTPART
260   NEXT L%
270 ENDPROC
280 :
290 REM Plots Parts of Figure
300 DEFPROCPLOTPART
310 MOVE S*X%(1),S*Y%(1):MOVE S*X%(2),S*Y%(2)
320 FOR J%=3 TO K%
330   PLOT85,S*X%(J%),S*Y%(J%):NEXT J%
340 ENDPROC
350 :
360 REM Coordinate Data on the Dancer
370 DATA 10,0,1,96,51,94,48,95,55,90,49,91,57
380 DATA 86,50,86,56,84,53,83,60,80,52
390 DATA 16,0,3,83,60,80,52,81,64,77,52,75,64
400 DATA 74,51,69,63,67,53,64,64,64,51,58
410 DATA 64,59,52,55,58,55,51,52,54,53,50
420 DATA 23,0,1,74,51,77,52,75,49,80,52,77,46
430 DATA 82,47,80,42,85,43,83,38,88,39,87,35
440 DATA 91,36,90,31,93,32,93,28,96,29,97,25,99
450 DATA 26,100,22,103,24,103,21,105,22,107,19
460 DATA 17,0,1,81,64,83,60,84,64,87,61,89,65
470 DATA 91,61,94,65,96,61,99,64,100,60,103,62,104
480 DATA 59,106,60,107,58,109,60,109,58,112,58
490 DATA 20,0,1,58,64,55,58,54,64,52,54,50,61
500 DATA 46,54,42,59,39,54,35,58,32,52,28,57,25,52
510 DATA 20,56,17,49,13,55,11,49,8,53,7,48,6,50,4,49
520 DATA 24,0,1,53,50,55,51,55,48,59,52,57,45
530 DATA 64,52,60,41,67,44,63,36,70,37,65,30,72
540 DATA 30,67,25,74,25,69,20,77,20,73,15,79,15
550 DATA 74,10,82,11,80,7,84,8,84,5,86,4
```

Program 7.2   continued

```
560 DATA 11,1,2,98,53,97,50,96,57,93,49,92,57
570 DATA 89,50,88,56,86,51,85,56,83,48,83,60
580 DATA 17,1,2,83,48,83,60,79,47,79,58,76,46
590 DATA 76,61,71,47,74,62,68,49,69,61,60,50
600 DATA 63,62,57,54,58,61,56,57,55,61,53,58
610 DATA 17,1,2,76,46,79,47,77,44,83,48,77,41
620 DATA 81,41,77,38,81,37,76,34,80,32,77,30
630 DATA 80,28,78,26,80,25,78,23,80,22,78,18
640 DATA 18,1,2,79,58,83,60,76,61,79,64,74,62
650 DATA 75,66,72,64,72,68,70,64,68,68,67,64,64,66
660 DATA 64,63,60,65,61,62,56,63,57,58,55,57
670 DATA 25,1,2,60,50,57,54,57,50,56,57,55,50
680 DATA 53,58,52,48,48,55,49,44,45,53,43,42,41
690 DATA 49,39,40,40,52,37,45,39,56,35,52,39,58
700 DATA 34,58,40,61,34,62,38,63,34,64,36,66,34,69
710 DATA 27,1,2,55,61,58,61,56,63,61,62,57,66
720 DATA 65,62,59,69,66,68,60,73,68,74,63,76,70,78
730 DATA 64,81,71,83,67,86,73,86,69,90,74,90,71,94,77,93
740 DATA 73,86,69,90,74,90,71,94,77,93
750 DATA 74,97,81,98,77,102,84,102,82,105,86,105,87,108
```

dance positions. Colours can also be varied. Readers are invited to scale the dancer so that the screen might be filled with dancers from a dance school!

7.3   REAL-TIME ANIMATION: DRAWING AND ERASING USING BOOLEAN OPERATIONS

The suitability of animation through simple colour switching will generally speaking depend on the number of distinct frames being displayed and whether or not they overlap. Clearly the upper limit for frames which all overlap each other is given by 2^n and where $n=4$, all 16 logical colours in MODE2 are required. Thus for an object such as the dancer in Program 7.2, the maximum number of frames describing the dance routine is 4 using the 16 colour mode. If there was no overlap as in the case of a figure running across the screen for example, a total of 15 frames could be defined in 15 of the 16 logical colours in MODE2, the 16th being the background colour. The degree of overlap will thus determine the number of frames possible but in general, there are many types of motion in which the number of frames required will far exceed the number of colours available. For example, consider an object like the pendulum in Fig. 7.1 which is to be made to rotate the full 360° of the circle. In MODE1, three separate non-overlapping positions of the pendulum are possible but there are nowhere near enough to generate a smooth circular rotation. In fact, even the 15 possible positions in MODE2 are probably not enough and in any case with the size of the block given in Program 7.1, these would overlap and require more colours.

The answer to this problem is both obvious and straightforward and

Fig. 7.2 Dance positions

Program 7.3   Three ballet dancers

```
10 REM Three Ballet Dancers
20 MODE1
30 DIM X%(27),Y%(27)
40 VDU23,1,0;0;0;0;
50 VDU19,0,6;0;19,1,4;0;19,2,6;0;19,3,4;0;
60 X0%=320:Y0%=512:S=5
70 XC%=60:YC%=55:DEL=50
76 FOR M%=1 TO 3
78    RESTORE 370
80    PROCFIGURE(X0%,Y0%)
82    X0%=X0%+320:NEXT M%
84 X0%=320
86 FOR M%=1 TO 3
88    RESTORE 560
90    PROCFIGURE(X0%,Y0%)
92    X0%=X0%+320:NEXT M%
100 REPEAT
110   AA=INKEY(DEL):VDU19,1,6;0;19,2,4;0;
120   AA=INKEY(DEL):VDU19,1,4;0;19,2,6;0;
130   UNTIL FALSE
140 END
```

involves not only drawing but erasing frames once they have been displayed. In this way, an indefinite number of frames can be generated and made to repeat themselves if so required. The algorithm used to implement this procedure however involves holding two frames at any one time. It is not appropriate to plot and display a frame, then erase it before the next one is displayed because there would be a moment when the screen would be blank. This discontinuity can be resolved by the judicious use of colour switching within the plotting and erasing process. It is possible to describe the algorithm without reference to the GCOL operations used to implement it because the principle is quite general. The algorithm begins by plotting the first frame using the first logical colour which is visible, and then plotting the second frame using the second logical colour which is invisible. These colours are then switched making the first frame invisible, hence displaying the second frame. While this second frame is switched on, the first is erased. Then a third frame is plotted invisibly, the second is switched off, the third switched on, the second erased while invisible, and so on. The essence of the algorithm is as follows: frame t is plotted invisibly, then frame $t-1$ which is visible is made invisible at the same time as frame t is being made visible. Frame $t-1$ is then erased. Frame t is then incremented to frame $t+1$ and the process cycles back to the beginning again. The flow chart in Fig. 7.3 illustrates this sequence.

Figure 7.4 shows a typical sequence of frames, the broken lines indicating frames which are invisible, the solid lines frames which are visible. The logical colour numbers used to draw each frame are also shown and it is clear that the area of overlap must be assigned a separate colour number. This implies that each frame must be plotted using the GCOL1 operation – the logical OR

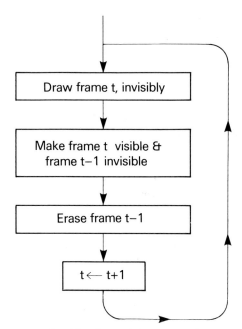

Fig. 7.3   The draw–erase algorithm for real-time animation

operator as in Program 7.2. Moreover, the algorithm in Fig. 7.3 begins with a frame displayed in one logical colour and ends with a different frame plotted in another. Thus the colours used to plot frames on each pass of the process alternate and therefore the switching of colours controlling visibility also alternates.

We are now in a position to discuss the logical operations appropriate to the drawing and erasing process. It is clear from Fig. 7.4 that the overlap of two frames in different logical colours involves a third colour which is generated when plotting the new over the old frame using GCOL1. However erasing the old frame involves transferring its logical colour to the background colour and

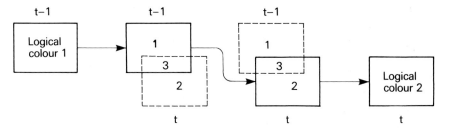

Fig. 7.4   Sequence of frames on a single cycle of the draw–erase algorithm

any overlapped frame area to the colour of the new frame. The logical operation to effect this is the AND operation given by GCOL2. For example in Fig. 7.4, consider the old frame $t-1$ plotted in logical colour 1 whose binary code is 01. To convert this to the background colour 00, it is necessary to remove the colour 01 by plotting frame $t-1$ using GCOL2 and logical colour 2 whose binary code is 10. Then from Table 7.1(b), 01 AND 10 = 00. The area of overlap between frames $t-1$ and t must also be restored to logical colour 2 from the overlap colour 3. This area which is formed by the inclusive disjunction 01 OR 10 = 11 can be unscrambled back to 10 by applying 11 AND 10 = 10. Thus the AND operation erases frame $t-1$ and restores its overlap with other frames to their appropriate colour. Just as the OR operation 'aggregates' colours, the AND operation 'disaggregates' colours back to their original form.

The other point to note is that when a new frame, say t, is plotted using logical colour 2, this presumes the old or existing frame is in logical colour 1. In the same sequence of operations, the same colour (logical 2) is used to erase logical colour 1. Thus the logical colours used in any single pass of the algorithm in Fig. 7.3 to draw the new and erase the old are the same. These colours also alternate between cycles of the draw-erase routine.

These concepts are combined together in a program which extends the pendulum motion of Program 7.1. This program sweeps the pendulum in circular fashion about its origin. In fact, it is more convenient to think of this sweep as akin to a gyroscope. The program is listed as Program 7.4. After initializations up to line 60, the original position of the pendulum is plotted at the start of conventional rotation where the angular variation is zero. The angular increment for each successive point in the circular sweep is 20° giving 18 positions for the pendulum around the circle. With the standard block size, these clearly overlap and thus the method of the previous section – colour switching – cannot be used. The rotation is contained in the REPEAT–UNTIL loop between lines 90 and 170 in which the angular variation is incremented (line 100), the position of the next frame invisibly plotted in lines 110 and 120, the colours switched in line 130, and the old pendulum frame erased in lines 140 and 150. In line 160, the logical colours for the next pass through the loop are fixed. The pendulum itself is computed and plotted in PROCLOCATE listed in lines 200 to 320 which is identical to the same procedure in Program 7.1.

In this program as in Program 7.1, the end of the pendulum is fixed. However a much simpler procedure can be defined which keeps the block of the pendulum horizontal. Lines 200 to 320 of Program 7.4 must be deleted and replaced by the following

```
200  REM Locates and Plots a Pendulum
210  DEFPROCLOCATE(ANG,R%,XS%,YS%)
220  ANG=RAD(ANG):XO%=R%*COS(ANG):YO%=R%*SIN(ANG)
```

Program 7.4 Motion of a gyroscope

```
10 REM A Gyroscope Based on Pendulum Motion
20 REM Drawing,Erasing & Colour Switching
30 MODE1
40 VDU23,1,0;0;0;0;29,640;512;
50 C1%=1:C2%=2:AD=0:INC=20
60 VDU19,C1%,1;0;19,C2%,0;0;19,3,1;0;
70 GCOL1,C1%:MOVE 0,0
80 PROCLOCATE(AD,350,80,80)
90 REPEAT
100   AD=AD+INC
110   GCOL1,C2%:MOVE 0,0
120   PROCLOCATE(AD,350,80,80)
130   VDU19,C1%,0;0;19,C2%,1;0;
140   GCOL2,C2%:MOVE 0,0
150   PROCLOCATE(AD-INC,350,80,80)
160   C3%=C1%:C1%=C2%:C2%=C3%
170   UNTIL FALSE
180 END
190 :
200 REM Locates and Plots a Pendulum
210 DEFPROCLOCATE(ANG,R%,XS%,YS%)
220 ANG=RAD(ANG):XO%=R%*COS(ANG):YO%=R%*SIN(ANG)
230 A=ATN(XS%/YS%):Z=SQR(XS%^2+YS%^2)
240 A1=ANG+PI+A:XA%=Z*COS(A1):YA%=Z*SIN(A1)
250 A2=ANG+2*PI-A:XB%=Z*COS(A2):YB%=Z*SIN(A2)
260 X1%=XO%+XA%:Y1%=YO%+YA%
270 X2%=XO%+XB%:Y2%=YO%+YB%
280 X3%=XO%-XA%:Y3%=YO%-YA%
290 X4%=XO%-XB%:Y4%=YO%-YB%
300 DRAW XO%,YO%:MOVE X2%,Y2%:MOVE X1%,Y1%
310 PLOT85,X3%,Y3%:PLOT85,X4%,Y4%
320 ENDPROC
```

230 DRAW XO%,YO%:MOVE XO%−XS%,YO%+YS%:MOVE XO%+XS%,
YO%+YS%
240 PLOT85,XO%−XS%,YO%−YS%:PLOT85,XO%+XS%,YO%−YS%
250 ENDPROC

Running this simpler program leads to a much more impressive kind of motion in which both ends of the rod are pivoted.

7.4 ANIMATING SINGLE OBJECTS: RANDOM MOTION AND REGULAR ROTATION

The key problem with real-time motion in which frames are drawn, then erased when no longer required, is speed. In Basic, the speed of animation is controlled by the complexity of the object it is necessary to draw, and in general, the more graphics primitives used, the slower the animation. Moreover erasing the object takes as long as drawing it and a reasonable indicator of the time each frame is displayed is twice the time taken to draw it.

Nevertheless quite effective animations can be produced in this way although so far our techniques are restricted to the movement of a single object. Our first computer movie utilizes the flexibility of real-time motion to move an object to any position on the screen through an unrestricted period of computer time. The object we have selected is a simple structure – a cartoon image of the Imperial space craft in the *Star Wars* movie saga known as a Tie-Fighter. The craft is composed of two T-bars as wings suspended horizontally about a one man cabin. Tie-Fighters move smoothly and very quickly but are very sensitive to their controls and thus operate in rather convoluted trajectories usually tracking some object. The best example of their motion is in the chase sequence at the end of the first *Star Wars* movie where Darth Vader and his Imperial Guard are in pursuit of Luke Skywalker and the rebel X-wing fighters along the Death Star trench.

It is worth introducing the program before commenting on the animation. The listing is given as Program 7.5 and the main program follows the structure of the algorithm in Figure 7.3 and the gyroscope program in Program 7.4. Initializations in terms of colour assignment, position and parameters controlling the craft's trajectory are set up in lines 20 to 70 while in line 80 the initial fighter position is drawn by a call to PROCFIGHTER. The REPEAT–UNTIL loop between lines 90 and 170 follows the structure of Fig. 7.3. In line 100, a call to PROCCOORD computes the screen coordinates for the next frame which is drawn invisibly in line 120. The visibility of the two existing frames is thus switched in line 130 and the earlier frame erased in line 140. In line 150, the coordinate positions of the current displayed frame are saved, and the colour for the next pass through the loop is switched using the EOR command. Note that where $C\%$ begins as logical colour 2, the sequence given by $C\% = C\%EOR3$ changes 2 to 1, 1 to 2, 2 to 1 and so on. (This is the exclusive OR operation which changes a 0 bit to a 1 and a 1 to a 0). In line 110, DIS is the distance parameter used to compute the distance of the Tie-Fighter from the viewpoint which is successively incremented while in line 160, SX and SY are the parameters controlling the position of the fighter on the screen; these values are also incremented.

We will now examine the procedure PROCFIGHTER which draws the space craft. This is listed in lines 200 to 280. The distance of the craft from the eye is controlled by a sinewave which varies continuously between 0 and 1. The value of this wave given as T in line 220 is applied to the screen coordinates of the fighter, and the regular variation from 0 to 1 and back to 0 shows the fighter getting smaller, then larger, then smaller again almost disappearing into the distance but then getting larger, and so on. The cabin of the fighter is plotted in line 230 and each wing in lines 240 and 250, and 260 and 270. The procedure PROCCOORD computes the horizontal and vertical trajectories of the fighter on the screen. A smooth trajectory is computed as trigonometric functions of the xy coordinates in lines 320 and 340; and the direction of the

Program 7.5 Tie-fighter simulation

```
10 REM Star Wars:Motion of a Tie Fighter
20 MODE1
30 *FX19
40 VDU23,1,0;0;0;0;
50 VDU19,1,5;0;19,2,0;0;19,3,5;0;
60 X%=80+RND(1140):Y%=64+RND(960)
70 C%=2:QX%=1:QY%=1:SX=0:SY=2:DIS=1
80 GCOL1,1:PROCFIGHTER(X%,Y%,DIS)
90 REPEAT
100   PROCCOORD
110   DS=DIS:DIS=DIS+0.02
120   GCOL1,C%:PROCFIGHTER(X1%,Y1%,DIS)
130   VDU19,3-C%,0;0;19,C%,5;0;
140   GCOL2,C%:PROCFIGHTER(X%,Y%,DS)
150   X%=X1%:Y%=Y1%:C%=C%EOR3
160   SX=SX+0.015:SY=SY+0.015
170   UNTIL FALSE
180 END
190 :
200 REM Draws the Tie-Fighter
210 DEFPROCFIGHTER(A%,B%,D)
220 VDU29,A%;B%;:T=SIN(D)
230 MOVE -T*40,0:MOVE 0,T*20:PLOT85,0,-T*20:PLOT85,T*40,0
240 MOVE -T*55,T*60:DRAW -T*75,T*40
250 DRAW -T*75,-T*40:DRAW -T*55,-T*60:MOVE -T*75,0
260 DRAW T*75,0:MOVE T*55,T*60:DRAW T*75,T*40
270 DRAW T*75,-T*40:DRAW T*55,-T*60
280 ENDPROC
290 :
300 REM Computes the Next Fighter Position
310 DEFPROCCOORD
320 X1%=X%+QX%*100*SIN(COS(3+SX))
330 IF X1%<80 OR X1%>1200 THEN QX%=-QX%:GOTO 320
340 Y1%=Y%+QY%*100*COS(SY)
350 IF Y1%<64 OR Y1%>960 THEN QY%=-QY%:GOTO 340
360 ENDPROC
```

trajectory is changed by the value of these functions as well as by the checks in lines 330 and 350 which keep the craft within screen limits. Essentially the program embodies a simple kind of perspective which assumes the viewer is moving to keep directly behind the craft wherever it is on the screen.

If you have ever seen the Star Wars movie, or played any of those amazing Star Wars arcade games involving Tie-Fighters, you will be disappointed by this simulation. Our Tie-Fighter moves in a reasonable looking trajectory across the screen but it is much slower than the real thing. In fact, the fighter is cruising rather than attacking. The other problem is that the movements are rather jerky. This could probably be improved a little by trial and error adjustment of the parameters but smoothing out the jerks involves reducing the increments of movement, and this in turn slows down the craft even further. Indeed simplifying the shape of the craft and cutting out some of the positional computations does not increase the speed of animation dramatically. Another way of increasing the effectiveness of the simulation would be to plot a quarry on which the fighter was homing in, possibly simulating occasional random fire between fighter and quarry, and even introducing a little sound. If this were done, and it does not involve much additional programming, attention would turn from the speed of the animation to the action itself, illustrating once again the fundamental principle that the ultimate effectiveness of computer graphics depends on very diverse relationships between the various components in the picture structure.

The second program which illustrates real-time motion is much more highly structured and once again represents regular rotation in circular fashion. The program involves setting up some circular object divided into regular segments about its origin, these segments being filled or open in various patterns. The typical example is a windmill in which alternate segments are filled or unfilled, the filled ones representing the windmill's sails. However the program is flexible enough to handle a wide variety of regular polygons inscribed within a circle such as stars, spoked wheels and cogs. The program is listed as Program 7.6. The coordinates describing the segment points on the perimeter of the circle are computed and stored in arrays $X\%$ and $Y\%$ each using 64 elements. After initialization of colours etc., PROCSETUP is called in line 70, and this procedure itself listed in lines 310 to 370, computes these coordinates in the standard circular trigonometric form and stores these in the $X\%$ and $Y\%$ arrays.

In lines 90 and 100, the first frame of the particular design is plotted in a call to PROCLOCATE, and the REPEAT–UNTIL loop between lines 110 and 190 plots new frames, switches colours, and erases old frames in the manner used previously in Programs 7.4 and 7.5. In line 80, parameter $K\%$ gives the starting point in terms of the number of segments to be switched and $L\%$ gives the number of segments (out of 64) through which the object is rotated on each cycle of the loop. Thus $L\%$ controls the speed of rotation, $L\% = 1$ being the slowest while $L\% = 64$ being the fastest, but the actual observed speed will depend on the design being plotted. The parameters $N\%$ and $M\%$ in line 80 control the shape of the design, and PROCLOCATE which is defined in lines 220 to 290, sets up and plots the design.

The parameter $N\%$ affects the number of filled segments which is $64/N\%$, and clearly $N\%$ must be an integer divisor of 64. $M\%$ is the width of a filled segment in terms of elemental segments. So if $N\% = 8$ and $M\% = 2$ as in Program 7.6, this sets up $64/N\% = 8$ sails, each sail being two segments in width. If $M\%$ were then changed to 8, the sails would be eight segments in width and would fill the circle giving an eight sided regular polygon. If $M\%$ were set as 16, a star shape would be formed. If $M\%$ were increased to 32, an eight spoked wheel would be the result, and so on. In PROCLOCATE, the

Program 7.6   Rotating a windmill

```
10 REM A Slow Rotating Windmill
20 MODE1
30 DIM X%(64),Y%(64)
40 VDU23,1,0;0;0;0;29,640;512;
50 C1%=1:C2%=2:A%=64
60 VDU19,C1%,1;0;19,C2%,0;0;19,3,1;0;
70 PROCSETUP(350)
80 K%=0:N%=8:M%=2:L%=1
90 GCOL1,C1%:MOVE 0,0
100 PROCLOCATE(K%,N%,M%)
110 REPEAT
120   K%=K%+L%
130   GCOL1,C2%:MOVE 0,0
140   PROCLOCATE(K%,N%,M%)
150   VDU19,C1%,0;0;19,C2%,1;0;
160   GCOL2,C2%:MOVE 0,0
170   PROCLOCATE(K%-L%,N%,M%)
180   C3%=C1%:C1%=C2%:C2%=C3%
190   UNTIL FALSE
200 END
210 :
220 REM Locates and Plots the Sails
230 DEFPROCLOCATE(KK%,N%,M%)
240 FOR I%=(A%+KK%) TO (2*A%-1+KK%) STEP N%
250   J%=I%MODA%:JJ%=(I%+M%)MODA%
260   MOVE 0,0:MOVE X%(J%),Y%(J%)
270   PLOT85,X%(JJ%),Y%(JJ%)
280   NEXT I%
290 ENDPROC
300 :
310 REM Sets Up the Positions of the Sails
320 DEFPROCSETUP(R%)
330 ANG=0:INC=2*PI/A%
340 FOR I%=0 TO A%-1
350   X%(I%)=R%*COS(ANG):Y%(I%)=R%*SIN(ANG)
360   ANG=ANG+INC:NEXT I%
370 ENDPROC
```

position of the next frame is determined by the parameter $KK\%$. The FOR–NEXT loop between lines 240 and 280 determines the position to which the design is rotated while the values of $J\%$ and $JJ\%$ determine the segments to be filled.

The resulting motion depends on $L\%$ and this is worth varying to see how fast the design can be rotated. Also change $N\%$ and $M\%$ to generate different designs. Four typical stills based on these variations are shown in Fig. 7.5 and the program enables these to be rotated at a variety of speeds. There is plenty of room for further exploration here matching the form of the design to an appropriate animation speed.

Fig. 7.5   Polygonal 'Windmill' designs

7.5 ANIMATING OVERLAPPING OBJECTS: MORE COMPLEX MOTION

When moving a single object using real-time motion, and when the object is in a single colour, the overlaps between successive frames are still dealt with by defining an appropriate number of logical colours. All that the draw and erase operations allow is an infinite number of frames to be handled but the fact that two of them need to be stored at any one time involves more than just a single colour. The previous rules apply: that is, for real-time animation of a single object with $n = 2$ frames, $2^n = 2^2 = 4$ logical colours are required, 1 for each frame, 1 for the area of overlap and 1 for the background. This is the logic of the two previous sections.

It is now easy to see how two objects might be handled. If the objects do not overlap, each will require two frames and a single background colour, thus generating seven colours in total. But if the objects themselves overlap in terms of their frames, then in essence the picture is now composed of four frames and $2^4 = 16$ colours are required. At this point we have reached the limit of what is possible using real-time motion in Basic on the BBC microcomputer. Any further animation in these terms would require a knowledge of the machine's internal architecture and assembly language; this would take us into technicalities which are outside the scope of this book, and beyond the design principles which are central to this treatment of computer graphics and art.

In this section, we will present a program in which two overlapping objects are animated; this will require all 16 colours in MODE2 and an essential first step involves assigning these colours. In fact, this section will be one of the most advanced in this book for it requires some deep logical thinking to enable the 16 colours to be properly assigned to areas of overlap so that no more than three actual colours appear on the screen. We will begin by assuming the first object has two frames which are coloured using colours A and B, and the second object two frames coloured by C and D. We will only assign logical colour numbers to these when we have discussed the structure of the problem.

Now any of these four frames can overlap any other, thus points can exist on the screen which are coloured by any pair of colours from the set {A B C D} as well as single colours. But points can also exist which are coloured by any triple of colours selected from the set, or even by all four colours. Thus what we require is a way of representing all possible overlaps of the four colours, and the appropriate structure is the so-called ordered set. Such a set can be represented as a network or lattice which not only shows all possible combinations of four colours on the screen but also all possible ways of assembling the colours into the appropriate combinations. The lattice of combinations is shown in Fig. 7.6(a) from which it is quite clear that there are 16 possible combinations of the four frames (colours) including the empty set which is the background colour. From this figure, it is also possible to trace any assemblage of colours which produce a specific combination or overlap by following a line through the lattice from the empty set {0} to the complete set {A B C D}.

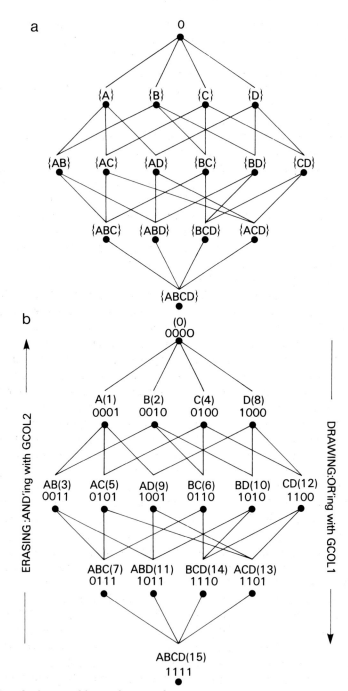

Fig. 7.6 The lattice of four colour combinations

The next step is to assign colour numbers to these combinations from the available set of 16 logical colour numbers. This is not an arbitrary matter as the way the overlapping colours are generated through the plotting must act as an essential guide to the assignment. In a previous section, it was shown how the logical OR statement (the inclusive disjunction) could be used to generate new colour numbers associated with the area of overlap. This suggests that the colour numbers relevant to the four frames {A B C D} must be elemental binary numbers – separate bit planes, for clarity of combination. With 16 colours, we are dealing with 4 bit words which have the following binary form – colour number 0:0000, 1:0001, 2:0010 and so on. The four appropriate colour numbers for the four frames are logical colour numbers 1:0001, 2:0010, 4:0100, and 8:1000 whose concatenation gives all numbers up to the maximum colour number 15:1111. We will assume that the two frames of object 1 are given by colour numbers 1 and 2, and of object 2 by 4 and 8 although this is quite arbitrary. From these definitions, it is clear that these four colour numbers define the 4 bit planes which compose the 4 bit word defining colours in MODE2.

We can now construct an OR lattice analogous to Fig. 7.6(a) which shows how these binary numbers combine to compose the areas of overlap. This is shown in Fig. 7.6(b). Several properties of these combinations are now apparent. First, logical colour numbers associated with combinations of original colours 1, 2, 4 and 8 can always be derived by simple binary addition. This is a feature of both the ORing process and the binary number system. Second, the ORing process in Fig. 7.6(b) can be seen as one of moving down the lattice from the empty set to the full set, composing combinations of colour on the way. This is a process of concatenation or aggregation.

The reverse process moving from the full to the empty set up the lattice can be seen as one of disaggregation in which combinations of colours are gradually unscrambled towards their elemental or bit plane form. Just as the composition process is associated with ORing, with drawing, this decomposition can be associated with ANDing or erasing. From Fig. 7.6(b) the erasing operation using GCOL2 can be easily seen. If I wish to erase all the colours from the screen which are not colour 1, I simply AND every colour on the screen with colour 1 (that is, GCOL2,1) and only colour 1. If I want to do the same but leave colours 2 and 8, then I must take the logical combination of 2 OR 8 = 10 (0010 OR 1000 = 1010), and AND every colour with colour number 10. The principle is entirely general and has wide applicability.

To give these ideas some visual coherence, consider Fig. 7.7 which is the four frame analogue of Fig. 7.4. The process of drawing and erasing two objects, each of which is composed of two frames, follows the algorithm in Fig. 7.3. We begin with the first frame of object 1 in colour 1, the first frame of object 2 in colour 4, and the area of overlap which is colour 5 (1 OR 4 = 5). Two additional frames, one for each object, are then drawn invisibly using

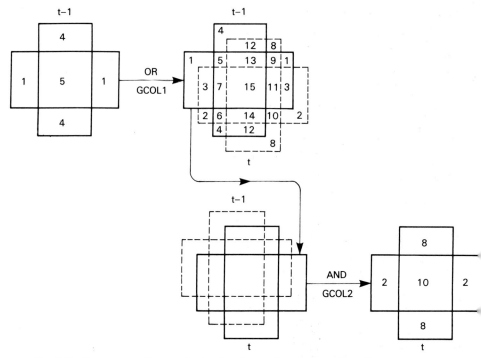

Fig. 7.7   Sequences of frames in the four frame draw–erase algorithm

colours 2 and 8 for the first and second objects respectively (shown by the broken lines), and this generates another 12 logical colours. Colour switching takes place in order to display the two new frames (the new positions of the two objects). The old frames are then erased in such a way that the basic colours 2 and 8 and their overlap colour 10 are restored.

The process of composing colours by overlapping frames is clearly determined by the use of GCOL1 as Fig. 7.6(b) suggests while the process of erasing frames is effected by GCOL2 but noting that the colour used to erase is 10(2 OR 8). Use of colour 10 ensures that only these colours including 10 which compose parts of 10 remain on the screen. We are now in a position to present a computer program which embodies these ideas, and we will extend Program 7.6 to rotate two circular objects which represent the sails of two windmills. The program which is listed as Program 7.7 is entirely straightforward being an extension of Program 7.6 incorporating the ideas just sketched.

The windmill's sails are set up and configured in the same way as in Program 7.6; that is, the coordinates of a typical set of sails around the circle are computed in PROCSETUP, and the particular object is plotted in its correct locational position in PROCLOCATE. These procedures are identical to those

Program 7.7   Overlapping windmills

```
 10 REM Two Overlapping Moving Windmills
 20 REM Draw,Erase & Complex Colour Switching
 30 MODE2
 40 DIM X%(64),Y%(64),C%(15)
 50 VDU23,1,0;0;0;0;
 60 CA%=1:CB%=0:CC%=4:CD%=0
 70 C1%=1:C2%=2:C4%=4:C8%=8:A%=64
 80 PROCPALETTE:PROCSETUP(350)
 90 K%=0:N%=8:M%=4:L%=2
100 XA%=465:YA%=614:XB%=815:YB%=410
110 GCOL1,C1%:VDU29,XA%;YA%;:MOVE 0,0
120 PROCLOCATE(K%,N%,M%)
130 GCOL1,C4%:VDU29,XB%;YB%;:MOVE 0,0
140 PROCLOCATE(K%,N%,M%)
150 REPEAT
160   K%=K%+L%
170   GCOL1,C2%:VDU29,XA%;YA%;:MOVE 0,0
180   PROCLOCATE(K%,N%,M%)
190   GCOL1,C8%:VDU29,XB%;YB%;:MOVE 0,0
200   PROCLOCATE(K%,N%,M%)
210   COL%=CA%:CA%=CB%:CB%=COL%
220   COL%=CC%:CC%=CD%:CD%=COL%
230   COL%=C2%+C8%:PROCPALETTE
240   GCOL2,COL%:VDU29,XA%;YA%;:MOVE 0,0
250   PROCLOCATE(K%-L%,N%,M%)
260   GCOL2,COL%:VDU29,XB%;YB%;:MOVE 0,0
270   PROCLOCATE(K%-L%,N%,M%)
280   COL%=C1%:C1%=C2%:C2%=COL%
290   COL%=C4%:C4%=C8%:C8%=COL%
300 UNTIL FALSE
310 END
320 :
330 REM Locates and Plots the Sails
340 DEFPROCLOCATE(KK%,N%,M%)
350 FOR I%=(A%+KK%) TO (2*A%-1+KK%) STEP N%
360   J%=I%MODA%:JJ%=(I%+M%)MODA%
370   MOVE 0,0:MOVE X%(J%),Y%(J%)
380   PLOT85,X%(JJ%),Y%(JJ%)
390   NEXT I%
400 ENDPROC
410 :
420 REM Sets Up the Position of the Sails
430 DEFPROCSETUP(R%)
440 ANG=0:INC=2*PI/A%
450 FOR I%=0 TO A%-1
460   X%(I%)=R%*COS(ANG):Y%(I%)=R%*SIN(ANG)
470   ANG=ANG+INC:NEXT I%
480 ENDPROC
490 :
500 REM Sets Up the Appropriate Logical Colour Palette
510 DEFPROCPALETTE
520 C%(1)=CA%:C%(2)=CB%:C%(4)=CC%:C%(8)=CD%
530 C%(3)=C%(1)ORC%(2):C%(5)=C%(1)ORC%(4)
540 C%(9)=C%(1)ORC%(8):C%(6)=C%(2)ORC%(4)
```

Program 7.7 continued

```
550 C%(10)=C%(2)ORC%(8):C%(12)=C%(4)ORC%(8)
560 C%(7)=C%(3)ORC%(4):C%(11)=C%(3)ORC%(8)
570 C%(13)=C%(5)ORC%(8):C%(14)=C%(6)ORC%(8)
580 C%(15)=C%(5)ORC%(10)
590 FOR I%=1 TO 15
600   VDU19,I%,C%(I%);0;:NEXT I%
610 ENDPROC
```

discussed in the previous section and do not need to be discussed any further. However there is one additional procedure PROCPALETTE which is used to assign actual to logical colours. PROCPALETTE which is defined in lines 500 to 610, makes extensive use of the OR statement in combining the original absolute colours in such a way that the correct overlap colour is specified. If you examine these, you will find that exactly the same rules of combination are used as those embodied in the lattice of Fig. 7.6(a) and (b), for the logic goes through entirely. Two of these colours are always background colours while the other two are absolutes. The procedure is also used to switch the colours as is required on each pass of the drawing and erasing algorithm.

After initialization up to line 70, the palette is defined and the coordinates of the sails set up by calls to PROCPALETTE and PROCSETUP in line 80. Parameters defining the type of 'windmills', their rotation speeds and positions are set in lines 90 to 100, and the two objects are first plotted in lines 110 to 140. The REPEAT–UNTIL loop between lines 150 and 300 now contains two frame plotting and two frame erasing calls to PROCLOCATE. The two new invisible frames (one for each object) are plotted in lines 170 to 200, colours switched and the palette reassigned in lines 210 to 230, and the old frames erased in lines 240 to 270. Note however that the erasure of the old frames is achieved using the combinations of the two logical colours used to plot the two new (invisible) frames.

When you run Program 7.7, the blue and red sails create the colour purple or magenta in the area of overlap. The colour of the overlap created will depend upon the concatenation of the two binary strings representing the original colours of the sails. It is easy to work this out by simply ORing the two colours in question, and this is essentially what PROCPALETTE does for the whole set of colours. For example when red which is actual colour 1 (binary 0001) is ORed with blue (actual colour 4 – binary 0100), the result is 0101 which is colour 5 – magenta. However if say cyan which is actual colour 6 (binary 0110) is ORed with blue (binary 0100), the result is still cyan (0110). Thus with this choice of colours, the windmill coloured cyan appears on top or in front of the windmill coloured blue. Several other combinations of colours lead to interesting overlaps, and a judicious choice of colour can thus enable priority of objects to be established on the screen. Even the appearance of transparency or at least opaqueness can be established in objects as shown in Program 7.7. To show how one of these objects takes priority, simply change $CA\% = 1$ to $CA\% = 6$ in line 60.

Other possibilities exist with this program. Explore the changing designs produced by varying $N\%$ and $M\%$. Also adapt the program to vary the speeds of rotation of each windmill, and the directions of rotation. With a little ingenuity, the program could even be adapted to simulate two interlocking cogwheels if the objects are repositioned and the parameters $N\%$ and $M\%$ given suitable values.

7.6 VERY SLOW ANIMATION: SUNRISE, SUNSET

A rather eccentric method for taking attention away from the rather jerky motion which originates from limits on controlling the speed of drawing and erasing in real-time animation, involves reducing the movement to as small a degree as possible, and applying the technique to pictures whose composition involves such 'gradual' motion. A classic example is a sunset (or sunrise) in which the motion is only appreciated by comparing views at different points in time. Without becoming too philosophic, we accept that the earth rotates diurnally about a 'fixed' sun, and that the earth's movement produces the effects of sunrise and sunset. But as a fixed observer, it appears to us that it is the sun, not the earth that is moving. Indeed, the very terminology of sunrise, sunset implies this. Thus, we immediately introduce an element of 'inaccuracy' into our characterization, and subsequent simulation which will involve moving the sun, not the earth. Accepting this piece of medieval physics, we are quite content to simply glance at the sun during sunrise or sunset and 'know' it is rising or setting without actually detecting movement. What we will do here is write a program based on such movement which takes as long to run as the sun actually takes to rise or set in these northern climes. Thus its impact only comes from running the program and occasionally examining its output.

The program itself produces a picture in which the sun and its rays are computed in the upper part of the screen – the sky window – and its shadow is cast in the lower part of the screen – in the foreground window. The program begins with the sun high in the sky and dropping one pixel unit at a time towards the horizon which is the line between the sky and foreground. As the sun sets, the shadow cast beneath the sun on the foreground widens and lengthens. By the time the sun has dropped below the horizon, the foreground has been entirely filled with an appropriate shadowed perspective vista. At this point, sunset becomes sunrise, and the process is reversed. As the sun begins to rise, the shadow is dragged back until the sun reaches its highest point in the sky, and the sunset begins once more. And so on *ad infinitum.*

Before we examine the program, we will describe the various techniques used to structure the scene, define the logical colours and operations, and generate the picture's geometry. The screen is divided into two graphics windows – the sky window in the upper screen, and the foreground window in the lower screen, and graphical operations in these windows alternate consistently. In the sky window, the sun and its rays are drawn one pixel up (sunrise) or down (sunset) from the previous frame within the given screen limits, but in such a way that the sun eventually disappears below or rises above the horizon: this effect of course is determined by the fact that the window determines what is visible. In the foreground window, shadows are cast or reduced, being drawn or erased afresh each time a new sun position is created.

The use of colours and logical plotting operations is as follows. The draw-erase algorithm is used to plot and replot the sun and its rays in the graphics window, thus four logical colours are required: colour 0 for sky (background), 1 and 2 for successive (and alternating) frames of the sun and its rays, and 3 for the overlap of any two successive frames. Colour 4 is used as the foreground colour and when the sun's rays are first plotted, these extend (only once) across the foreground to give a perspective effect: colour 5 is reserved for these foreground rays. Finally the shadows are drawn using colour 8 but as these overlap the foreground colour 4 and the perspective ray colour 5, colours 12 and 13 respectively are reserved for these overlaps. Colour numbers 3, 5, 12 and 13 are all produced using the logical OR operation in GCOL1 which controls the following juxtaposition of colours: 1 OR 2 = 3; 1 OR 4 = 5; 4 OR 8 = 12; 5 OR 8 = 13. In total, nine logical colours are defined, leaving seven for further possible elaboration of the program.

The sun itself and its rays involve both circular and elliptical geometry. The rays are drawn using 128 angular increments describing rotation around an ellipse whose horizontal axis is about 1.6 times the length of its vertical axis. The rays which splay out from the centre of the ellipse 'interfere' with one another, that is merge with one another, close to the centre, and produce characteristic moiré patterns due to the screen's resolution. This by itself produces the effect of diffusing rays but to give added impact a circular sun is plotted over the centre of these rays. The elliptical coordinates of the rays are also used for the sun using an appropriate scaling back to circular form. The shadows are drawn beneath the sun as lines across the screen with one pixel width separating them, and their length tapering to a point as distance from the horizon increases in terms of the setting sun. This effect is reversed for the rising sun. This provides an appropriate perspective which is also aided by the fact that when the shadows cut the original rays, perspective is enhanced for these rays become visible. The shadows are given a ragged edge using the PLOT21 command in their drawing.

The program is listed as Program 7.8. Initializations are made up to line 90 with the sky and foreground windows coloured light blue (cyan) and dark blue respectively. In line 100, PROCSETUP is called which sets up the elliptical

Program 7.8 Very slow animation: sunrise, sunset

```
 10 REM Very Slow Animation:Sunrise,Sunset
 20 MODE2
 30 DIM X%(128),Y%(128)
 40 VDU23,1,0;0;0;0;
 50 C1%=1:C2%=2:A%=128:YINC%=4
 60 VDU19,C1%,6;0;19,C2%,4;0;19,3,1;0;
 70 VDU19,0,4;0;19,4,6;0;19,5,6;0;
 80 VDU19,8,6;0;19,12,6;0;19,13,6;0;
 90 VDU24,0;0;1279;300;:GCOLO,132:CLG
100 PROCSETUP(1200)
110 OP%=1:COL%=8:BE%=292:ST%=-8:KG%=1
120 X0%=900:Y0%=900:KC%=0:GCOL1,C1%
130 PROCLOCATE
140 AA=INKEY(250):KC%=1
150 VDU19,C1%,1;0;19,4,0;0;19,5,0;0;
160 VDU19,8,1;0;19,12,1;0;19,13,0;0;
170 REPEAT
180   Y0%=Y0%-YINC%:GCOL1,C2%
190   PROCLOCATE
200   VDU19,C1%,4;0;19,C2%,1;0;
210   Y0%=Y0%+YINC%:GCOL2,C2%
220   PROCLOCATE
230   C3%=C1%:C1%=C2%:C2%=C3%:Y0%=Y0%-YINC%
240   IF Y0%<-300 OR Y0%>900 THEN PROCSWITCH
250   UNTIL FALSE
260 END
270 :
280 REM Draws or Undraws Sun and Shadows
290 DEFPROCLOCATE
300 VDU26:IF KC%=0 THEN GOTO 320
310 VDU24,0;304;1279;1023;
320 VDU29,X0%;Y0%;
330 FOR I%=0 TO A%
340   MOVE 0,0:DRAW X%(I%),Y%(I%):NEXT I%
350 MOVE 0,0
360 FOR I%=0 TO A% STEP 8
370   MOVE 0,0:PLOT85,0.075*X%(I%),0.12*Y%(I%):NEXT I%
380 VDU26:VDU24,0;0;1279;300;:VDU29,X0%;0;
390 YL%=(Y0%-600)/2+50:GCOLOP%,COL%
400 IF KG%=-1 THEN YL%=YL%+475
410 FOR YI%=BE% TO YL%+4 STEP ST%
420   XI%=(YI%-YL%)/10:XI%=XI%^2
430   MOVE -XI%-RND(XI%),YI%:PLOT21,XI%+RND(XI%),YI%
440   NEXT YI%
450 ENDPROC
460 :
470 REM Sets Up Elliptical Coordinates
480 DEFPROCSETUP(R%)
490 ANG=0:INC=2*PI/A%
500 FOR I%=0 TO A%
510   X%(I%)=2*R%*COS(ANG):Y%(I%)=1.25*R%*SIN(ANG)
```

Program 7.8 continued

```
520    ANG=ANG+INC:NEXT I%
530 ENDPROC
540 :
550 REM Controls the Direction of the Sun's Motion
560 DEFPROCSWITCH
570 IF KG%=1 THEN OP%=2:COL%=5 ELSE OP%=1:COL%=8
580 YINC%=-YINC%:BE%=-BE%:ST%=-ST%:KG%=-KG%
590 ENDPROC
```

coordinates of the rays in the $X\%$ and $Y\%$ arrays which each contain 129 elements. PROCSETUP which is defined in lines 470 to 530 is similar to the same procedure in Programs 7.6 and 7.7. In lines 110 and 120, the sunset positions are established, and the sun and its rays then plotted by a call to PROCLOCATE in line 130. PROCLOCATE itself which is defined in lines 280 to 450 does two things. It first sets up the sky window and plots the next frame of the sun and its rays – lines 310 to 370, and then sets up the foreground window and plots the shadows in lines 380 to 440. On the first call to this procedure, the sun and its rays are plotted across the whole screen in GCOL1, and the rays which cover the foreground window act as an aid to perspective defined by logical colour 5. The FOR–NEXT loop in lines 330 and 340 draws the rays, and the loop in lines 360 and 370 draws and fills the sun. In line 380, the foreground colour is established and in lines 390 and 400, the parameters of the shadows relating to colour, length and direction (for sunset or sunrise) are established. The FOR–NEXT loop between lines 410 and 440 compute and draw each line of the shadow in such a way that they are red on a black foreground in the setting sun, black on red in the rising sun.

With the first call to PROCLOCATE, the sun and its rays, and the shadows are coloured cyan as is the foreground, and thus the shadows cannot be seen. In lines 150 and 160, the colours are switched to those used for the sunset – red sun and rays on a blue sky, and red shadows on a black foreground. The REPEAT–UNTIL loop between lines 170 and 250 needs no explanation as it follows the draw, switch, erase procedure of Fig. 7.3 and previous programs. However in line 240, the parameters controlling the direction of the sun's motion are switched by a call to PROCSWITCH if the sun has reached its zenith or nadir. PROCSWITCH defined in lines 560 to 590, simply effects the appropriate switch in direction.

With the present parameters, the sun takes about one hour to set, and the same time to rise. A sequence of typical sun positions is shown in Plate 18. Readers should explore different speeds of sunrise and sunset by increasing $YINC\%$ in line 50. Different colours can also be tried. Perhaps a more effective shadowing would involve defining the foreground in green with black shadows for sunset, green for sunrise. There are many such possibilities and by this point in the book such extensions should quite literally jump out of the pages at you. Only in this way can the liberating effects of computer art be realized.

7.7 VERY FAST ANIMATION THROUGH SCREEN SCROLLING

The third major method involving animation to be introduced here is much closer to the hardware of the BBC machine than any of those already explored. This involves actually moving a frame which is set up within the screen memory by moving this memory itself within the computer's RAM. This sounds rather specific but in fact, it is no more than scrolling the screen and is a facility which is available on many computers, indeed all of those which have raster graphics capability (see Fox and Waite, 1984). As before the principles presented here are entirely general.

On the BBC machine, the screen memory can be scrolled either sideways or vertically using VDU commands. The command

   VDU23;13,value;0;0;0;

controls sideways scrolling. In essence this command resets the 'Value' of register 13 which contains the 8 lowest bits of the 14 bit start address of the screen memory. If the value is negative, the screen will scroll right from its present position, if positive it will scroll left. There is a major limitation on this sideways scrolling capability and that is that if the screen memory is scrolled one full screen in width left or right, the vertical height of the screen will be displaced one unit up or down respectively. This unit displacement is one character position where there are 32 text characters defining the height of the screen in MODE 0, 1 and 2. Thus effective screen scrolling must take account of this limitation which in essence means that actual scrolling sideways always involves a dislocation in height which is usually unacceptable. This means the objects on the screen must not touch the edge of the screen, and that if dislocation of any kind which raises or lowers the height of the object is unacceptable, screen scrolling can only take place within a much narrower range.

The value of the register is in fact measured in the units which describe the 80 columns of text in MODE0. Setting *value* = 80 above will scroll the screen leftward 1279 screen units. Thus if an object of width 20 text or 320 screen units is to be moved, then for the object to remain on the screen but move left or right, the value of the register must range between -20 and $+20$. Vertical scrolling of the screen is a little coarser in terms of special commands VDU10 and VDU11 which move the screen down and up respectively a height of one text line. However in both cases, this type of scrolling is very fast and usually requires the use of the INKEY command to enable a delay to be introduced.

The simplest method of scrolling is to plot a single frame on the screen, perhaps based on a very elaborate picture, and just move it sideways, up or down to simulate motion. Clearly this kind of simple motion is only appropriate to a very small number of objects, for example those based on repetitive mechanical motion although the idea can be used to good effect as is illustrated in the Mickey Mouse Movie at the end of this chapter. However it is not possible to combine these types of scrolling to produce trajectories other than either horizontal or vertical, and thus other methods of extending the screen scrolling must be explored.

It is possible to produce more elaborate types of animation by combining scrolling with colour switching. For example, by a judicious combination of different frames on the screen implying different movements, and the ability to display any of these frames by colour switching together with screen scrolling, a variety of movement patterns can be simulated. Consider four separate frames placed side by side across the screen, each one plotted using different logical (not actual) colours. Each frame might represent a different position of the object, for example different positions of a man running. Now if only one frame were to be displayed in sequence, the runner would appear to move across the screen but would also quickly disappear. However if each time the frame were switched on, the screen were scrolled to a fixed position on the screen, the runner would appear to be running on the spot.

This process can be easily extended to encompass vertical motion as well. If the runner were hurdling say, then the frames could be displaced up or down the screen. When scrolled, vertical motion would also be generated. If the object were to rise and fall steadily, then diagonal placement of the frames on the screen combined with colour switching and scrolling would engender this. Finally, much more complex trajectories could be designed which would combine differential scrolling and positioning but in every case, the limits on screen scrolling indicated above would have to be observed.

We have illustrated this last type of scrolling in a program which simulates the vertical motion of a World War 2 bomber. The program is listed as Program 7.9, and it is based on the construction of five frames, each one based on the same bomber which are located diagonally and non-overlapping from the bottom centre to the top right of the screen. All frames but the first are then switched off; the animation begins by switching off the first frame, scrolling the screen one frame left, switching on the second frame, switching it off, scrolling again and so on. The vertical upwards motion of the bomber is then replaced by downward motion in which the sequence of the display is reversed. Before the scrolling takes place, the entire set of frames is displayed and these are illustrated in Fig. 7.8. Imagine, if you can, the screen being scrolled so that each successive frame is only switched on when it is in the centre position of the VDU screen. This action based on sideways scrolling back and forth leads to the vertical motion of the plane.

The program itself is straightforward. As each bomber is identical, the same coordinate data are used but each frame requires different logical colours. The

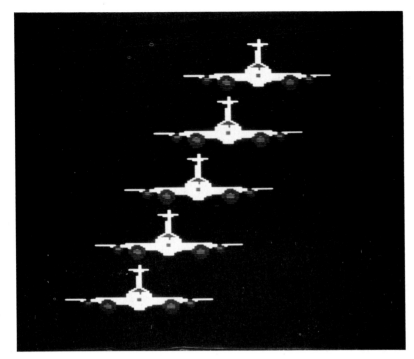

Fig. 7.8 Bomber positions, prior to animation

background colour is black, and as there are five frames to be positioned, this means three colours can be assigned to each frame in MODE2. The wings and fuselage of the plane are coloured white, the outer propeller shafts, the nose cone and the cockpit blue, and the inner propellers (or jets!) red. These colours are stored in the array C% and are defined and assigned in the FOR–NEXT loop between lines 70 and 110. The FOR–NEXT loop between lines 130 and 170 positions the relevant frame, defines its colours, and calls PROCBOMBER (line 150) which draws the plane. The FOR–NEXT loop in lines 180 and 190 switches off all colours except for those in the first frame, and then scrolling begins in the REPEAT–UNTIL loop bounded by lines 200 and 250. In this loop, two calls are made to PROCSCROLL in lines 220 and 240 which initiate leftward scrolling implying upward motion, and rightward scrolling implying downward motion respectively.

PROCBOMBER is defined in lines 420 to 700. As the plane is viewed front on, it is symmetrical and thus one set of coordinate data is read twice, the first for the left side of the plane, the second for the right side. This symmetry is controlled by the FOR–NEXT loop between lines 440 and 690, and the RESTORE statement in line 450. Within this loop, the inner FOR–NEXT loop

Program 7.9   Very fast animation: a low flying aircraft

```
 10 REM Simulating the Motion of a WW2 Bomber
 20 REM Through Screen Scrolling & Colour Switching
 30 MODE2
 40 DIM C%(15)
 50 I%=7:J%=1:K%=4:C%(0)=0:T=2.5
 60 VDU23,1;0;0;0;0;19,0,C%(0);0;
 70 FOR II%=0 TO 12 STEP 3
 80   F%=II%+1:G%=II%+2:H%=II%+3
 90   C%(F%)=I%:C%(G%)=J%:C%(H%)=K%
100   VDU19,F%,I%;0;19,G%,J%;0;19,H%,K%;0;
110   NEXT II%
120 SX%=640:SY%=150:IC%=0
130 FOR II%=1 TO 15 STEP 3
140   I%=II%:J%=II%+1:K%=II%+2
150   VDU29,SX%;SY%;:PROCBOMBER
160   SX%=SX%+96:SY%=SY%+160
170   NEXT II%:AA=GET
180 FOR K%=4 TO 15
190   VDU19,K%,C%(0);0;:NEXT K%
200 REPEAT
210   Z%=1:M1%=4:M2%=13:M3%=3
220   PROCSCROLL
230   Z%=-1:M1%=12:M2%=3:M3%=-3
240   PROCSCROLL
250   UNTIL FALSE
260 END
270 :
280 REM Controls the Sideways Scrolling of the Screen
290 DEFPROCSCROLL
300 FOR I%=M1% TO M2% STEP M3%
310   FOR M%=1 TO 3
320     VDU19,I%-M%*Z%,C%(0);0;:NEXT M%
330   FOR J%=1 TO 6
340     IC%=IC%+Z%
350     VDU23;13,IC%;0;0;0;:NEXT J%
360   FOR M%=0 TO 2
370     Q%=I%+M%*Z%
380     VDU19,Q%,C%(Q%);0;:NEXT M%
390   AA=INKEY(10):NEXT I%
400 ENDPROC
410 :
420 REM Plots the Bomber By Symmetrical Reflection
430 DEFPROCBOMBER
440 FOR N%=1 TO 2
450   RESTORE 820:GCOLO,I%:MOVE0,0
460   READ X%,Y%:IF N%=2 THEN X%=-X%
470   MOVE T*X%,T*Y%
480   FOR M%=1 TO 5
490     READ X%,Y%:IF N%=2 THEN X%=-X%
500     PLOT85,T*X%,T*Y%:MOVE 0,0:NEXT M%
510   FOR M%=1 TO 6
520     READ X1%,Y1%,X2%,Y2%,X3%,Y3%
530     IF N%=2 THEN X1%=-X1%:X2%=-X2%:X3%=-X3%
540     MOVE T*X1%,T*Y1%:MOVE T*X2%,T*Y2%
550     PLOT85,T*X3%,T*Y3%:NEXT M%
```

Program 7.9   continued

```
560    FOR M%=1 TO 2
570      READ X%,Y%,R%:IF N%=2 THEN X%=-X%
580      X%=X%*T:Y%=Y%*T:R%=R%*T
590      GCOLO,K%:PROCCIRCLE
600      R%=R%*0.3:GCOLO,J%
610      PROCCIRCLE:NEXT M%
620    GCOLO,K%:X%=0:Y%=0
630    READ R%:R%=T*R%:PROCCIRCLE
640    FOR M%=1 TO 3
650      READ X1%,Y1%,X2%,Y2%,X3%,Y3%
660      IF N%=2 THEN X1%=-X1%:X2%=-X2%:X3%=-X3%
670      MOVE T*X1%,T*Y1%:MOVE T*X2%,T*Y2%
680      PLOT85,T*X3%,T*Y3%
690      NEXT M%:NEXT N%
700    ENDPROC
710    :
720    REM Computes & Fills a Standard Circle
730    DEFPROCCIRCLE
740    MOVE X%+R%,Y%:MOVE X%,Y%
750    FOR KK%=0 TO 360 STEP 24
760      XX%=X%+R%*COS(RAD(KK%))
770      YY%=Y%+R%*SIN(RAD(KK%))
780      PLOT85,XX%,YY%:MOVE X%,Y%:NEXT KK%
790    ENDPROC
800    :
810    REM Coordinate Data on Right Side of Bomber
820    DATA 0,15,6,13,10,10,13,-6,5,-10,0,-10
830    DATA 0,14,2,14,0,40,0,35,10,35,0,32
840    DATA 0,-10,5,-10,0,-12,0,-12,5,-10,5,-12
850    DATA 13,-6,10,10,14,3,14,3,13,-6,90,0
860    DATA 40,-8,9,65,-5,5,2,0,6,0,12,3,12
870    DATA 3,12,0,6,3,9,3,9,3,12,7,10
```

between lines 480 and 500 plots the fuselage in white using PLOT85 commands, the loop from 510 to 550 plots the tail and wing span also in white, and the loop from lines 560 to 610 plots the two propellers or jet shafts, the outer shafts in blue, the inner in red using calls to PROCCIRCLE. This procedure listed in lines 720 to 790, is based on the standard slow circle filling routine introduced in Chapter 2. The nose cone and the cockpit are also plotted in blue in the loop between lines 640 and 690.

PROCSCROLL in lines 280 to 400 is composed of three FOR–NEXT loops. The first from lines 310 to 320 switches off the currently displayed frame, the second (lines 330 to 350) makes the appropriate sideways scroll, and the third in lines 360 to 380, switches on the current centrally positioned frame. These three loops are embedded in a fourth outer loop which controls the sequence of frames being displayed. In fact, one of our general rules of animation is violated here. Although implicit, we have assumed that in good animation, there should always be a frame on the screen. Just for a moment here, there is no frame on the screen while scrolling takes place but the moment is small and the motion sufficiently fast and robust for this to contribute rather than detract from the simulation.

As in all previous programs, many extensions are possible. The frames could be tilted slightly to simulate wind currents and there is even the possibility that a roll-over motion could be simulated although with only five frames, this would be a little tight. Nevertheless, there is plenty of scope for improvements to this particular program and readers should attempt some of these.

7.8   THE MICKEY MOUSE MOVIE

To illustrate how the three principles of animation illustrated in this chapter can be combined but also by way of more lighthearted entertainment in concluding this chapter and indeed this book, we have written a program to animate that most famous of cartoon characters, Mickey Mouse. The techniques of colour switching, real-time motion and the idea of screen scrolling will all be illustrated here with respect to Mickey and the program will also illustrate a couple of other principles relevant to cartooning.

For purposes of both clarity and feasibility, we have divided these programs into three relatively independent program segments. First we will describe a master program which essentially plots Mickey from the coordinate data we have measured. This master program can then be used to call two other programs, the first which shows one happy Mickey delighting in wagging his tail, twinkling his eyes and stringing a Yo-Yo, the other showing Mickey rolling back and forth on a skate board. If you intend to key in these programs and store them on your filespace, call the master program MICKEY, the Yo-Yo animation segment YO-YO and the skate board animation SKATE. We will refer to these as such in the sequel. We will not show here how YO-YO and SKATE can be combined but this is a straightforward extension of the animation and can be left to the reader.

We will first present the master program which plots and transforms Mickey from the given coordinate data. Mickey has been divided up into 26 parts, each of which is described by a sequence of xy coordinates arranged in such a way as to facilitate the colour fill using the PLOT85 triangle fill commands. These parts are read in in the following order which is worth giving to indicate the elaborate nature of the graphical coding. The parts whose coordinates begin at line 660 in the program refer to the following sequence: right ear, left ear, head, body, right arm, left arm, sleeve, hand, tail, right leg, left leg, right shoe top, left shoe top, right foot, left foot, first trouser, second trouser, face, mouth, tongue, right eye panel, left eye panel, right eye, left eye, right button, and left button. There are eight further lines describing how the edges of Mickey are rendered, and these are given in order as: right eyebrow, left eyebrow, thumb crease, hand edge, first finger crease, second finger crease, edge of right foot, and edge of left foot.

The master program plots several transformations of Mickey in different positions on the screen, thus illustrating limits on the level of resolution in MODE2 in which the cartoon is drawn. These transformations are read from DATA statements along with data on the screen position of each Mickey to be plotted. Because of limits on memory, it is not possible to store the coordinates of all the points describing this complex cartoon; thus each time the cartoon is drawn at whatever scale, the data is reread. The fact that the figure is divided into 26 parts enables a manageable number of coordinate pairs to be stored while plotting although it would be a simple matter to read and immediately plot the point in its sequence if so required.

The master program is organized to plot 11 Mickeys using different transformations. First a full screen version is plotted in the centre of the screen, then three smaller versions are plotted in a band across the screen. After this, six even smaller cartoons are plotted on a full screen but this really touches the limits of resolution in terms of the detail contained in the character. Finally a full screen version is plotted but this time it is off-centre so it can be retained in the frame buffer as a basis for the subsequent animations referred to above. The colours used are characteristic of the well-known cartoon. Mickey's body is in black, his feet, hands and face in white, his trousers in red and his eyes in light blue. He is also displayed on a light blue (cyan) background. The logical colour numbers (0 – cyan background), 4 (black), 5 (white) and 6 (red) are assigned to plot the figure. Note that colours 1, 2 and 3 have been reserved for the animation sequences which will be presented below.

The program is listed as Program 7.10. In line 30, the dimension statements refer to the coordinates of a relevant part of Mickey ($X\%$ and $Y\%$), the number of coordinates in each part ($C\%$), the logical colour number of each part ($COL\%$), the number of line edges to be plotted ($CC\%$), the transformations used (TT) and the associated screen positions ($CN\%$). The FOR–NEXT loops in lines 60 and 70, and 80 and 90 read in the 11 transformations TT and screen positions $CN\%$ from DATA statements, while the loops between 100 and 130, and 140 and 150, read in the 26 colour numbers $COL\%$, and the number of coordinates in each part $C\%$. The main body of the program is contained in the FOR–NEXT loop which is bounded by lines 170 and 390 which controls the 11 transformations. In line 180, DATA statements are restored for each pass through the loop, and screen positions of each relevant Mickey set. In line 190, the screen is cleared if the appropriate number of Mickeys have been plotted.

The FOR–NEXT loop between lines 200 and 270 controls the reading and plotting of the data in its 26 parts. The inner loop between 220 and 250 reads in the relevant data; in line 260, the colour of the part is set and then it is plotted by a call to PROCPLOTPART in line 270. In lines 280 and 290, the number of edge lines to be plotted is read in and the FOR–NEXT loop between

Program 7.10   The master program for the Mickey Mouse movie

```
 10 REM Transformations of Mickey Mouse
 20 MODE2
 30 DIM X%(35),Y%(35),C%(26),COL%(26),CC%(8),TT(11),CN%(11,1)
 40 VDU23,1,0;0;0;0;29,440;512;
 50 VDU19,0,6;0;19,4,0;0;19,5,7;0;19,6,1;0;
 60 FOR L%=1 TO 11
 70    READ TT(L%):NEXT L%
 80 FOR L%=1 TO 11
 90    READ CN%(L%,0),CN%(L%,1):NEXT L%
100 FOR I%=1 TO 26
110    READ COL%(I%)
120    IF COL%(I%)<>0 THEN COL%(I%)=COL%(I%)+3
130    NEXT I%
140 FOR I%=1 TO 26
150    READ C%(I%):NEXT I%
160 YC%=95:XC%=72
170 FOR L%=1 TO 11
180    RESTORE 660:T=TT(L%):VDU29,CN%(L%,0);CN%(L%,1);
190    IF L%=1 OR L%=2 OR L%=5 OR L%=11 THEN CLS
200    FOR I%=1 TO 26
210       K%=0
220       FOR J%=1 TO C%(I%)
230          K%=K%+1:READ Y%(K%),X%(K%)
240          Y%(K%)=Y%(K%)-YC%:X%(K%)=X%(K%)-XC%
250          NEXT J%
260       GCOL0,COL%(I%):K%=0
270       PROCPLOTPART:NEXT I%
280    FOR I%=1 TO 8
290       READ CC%(I%):NEXT I%
300    FOR I%=1 TO 8
310       K%=0
320       FOR J%=1 TO CC%(I%)
330          K%=K%+1:READ Y%(K%),X%(K%)
340          Y%(K%)=Y%(K%)-YC%:X%(K%)=X%(K%)-XC%
350          NEXT J%
360       GCOL0,4:K%=0
370       PROCLINE:NEXT I%
380    IF L%=1 OR L%=4 OR L%=10 OR L%=11 THEN AA=INKEY(200)
390    NEXT L%
400 CHAIN"YO-YO"
410 END
420 :
430 REM Plots a Segment of Mickey using Triangle Fill
440 DEFPROCPLOTPART
450 K%=K%+1:MOVE T*X%(K%),T*Y%(K%)
460 K%=K%+1:MOVE T*X%(K%),T*Y%(K%)
470 FOR J%=3 TO C%(I%)
480    K%=K%+1:PLOT85,T*X%(K%),T*Y%(K%)
490    NEXT J%
500 ENDPROC
510 :
520 REM Plots an Edge Line of Mickey
530 DEFPROCLINE
540 K%=K%+1:MOVE T*X%(K%),T*Y%(K%)
550 FOR J%=2 TO CC%(I%)
560    K%=K%+1:DRAW T*X%(K%),T*Y%(K%)
```

Program 7.10   continued

```
570   NEXT J%
580 ENDPROC
590 :
600 DATA 4.5,3.0,3.0,3.0,2.5,2.5,2.5,2.5,2.5,2.5,4.0
610 DATA 640,512,250,512,640,512,1030,512,250,256
620 DATA 640,256,1030,256,250,768,640,768,1030,768,440,512
630 DATA 1,1,1,1,1,1,3,2,1,1,1,3,3,2,2,3,3,2,2,3,2,2,0,0,2,2
640 DATA 11,17,26,17,9,7,12,32,35,10,11,14,10,15,22
650 DATA 17,7,29,19,6,28,15,8,8,7,6
660 DATA 140,10,150,14,127,11,156,24,119,17
670 DATA 153,31,117,28,147,36,120,34,142,39
680 DATA 130,29
690 DATA 165,33,172,31,162,36,179,33,161,40
700 DATA 183,36,160,45,186,41,160,50,188,47
710 DATA 166,63,189,53,170,67,189,59,175,68
720 DATA 186,64,181,68
730 DATA 142,39,130,39,153,44,118,42,160,50
740 DATA 114,46,166,63,108,62,164,79,108,77
750 DATA 160,85,111,86,157,89,113,92,150,93
760 DATA 115,96,140,95,118,99,140,97,120,102
770 DATA 144,99,125,105,146,103,137,105,145,105
780 DATA 142,107
790 DATA 108,62,108,77,95,67,111,86,87,68
800 DATA 100,101,72,67,92,107,64,66,80,109
810 DATA 58,63,72,108,53,71,64,106,51,81
820 DATA 56,104,53,92
830 DATA 108,62,95,67,99,58,87,68,88,57
840 DATA 81,67,76,61,73,68,72,67
850 DATA 111,86,100,101,104,102,94,106,103,108
860 DATA 94,110,102,113
870 DATA 91,111,94,110,90,114,98,112,97,114
880 DATA 102,113,98,117,104,117,99,118,105,120
890 DATA 103,121,104,122
900 DATA 117,133,118,136,113,131,116,138,110,130
910 DATA 112,139,106,129,106,138,104,122,101,135
920 DATA 99,118,97,135,97,114,94,135,90,114
930 DATA 92,135,84,118,89,136,80,120,85,137
940 DATA 77,122,82,138,73,123,78,139,70,124
950 DATA 75,139,67,126,70,137,65,128,68,136
960 DATA 65,132,65,135
970 DATA 55,67,56,64,50,63,52,60,46,58
980 DATA 48,56,43,51,45,50,40,44,42,43
990 DATA 38,37,39,36,36,30,38,29,35,24
1000 DATA 37,23,35,17,36,16,34,13,35,12
1010 DATA 32,10,33,8,31,7,30,6,29,8
1020 DATA 28,7,27,9,26,9,27,13,25,14
1030 DATA 27,18,25,19,27,23,26,24,29,30
1040 DATA 51,81,45,77,54,69,42,74,43,65
1050 DATA 34,70,36,61,31,68,33,60,30,65
1060 DATA 53,92,51,81,45,86,44,77,38,82
1070 DATA 37,73,34,79,34,72,31,77,31,73
1080 DATA 27,74
1090 DATA 36,57,36,61,33,53,33,60,27,53
1100 DATA 31,62,27,63,30,65,26,67,31,68
1110 DATA 25,71,34,70,25,73,34,72
```

Program 7.10   continued

```
1120 DATA 25,75,30,74,25,78,31,77,27,80
1130 DATA 34,79,28,84,33,83,29,86,32,85
1140 DATA 25,45,27,53,18,40,27,63,11,40
1150 DATA 26,67,6,43,25,71,3,55,21,76
1160 DATA 3,68,19,78,5,75,15,80,11,79
1170 DATA 25,71,25,73,21,76,25,78,19,78
1180 DATA 28,84,15,80,31,91,11,79,33,97
1190 DATA 10,83,32,97,9,89,30,107,9,95
1200 DATA 28,111,9,100,24,114,11,106,21,114
1210 DATA 15,111,17,113
1220 DATA 87,68,91,78,81,68,96,92,73,68
1230 DATA 100,101,67,68,95,103,61,66,90,107
1240 DATA 57,65,84,108,54,72,80,109,51,81
1250 DATA 77,108,52,88
1260 DATA 54,95,73,95,55,96,77,108,55,100
1270 DATA 67,105,56,103
1280 DATA 135,103,126,104,133,102,122,101,132,99
1290 DATA 118,98,138,97,116,96,137,92,113,90
1300 DATA 133,85,112,83,132,83,112,77,130,78
1310 DATA 113,74,129,76,115,68,129,70,120,62
1320 DATA 131,64,124,58,132,59,126,55,133,54
1330 DATA 125,53,130,44,122,51,123,42
1340 DATA 123,42,122,51,117,44,123,57,113,53
1350 DATA 119,61,110,59,114,64,110,63,111,65
1360 DATA 107,65,107,67,104,68,106,71,104,72
1370 DATA 107,73,106,75,109,76,108,78
1380 DATA 110,66,110,69,108,68,109,71,107,72
1390 DATA 109,73
1400 DATA 130,78,131,77,129,76,133,75,129,70
1410 DATA 136,73,131,64,139,72,135,61,141,72
1420 DATA 141,58,143,72,148,57,144,72,151,57
1430 DATA 146,73,160,60,144,74,162,65,146,76
1440 DATA 157,74,144,79,150,80,140,81,140,84
1450 DATA 136,82,135,86,133,85
1460 DATA 150,80,157,74,148,83,162,79,149,85
1470 DATA 159,84,150,86,155,88,148,88,149,92
1480 DATA 145,90,145,93,141,91,143,92,141,91
1490 DATA 143,73,138,74,145,75,140,76,143,79
1500 DATA 139,78,139,80,133,81
1510 DATA 145,82,143,83,147,85,144,85,146,88
1520 DATA 143,88,143,89,138,90
1530 DATA 91,91,92,93,85,91,90,95,80,94
1540 DATA 86,96,80,95
1550 DATA 91,102,86,101,92,104,81,102,87,106
1560 DATA 82,105
1570 DATA 3,3,3,11,3,3,9,10,148,65,152,66,154,70
1580 DATA 157,80,157,83,155,86,99,118,97,122,94,123
1590 DATA 89,136,85,137,82,138,78,139,75,139,70,137
1600 DATA 68,136,65,135,65,132,65,128,67,126
1610 DATA 65,132,69,132,75,130,70,137,76,136,81,134
1620 DATA 27,53,27,63,26,67,25,71,21,76
1630 DATA 19,78,15,80,11,79,5,75
1640 DATA 28,84,31,91,33,97,32,97,30,107
1650 DATA 28,111,24,114,21,114,17,113,15,111
```

lines 300 and 370 mirrors the earlier one between 200 and 270 except that lines, not parts are plotted. The loop from lines 320 to 350 reads the relevant data, the colour is set in line 360 and a call to PROCLINE in line 370 draws the line. PROCPLOTPART and PROCLINE which are defined respectively between lines 430 and 500, and 520 and 580 need no explanation as they use the standard sequences of graphical primitives to fill shapes and plot lines which we have used many times before.

A picture of the six smallest Mickeys on the screen is shown in Plate 19. There is plenty you can experiment with here particularly in terms of changing the colours. Only four colours are used and thus there is a lot of room for elaboration. Even if the two animations now to be described were to be merged, this would require $8 + 3 = 11$ additional logical colours, still leaving an additional colour which could be used to render Mickey. Try changing the parts coloured white to yellow and Mickey's trousers to green. Whatever you do will lead to a colourful picture as long as you use at least four colours including the background.

If you look at Program 7.10, you will see that the animation is initiated at line 400 where the command CHAIN "YO-YO" loads and runs the Yo-Yo program which must exist on your filespace. The same principle of adding to the frame buffer using another program as was illustrated for the space scene in the last chapter is used here. Note that if you wish to animate Mickey on his Skate Board, you must replace line 400 with CHAIN "SKATE". First however we will look at the more complex Yo-Yo program.

The Yo-Yo program animates Mickey by plotting a Yo-Yo which Mickey strings back and forth using the real-time motion technique to draw and erase, by plotting different tail positions and wagging the tail through colour switching, and by flashing the eyes and tongue, also through colour switching. The program which is listed as Program 7.11, does not contain any MODE command to clear the frame buffer but assumes the Yo-Yo, tail, eye and mouth animation takes place on whatever is already in the MODE2 buffer. If chained from the program MICKEY, this will be Mickey himself, correctly positioned. After initializations up to line 90, the Yo-Yo thumb string is read from data and plotted in lines 110 to 150. Then in the FOR–NEXT loop between lines 180 and 200, the tail is read in once again and plotted in line 210. The tail is then transformed to a second position through a call to PROCTRANS, plotted again using a different colour in line 220, transformed further to a third position and plotted finally in line 230. The next two FOR–NEXT loops between lines 260 and 280, and 310 and 370 then read in the mouth and eyes and replot these. Note that these parts of Mickey are read from the same coordinate data used in Program 7.10 for it is easier to assign the appropriate logical colours in this segment than in the earlier master program.

The tail, eye and mouth parts are all assigned different logical colours from those used in the master program so that these colours might be switched for

Program 7.11   The Yo-Yo animation

```
 10 REM Mickey with a Yo-Yo
 20 REM Drawing,Erasing & Colour Switching
 30 DIM X%(35),Y%(35)
 40 VDU23,1;0;0;0;0;29,440;512;
 50 VDU19,0,6;0;19,4,0;0;19,5,7;0;19,6,1;0;
 60 T=4.0:XC%=72:YC%=95:AG=25
 70 CA%=4:C1%=1:C2%=2:G%=1
 80 VDU19,3,CA%;0;19,C1%,CA%;0;19,C2%,6;0;
 90 K%=0:M%=35:N%=20:GCOLO,3
100 REM Reads and Plots Coords of Yo-Yo String on Thumb
110 READ XX%,YY%:XX%=XX%-XC%:YY%=YY%-YC%
120 MOVE T*XX%,T*YY%
130 FOR I%=2 TO 5
140    READ XX%,YY%:XX%=XX%-XC%:YY%=YY%-YC%
150    DRAW T*XX%,T*YY%:NEXT I%
160 VDU19,8,0;0;19,9,6;0;19,10,6;0;
170 REM Reads,Transforms and Plots the Tail in 3 Positions
180 FOR I%=1 TO M%
190    READ Y%(I%),X%(I%)
200    Y%(I%)=Y%(I%)-YC%:X%(I%)=X%(I%)-XC%:NEXT I%
210 GCOLO,8:KB%=0:PROCPLOTPART:PROCTRANS(RAD(AG))
220 GCOLO,9:KB%=1:PROCPLOTPART:PROCTRANS(RAD(AG))
230 GCOLO,10:KB%=2:PROCPLOTPART
240 VDU19,14,1;0;19,15,6;0;
250 REM Reads and Plots the Mouth
260 FOR I%=1 TO 6
270    READ Y%(I%),X%(I%)
280    Y%(I%)=Y%(I%)-YC%:X%(I%)=X%(I%)-XC%:NEXT I%
290 GCOLO,14:M%=6:KB%=2:PROCPLOTPART
300 REM Reads and Plots the Eyes
310 FOR J%=1 TO 2
320    FOR I%=1 TO 8
330       READ Y%(I%),X%(I%)
340       Y%(I%)=Y%(I%)-YC%:X%(I%)=X%(I%)-XC%
350    NEXT I%
360    GCOLO,15:M%=8:KB%=3:PROCPLOTPART
370 NEXT J%
380 REM Plots Yo-Yo String,Sets up Shape and Plots It
390 X1%=T*(189-XC%):Y1%=T*(30-YC%)
400 X2%=T*(138-XC%):Y2%=T*(98-YC%)
410 IX%=(X1%-X2%)/N%:IY%=(Y2%-Y1%)/N%
420 PROCSETBALL
430 GCOL G%,C1%:MOVE X2%,Y2%:DRAW X1%,Y1%
440 PROCPLOTBALL(X1%,Y1%)
450 T1%=0:T2%=6:T3%=6:KK%=5
460 M1%=1:L1%=-6:M2%=6:L2%=2
470 REM This Loop Plots and Erases the Yo-Yo in Various
480 REM Positions and Switches Colours to Simulate
490 REM Movement in the Tail,Eyes and Mouth
500 REPEAT
510    XX%=X1%:YY%=Y1%:IX1%=-IX%:IY1%=IY%
520    FOR I%=1 TO 28
530       L1%=-L1%:L2%=-L2%:KK%=KK%+1
540       M1%=M1%+L1%:M2%=M2%+L2%
550       IF KK%MOD4=1 THEN T1%=0:T2%=6:T3%=6
560       IF KK%MOD4=2 THEN T1%=6:T2%=0:T3%=6
```

Program 7.11   continued

```
570     IF KK%MOD4=3 THEN T1%=6:T2%=6:T3%=0
580     IF KK%MOD4=0 THEN T1%=6:T2%=0:T3%=6
590     IF I%>14 THEN IX1%=IX%:IY1%=-IY%
600     G%=1:IF C1%=1 THEN C1%=2:C2%=1 ELSE C1%=1:C2%=2
610     PROCPLOTBALL(XX%+IX1%,YY%+IY1%)
620     G%=2:VDU19,C1%,CA%;0;19,C2%,6;0;
630     PROCPLOTBALL(XX%,YY%)
640     YY%=YY%+IY1%:XX%=XX%+IX1%
650     VDU19,14,M1%;0;19,15,M2%;0;
660     VDU19,8,T1%;0;19,9,T2%;0;19,10,T3%;0;
670     NEXT I%
680   UNTIL FALSE
690 END
700 :
710 REM Plots a Segment using Triangle Fill
720 DEFPROCPLOTPART
730 MOVE T*X%(KB%+1),T*Y%(KB%+1)
740 MOVE T*X%(KB%+2),T*Y%(KB%+2)
750 FOR K%=KB%+3 TO M%
760   PLOT85,T*X%(K%),T*Y%(K%):NEXT K%
770 ENDPROC
780 :
790 REM Transforms Coords of a Segment by ANG Degrees
800 DEFPROCTRANS(ANG)
810 CS=COS(ANG):SS=SIN(ANG):TX=X%(1):TY=Y%(1)
820 AX=TX*(1-CS)-TY*SS:AY=TY*(1-CS)+TX*SS
830 FOR K%=1 TO M%
840   ZZ=X%(K%)*CS+Y%(K%)*SS+AX
850   Y%(K%)=-X%(K%)*SS+Y%(K%)*CS+AY
860   X%(K%)=ZZ:NEXT K%
870 ENDPROC
880 :
890 REM Sets up Coords of a Yo-Yo using a Fast Circle Fill
900 DEFPROCSETBALL
910 R%=T*11:Z%=R%/SQR(2):K%=0
920 FOR XQ%=Z%+4 TO R% STEP 4
930   K%=K%+1:YQ%=SQR(R%*R%-XQ%*XQ%)
940   X%(K%)=XQ%:Y%(K%)=YQ%:NEXT XQ%
950 FOR YQ%=Z%+4 TO R% STEP 4
960   K%=K%+1:XQ%=SQR(R%*R%-YQ%*YQ%)
970   X%(K%)=XQ%:Y%(K%)=YQ%:NEXT YQ%
980 ENDPROC
990 :
1000 REM Plots the Yo-Yo
1010 DEFPROCPLOTBALL(X0%,Y0%)
1020 K%=0:GCOL G%,C1%:MOVE X2%,Y2%
1030 DRAW X0%,Y0%:VDU29,X0%+440;Y0%+512;
1040 MOVE Z%,Z%:MOVE Z%,-Z%:PLOT85,-Z%,Z%
1050 MOVE -Z%,Z%-4:MOVE -Z%,-Z%:PLOT85,Z%-8,-Z%
1060 FOR J%=Z%+4 TO R% STEP 4
1070   K%=K%+1:MOVE X%(K%),Y%(K%):DRAW X%(K%),-Y%(K%)
1080   MOVE -X%(K%),Y%(K%):DRAW -X%(K%),-Y%(K%):NEXT J%
1090 FOR J%=Z%+4 TO R% STEP 4
1100   K%=K%+1:MOVE X%(K%),Y%(K%):DRAW -X%(K%),Y%(K%)
1110   MOVE X%(K%),-Y%(K%):DRAW -X%(K%),-Y%(K%):NEXT J%
```

Program 7.11   continued

```
1120 VDU29,440;512;
1130 ENDPROC
1140 :
1150 REM Data on Coords of String,Tail,Mouth and Eyes
1160 DATA 130,107,131,101,135,97,138,98,138,100
1170 DATA 55,67,56,64,50,63,52,60,46,58
1180 DATA 48,56,43,51,45,50,40,44,42,43
1190 DATA 38,37,39,36,36,30,38,29,35,24
1200 DATA 37,23,35,17,36,16,34,13,35,12
1210 DATA 32,10,33,8,31,7,30,6,29,8
1220 DATA 28,7,27,9,26,9,27,13,25,14
1230 DATA 27,18,25,19,27,23,26,24,29,30
1240 DATA 110,66,110,69,108,68,109,71,107,72
1250 DATA 109,73,143,73,138,74,145,75,140,76,143,79
1260 DATA 139,78,139,80,133,81
1270 DATA 145,82,143,83,147,85,144,85,146,88
1280 DATA 143,88,143,89,138,90
```

animation. The three tail positions are given colour numbers 8, 9 and 10, the mouth colour 14 and the eyes 15. At this point in the program the Yo-Yo is constructed. The string is first set up in lines 390 to 430. In line 420, the coordinates of the Yo-Yo itself are first set up using a call to PROCSETBALL and the first frame of the ball is plotted using the fast circle fill routine called in PROCPLOTBALL in line 440. The animation then begins. The REPEAT-UNTIL loop in lines 500 to 680 mirrors the algorithm in Fig. 7.3. Within this loop, the Yo-Yo occupies 28 positions moving up and down the string, a new invisible frame being plotted in line 610, the old one being erased in line 630. Colour numbers 1, 2 and 3 are used in this sequence. Within this REPEAT–UNTIL loop, a variety of parameters are reset, for the colour switching of the tail, eyes and mouth takes place as well as the colour switching relevant to the Yo-Yo's frames. $T1\%$, $T2\%$ and $T3\%$ determined in lines 550 to 580 and switched in line 660, fix the particular tail to be displayed. $M1\%$ and $M2\%$ determined in lines 530 and 540 and switched in line 650, fix the flashing of the mouth and eyes respectively.

The various procedures called from the main program are quite straightforward. PROCPLOTPART in lines 710 to 770 is identical to that used in Program 7.10 above. PROCTRANS defined in lines 790 to 870 involves a two-dimensional transformation based on equations (3.6) and (3.7) but note that a displacement of the xy coordinates is incorporated so that the tail positions do not overlap. PROCSETBALL in lines 890 to 980 computes the coordinates of the circle associated with the fast fill technique given in equations (2.22) and (2.23). Finally PROCPLOTBALL defined in lines 1000 to 1130 draws the Yo-Yo string to an appropriate length and fills the Yo-Yo ball itself using the fast fill circle technique whose coordinates are established in PROCSETBALL.

A typical still from this animation is shown in Fig. 7.9. Imagine the tail

Fig. 7.9 Mickey with a Yo-Yo
         © 1987 The Walt Disney Company

being switched regularly over three positions, and the eyes and tongue flashing. The Yo-Yo goes up and down the string at about the speed you would expect an expert Yo-Yo player to work it. There is still potential here for it would be possible to arrange for Mickey to tap his foot or move his hand in time to the Yo-Yo using the real-time animation technique.

Our second and final animation involves placing Mickey on a skate board, scrolling the screen back and forth to move the board and Mickey, and rotating the spokes of the skate board's wheels in the appropriate direction. What we have done is to scroll the screen sideways implying that Mickey's hand is propelling himself and the skate board off the edge of a wall – the edge of the screen. This program is called from Program 7.10 by setting line 400 to CHAIN"SKATE"; this is listed as Program 7.12. Like the Yo-Yo program, the frame buffer is not cleared by defining a MODE statement. After initialization up to line 60, the xy coordinates of the skate board are read in and the board plotted using PROCPLOTPART called in line 110. This procedure defined in lines 370 and 420 is similar to that used in Programs 7.10 and 7.11. The skate board is then edged between lines 120 and 180. The two wheels under the board are then plotted using calls to PROCWHEEL in lines 210 and 220. This

Program 7.12   The skate board animation

```
 10 REM Mickey on a Skate Board
 20 REM Animation Through Screen Scrolling
 30 DIM X%(16),Y%(16)
 40 VDU23,1;0;0;0;0;29,440;512;
 50 VDU19,0,6;0;19,4,0;0;19,5,7;0;19,6,1;0;
 60 T=4.0:XC%=72:YC%=95:M%=16
 70 REM Reads and Plots the Coords of the Skate Board
 80 FOR I%=1 TO M%
 90   READ Y%(I%),X%(I%)
100   Y%(I%)=Y%(I%)-YC%:X%(I%)=X%(I%)-XC%:NEXT I%
110 GCOLO,6:PROCPLOTPART
120 GCOLO,4:MOVE T*X%(1),T*Y%(1)
130 REM Edges the Skate Board
140 FOR I%=2 TO M% STEP 2
150   DRAW T*X%(I%),T*Y%(I%):NEXT I%
160 GCOLO,5:MOVE T*X%(1),T*Y%(1)
170 FOR I%=3 TO M%-1 STEP 2
180   DRAW T*X%(I%),T*Y%(I%):NEXT I%
190 VDU19,11,3;0;19,12,3;0;19,13,3;0;
200 REM Plots the Wheels under the Skate Board and Draws Spokes
210 X0%=T*(50-XC%):Y0%=T*(-14-YC%):PROCWHEEL
220 X0%=T*(100-XC%):IC%=10:ZZ%=1:PROCWHEEL
230 REM Scrolls the Screen and Rotates the Wheels Back
240 REM and Forth using Colour Switching on the Spokes
250 REPEAT
260   IC%=IC%+ZZ%
270   IF IC%MOD3=0 THEN Z1%=3:Z2%=0:Z3%=0
280   IF IC%MOD3=1 THEN Z1%=0:Z2%=3:Z3%=0
290   IF IC%MOD3=2 THEN Z1%=0:Z2%=0:Z3%=3
300   VDU19,11,Z1%;0;19,12,Z2%;0;19,13,Z3%;0;
310   VDU23,13,IC%;0;0;0;
320   IF IC%>90 THEN ZZ%=-1
330   IF IC%<46 THEN ZZ%=1
340   UNTIL FALSE
350 END
360 :
370 REM Plots a Segment using Triangle Fill
380 DEFPROCPLOTPART
390 MOVE T*X%(1),T*Y%(1):MOVE T*X%(2),T*Y%(2)
400 FOR K%=3 TO M%
410   PLOT85,T*X%(K%),T*Y%(K%):NEXT K%
420 ENDPROC
430 :
440 REM Plots a Circle(Wheels) and Draws Radii(Spokes)
450 DEFPROCWHEEL
460 IC%=2:R%=T*10:VDU29,X0%+440;Y0%+512;
470 MOVE 0,0:MOVE 0,R%
480 FOR I%=0 TO 360 STEP 24
490   XX%=R%*COS(RAD(I%)):YY%=R%*SIN(RAD(I%))
500   GCOLO,4:PLOT85,XX%,YY%:MOVE 0,0:NEXT I%
510 FOR I%=360 TO 0 STEP -24
520   IC%=IC%+1:Z%=11+IC%MOD3
530   XX%=R%*COS(RAD(I%)):YY%=R%*SIN(RAD(I%))
540   GCOLO,Z%:MOVE 0,0:DRAW XX%,YY%:NEXT I%
```

Program 7.12   continued

```
550 ENDPROC
560 :
570 REM Data on X-Y Coords of Skate Board
580 DATA -1,32,3,35,-5,35,3,105,-5,105
590 DATA 3,110,-4,110,4,115,-3,115,5,120
600 DATA -1,120,7,123,2,123,9,126,5,126,11,130
```

procedure which is listed in lines 440 to 550 fills each wheel in black using the slow circle fill, and then draws 15 yellow spokes alternating through the sequence of colour numbers 11, 12 and 13. The REPEAT-UNTIL loop between lines 250 and 340 effects the animation. Logical colours of the spokes are changed in lines 270 to 290 and the colours switched in line 300. The screen is also scrolled back and forth over a narrow range (thus avoiding any sideways discontinuity) and a novel feature of the animation is that the direction of scroll is linked to the colour switching of the spokes, thus enabling the direction of scrolling to influence the direction in which the wheels are turning.

Plate 20 shows a still of Mickey on his skate board. As mentioned earlier, it would be quite easy to chain this program from the Yo-Yo program but if this were done, the Yo-Yo would no longer move. To get Yo-Yo, tail, eyes, tongue and skate board to move would involve merging Programs 7.11 and 7.12. This would not be difficult as the logical colour numbers are already complementary, but if this is attempted, it would probably be advisable to separate the initial plotting from the subsequent animation to conserve memory space. This was the technique used in the space picture Off Moon Base Alpha in Chapter 6 and it implies that an animation program has the following segment structure: background, object plotting, and animation of objects, the second segment being chained from the first, the third from the second.

There are very strong limits to animations on microcomputers at the present time for none of the presently available techniques is entirely satisfactory. In fact, the usual technique of drawing different frames in a sequence across the screen and just switching them on and off is something we have avoided because this type of animation is often rather pointless. A man running across a screen soon disappears off the edge and the animation ends. We have avoided such animation here in the interests of constructing pictures in which motion occurs indefinitely. All the programs in this chapter contain the animation sequence REPEAT–UNTIL FALSE which indicates this. This may sometimes be boring but at least it offer the possibility of the computer itself acting as both camera and film projector.

In professional movies in which computers are used to assist in producing frames, the norm is still in using computers to construct elaborate stills which are filmed as single frames. Real-time motion of the kind alluded to above is rarely used, for pictures of the requisite resolution and complexity are near impossible to produce on any but the largest computers at the required speeds of 24 or 30 frames per second. For a long time yet, the movie industry will be using computers to produce stills, but real-time animation will come and the rudiments established here will be central. In the meantime, research on computer animation is likely to lead to improved methods of constructing still pictures more quickly and more efficiently, for very often the most effective process of constructing a picture is an analogue of the way the picture is actually produced – evolved naturally or constructed artificially in real-time. As was mentioned at the beginning of this chapter, this area is likely to be the one in which the greatest progress will be made in the next decade.

8

Conclusions

If computer graphics can be art then the question arises
as to where precisely the art is located. Is it in the
program or in the output?

(Annabel Jankel and Rocky Morton,
Creative Computer Graphics, 1984)

This book has attempted to answer Jankel and Morton's question: the art in
computer graphics is in both the program *and* the output, and an appropriate
understanding and appreciation of such art can only come through some
sympathy with this viewpoint. The main theme elaborated here that picture
structure is reflected in program structure and vice versa is an important
element in this viewpoint but it is by no means the only element. What is
possible with this type of art and graphics depends on the constraints and
potential imposed by the hardware and the software as well as the intuition
and artistic abilities of the artist/programmer, and the ability to translate
algorithms in the artist's mind to those in the computer is central.

Different types of computer as reflected in their architecture and in the
various languages and their dialects available provide the materials of
computer graphics. The art produced depends as much on ingenuity in
programming and the insights required in the synthesis of program and output
as in the sort of manual dexterity and ability to translate ideas into physical art
forms essential to conventional art. The medium of computer art is not
quantitatively or qualitatively any less or greater than conventional art but as
this book has attempted to demonstrate, it is simply different, requiring a
different blend of skills, insights, knowledge, emotions, perhaps cultures. At
present, the materials of computer art do seem more significant than those of
conventional art but this is unlikely to remain a distinction for all time,
perhaps only for a few years longer. Appreciating art in this medium as well as
engaging in it is equally different for it demands a different knowledge base.
And again, computer art should be no harder to understand or appreciate but
it does require a different type of involvement from traditional modes of art
appreciation and criticism. These points are disputable but at least, there is
now the realization that computer art cannot be judged as traditional art, just

as it has always seemed outrageous to judge traditional art in terms of what the computer can produce.

We have only dealt with what in Chapter 1 we called computer art as programming, rather than painting, and the point must be made time and again that the viewpoint espoused here is not meant to exclude the legitimacy of computer art as painting. The principles introduced apply largely to the way art and graphics have been conceived about the relationship between picture and program structure, but some of these ideas are also relevant to the development and use of computer painting systems. Doubtless there are many other principles not noted here which apply to computer painting systems, and currently, Prueitt's (1984) book is as good a non-technical illustration of these ideas as one might find. In time, more technical expositions of computer painting systems will be developed as more experience is gained with the use of such systems. But at present, such ideas are rudimentary.

8.1   COMPUTER ART AS CREATIVE MODELLING

Thirty years ago, many areas of the visual arts and design were affected by the quest to make the process of invention, innovation, creation and design more explicit, and in some cases, more formal. This view was founded on the assumption that although much art might remain mysterious, hence inaccessible to systematic study, it was an entirely worthwhile task to see how far such intuitive processes could be made clearer. The development of computers had as much to do with this effort as anything else. It was felt that much of the mystery of art and design which was usually considered to be the province of intuition, could be revealed by more systematic study, and the most optimistic expression of this ideology was to be found in the then emergent field of artificial intelligence. Since then, this optimism has been tempered, but the value of an explicit approach to art still remains, and some of these advantages have been liberally illustrated throughout this book. Although a multitude of insights and decisions which can never be made explicit, go into the making of any single computer picture, at least the key steps in the process are open to inspection and reflection. As with music which can only be taught as a highly structured affair to the majority, computer art with its emphasis on formality and system is likely to attract a very different following than art for those with manual dexterity; and thus, its liberating effects are very different from conventional art.

The theory of creative design usually revolves around two critical phases which interact in subtle and surprising ways; these are often referred to as problem definition and solution. The domain of problem definition is largely analytic while solution is synthetic. Sometimes the design process is structured as one in which induction and deduction interact, while another notion considers the process as one involving a synthesis of realism and idealism. In the language adopted here, self-conscious design of the art object would involve a detailed analysis of the picture structure in terms of the ways its component 'parts' produce the 'whole' picture, followed by a synthesis of these same components using program algorithms to effect a computer representation of the same picture. However, much of the art and graphics developed here has concentrated on the latter stage of the process rather than the former which involves the analysis of picture structure. The concern here is thus more with idealism, than realism, and analysis has remained implicit, notwithstanding the fact that the way pictures have been synthesized, has been made explicit.

In this context, we have invoked little art theory to guide our construction of pictures because so little exists but also because the emphasis has been on synthesis rather than analysis. Nevertheless, the need for more formal theory in computer graphics and art is very clear for computers are well-suited to the treatment of explicit structure and form. It is interesting that the search for structure in art is strongly influenced by developments in computer graphics. For example, fractal geometry, the art of generating irregular graphics, is influenced by the analysis of irregularity in real systems such as landscapes, and such analyses are directly affecting the production of idealistic computer graphics and art such as that being developed in the film industry (Mandelbrot, 1982; Jankel and Morton, 1984). At a more abstract level, Hofstadter's (1979) search for structure in music, art and mathematics is underpinned by the power of formal algorithms based on notions of recursion which in turn represent the lifeblood of contemporary computer programming.

Another central principle of design theory which finds its expression in computer graphics is the idea that there are alternative and often conflicting solutions to design problems. The notion of constrained randomness which is best seen in the Random Landscapes program in Chapter 4 and various recursive designs in Chapter 5 illustrate that quite different designs can emerge from variations within the same general structure. The other principle which leads to alternative designs involves integrating primitives or segments in different combinations. For example, the Vale of Glamorgan picture involved combining cloud, hill and tree forms from separate programs. Different repetitions of the same modules can lead to very different pictures and ever greater diversity can emerge if additional modules are incorporated. As much ingenuity and insight is required in the synthesis of relatively independent program segments as in the design of these segments in the first place. More fundamental types of computer art involves embodying some intelligence or learning function into the algorithm producing the picture, so that the program itself might represent some creative function. This might seem a little far-fetched but the art of Harold Cohen which is richly illustrated in his recent book (Cohen, Cohen and Nii, 1984) demonstrates that a style of computer art is emerging which in Simon's (1969) terms can be truly called a science of the artificial.

8.2   THE NEXT TWENTY YEARS

Carl Sagan's (1984) challenge that we try imagining where computer art will be in twenty years is symptomatic of the rapid development this field will continue to see. As pointed out in Chapter 1, a qualitative change in the type of art which is possible, has already come about with the development of cheap memory which has replaced the art based on vector graphics and line plotters with the art of the raster graphics screen. Within the next decade, microcomputers will surely be endowed with massive amounts of cheap memory which will herald the availability of high resolution screens and many colours. The limitations posed by the constraints on resolution and colour which have influenced most of the art and graphics in this book, will effectively disappear, and many of the more sophisticated computer graphics techniques involving hidden lines, varieties of rendering, lighting and other techniques used to engender 'realism', will become commonplace on micros.

Already, new microprocessors exist in which many of the primitives used in this book are embodied in hardware, while a variety of menu-driven programming systems for writing graphics software are now available. Yet in one sense, the principles developed here are unlikely to change. There is a limit to the number and type of graphics primitives which can be set in hardware, and the real challenge in computer graphics is not the definition or even use of these primitives independently but their combination or integration in producing good pictures. Thus principles of picture composition in terms of their analysis and synthesis using computers will remain as important as at present.

To this end, it is clear that there will be much more research into the formal properties of picture composition. Classical approaches of which for example, fractal geometry is one, have been noted as have emergent approaches based on artificial intelligence. However, models of the design process using shape grammars which herald new forms of picture language are likely to become increasingly important (Stiny and Gipps, 1978). One widely influential example is the development of the LOGO language which was fostered by artificial intelligence researchers to teach children relational mathematics (Abelson and DiSessa, 1980).

Advances in the ability to animate using microcomputers will perhaps represent the most dramatic of all changes in the ideas illustrated here. This will be a direct consequence of the falling cost of computer memory but the increasing ability to animate in real time on a computer will hasten the elaboration of appropriate principles which extend those introduced by Fox and Waite (1984) and in Chapter 7. Similar advances will of course take place with painting systems although the quality of the art produced, its style, its diversity, its form and so on is much less easy to predict, for this depends in the last analysis on the artist, not the computer.

The principles we have begun to sketch here and those which are contained in complementary treatments of computer art and graphics are likely to remain fairly central to the field. In art and design, there is an enormous dearth of theory although the computer is one of the most potent forces in raising awareness about the nature of art. This is evident from the fact that new minds are being attracted to art through the computer, and as in all disciplines where progress occurs in analogy to other fields of knowledge, this can only lead to new insights, interpretations and principles. From this milieu, will surely arise new art forms as difficult to foresee as any of those which emerged in the past. Already the idea of watching a picture unfold as the computer 'makes' it – a central principle of the structures developed here – provides an unusual and sometimes stimulating experience. The way various designs unfold such as the way landscapes are built up here, evokes surprise and pleasure among those who watch. In a sense, this represents the fundamental interaction between picture structure and program structure which is the essence of this treatment and although many of the ideas in this book may date quickly, these principles will remain central to computer graphics and art in the foreseeable future.

Further reading

There are several directions which readers can take once they have absorbed the contents of this book but much will depend upon future intentions. Here we will emphasize six different areas for further reading which involve both complementary and advanced treatments of many of the ideas introduced in this text. We will deal with the context to computer graphics and art, intermediate treatments of microcomputer graphics, machine-specific treatments, advanced reading concerning mainstream computer graphics, general texts on formal geometry and patterns, and books on creativity involving computers. We will conclude these six areas with some indications of the main journals in these fields.

First for readers who wish to review the history and scope of computer graphics and art, there are several books of a non-technical and pictorial nature. If you wish to examine early developments, Reichardt's (1968) *Cybernetic Serendipity*, and Leavitt's (1976) *Artist and Computer* contain comprehensive and systematic selections of articles describing computer art in the 1950s, 1960s and early 1970s. This was the era when computer art and graphics was dominated by line drawing using vector graphics and plotters. A much more up-to-date account is provided by Deken (1983) whose book *Computer Images* contains a useful selection of examples of all kinds of digital imagery based on raster-scan devices. The best book however, in my opinion, is Jankel and Morton's (1984) *Creative Computer Graphics* which presents a comprehensive review of the state-of-the-art, together with some of the best work. In a more idiosyncratic style is Prueitt's (1984) *Art and the Computer* which contains much of his own personal work and represents a combination of art through creative modelling and painting systems. These books are all coffee-table style books but nevertheless contain good summaries of the field in a non-technical sense, and are thus worth perusing. If you are interested in a slightly more technical but readable exposition, Greenberg, Marcus, Schmidt and Gorton's (1982) *The Computer Image* is quite excellent and will provide you with some useful background for a systematic study of the field.

The second area of interest which readers may have, involves a more serious exposition of computer graphics but still at a comparatively elementary or intermediate level, and still involving microcomputers which are easiest to proceed with if you have not been exposed to mainframe computing. Myers' (1982) *Microcomputer Graphics* is a very readable treatment of two- and three-dimensional graphics at about the same level as this text but is less concerned with art and design, more with traditional graphics. Myers' book is available with programs for the Apple II and IBM-PC (in Basic) while the book by Park (1985) *Interactive Microcomputer Graphics* is slightly more formal than Myers, has a hardware bias, and contains examples in Basic also for the IBM-PC. Both these books contain programs at about the same level as those included here and thus will indirectly provide you with hints as to how BBC Basic might be translated into Apple and Microsoft Basics.

The third area of interest involves readers who are working with the BBC Micro. A conventional treatment of computer graphics in BBC Basic which is more advanced than in this book is given in Angel and Jones' (1983) *Advanced Graphics with the BBC Model B Microcomputer*, while a book with a graphic design orientation is McGregor and Watt's (1984) *The Art of Microcomputer Graphics* which has interesting sections on tessellations, transformations and Escher-like designs. However by far the best book on graphic design and creative modelling is Cownie's (1982) *Creative Graphics on the BBC Microcomputer* which contains some brilliant pictures and programs. The book however is just a collection of annotated listings and is much less pedagogic than our own treatment here.

The intermediate and machine-specific texts listed above can all be easily read either alongside this book or immediately this book has been studied. However our fourth area involves more mainstream computer graphics at a more advanced level. If it is your intention to follow the mainstream, it is likely you will require another computer language. Pascal is probably the best because so many mainstream texts use a Pascal-like pseudo-code in presenting programming ideas; but be warned, Pascal is not always available with graphics facilities; Fortran almost always is, as is Basic, on mainframe machines. Nevertheless, Pascal is worth learning and Brown's (1982) *Pascal from BASIC* provides an excellent introduction.

The classic computer graphics text is Newman and Sproull's (1979) *Principles of Interactive Computer Graphics* which was originally written for vector graphics devices. This book covers the normal topics of 2-D and 3-D graphics, lighting, rendering, geometrical approximations and suchlike. The current edition is now orientated to raster-graphics devices but the book which seems to be taking its place as the classic is Foley and Van Dam's (1982) *Fundamentals of Interactive Computer Graphics*. The topics covered are similar to those in Newman and Sproull and both books are hardware orientated in the mainframe context. If you are less interested in hardware, Harrington's (1983) *Computer Graphics: A Programming Approach* is very readable and covers much the same ground while Rogers' (1985) *Procedural Elements of Computer Graphics*, although advanced, contains a good treatment from the mathematical/programming standpoint. For those who wish to follow a route from this book to the mainstream, I would advise you to first look at Myers (1982) and then study Foley and Van Dam (1982) or Harrington (1983). In this way, a comprehensive knowledge of 2-D and 3-D graphics, hidden line, splines, clipping, lighting and rendering can be acquired. But if you are interested in pictures, be warned that the mainstream of computer graphics can be a pretty dry affair and several books on the subject exist without *any* pictures at all!

I am not recommending a book on mathematics for computer graphics because so many of the texts cover the appropriate mathematics, and reference is always then made to rather more general mathematics texts. Our fifth area however deals with mathematics and pattern which is the essence of much of the design contained in this book. A good basic book is March and Steadman's (1971) *The Geometry of Environment* which covers many of the basics used to construct spatial designs, while a more general treatment is in Stevens (1974) *Patterns in Nature* which is especially good on natural forms such as trees. Abelson and DiSessa's (1980) book on *Turtle Geometry* is worth looking at too while Thornburg's (1983) *Discovering Apple Logo* is as good a treatment of recursion, natural patterns and art forms as you will find at the elementary level. McGregor and Watt's (1984) *The Art of Microcomputer Graphics* is also worth looking at here.

Our last section deals more generally with books on creative computing. Michie and Johnston's (1984) *The Creative Computer* is an excellent, general introduction, especially Chapter 7 which deals with computer art, while Hofstadter's (1979) *Gödel, Escher, Bach: An Eternal Golden Braid* must be looked at. This book, which has become the bible of artificial intelligence and computer science students in the top US universities such as MIT and Stanford, deals with structure in music, art and mathematics and particularly emphasizes ideas about algorithms and recursion as the basis of art. Mandelbrot's (1982) *The Fractal Geometry of Nature* is also a must if only because of its excellent computer graphics, illustrating the sorts of pictures which *only* computers can produce. Very few books referred to here will outlast the century but Hofstadter and Mandelbrot's contributions will still be referred to in 50 years time. Finally, to see how formal approaches to art are developing, Stiny and Gipps' (1978) *Algorithmic Aesthetics* is worth looking at.

In conclusion, it is worth saying a little about the key journals and periodicals. In the UK, popular monthly magazines such as *Acorn User* and *BEEBUG* deal specifically with the BBC Micro and about three or four times a year contain good articles on graphics. More general popular computing magazines in the UK only occasionally deal with graphics but in the USA, the monthly journals *Byte* and *Popular Computing* often have good sections on state-of-the-art graphics. At a more professional level, by far the best journal is the publication of the ACM (Association for Computing Machines) Special Interest Group on Graphics (SIGGRAPH) publication *Computer Graphics* which is quarterly. More recently the ACM have begun to produce a *Transactions on Graphics* while the *IEEE Computer Graphics and Applications* contains some excellent articles. These are the journals to look at if you are interested in following the state-of-the-art.

References

Abelson, H. and DiSessa, A. (1980) *Turtle Geometry: The Computer as a Medium for Exploring Mathematics*, The MIT Press, Cambridge, Massachusetts.

Alexander, C. (1966) A City is not a Tree, *Design*, **206**, 46–55.

Alexander, C. (1979) *The Timeless Way of Building*, Oxford University Press, New York.

Angel, I.O. and Jones, B.J. (1983) *Advanced Graphics with the BBC Model B Microcomputer*, Macmillan Press, London.

Aoni, M. and Kunii, T.L. (1984) Botanical Tree Image Generation, *IEEE Computer Graphics and Applications*, **5**, 10–34.

Ballard, J.G. (1975) *Vermilion Sands*, Panther Books, London.

Banthorpe, M. (1984) Adding a New Dimension to Life, *Acorn User*, **20**, 91–101.

Batty, M. (1985) Fractals – Geometry between Dimensions, *New Scientist*, **105** (1450), 31–35.

Booth, K.S., Kochanek, D.H. and Wein, M. (1983) Computers Animate Films and Videos, *IEEE Spectrum*, February, 44–51.

Brown, P. (1982) *Pascal from BASIC*, Addison–Wesley, Reading, Massachusetts.

Cohen, H., Cohen, B. and Nii, P. (1984) *Art and Computers: The First Artificial Intelligence Coloring Book*, William Kaufmann, Los Altos, California.

Coll, J. (1982) *The BBC Microcomputer System User Guide*, British Broadcasting Corporation, London.

Cooper, D. (1984) Computer Landscapes, *Byte*, **9** (10), 211–18.

Cownie, J. (1982) *Creative Graphics on the BBC Microcomputer*, Acornsoft, Cambridge, England.

Crow, F.C. (1978) Shaded Computer Graphics in the Entertainment Industry, *Computer*, **11**, 11–22.

Deken, J. (1983) *Computer Images: State of the Art*, Thames and Hudson, London.

Eigen, M. and Winkler, R. (1983) *Laws of the Game: How the Principles of Nature Govern Chance*, Harper and Row, New York.

Foley, J.D. and Van Dam, A. (1982) *Fundamentals of Interactive Computer Graphics*, Addison–Wesley, Reading, Massachusetts.

Fournier, A., Fussell, D. and Carpenter, L. (1982) Computer Rendering of Stochastic Models, *Communications of the ACM*, **25**, 371–84.

Fox, D. and Waite, M. (1984) *Computer Animation Primer*, McGraw–Hill, New York.

Franke, H.W. (1971) *Computer Graphics, Computer Art*, Phaidon Press, London.

Ghyka, M. (1946) *The Geometry of Art and Life*, Dover Publications, New York.

Glassner, A.S. (1984) *Computer Graphics User's Guide*, Howard W. Sams and Company, Inc., Indianapolis, Indiana.

Greenberg, D. (1982) An Overview of Computer Graphics, in *The Computer Image: Applications of Computer Graphics* (eds D. Greenberg, A. Marcus, A. Schmidt and V. Gorter), Addison–Wesley, Reading, Massachusetts, pp. 7–35.

Greenberg, D., Marcus, A., Schmidt, A. and Gorter, V. (1982) *The Computer Image: Applications of Computer Graphics*, Addison–Wesley, Reading, Massachusetts.

Hadley, G. (1961) *Linear Algebra*, Addison–Wesley, Reading, Massachusetts.

Haggett, P. and Chorley, R.J. (1969) *Network Analysis in Geography*, Edward Arnold, London.

Haggett, P., Cliff, A.D. and Frey, A. (1977) *Locational Analysis in Human Geography, Volume 1: Locational Models*, Edward Arnold, London.

Harrington, S. (1983) *Computer Graphics: A Programming Approach*, McGraw–Hill, New York.

Harris, D. (1984), *Computer Graphics and Applications*, Chapman and Hall Ltd., London.

Hofstadter, D.R. (1979) *Gödal, Escher, Bach: An Eternal Golden Braid*, Basic Books, New York.

Ihnatowicz, E. (1976) Towards a Thinking Machine, in *Artist and Computer* (ed. R. Leavitt) Creative Computing Press, Morristown, New Jersey, pp. 32–34.

Jankel, A. and Morton, R. (1984) *Creative Computer Graphics*, Cambridge University Press, Cambridge, England.

Kolomyjec, W.J. (1976) The Appeal of Computer Graphics, in *Artist and Computer* (ed. R. Leavitt) Creative Computing Press, Morristown, New Jersey, pp. 45–51.

Kosniowski, C. (1983) *Fun Mathematics on Your Microcomputer*, Cambridge University Press, Cambridge, England.

Laposky, B.F. (1976) Oscillons: Electronic Abstractions, in *Artist and Computer*, (ed. R. Leavitt) Creative Computing Press, Morristown, New Jersey, pp. 21–22.

Leavitt, R. (1976) Preface, in *Artist and Computer* (ed. R. Leavitt) Creative Computing Press, Morristown, New Jersey, pp. vii–viii.

Malina, F.J. (ed.) (1979) *Visual Art, Mathematics and Computers: Selections from the Journal Leonardo*, Pergamon Press Ltd, Oxford, England.

Mandelbrot, B.B. (1967) How Long is the Coast of Britain? Statistical Self-Similarity and Fractional Dimension, *Science*, **156**, 636–8.

Mandelbrot, B.B. (1981) Scalebound or scaling shapes: a useful distinction in the visual arts and in the natural sciences, *Leonardo*, **14**, 45–47.

Mandelbrot, B.B. (1982) *The Fractal Geometry of Nature*, W.H. Freeman and Company, San Francisco, California.

March, L. and Steadman, P. (1971) *The Geometry of Environment: An Introduction to Spatial Organization in Design*, RIBA Publications, and Methuen and Company, London.

McDermott, J. (1963) Geometrical Forms Known as Fractals Find Sense in Chaos, *Smithsonian*, **14** (9), 110–17.

McGregor, J. and Watt, A. (1983) *The BBC Micro Book: BASIC, Sound and Graphics*, Addison–Wesley, London.

McGregor, J. and Watt, A. (1984) *The Art of Microcomputer Graphics*, Addison–Wesley, Wokingham, Berkshire, England.

McLuhan, M. and Fiore, Q. (1967) *The Medium is the Massage*, Allen Lane, Harmondsworth, Middlesex, England.

McMahon, T.A. (1975) The Mechanical Design of Trees, *Scientific American*, **233** (1), 92–102.

Mezei, L. (1976) Untitled contribution in *Artist and Computer* (ed. R. Leavitt) Creative Computing Press, Morristown, New Jersey, pp. 23–26.

Michie, D. and Johnston, R. (1984) *The Creative Computer: Machine Intelligence and Human Knowledge*, Penguin Books Ltd, Harmondsworth, Middlesex, England.

Mufti, A.A. (1982) *Elementary Computer Graphics*, Reston Publishing Company, Reston, Virginia.

Myers, R.E. (1982) *Microcomputer Graphics*, Addison–Wesley, Reading, Massachusetts.

Nees, G. (1968) Programming Stochastic Computer Graphics, in *Cybernetic Serendipity* (ed. J. Reichardt), The Institute of Contemporary Arts, London, p. 79.

Negroponte, N.P. (1979) The Return of the Sunday Painter, in *The Computer Age: A Twenty-Year View* (eds M.L. Dertouzas and J. Moses), The MIT Press, Cambridge, Massachusetts, pp. 21–37.

Nevison, J.M. (1978) *The Little Book of Basic Style: How to Write a Program You Can Read*, Addison–Wesley, Reading, Massachusetts.

Newman, W.M. and Sproull, R.F. (1979) *Principles of Interactive Computer Graphics*, McGraw–Hill, New York.

Norton, A. (1982) Generation and Display of Geometric Fractals in 3-D, *Computer Graphics*, **16** (3), 61–7.

Papert, S. (1980) *Mindstorms: Children, Computers and Powerful Ideas*, Basic Books, New York.

Park, C.S. (1985) *Interactive Microcomputer Graphics*, Addison–Wesley, Reading, Massachusetts.

Pedersen, C.F. (1971) *The International Flag Book*, Blandford Press, Poole, Dorset, England.

Peterson, D. (1983) *Genesis II: Creation and Recreation with Computers*, Reston Publishing Company, Reston, Virginia.

Prueitt, M.L. (1984) *Art and the Computer*, McGraw–Hill, New York.

Reffin-Smith, B. (1984) *Soft Computing: Art and Design*, Addison–Wesley, Wokingham, Berkshire, England.

Reichardt, J. (ed.) (1968) *Cybernetic Serendipity*, The Institute of Contemporary Arts, London.

Rogers, D.F. (1985) *Procedural Elements of Computer Graphics*, McGraw–Hill, New York.

Sagan, C. (1984) Introduction, in *Art and the Computer* (M.L. Prueitt), McGraw–Hill, New York, pp. viii–ix.

Simon, H.A. (1969) *The Sciences of the Artificial*, The MIT Press, Cambridge, Massachusetss.

Smith, A.R. (1983) Digital Filmmaking, *Abacus*, **1**, 28–45.

Sorensen, P.R. (1984a) Simulating Reality with Computer Graphics, *Byte*, **9** (3), 106–34.

Sorensen, P.R. (1984b) Fractals, *Byte*, **9** (10), 157–72.

Stevens, P.S. (1974) *Patterns in Nature*, Little, Brown and Company, New York.

Stiny, G. and Gipps, J. (1978) *Algorithmic Aesthetics: Computer Models of Criticism and Design in the Arts*, University of California Press, Berkeley, California.

Strauss, W. (1972) *The Human Figure by Albrecht Dürer*, Dover, New York.

Sutherland, I.E. (1963, 1980), *Sketchpad, A Man-Machine Graphical Communication System*, PhD Thesis, Department of Electrical Engineering, Massachusetts Institute of Technology; and *Outstanding Dissertations in the Computer Sciences*, Garland Publishing, New York.

Sutherland, I.E., Sproull, R.F. and Schumacker, R.A. (1974) A Characterization of Ten Hidden-Surface Algorithms, *Computing Surveys*, **6**, 1–55.

Thompson, D.W. (1961) *On Growth and Form*, Abridged Edition, Cambridge University Press, Cambridge, England.

Thornburg, D. (1983) *Discovering Apple Logo: An Invitation to the Art and Pattern of Nature*, Addison–Wesley, Reading, Massachusetts.

Tobler, W.R. (1979) Cellular Geography, in *Philosophy in Geography* (eds S. Gale and G. Olsson), D. Reidel, Dordrecht, Holland, pp. 379–86.

Tobler, W.R. (1983) *Durer Transforms*, Department of Geography, University of California, Santa Barbara, California.

Van Dam, A. (1984) Computer Software for Graphics, *Scientific American*, **251** (3), 102–13.

Whipple, F.L. (1968) Stochastic Painting, *Leonardo*, **1**, 81–83.

Whitney, J. (1980) *Digital Harmony: On the Complementarity of Music and Visual Art*, Byte Books, McGraw–Hill, Peterborough, New Hampshire.

Wittgenstein, L. (1961) *Tractatus Logico – Philosophicus*, Routledge and Kegan Paul, London.

Woldenberg, M.J. (1971) A Structural Taxonomy of Spatial Hierarchies, in *Regional Forecasting* (eds M. Chisholm, A.E. Frey and P. Haggett), Butterworths, London, pp. 147–75.

Author index

326   *Author index*

Subject index